ALSO BY BEVERLY LOWRY

Fiction

Come Back, Lolly Ray

Emma Blue

Daddy's Girl

The Perfect Sonya

Breaking Gentle

The Track of Real Desires

Nonfiction

Crossed Over: A Murder, a Memoir

*Her Dream of Dreams: The Rise
and Triumph of Madam C. J. Walker*

Harriet Tubman: Imagining a Life

WHO KILLED THESE GIRLS?

WHO KILLED THESE GIRLS?

COLD CASE:

THE YOGURT SHOP MURDERS

BEVERLY LOWRY

ALFRED A. KNOPF · NEW YORK · 2016

THIS IS A BORZOI BOOK PUBLISHED BY ALFRED A. KNOPF

Copyright © 2016 by Beverly Lowry

All rights reserved. Published in the United States by Alfred A. Knopf, a division of Penguin Random House LLC, New York, and distributed in Canada by Random House of Canada, a division of Penguin Random House Canada Limited, Toronto.

www.aaknopf.com

Knopf, Borzoi Books and the colophon are registered trademarks of Penguin Random House LLC.

Grateful acknowledgment is made to Will Sheff for permission to reprint excerpted lyrics from "Westfall" by Okkervil River, copyright © 2016 by Joundsongs. Reprinted by permission of Will Sheff.

Library of Congress Cataloging-in-Publication Data
Names: Lowry, Beverly, author.
Title: Who killed these girls? : cold case : the yogurt shop murders / Beverly Lowry.
Description: New York : Knopf, 2016.
Identifiers: LCCN 2016011074 (print) | LCCN 2016017645 (ebook) | ISBN 9780307594112 (hardcover) | ISBN 9781101947999 (ebook)
Subjects: LCSH: Murder—Texas—Austin—Case studies. | Murder—Investigation—Texas—Austin—Case studies. | Cold cases (Criminal investigation)—Texas—Austin—Case studies. | BISAC: TRUE CRIME / General. | SOCIAL SCIENCE / Criminology. | HISTORY / United States / State & Local / Southwest (AZ, NM, OK, TX).
Classification: LCC HV6534.A8 L69 2016 (print) | LCC HV6534.A8 (ebook) | DDC 364.152/30976431—dc23
LC record available at https://lccn.loc.gov/2016011074

Jacket design by Oliver Munday

Manufactured in the United States of America
First Edition

For Gary Fisketjon

Contents

I. THE CRIME

December 6, 1991	3
The Girls	15
The Sisters: Jennifer and Sarah Harbison	17
Eliza Thomas	22
Amy Ayers	24
On the Street All the Time	27
Missing Boys	34
Crime Scene	36
Your Yogurt Girl	41
Task Force	53
The First Week: Innocence	62
Dark Days, Black Nights	69
Until This Case Is Solved	73
Billboards	81
Anniversary	97
Father Confessor	101
PTSD	108

II. THE PAUL JOHNSON SHOW

The New Guy	119
Northcross	124

CONTENTS

Rob 127

Mike 130

Forrest 133

Ringleader 135

Pathfinder 138

Wired 141

The Boys, 1997 144

Not a Task Force 146

PowerPoint 150

The Pursuit of Maurice Pierce, Round One 154

The Pursuit of Maurice Pierce, Round Two 163

The Pursuit of Maurice Pierce, Round Three 186

The Pursuit of Maurice Pierce, Round Four 192

Arrests 203

III. THE COURTS: LAW, SCIENCE, BLUNDERS AND LUCK

Certification 213

The Judge 222

Sawyer 225

Garcia 227

The Stiletto 229

Pretrial 231

Fire 238

Jury Selection 240

Jury Trials 244

Always Pierce 297

Scalia 301

Everything Happens in the Spring 304

Science 307

Downhill Roll 309

Rose 314

Rose's Choice 318

IV. UNANSWERED QUESTIONS

Who Killed These Girls?   327
What Really Happened?   328
Paul Johnson and the Disease of Certainty   338
The Storage Room   342
Jones at the Embassy Suites   344
2015   349
2016   351

Epilogue   357
Appendices   363
Acknowledgments   375
Bibliography   379

I

THE CRIME

DECEMBER 6, 1991

When the call came in, Austin Police Department's Sgt. John Wilson Jones was the only homicide cop on the street. That's how small and safe a city Austin was back then. Close to midnight on a Friday night and Jones was it. When his mobile rang the first time, he was on the other side of town, at Airport and Martin Luther King boulevards, following up an earlier call, a guy who'd barricaded himself inside a building and was threatening to kill himself.

Jones punched in.

"Two fatalities," the dispatcher told him, "suspected arson, suspected homicide, looks like gunshot wounds." And he gave him the address: I Can't Believe It's Yogurt!, 2949 West Anderson Lane. Everything about that night was unusual, including the fact that two people had ridden out with Jones, a reporter and videographer from KTBC-TV, a local CBS affiliate doing a series on homicides in Texas. So far, except for a couple of weenie calls, the ride had been a bust. "Nothing happens in Austin," the reporter complained. But never mind. They were heading to Houston the next day, where they'd surely score.

Abandoning the would-be suicide, Jones cranked his unmarked sedan, switched on his lights and siren and, once his riders were settled in the backseat, hit the ramp leading to the interstate. If working in law enforcement had taught him anything, it was that there was no such thing as a routine call, but this one sounded ominous. Crime in northwest Austin was rare, murders all but nonexistent—and in a frozen-yogurt shop?

In no time the next call came in. They'd found another body.

From the backseat, the cameraman videotaped John—dressed in dark pants, a black windbreaker and a long-sleeved white dress shirt with pale green stripes—as he blazed north on I-35. After tonight, he will hang the shirt on a wall at APD headquarters, a symbol of Homicide's determination to find the killers. "When you see me wearing this shirt," he'd told the victims' families, "you'll know the case is solved." It will remain on the wall for months. It hangs in his closet to this day.

He was in sight of Highway 183 when the numbers of his mobile lit up again.

"Jonesy," said a cop on the scene. "Make that four."

"Okay," Jones said. "Here we go."

Girls. Kids. Bound, gagged. Naked. Stacked. Burned to the bone.

When I tell people about the case, one of the first things they want to know is, How old were they? Two were seventeen, I tell them. One was fifteen and the youngest, thirteen, was still in the eighth grade. Two were sisters.

And was robbery the motive?

Absolutely not.

The next thing they ask is, Was race an issue? Were the girls black? Latina? What about the suspects?

So far, the only person of color known to have been directly involved in what is unfailingly called the "Yogurt Shop Murders" was the lead cop, Sgt. John W. Jones, who arrived at the scene shortly after midnight. By then, Hillside Center was lit up like a nighttime movie set. Fire trucks, police cars, flashers. Harsh generator-powered lights in the alley mounted on steel girders high above the flat rooftops.

He pulled in. Hillside's an ordinary strip center, concrete blocks, concrete flooring, each store with its name and logo on a ledge above the door. The yogurt shop was dark, its wide front window blackened from smoke and soot, the sign above reading I CAN'T BELIEVE IT'S . . . in modern sans serif and YOGURT! in swirls, like the cones it sold. Next door, the Party House logo featured red balloons tied together in a bunch, heading skyward as if to escape. After telling the reporters to stay put, Jones headed toward one of the police-men stretching the yellow crime-scene tape. Earlier in the night, the videographer had clipped a microphone to Jones's belt, but, much to John's relief, its batteries had gone dead; otherwise, CBS would have recorded his every word, including a few choice expletives. Because the fire department had set up its staging area in the parking lot, the APD cop advised him to go through the Party House.

When he got to the alley, the steel doors to the storage room of the yogurt shop were wide open. Jones stepped inside.

"I look in there and I go, *Oh my God*. There were puddles of water all over the place. The bodies were still smoldering. There was insulation from the ceiling that had dropped down. And it was hot. It was smoky. And I was by myself."

His next thought? "I needed help. I'd been a policeman for twenty-one years and I'd never seen anything like it."

First homicide cop on the scene, old-school protocol says the case is his. Jones went to work.

I didn't live in Austin then, but I had family here and visited often. I heard about the murders immediately, and every time I went back it seemed something new had happened: another whacked-out confession, a new tip, a bigger reward, the arrests, trials, Supreme Court decisions, reversals. You didn't have to live here at the time to know the story. Say "yogurt shop" in Austin even today and locals jump to "murders" before you get there. Lawyers just say Yogurt Shop. Some even cut that short. *You here for Yogurt?* is a question I've been asked more than once.

We tag unspeakable crimes for a number of reasons, one of which springs from our wish never again to have to describe or even imagine the horrible event. Sometimes the name emerges from the killer (Manson, Jack the Ripper, the Boston Strangler) or the victim (Jon-Benét, Lindbergh, the Black Dahlia), or, now and then, the weapon, whether Pickax or Broomstick. When the World Trade Center buildings went down, we focused on the date and used only the two numbers. Like the mass shootings at Columbine High and at Luby's Cafeteria in Killeen, Texas, the rape, murder and burning of the four

Austin girls was named for the place where the crime occurred and for the same reason: A more unlikely place for random savagery could hardly be imagined (if it turns out that *random* even applies).

In 1991, Austin was on the verge of becoming what it is today, but back then nobody had a clue. The go-to Texas cities were Houston, Dallas, San Antonio. With its big-time celebration of Eeyore's birthday, its dog parades, costumes and flummery, Austin was Slackerville, rock music, goofball pot smokers and drunken legislators, a city where unreconstructed hippies and university students swam naked in nearby lakes and sometimes had sex in the bushes. While Houstonians liked to say Austin was hoping to become a grown-up city, too, someday, nobody here took offense. Who wanted to be like Houston?

Then came Yogurt Shop. *We lost our innocence that night* became an official mantra among politicians and self-congratulating residents who considered innocence a concrete possibility instead of a handy, if unrealistic, construct. And then, when the crime remained unresolved year after year after year, it became a permanent part of our history.

I once asked my son, who lived here then and still does, "Will the Yogurt Shop Murders ever be out of our lives?"

His answer came fast. "No," he said. "They're with us forever."

He might be right.

B y the summer of 2009, when I stepped into the long, tortured path of the story, I'd lived in Austin for three years. The crime was eighteen years old by then, but resolution—the exorcism we all longed for—still seemed a distant hope. Between 1991, when John Jones became lead investigator, and 1994, when he was removed from the case, a high-stakes investigation had yielded hot tips, FBI assurances and urgent confessions but no arrests. Then nothing. The case went cold until 1999, when, after a new task force was appointed, two boys confessed and implicated two of their running buddies. All four were arrested and charged with capital murder. Those who'd confessed were indicted, tried, found guilty and, by 2003, had been sent to state prison: one for life, the other to await execution. The third—called "Action Man," widely assumed to be the ringleader—was indicted and locked up in county jail for a while but, for lack of evidence, was eventually released: no trial. The fourth—a boy of fifteen when the crime occurred—was never indicted. Nobody on the prosecutorial team was happy about those two going free, especially Action Man, though at least they'd nailed the first pair, who the DA figured would surely flip on their cohorts once prison life got to them.

For a while, that seemed to be that. But even then, some people thought the equation of four bad guys for four good girls, while satisfying, might be, if anything, a little too perfect. And the story kept jumping back to reset, with disruptions of one kind and another: appeals, reversals, higher-court decisions. Shortly after I made Austin my home, both convictions were overturned and the suspects remanded to Travis County District Court 167, where they had been tried originally. By 2009, retrials had been lined up. Same courtroom, same defense attorneys, defendants and judge, different prosecutors, new district attorney. Jury selection for the first trial had been scheduled for early July, the second to follow immediately after. The judge, whose rulings had been publicly slammed, was pushing hard; he wanted this thing, by God, to be *over*.

All of this was in the air when, in June of that year, I went to a Yogurt Shop hearing. I hadn't decided what I wanted to do with whatever I saw, heard or learned there but did know why the long, unsettled history of the case drew me to it and why I thought it might be my story to tell. So did my family and friends.

I sat on the left side of the aisle, unaware that courtrooms have seating conventions, like weddings, and that I'd chosen the prosecutorial side of the room, along with police and families of the victims. Not that it mattered. Only to say, that's how much I knew.

In movies, courtrooms are usually grandly appointed sanctuaries, all dark and with ornately carved mahogany and high arched ceilings, perhaps an upstairs gallery and sometimes a bronze statue of blindfolded Lady Justice holding the scales. In *And Justice for All*, Al Pacino makes his plea to a judge sitting so high above the defense table that the lawyers have to crane their necks to make eye contact. Behind the judge, a wall of marble extends to the ceiling. Even small-town courtrooms like those in *To Kill a Mockingbird* and *A Time to*

Kill manage to communicate the fearful dignity and weight of the law. They are like consecrated vaults.

Courtrooms in the Travis County Blackwell-Thurman Criminal Justice Center exude no such grand sense of purpose. They are just rooms, utilitarian and unremarkable. Fluorescent tubing inserted into a low ceiling of ordinary soundproofing casts an unflattering yellowish glare down gray grainy-surfaced walls. And while the judge sits properly elevated above everybody else, the bench—his desk—does not parallel the back wall but is situated in a corner, at an angle to participants and spectators.

For the press, Yogurt Shop had been a honeypot from day one. Call a hearing or mention a name and everybody showed up. On this occasion, print reporters—many of whom had attended the original trials—sat together on the defense side of the aisle, chatting amiably. Photographers and videographers had gathered along the front row of the jury box, their cameras aimed at the door the defendant would walk through: not the placid, loopy guy, but the snarly one with the scary eyebrows, the mullet haircut and the famous rock 'n' roll surname. Behind the camera crew were fourteen black leather chairs with high backs and headrests. Wooden benches in the spectator section were padded, a blessing when a trial goes on and on, as death-penalty trials like Yogurt Shop always do. There was seating for maybe sixty observers, if that. During the earlier trials, the judge had sent a live video feed to a nearby room for the daily overflow.

When the armed deputy from the sheriff's department ushered in the defendant, cameras whirred and clicked. Dressed in a navy sport coat, black leather shoes and dark gray pants, Robert Burns Springsteen IV looked calm and pulled together—respectable instead of unkempt and defiant, as he had during his trial. He sat at the defense table between two lawyers: a handsome silver-haired man and a large woman carrying an open briefcase jammed with files and knitting.

When the bailiff instructed us to "All rise," the judge swooped in. A small man, wiry, goateed, as quick-witted and intense as a terrier, Mike Lynch took his seat and, after a quick "Good morning," brusquely addressed the courtroom.

"The only reason we're here," he said, "is for me to hear both sides argue about the *significance* of the new DNA test results." The session, he declared, would be short. There would be no expert witnesses and he didn't want to hear a lot of technical data about what had been done or why it was or wasn't valid. He didn't want to hear about the *science* of DNA. All he wanted to know was, from each perspective, *what* the results were and *why* they mattered. Was that clear?

His glittering blue eyes scanned the courtroom. Having been born and raised in Arkansas, Lynch made use of his cracker-tinged accent much like Lyndon Johnson had, gaining advantage by emphasizing his aw-shucks country-hick roots and subsequent lack of sophistication, a ruse that, in both instances, worked startlingly well. Often called the best-liked judge in Travis County, he'd sat on the 167 bench since 1993.

After lawyers on both sides promised to follow the judge's instructions, the lead defense attorney stood. Perfectly tanned and immaculately dressed in his seasonal best—wheat-colored linen jacket, dark trousers, a crisp white shirt perfectly accessorized with a silk tie and cuff links made of gold coins—he epitomized the "white-shoe lawyer," his silver hair shaped in a perfect razor cut and his black cowboy boots polished to a high sheen. You will rarely see him dressed less elegantly. Joe James "Jim" Sawyer was known for his flamboyance, literary references and courtroom maneuvers, as well as his movie-star smile and love of the camera. When I asked why he took on Yogurt Shop, he smiled broadly. "I have a big ego," he said. "It was the biggest thing to hit Travis County and I wanted in."

It was Sawyer who'd requested the hearing. During the past few weeks, press reports had been constant. In addition to the reversals, it seemed, a new kind of DNA test result had damaged the state's case. The defense had become aggressive.

Sawyer addressed the bench. He was in court today, he assured the judge, only to discuss results and to ask that his client be released from jail pending a trial. "We can't replace or give Robert Springsteen back the ten years he's lost sitting in jail," he pointed out, but there was a scientific incentive to give him his freedom now. Loath to wearing reading glasses in court, Sawyer nonetheless donned them now. The Y-STR DNA report, issued by an identity lab in Fairfax, Virginia, was complicated and he wanted to get it right. He read it word for word.

When he was finished, the lead prosecutor said only that they were continuing to do their own testing and that those DNA results were not conclusive.

Lynch looked up, making sure nobody had anything else to say, then promised to make his decision on Monday, banged his gavel and swept out. It was Thursday. Springsteen was escorted back to a holding cell in county, where he would remain for the next four days. The hearing had lasted maybe twelve minutes.

I had not come to District Court 167 to find out whether or not Rob Springsteen would be granted bail reduction or even released, as Sawyer had requested. I'd already gone to the basement of the Texas Court of Criminal Appeals to read the original trial transcripts. I knew what the customers who'd been to the shop that night had reported having seen and heard. I'd read how the parents of the murdered girls described their daughters on the stand. And I'd seen photocopies of the gruesome crime-scene photos, including close-ups of the girls' genitals. From autopsy shots, I knew what death looks like when incinerated corpses have been cleaned up and laid stiff and medically prepped on a table in the morgue. By the time I went to the hearing, I knew a lot. Bail reduction didn't mean much by comparison.

Nor did any other legal shenanigans. Writers don't pick their subjects out of the clear blue. What mattered to me and drew me to this particular story was the uncertainty of the parents of the dead girls, the not-knowing they might well have to accept as their lifelong fate. This was something I knew about myself, having lived with it since 1984, when my son Peter was killed by a hit-and-run driver who was never identified.

Jury selection was scheduled to begin three weeks later in the retrial of Robert Springsteen's onetime roommate and convicted collaborator, Michael James Scott. His case had, in fact, already moved into pretrial. Scott's lead attorney, Carlos Garcia, had chosen not to participate in the bail-reduction hearing. He was too busy working on his client's case, which he thought he had a good shot of winning this time around.

In the meantime, the press, the families of the victims and the city of Austin itself geared up to suffer through a rehash of a case they'd thought was finished. Until then, we awaited Lynch's decision, after which the Travis County DA, Rosemary Lehmberg, would announce hers. In the face of a failed, outlawed strategy and the new DNA test results, she'd been ordered to come up with a new case to present.

Or else what? Lynch had not spelled that out.

Only six months into the job, Lehmberg had become DA in a special election after her boss, Ronnie Earle, who'd held the job for thirty-two years, retired. When I asked a friend of hers if dismissal was likely, she shook her head. "Rose never gives up on anything," she firmly declared. When I started to protest, my friend shushed me and said, "She'll find a way."

But justice is local, and it's culturally affected. In the ten years since the four boys were arrested, public attitudes had shifted. In 1999, we hadn't yet become dependent on forensics and DNA to solve cold cases and correct old mistakes. The first episode of the *CSI* series hadn't yet run. Colleges hadn't added special degrees in crime-scene forensics. Bookstores didn't display copies of *Forensics for Dummies*. Even into the new century, confessions were considered golden. Juries loved them and, as a result, so did DAs. We all did. We still do. "Just tell me what happened," we say to those who betray or assault us. "Then tell me *why*." So what if there wasn't a shred of evidence linking the two convicted guys to the crime? They *confessed*.

As for the suggestion that someone might be convinced to give what is called a "false confession," few among us think we'd confess to something we didn't do.

By 2009, however, a number of confession-based convictions had been overturned when DNA testing offered scientific proof that police departments and DAs all over the country had bagged the wrong person. It turned out that getting a suspect to falsely confess wasn't all that difficult, even without rubber hoses or a telephone book to the kidneys. These were big-time cases, widely covered. And when those wrongly convicted individuals were exonerated after spending a significant chunk of their lives in prison, the public mind turned a corner. Was it possible that you or I could fall for an interrogator's tricks, as the five boys arrested in the Central Park Jogger Case had? The Norfolk Four?

I left the courtroom without saying anything to anybody. In the hall outside, Jim Sawyer was giving a dramatic interview while reporters scribbled and photographers snapped his handsome picture.

I was in. I knew that. *This is right,* I wrote in my notebook.

Sometimes a homicide rocks a city to its bones. People wake up and find themselves living in a place they no longer recognize. The extent of the shake-up depends on many things: the age, sex and skin color of the victims; the specific location of the murders (home being possibly the most horrific, as the sanctity of our safest refuge is destroyed, as when twelve-year-old Polly Klaas was taken from her home in Petaluma, California); whether the nature of the crime is familiar—man shoots wife, children and self, wife shoots husband and girlfriend, drug dealer shoots customer, customer shoots dealer—or so outside the norm that it makes residents wonder what kind of place they're living in and even if they should move.

When the Herb Clutter family was murdered in their wheat-field home in western Kansas, the local response was, These things don't happen here. A "senseless" killing particularly disturbs a community that has defined itself as the ideal spot to raise a family. There are many examples of this: the murder of JonBenét Ramsey in Boulder; the trail of dismembered body parts scattered by Edmund Kemper around Santa Cruz; the sixteen-year spree of Gary Ridgway, dubbed the Green River Killer, in Seattle; Lizzie Borden in Fall River; the boys from Columbine High; the horrific murder, rape and burning of the family in wealthy Cheshire, Connecticut; the children in Newtown.

Austin was never without its high-profile homicides, but most are easier to understand. In 1966, when Charles Whitman climbed to the top of the Texas Tower at the University of Texas and—having already murdered his wife and mother—killed fourteen people and wounded thirty-one others with his deer rifle, UT, the city and the nation were shocked, without question. Soon afterward, the top floor of the tower was closed, and today it can be visited only on strictly regulated tours that prohibit—among other things—bags, backpacks and "wristlets." In a part of town with few tall buildings, the light on the tower remains a fixed point, both as a signal of victory by a Longhorn sports team and a reminder of the day when Whitman opened fire. But he was a familiar kind of guy: ex–Eagle

Scout, ex-Marine, owner of a rifle used by many hunters. He didn't emerge from the shadows, but operated in broad daylight and was soon shot down himself when police stormed the tower. We knew Whitman. He was a Lone Star guy gone haywire. And we killed him on the spot.

The murder of the four girls was different. The predators came, it seemed, from out of nowhere, as if from the winds of El Niño, or perhaps from the trashy vacant fields along the banks of nearby Shoal Creek or a transport truck passing through on Highway 1. And once they'd done their quick, ugly work, they vanished into a moonless fog, not through the parking lot of one of the many boozy music halls that line Sixth Street downtown, and not on the east side of town, where crack killings had reached a new high, but from a family-friendly frozen-yogurt shop on the west side of town. There wasn't much money to steal and the killers left behind a good bit of what there was.

Did this mean that Slackerville had grown up and become Houston? Were we a real city now? As Barbara Ayres-Wilson (then Barbara Suraci), both of whose daughters were killed that night, told *People* magazine in 1992, "What did we do wrong here? We moved to a nice house in a good neighborhood. We did all the middle-class American things that you do to protect your family and make it wholesome and right. If this can happen to us, it can happen to anyone."

In *Crossed Over: A Murder, a Memoir,* I wrote about Karla Faye Tucker, who had confessed to participating in a gruesome double murder in Houston. Over the course of our many conversations in the maximum-security unit of the Texas women's prison system, Karla and I became friends. We talked about her life and the lives of her victims, and we talked about the violent death of my son. Our situations, of course, were very different. She knew what she'd done and why she'd been sent to death row. In the early years of her incarceration, she felt pretty sure she deserved execution. I, on the other hand, had come to understand that I would never know what happened to Peter that night, whether the driver realized what had happened and just didn't stop or never even felt the impact. We talked about how hard it was to accept uncertainty and if it was possible to do what people almost always suggest, which is to "move on" from a terrible event. We agreed that what psychologists call "closure" was not a possibility for either of us. After the arrests of the four suspects in 1999, the father of the youngest murdered girl told the press his wife hated the word. "There's no such thing as closure," she had declared.

This book is about memory and uncertainty, loss and grief. It is about how we know what we think we know and where the information comes from, and how we sometimes manage to dream up memories of an event that never took place and at other times conversely remember what we perhaps most wanted to forget, despite our best efforts. It is about an overworked, dedicated homicide cop who was later branded a failure when a different single-minded cop was given credit for cracking the case after using questionable interrogation techniques. It's about persuasion, suggestion, science and law. The sadness that won't end for the parents of dead children. The effect an event can have . . . on a family, an entire police department, a city and on hapless strangers who, walking down a certain street, might suddenly realize where they are and say, "Isn't that where the yogurt shop was?"

Dark things attract us. We criticize the media for its overwrought coverage of such events. Yet we watch, we read and reread, because we're relieved it's not us and to imagine what it would be like if it *were* us, because the unfolding narrative speaks to our deepest fears, to figure out why these things happen and what we should do next. Wondering why anybody would confess to something he or she didn't do, we long to know who did the unspeakable thing if the one who claimed to have done it in fact hadn't. And when, twenty-five years later, we still don't know, we're downright flummoxed by how badly things have gone. Could these four layabout teenagers have been guilty? Or did the cops figure out how to make two of them *think* they were? And what about those other guys who confessed and the ones in the hoodies who were there that night? Would we ever know *anything*?

Uncertainty jangles the nerves, but sometimes it's what we have to live with.

And now everything was starting all over again.

THE GIRLS

December 6, 1991, fell on a Friday, for public school kids the end of the next-to-last week of the fall semester. The day had dawned gray and sour, with no sign of a breeze. By the time classes ended, nothing had changed. Early December had brought a damp chill, down into the thirties at night, but by Thursday the air had turned sulky, with an unnatural stillness that makes people testy as they wait for whatever's about to happen next. Austin winters can be like that. Not cold, exactly, but rank and unsettling.

Nineteen ninety-one was an El Niño year, the first since the winter of 1986–87. Born of unusually warm temperatures in the Pacific, these unruly, mad-dog weather systems sometimes roll in from the ocean east across California and into the Southwest, bringing nonstop downpours and lower temperatures. In October, *The Washington Post* predicted a "wimpy" El Niño this year, although in the end, of course, nobody really knew.

On December 6, the moon was new and the night sky black, the darkness further compounded by fog that by nine o'clock had settled in, bringing with it a spitting drizzle. More than likely, the four girls paid little attention. Friday offered better things to think about than meteorology.

As soon as the bodies had been identified and their names made public, the girls quickly merged, as if they were alike or even the same. They were good girls, white girls, *our angels*. "We know them," one city official declared; "they are ours." In newspaper, magazine and television coverage, in the billboard announcing a reward for information leading to the conviction of their killers, they became representatives of a highly desirable kind of American girlhood. Beneath their posed photographs, the billboard asked, WHO KILLED THESE GIRLS?

It is important to know them separately and not as angels, symbols or the personification of innocence, but as four very young girls who at the time of their deaths were doing no harm to anyone. Nothing else matters, really.

THE SISTERS: JENNIFER AND SARAH HARBISON

By four-thirty that afternoon, when Barbara Suraci came home from work as a credit officer at Team Bank, her younger daughter was already there, sitting on the living room couch and peeling an orange. Fifteen-year-old Sarah Harbison was in a good mood. She had a new boyfriend, who after only three weeks of dating had given her his senior ring. And since she didn't have basketball or volleyball practice the next day, she told her mother she was going out.

Barbara's a feisty, passionate woman, warm, forthright and pure Texas. "Oh, yeah?" she said. She and her girls were close, almost like sisters. She'd grown up in New Boston, a small town in East Texas near the Arkansas line. Having married her high school sweetheart, she'd been young when she had her babies; then, when her husband decided to enroll in graduate divinity courses at the university, they all moved to Austin, where Barbara worked to support the family until he got his degree and they could go back home. But city life had opened her mind to new possibilities, and when the girls were five and two and a half, she left both Mike Harbison and New Boston and set off in her little hatchback, figuring she and her daughters could lead more interesting, informed lives in Austin. And have more fun.

Sarah's big sister, Jennifer, had driven her home in her 1991 dark blue Chevy S-10, then turned around and gone on. Before showing up for work, she wanted to spend some time with her boyfriend, who, because of his grandfather's funeral, hadn't been at school that day. The Harbison sisters lived with their mother and stepfather in a big brick house in a secluded suburban development with curvy streets in northwest Austin. Jennifer's boyfriend, Sammy Buchanan, lived in a nearby apartment complex with his mother. She also had to go by a friend's house to retrieve her wallet and then back to school to pick up a form she needed to fill out to run for queen of the local chapter of the Future Farmers of America (FFA). She'd return home sometime around seven to put on her work clothes.

Soon after arriving in Austin with her two little girls, Barbara had met Frank Suraci, a technician at Dell Computers, whom she married in 1980. For Barbara, "Skip" was exotic: easterner, Italian, Catholic, sexy. A woman of impromptu choices, she dove full force into the relationship. To enable them to exchange marriage vows in church, she and her daughters had taken lessons at St. Louis King of France on Burnet Road. She says her girls liked going to Catholic middle school and attending Mass, but they were eager to transfer to a public high school when the time came.

Only eighty-six pounds and five feet tall, a relay runner on the Sidney Lanier High School varsity track team, Jennifer was a mosquito-size girl who had little time for meals and no patience for standing still or waiting around. Seniors, she and Sammy were already wearing their 1992 graduation rings—gold, with a green stone—and hoping he'd win a baseball scholarship to a college Jennifer could also attend, so that after graduating they could get married and move forward into a life together.

The S-10's a small, peppy pickup, especially prized among the country-western set. Mike Harbison had bought the truck new, and Jennifer took a job at the I Can't Believe It's Yogurt! (ICBY) shop in part to help him make payments on the loan. Before that, she'd worked at a nearby Albertson's, sacking groceries and, despite her size, hauling them through the parking lot into customers' cars. She'd hired on at ICBY in July, after her friend Eliza Thomas, who'd been working there for six months, told her what a great job it was. Brice Foods, which owned the franchise, was a Texas operation, founded in 1977 by a brother and sister from Dallas, Bill and Julie Brice, while they were enrolled at Southern Methodist University, using their tuition money as collateral for a loan to buy and revamp two existing yogurt shops. They came up with a logo and a name, emphasized the product's nonfat status and forgot about college.

The shop was pleasant and nicely furnished, the customers friendly. No cooking, no waitressing. And although Brice had a lot of rules, for the duration of a shift you were pretty much on your own. The Anderson Lane ICBY shop was a neighborhood gathering place, where families and young couples went after shopping or a movie, and sometimes Governor Ann Richards stopped in. Both girls worked mostly weekend nights, although Eliza did take an occasional weeknight shift.

As always, Jennifer operated on a tight schedule. To keep up, she wore a Timex wristwatch with a big face and a sturdy black band. She will die wearing the watch; it will stop at 11:48, marking the time of the fire's most intense burst of heat.

Curled on her side, she'll lie close to the melted steel shelves against the south wall, wrists pressed against her spine—one in the thoracic area, the other nearer her waistline—exploded cans of toppings, paint and cleaning supplies on the floor around her, her face obliterated, a steel girder between her legs. She will be burned worse than the other three girls, the curled brown skin of her top leg peeled back like a stocking. When store manager Therese "Reese" Price comes, she won't be able to identify the two girls who worked for her. "They had no faces," she will testify.

Sarah also attended Lanier, where, now a sophomore, she played basketball and volleyball and was a member of the FFA and the student council. For an FFA project, she and Jennifer were raising lambs to show at the annual Austin Livestock Show and Rodeo the next spring. That morning after breakfast, the sisters had gone to the ag barn—some three miles away—to feed the lambs and muck out their stall. The barn wasn't much more than a shed in the middle of a fenced field donated by its owner, but they went there twice every day. In the morning, they'd return home to shower and change before Jennifer then drove them to school. That was part of the arrangement she'd made with her father, to give her sister—who wasn't old enough to drive—rides wherever she needed to go. After school that day, Jennifer had also driven Sarah's new boyfriend home, after which the two girls made their second stop at the ag barn.

Later that night, when ordered to strip, Sarah will slide Mike

McCathern's ring from her finger and place it between items of her own clothing, along with her wallet and her Mickey Mouse watch. She would die, however, wearing her own ring and the gold cross around her neck, both of which melted. From the witness stand, McCathern will identify his ring, gold, with a green stone, with a tractor on one side and his initials on the other.

In death, Sarah will lie less than three feet from her sister, on her back, still gagged, wrists bound behind her, blackened legs spread and an ice scoop on the concrete floor between her thighs, its handle pointed toward her pubic bone.

At five one and 125 pounds, Sarah was a little heavy, especially compared to her sister. "Why," she often asked Barbara, "do I have to be the big one?" But like her mother, Sarah loved food. "She was always hungry," Barbara says. "And she would eat anything." As for Jennifer, she took after Barbara's mother, who never hit 100 pounds in her life.

When festivalgoers come to Austin, they experience only the smallest part of the city and never quite understand that we are a city perched on an edge, straddling a divide. Two highways run crookedly north and south through town: Interstate 35, which extends from Laredo, Texas, to Duluth, Minnesota, and west of the interstate, State Highway 1, called MoPac for the railroad it parallels, the Missouri Pacific. MoPac runs along the Balcones Escarpment, which separates the coastal plains from the Edwards Plateau. East of the highway, the land goes flat pretty quickly and rolls on from there to Houston, where the topsoil runs deep and dark and ancient live oaks guard the sidewalks, and then into bays and bayous and, eventually, the Gulf of Mexico. Due west of Highway 1, the countryside changes astonishingly fast, the land suddenly cratered with fault lines and rocky jags, the soil thin and sandy, the trees small, with scrubby, short limbs gnarled like arthritic fingers. Out there, you might well think you're in the West.

But you're not. In the late nineteenth century, when geologists tried to distinguish the generally moist East from the arid West, they settled on the 100th meridian, which stretches through the Dakotas, Nebraska, Kansas, Oklahoma and then to Texas, where it falls past Abilene, San Angelo and Laredo to Mexico. The longitude was chosen because the country east of it generally received upwards of twenty inches of rainfall annually, while everything to the west got much less. Crops planted in the former needed little or no irrigation, but watering was essential in the latter. Austin's some two hundred miles east of the line.

Lanier High School and the ICBY shop were both situated east of MoPac, between rocky Shoal Creek—which runs south through downtown and sometimes overruns its banks—and Burnet Road, a north-south farm-to-market road that connects Travis and Williamson counties. In 1990, Skip and Barbara and her daughters had moved from a small house in a dicey neighborhood into a roomy, barnlike structure west of MoPac, on a street called Tamarack Trail, seven miles from the school.

By seven-thirty that evening, in addition to running errands and giving rides, Jennifer would have made two round-trips up and down either MoPac or a through street. The S-10 had a standard transmission. With traffic, she'd have been shifting down, working the clutch, waiting, shifting up, making lists, figuring out times and schedules, checking her Timex. A tiny, light-haired, doll-like girl. Organized. Always thinking ahead. Keeping secrets. Once her beloved S-10 has been thoroughly checked by the police, Mike Harbison will come get it and park it in his yard in New Boston.

ELIZA THOMAS

For her FFA project, dark-haired Eliza Thomas was raising another pig. She'd done well at last year's show, when her pig won a ribbon and was auctioned off for a good price. She was hoping to win again, but Stony was ailing. The vet had prescribed shots twice a day. On the morning of December 6, Eliza asked her mother to go with her to the ag barn and help her give 254-pound Stony an injection.

Maria Bancheri Thomas wasn't particularly drawn to animal husbandry, but because she especially doted on her elder daughter, she agreed to try. Eliza drove her bright green 1971 Karmann Ghia to Lanier and parked it there. Maria followed in her car and the two drove together to the barn.

A beautiful girl with deep brown eyes and a wide, lush mouth, Eliza had taken the $4.35-an-hour job at the ICBY shop in January, to supplement another job—escorting a nine-year-old boy to gym lessons twice a week. A lot of what she made went to maintain the VW, which was extremely sporty back then. That car, Maria would tell *People* magazine, was Eliza's pride and joy. "Her birthstone was an emerald so she just knew that car was meant for her." Another girl who worked at the yogurt shop told a police officer that Eliza was always trying to make more money because her mom, whose current job was as an artist's assistant, didn't bring in all that much and she often switched interests and careers.

Bereaved parents rarely talk about what their dead children might have grown up to be, but Maria Thomas went all out. Eliza, she declared, was special. She read constantly and had a gift for language;

she could have become a writer, maybe a poet. But Eliza's father, James, took his daughter at her word when she said she wanted to go to Texas A&M and become a vet, that she "had always been nuts about animals." For a couple of years she'd kept a bowl of crawfish, then white rats. James Thomas thought FFA was the best thing that ever happened to Eliza. Mechanically inclined, she could also weld and keep up with repairs on the Karmann Ghia. For Christmas this year, she'd asked for car parts.

At the ag barn, Maria wasn't much help. "I'm not too good with pigs," she said on the stand. In the end, Eliza found a fellow FFA member to help with the injection while her mother—anxious to contribute—mucked out the pen.

Divorced since 1981, when Eliza was seven, James and Maria Thomas had shared custody until she turned fourteen, when they let her decide for herself which parent she wished to live with. During the spring and early summer of 1991, she'd lived with her father and his second wife, but in July she'd moved in with her mother. That week in early December, Eliza's younger sister, Sonora, thirteen, was staying with their father in his home on Skylark Drive, only blocks from the yogurt shop. Sonora described her sister as popular, friendly and chatty, which made ICBY a perfect place for her to work. Eliza often called from there and asked her to ride her bike over, to bring something she'd forgotten or just to visit.

Neither Barbara Suraci nor Maria Thomas had raised their daughters to be country-western girls. Barbara had, after all, escaped small-town rural life. As for Maria—born in Italy, naturalized at an early age—she assumed her daughter's Aggie phase was just a teenager's infatuation and soon would fade.

Once she dropped Eliza off at Lanier at around 8:45, Maria went home to prepare for her workday, which began at 11:00 a.m.

After being forced to strip, Eliza will place her run-over white Reeboks alongside Jennifer's black pair in a neat pile against the wall next to the steel back doors. She'll be found lying spread-eagle on top of Sarah, placed there by the killers, the skin of her athletic young legs split apart by the radiant heat of the sweeping flames. Bound, gagged and, like Jennifer, burned bald and faceless. In years to come, Maria Thomas will refer to December 6, 1991, as the night "they burned up my daughter."

AMY AYERS

When Sarah said she was going out, Barbara Suraci knew what she meant. She wanted to go to Northcross Mall, not especially to buy anything—according to the incident report, Sarah's wallet contained the same five-dollar bill she'd left home with—but just to go out. In the early nineties, mall crawling had become a fact of life for suburban kids all over the country, a new version of hanging out on Main Street or driving up and down it in their cars. Austin was no different. Weekend nights, kids from all over the city either drove to or were dropped off at Northcross to window-shop, eat pizza, smoke cigarettes, drink sodas, maybe go to a movie or even ice-skate on the only rink within two hundred miles.

Located at the intersection of Burnet Road and West Anderson Lane—at that time the city's northernmost major intersection—the mall had opened with huge fanfare in 1975, when developers were trying to improve Austin's reputation as a stoners' paradise. Even former first lady Lady Bird Johnson was there, showing her gratitude to the Northcross founders for the donation they'd made to the ten-mile hike-and-bike trail that encircled Town Lake. Diana Hobby, the wife of Texas's lieutenant governor, had cut the ribbon to allow the first customers to enter. Touted as one of Austin's biggest retail attractions ever, the mall had a high-fashion Frost Bros. store, a six-screen movie theater, the ice-skating rink, wheelchair accessibility and artwork throughout the concourse. It offered, as all the ads promised, a new world of shopping.

But Austin wasn't Dallas, and by 1989 Frost Bros. had been liquidated. When other upscale stores closed, Northcross became a major teenage scene. For a while, LSD was the drug of choice among mall moles, especially those who came to the midnight movies on Friday and Saturday nights: the animated *Heavy Metal*, Pink Floyd's *The Wall* and, beginning in 1983, *The Rocky Horror Picture Show*. The Goth element—pierced and tattooed kids whom local cops tagged "PIBs," for people in black—showed up wearing studded dog collars, their lips inked black and their hair cut in Mohawks dyed fluorescent pink or blue, in time to see the movie they called the Rocky Show and watch the shadow cast of costumed and made-up locals act out the story as it progressed on-screen.

Sarah had no interest in going to the mall alone, so she asked her mother's permission to invite thirteen-year-old Amy Ayers to go along and afterward have a sleepover. Because Amy was younger and attended Burnet Middle School, these two best friends of the closest sort hardly ever got to see each other. Barbara agreed and suggested that if Sarah went with her sister when she drove to work, they could pick Amy up en route; then Jennifer could drop them off at the mall and go get them when they were ready to leave. They could also help Jennifer and Eliza close up: with all four of them pitching in, they'd be out of there in no time.

Sarah called Amy, whose parents were going Christmas shopping. Pamela Ayers had seen a watch she wanted to buy for her son, Sean, at Sheplers, a western store only ten or fifteen minutes away. She and her husband, Bob, were also planning to buy western clothes for Amy.

The Ayerses are small people, quiet, reserved, religious. On the witness stand, Amy's father will describe his daughter as a private girl who kept to herself. Having spent a good part of her childhood on a ranch, Amy had been riding horses since she was three. She could, Bob Ayers testified, ride all day without getting tired or bored. She often wore a cowboy hat to school, and sometimes she leashed up one of the two pigs she and Sean were raising and took it for a walk. She liked to do needlepoint. Like Eliza and a lot of other adolescent girls, she wanted to grow up to be a veterinarian. Though still an eighth grader, she'd been given permission to become an active junior member of the Lanier FFA. When asked if his daughter was "something of a cowgirl," Bob Ayers said no. She was *all* cowgirl.

Knowing that the Harbison girls took special precautions to look after their young daughter—they'd often promise that nothing would happen to Amy when she was with them—the Ayerses said yes to the sleepover and, presumably, to Northcross, which was a first. "That's the thing," Barbara Ayres-Wilson told me. "That was the first time either one of those girls had been to the mall on their own."

When Jones and the other investigators walk through the back doors, they might not immediately realize that the pale, shimmering mass beyond the worst of the destruction and away from the three hideously burned bodies is actually another body, another girl. There will be much speculation about Amy's position and why she wasn't lined up with her friends near the seat of the fire; as a result, she was burned less severely, her skin blistered and raw but not charred. In police photos taken from the back door, she looks almost like the distant ghost of a naked dead girl.

ON THE STREET ALL THE TIME

By the time Jennifer arrived home, the sky was dark. Greeting her mother, she looked quickly away and, after agreeing to drive Sarah and Amy to Northcross, rushed upstairs to change. Noting her evasiveness, Barbara figured she was keeping a secret that more than likely had to do with Sammy. Probably, she assumed, they were having sex, a suspicion confirmed when vaginal DNA swabs were taken and Sammy was questioned and then summoned to testify.

Upstairs, Jennifer changed into work clothes. Both her bedroom and Sarah's were decorated with FFA and sports memorabilia, stuffed animals, school photographs and country music CDs. On her wall Jennifer had hung a collage she'd made of pictures of barrel-racing girls on horseback that was captioned *The Boots, the Jeans, the Dream.*

ICBY regulations required employees to wear Brice's official open-necked knit polo shirt—white, with pink-and-green trim and the company's logo—tucked into dark jeans, and white or black athletic shoes. Once she'd changed, she tied her black high-top Reeboks, put on a jacket, grabbed her purse and went downstairs.

A young woman I met, Kate Wallace McClung, was fourteen when the girls were killed. She and her parents and her younger sister lived on Janey Drive in the Allandale neighborhood, some twenty blocks from Northcross Mall. A bright, headstrong girl, Kate had cut a secret flap in her bedroom window screen so that at eleven on

Friday and Saturday nights she could scramble out to the mall and, as a member of the Rocky Show shadow cast, dress up like Magenta and act out her part.

"Kids were on the street all the time," she said. "Nobody thought anything about it." She was never afraid, even though some of the streets were heavily shadowed.

In the coming years, new growth would push the desirable residential and commercial properties farther north and west, in the process stealing away not only many businesses but also much of the resale value. In a rapidly growing city where real estate inventory is low, prices in this area temporarily stalled. Out to the north and west, the Domain shopping center—with Neiman Marcus, Tiffany, Ralph Lauren and Louis Vuitton—has erased any chance of a Northcross revival. Even though each turnover or reinvention is cheerily announced in the *Austin American-Statesman* and the *Austin Business Journal* as a "makeover," Northcross is all but dead now. No anchor store, no movie theater, only a mattress shop, a guitar shop, a business center for annual meetings, a slew of beauty salons, a ballroom-dance studio and the ice rink. Everything else is gone. The once-grand venue has become a beige creep show, so empty that when you walk the halls, your footsteps echo. Residents who tried to forestall the construction of a Walmart next door lost that battle, and the giant discount store is thriving.

A t six-thirty, Eliza had arrived home and was getting ready for the short drive to the yogurt shop when her mother phoned to ask if Eliza wanted her to bring her a sandwich. Eliza was in an especially good mood because both she and Jennifer had been nominated for FFA queen, but she wasn't hungry. After their brief conversation, she donned her ICBY outfit, pulled her thick dark hair into a scrunchie and left home in time to make her seven o'clock shift. She'd had a difficult time the previous night, when she'd subbed for another girl and her former boyfriend, Roger Kerduka, had convinced a pal to call the shop and ask about all the flavors of yogurt they had. Eliza could hear Roger in the background, laughing and making remarks. Something about the prank had really upset her, leading cops to consider Kerduka a possible suspect, but, as John Jones says, "Back then we considered everybody a suspect."

Around this same time, Jorge Barney was closing the Party House for the night. He'd owned the store—previously called the Party Pig—for only three months and was working late in anticipation of the Christmas season. He already had a Santa Claus on his roof, complete with sleigh and reindeer. He then walked three stores down to Mr. Gatti's for some takeout. Barney's office was in the back of the store, near the wall he shared with the yogurt shop's storage room, and that's where he would work on his books while watching a little TV and eating his pizza.

How do we know all of this, and why does it matter what time anybody did anything or that Eliza's ex-boyfriend was mad at her? We know because we are still trying to figure out what happened and who the killers were—how they entered the shop, where the exit point was—and because the state, in order to negate reasonable doubt, had to re-create, from police reports, a detailed time line of the night on which the crime occurred. Everything matters, especially in a capital case. The fact that Jorge Barney ate supper at his desk while working on Christmas plans and watching a Cheers rerun mattered. He doesn't remember hearing pistol shots but, on the other hand, was the first person to smell smoke and take note of the flames from the adjacent store. The layout of the yogurt shop's back room and the position of the bodies relative to walls, shelves, sink, doors and one another will be of prime importance. "Evidence is everything," Jones will remind his people, his job being to find, record, collect and preserve.

Eliza took the office keys from the cash register's ledge and walked to the end of the counter and through an open door on her left into the storage area. Past the two bathrooms, mop sink and walk-in cooler, she swung to the right and unlocked the ICBY office door. Inside, she laid her jacket, car keys, purse and maroon-and-white Texas Aggie backpack on a filing cabinet, then locked the door behind her and retraced her steps. Following Brice rules, she put the keys back on the cash register, where they'll be found hours from now, long after the flames have been doused and the four bodies discovered.

Once the girl finishing her shift had left, Eliza would run the store alone until Jennifer arrived at eight; then they'd share responsibility. Ten minutes before the eleven o'clock closing time, they would lock the front door from the inside, turn the OPEN sign to CLOSED and leave the key in the lock, even if last-minute customers were still in the shop. They would deposit the night's proceeds in a floor safe in the office and clean up according to Brice's precise schedule. When they were finished, they'd remove the key and lock the door again from the outside, then put the key in an envelope and slide it under the door, where the manager would retrieve it in the morning. Because Eliza arrived first, she would run the cash register while Jennifer took orders. The tape in the machine—an old-fashioned paper roll—would record every transaction Eliza—cashier 13—rang up, including the last one of the night, a "No Sale" at 11:03 p.m., some thirteen minutes after the front door was locked and three minutes after the shop was officially closed.

In 2010, I talked to Peggy Sanders, the general manager of a locally owned coffee and tea store not far from Hillside Center, who spoke of the risks of working in retail, especially in small shops without a security guard. "You never know who's coming in that door," she said. In her view, those little girls wouldn't necessarily have realized if somebody might be suspicious, or if it was okay to let somebody use the bathroom, or when, maybe, they should call the police.

A late-night ICBY regular will echo her thoughts. Having noticed the lack of adult supervision, he'd often wondered if the girls who worked there were too trusting and naïve to recognize a potentially dangerous situation and if security shouldn't have been a pressing concern.

All the West Anderson ICBY girls were close to the same age, seventeen. For Brice, this was normal. When Reese Price began working there seven years earlier, that's how old she was. Afterward, people did raise the issue of workplace safety, but back then Austinites didn't worry that much about crime and, besides, this was a safe part of town. One Hillside business didn't even bother to switch out a defective lock. Anyway, who was going to make trouble in a frozen-yogurt shop?

In a city that prides itself on its liberal, classless attitudes, the murders brought a few surprising opinions to the surface. "We never thought our daughters would have to have a job," one mother told me. "I felt bad for those girls that they did."

"What were they thinking," another woman wondered, "letting those little girls work by themselves after nine, when the other stores were closed? I would *never* have allowed it."

Actually, Barbara Suraci had encouraged Jennifer *not* to take a job during her senior year, to, instead, "do wild and crazy things and have fun." But she wasn't surprised when her daughter insisted. "It's what we *do* in our family. We work. We build things. We have jobs."

By seven-thirty, Sarah had donned a black denim jacket with a pseudo-Aztec lightning bolt across the front. As she and Jennifer headed to the S-10, their mother shouted out her usual "Be safe!" and Jennifer backed down the driveway and drove toward Amy's house on Ohlen Road in a neighborhood of smallish brick bungalows on rather large flat lots, only five blocks from Burnet Middle School and seven from West Anderson Lane.

At the front door, Bob and Pamela Ayers had kissed their daughter good night and told her they loved her; outside, they heard the lock turn behind them. Once her parents had left to go shopping, Amy packed her pajamas and other necessities in her Jiminy Cricket tote bag.

When the S-10 pulled up, she emerged wearing her brother's leather bomber jacket, her turquoise Wranglers and black lace-up boots; her watch, her shrimp earrings, the three-string friendship bracelets she never took off and, around her waist, a wide leather belt threaded with multicolor lacing and fastened with a large heart-shaped buckle she'd borrowed from her mother. The buckle will be among the items of clothing found on the yogurt shop's floor, but neither the belt nor the bomber jacket will ever be recovered.

Minutes later, Jennifer dropped the two girls off at the mall and, after settling on a time and place to pick them up, drove past Hooters, Walgreens and a number of strip shopping centers to the Hillside lot, where she parked next to Eliza's Karmann Ghia and went inside, leaving Amy's tote bag on the seat. Four hours from now, police will begin to figure out who the murdered girls are by examining registration papers in Jennifer's truck and Eliza's VW.

A woman who worked at Suzanne's, an adjacent dress shop, described Jennifer and Eliza as "squeaky-clean." Another Hillside shop owner called them "innocent little girls." The day after the murders, John Jones sent a cop he considered the most cynical guy in Homicide to examine the girls' bedrooms to see if he could find something indicating drugs, secrets, a bad-guy boyfriend, uncle or stepfather; anything at all. He came back shaking his head. Those girls, he reported, were *pure*. Both of them got good grades, had dreams of college and were true to the popular image of middle-class Texas girls who loved animals, family, George Strait, Garth Brooks and western gear. Whether or not they became farmers, ranchers or even veterinarians, thinking they might gave them energy and structured their lives. They wore their FFA jackets proudly, raised their animals devotedly, listened to country music, wore tight jeans with belts, rooted for the Aggies, liked their snap-button shirts tight and their jeans long enough to reach past the arch of their boots.

Walking my dog along a leash-free trail on Austin's Redbud Isle, I once ran into a man named Doug Tash, whose mother still ran a pet-grooming shop two doors down from where ICBY used to be.

Oh, yeah, he told me, his family was in business when the murders occurred. Their shop had filled with smoke from the fire. A window got broken and some cats they were boarding escaped. They managed to catch them, but it wasn't easy.

As for the girls, he said, "They were rednecks, you know. Their friends put FFA jackets on the caskets. I was there. I saw it."

Tash went to a different high school, McCallum, where a lot of kids were more into acid than pigs. When subpoenaed as a potential witness, he asked the judge to release him. When Lynch asked why, Doug said, "I'd like not to be a part of this."

"Kickers," another McCallum student called the girls. "You don't want to fool around with shitkickers."

———

At Northcross, APD officer Malcolm Wilson moonlighted weekend nights as a uniformed private security guard. From six until closing at nine, he and his partner walked a regular beat: around the concourse, outside to the parking lot, back inside. Shown photographs of Sarah and Amy, Wilson (who would soon play a significant role in the ICBY investigation) couldn't remember having seen them, probably because the mall had been packed with kids all night long. After the murders, a boy who knew Sarah from Catholic school would call the special APD tips line to report having seen her with Amy near the Hallmark shop. He didn't know Amy, but Sarah introduced them, then laughed about not having any money for Christmas presents. When the boy's mother showed up, everybody wandered away and he didn't see the girls again. He remembered the leather bomber jacket but thought Sarah was wearing it, not Amy. And maybe he had it right. The girls might well have switched.

MISSING BOYS

That same morning, at 8:44, about when the girls were entering their classrooms, Austin Teleserve received a missing-person report. Identifying himself as Robert Springsteen, Sr., the caller said he hadn't seen or heard from his son since ten o'clock on Wednesday night, December 4. The boy hadn't attended school on Thursday and wasn't there today, either.

Teleserve had been set up to field calls about minor incidents that didn't require sending out an officer: old burglaries, lost pets, missing adults. Sidelined from street duty by an injury, ten-year APD veteran Mary Ann Hueske took the call.

Springsteen gave his address as 3839 Dry Creek Drive, Apartment 129, and his date of birth, January 18, 1945. His son's name, he said, was Robert Burns Springsteen, Jr., known as Rob, whose date of birth was November 26, 1974, his address the same as his father's but one apartment over. He described Rob as six feet tall, slim, 150 pounds, light complexion, hazel eyes, brown hair styled in a buzz cut with a tail—a mullet. He then noted that Rob's roommate, Michael James Scott, was also missing. The two had been sharing the apartment for three, maybe four weeks. The last time he'd seen Mike was also on Wednesday at ten. He happened to know that Mike's date of birth was February 6, 1974.

After asking a few more questions, Hueske asked Mr. Springsteen to please call back if his son returned.

He said he would. The officer filed the report.

And that was it. There was no follow-up call on either side. And no way to know why Rob's father had added "Sr." and "Jr." to his and his son's surnames when, legally, they were "III" and "IV."

CRIME SCENE

The first report was made at 11:48 by Troy Gay, an APD rookie on DWI patrol who—crossing Highway 1 on Anderson Lane—spotted a column of smoke rising from the hackberry trees lining Shoal Creek and drove toward it. When he came to the alleyway behind Hillside and saw yellow flames shooting out between two steel doors, he turned in. Beyond a blue dumpster, a man appeared in the next set of doors and waved him forward. When Jorge Barney saw smoke seeping around the electric panel in the north wall of his shop, he'd opened his back doors in time to see the police car edging toward him.

Gay drove to the front of the strip center and called in a general dispatch: "Have a fire inside a business," he said. Unfamiliar with the neighborhood, he gave the wrong address, but his mistake was soon corrected by another officer, Dennis Smith, who headed to the scene. By then, the yogurt shop's window and the glass panes in the front doors were completely black and smoke was pouring from the roofs of adjacent businesses.

An ordinary kitchen fire, people thought. *Somebody left a burner on, closed up the shop and went home. Happens all the time.*

Station Eight of the Austin Fire Department sent four units: an aerial ladder company, an engine company carrying hoses and water, an Emergency Medical Service ambulance and a battalion chief's car. A separate victims' rescue team rode in a Chevrolet Suburban. Because the engine company's job was to "make entry, find the fire and put it out with the water and hoses," that unit parked closest to the shop so that two of its specialists, Rene Hector Garza and David Deveau, could quickly connect and charge the hoses. Once they'd done that, the two men, already dressed in turnouts and equipped with a Handy-Pak radio, donned air packs, face masks and gloves.

Garza pulled on the front door, but the lock didn't give, so he used a crowbar to pop it open, and smoke banked to the ceiling and poured out. To get under it, he and Deveau dropped to their hands and knees. After bumping headfirst into the service counter, they regrouped and crawled into the back room, where they stood up and took in the situation.

Garza: "We located the fire. We began knocking it down. We found the seat, went and put the fire out. After we had knocked it down, there were some hot spots, just small bits and flames here and there. And once you put water on a fire, it creates steam, so it knocks down the visibility some." The hottest flames, he testified, came from halfway up the south wall of the storage room, where they assumed the stove was located.

Hoping to ventilate the room, Garza had taken a tentative step into the darkness when he felt Deveau's hand on his shoulder. Because of the masks and packs, the firefighters communicated primarily through gestures and touch. "Deveau kind of shakes me . . ." Garza remembered. "He's got a hand light; he points it at the floor."

"Is that a foot?" Deveau yelled through his mask.

Garza looked down and then, to get a better view, stepped back and saw it, too.

"I proceeded to back up, you know, startled a little bit," Deveau said, "and we found the second body."

Garza told him to stay put. Outside in the staging area, where firefighters were climbing ladders and knocking open doors of the other businesses, he told his battalion chief what they'd found. Two victims, he said. Kids. Nude. When a member of the rescue team wanted to go in, he shook his head. "Let's not move them," he said. "Something is *wrong.*" Then he walked toward the alley, to try to open the back doors.

Rene Garza will relive these moments at least three times: once for the official AFD incident report and, years later, during the two trials. His testimony will be among the most compelling and moving the juries will hear, a tribute to articulate simplicity and honest recall.

When he pushed at the back doors, they swung open easily, allowing smoke and steam to pour out. He looked inside. There was no kitchen, no stove. When he stepped in, he saw the lower half of yet another dead girl. Asked to describe his experience that night, Garza always said the same thing. "The foot," he said. "I remember the foot."

Just as the battalion chief was telling the two policemen on the scene about the bodies, another cop, Joe Pennington, showed up, and the three officers entered the shop together. Once inside, they could see enough to verify the information, but the storage area was still full of smoke and steam, and without masks it was hard for them to breathe. "So it was walk in, look around, walk right back out. Maybe a minute, minute and a half tops."

That was when Gay called for a homicide cop: "Two bodies, probable arson, probable homicide." This brought other policemen and an arson investigator. Having been released from further duty, Garza and Deveau walked away together and sat talking in the cab of their truck until they felt ready to emerge, when they were reassigned.

Cops hate arson. Any trace evidence left untouched by fire gets either soaked or washed away once firefighters arrive. John Jones knew all about this. Fourteen months earlier, barely into his second week in Homicide, he caught his first case of arson-murder after a man with a grudge over an eight-dollar drug debt torched an apartment complex with a flare gun and burned it to the ground. It was nighttime, and people were sleeping; there were numerous injuries and two fatalities. One man suffered burns over 80 percent of his body when he carried his wife out through the flames and went back to find their baby. It was Jones who had to travel to the burn center in San Antonio to tell him that his wife and child were dead. What he didn't say was how long it took cops and firemen to find the baby's body.

In a trial, crime-scene photographs are called "exhibits." They are not evidence, merely pieces of information that both the prosecution and the defense use to support their version of events: the position of the bodies; location and trajectory of wounds; fire damage to particular objects and burn patterns on the walls; blood spatter, fallen debris, the placement of ligatures, the tying of knots. These exhibits tell us how things looked afterward, leaving interpretation and imaginative scenarios to the viewer.

For me, everything changed when I saw those photographs. After that, I understood why the firefighters couldn't bear to leave and why in the coming months Homicide would go all out in pursuit of Austin's self-proclaimed Satanists and devil worshippers. Garza said *wrong*. I thought *evil,* without knowing whether I even believed in it. As for Jones, he looked at the photos only once, a couple days after the murders. "I don't need pictures," he declared. "That scene is *burned* into my memory."

Months from now, when a television reporter asks what he saw when he first stepped into the shop, Jones will give a quick answer: "Wholesale carnage." But he's good at sound bites and in person he agrees with me: The real horror, beyond the unspeakable condition of the bodies, was that the girls had become one with the scene— melted, merged, blackened—and all but indistinguishable from the fallen girders, insulation and soundproofing tiles, the exploded cans and spilled syrups, the wet black splatters of muck and char, the aluminum ladder missing its top two rungs, the metal shelves along the south wall softened into swooping hammocks, as if made of candle wax. "Everything looked black at first," he says now, "except, of course, Amy." He shrugs. "But that's fire."

My grandson is a welder. To determine the composition of the shelves, I showed him a photograph. "Stainless," he said. "Standard restaurant supply—but wait." He took a breath. "Is that a body?"

It was Jennifer, burned beyond recognition. I shut down my computer screen.

Ignoring the firefighters, who either milled around or just stood there looking down, Jones stepped gingerly around the bodies. Having been schooled in evidence collection and processing, he felt competent to handle 95 percent of most crime scenes, but this one lay well beyond his expertise. In a memo to the DA's office, he will describe the situation as "Robbery + Sexual Assault + Multiple Child Victims + Bondage + Gunshot Wounds + Fire/Heat/Smoke/ Water Damage + No Known Witnesses = the Homicide, Arson and DA's worst nightmare."

In old-school police work, a lead cop struggled to solve the crime on his own. From the beginning, Jones knew he needed a team and he needed experts. But an officially sanctioned task force wasn't easy to come by, and besides, protocol said he couldn't make significant decisions without the approval of a unit supervisor—either Senior Sgt. Hector Polanco or Lt. Andy Waters. Since Polanco was out of town, he called Waters, who quickly dressed and headed over. Awaiting him, Jones began snapping black-and-white Polaroids, as he'd been taught to do when processing a fire scene. By then, longtime AFD arson investigator Melvin Stahl had arrived and was also taking pictures. But according to Jones, "We were photographing for different reasons. He was looking for signs of arson and to find out how the fire started and progressed. I was trying to solve a crime."

In his official report—written Saturday, December 7—Stahl would estimate that the fire had been set somewhere high along the south wall of the storage room toward the east end of the steel shelves at approximately 11:42, thirty-nine minutes after Eliza rang up "No Sale."

YOUR YOGURT GIRL

In many instances, to write about a murder is to write about a trial. Consider O.J., or Lizzie Borden, Ted Bundy, Smith and Hickock, McVeigh, the West Memphis Three. Information comes slowly but in minute detail. In this instance, *Precisely at what time did you arrive, who else was there and who arrived next and when exactly; can you describe the path of the bullet and tell us about latent fingerprints, blood spatter, backdraft, accelerant, fire science, flashover? How do you know the girls were dead before the fire was ignited? Can you explain that for us?*

From testimony and transcripts we learn things—the woman who heard the dog bark at the very instant forensic investigators say the knife sliced across Nicole Brown Simpson's jugular; the bloody dress taken from Lizzie Borden's washtub; Karla Faye Tucker's taped boast that murdering victims with a pickax gave her sexual satisfaction ("I come with every stroke"); the celebrated expert witness who helped convict the West Memphis Three by citing examples of Satanism among fans of Iron Maiden and Metallica. . . . From photographs of the accused, by checking out the look in their eyes for signs of otherness and guilt, we make judgments. From all such fragments we can create a story that after a while seems real. We think we were there. If the victims are all dead, how else could we know?

The Hillside parking lot extends for a city block and can accommodate about two hundred cars, with an additional four or five head-in spots in front of each business. But by eight o'clock, when Jennifer began her shift, only Sun Harvest (a large natural-foods grocery store), Mr. Gatti's and the yogurt shop remained open, so there was plenty of space. At nine, Sun Harvest—now called Fresh Plus Grocery—would close as well.

Between eight-fifteen and eight-thirty, fifty-one-year-old Lusella Jones parked in one of the ICBY spots and got out. A resident of nearby Allandale, she'd come to get a quick takeout for her husband, who'd had dental surgery and could eat only soft food.

By then, the four girls' parents had relaxed into their normal Friday-night routines. Barbara and Skip Suraci had eaten a quiet dinner and retired to their bedroom to watch television. Mike Harbison was in New Boston with his second wife, Debbie; they had no children of their own. When Maria Thomas got off work, she drove to the HQ Fitness Center on Far West Boulevard, hoping to do a short workout before dropping by the yogurt shop to say hi to Eliza. Having finished their shopping, Bob and Pam Ayers returned home with Sean's Christmas watch and new jeans and a fancy belt buckle for Amy. James Thomas, a social worker, and his second wife, Norma Fowler, a University of Texas economics instructor, were attending a graduate student party but planned to leave early and pay Eliza a visit at work. Because Sonora was home alone, they wouldn't stay long.

Heading inside, Lusella Jones noticed only two other vehicles in the lot: Eliza's VW and Jennifer's S-10. Had she bothered to look through the ICBY front window, she could've seen the entire service area—booths, tables, chairs, customers, the toppings display and yogurt machines, the girls working there. To the right of the window were two heavy wooden doors with plate-glass inserts. The left-hand door—bolted shut with top and bottom sliding locks—held product-display posters and a cardboard OPEN sign. A frequent customer, Jones went in through the other door.

The interior had a cheerful southwestern look, with dark red Mexican tile floors and walls lined with light oak-toned wood paneling. Along the north wall were three booths covered in forest green vinyl, each with a blond wooden chair at the end. There were five more booths against the south wall and, in the middle of the room, three tables. The serving counter extended from the cash register on

Jones's left to within five feet of the other wall, where there was a freezer chest filled with prepackaged cakes, pies, frozen-yogurt sandwiches and treats for special occasions. Beyond the space at the end of the counter, an open door led into the back room. Today, the storage area is pretty much as it was then: an open space sectioned off into partitions using fake, or stub, walls. Dark. Efficient. Windowless. Smaller than you might think, given the events that took place there.

Eliza stood behind the cash register while Jennifer manned the toppings display—chocolate, hot fudge, caramel, strawberry, cherry, carob chip, chopped nuts, M&M'S, granola, chunks of syrupy fruit, aerosol cans of whipped cream—as well as the five large dispenser cans on a shelf behind her, each filled with a particular flavor of yogurt. The chocolate and vanilla cans sat side by side, with a common spigot that delivered ICBY's favorite selection, the vanilla-chocolate swirl.

As the door closed behind her, Lusella Jones came to an abrupt halt. Only two other customers were in the shop, teenage boys who'd taken the table nearest the door and were focusing intently on something between them, a small sack of some kind. One sat with his back to her, leaning on his elbows and slumped over the table, while the other stood behind it, facing her.

Something about them unnerved Jones, though she couldn't say exactly what, only that she felt immediately fearful.

They were, she testified, probably between fourteen and seventeen and had a kind of "hippie" look. The one facing her was between five four and five seven, had medium-dark hair and weighed something like 130 to 140 pounds. She wouldn't call his hair messy, but it certainly wasn't clean-cut. Since the other boy never turned around, she couldn't describe him at all. As for ethnicity, they were "possibly Hispanic but may have been Anglo." Dark-skinned, in other words, in a white neighborhood.

When the standing boy stuck his hand down in the sack and stirred it around, there was, Jones said, a clicking sound, like marbles striking one another. Or coins. Maybe keys.

There was no sense to it. For one thing, Jones told a BATF (Bureau of Alcohol, Tobacco and Firearms) agent who was trying to help her analyze her suspicions, neither of them appeared to be eating anything. In the next moment, however, she modified her statement. "I don't remember," she said, "any containers on the table." And then she softened her certainty again: "I did not have a clear view of the entire table."

Pulling herself together, Jones eventually moved past the boys to the counter, where she ordered a fresh strawberry sundae from Jennifer, then went to the cash register to pay. She remembered wondering if maybe she should ask the girls if they were okay there by themselves or if they wanted her to call somebody, but Eliza and Jennifer were chatting happily and so Jones figured perhaps her premonition didn't amount to anything. She paid by check, took her sundae and left without looking back.

Memory's fungible, eyewitness accounts notoriously unreliable. People call in a tip or show up at a police station for many reasons, one of which is to contribute to the righting of a wrong, which sometimes causes potential eyewitnesses to embroider or imagine particular details in order to shape events to match either what they *think* happened or what somebody else had reported or suggested. Knowing this, cops withhold certain details, hoping a witness will cite them without being prompted.

By the time Lusella Jones testified in 2001, her memory had sharpened enough that she could come up with previously unmentioned details, one of which was that the standing boy had rolled his hand around inside the sack in a *threatening* manner. This, in retrospect, made her wonder if the clicking she'd heard hadn't been marbles, but bullets. What she emphasized most strongly, ten years later, was a sense of foreboding, a feeling that these boys were up to no good.

It could well be that the more Jones concentrated on dredging up her memories of that night and the more she told friends and family about being in the yogurt shop only hours before the girls were killed, the more positive she became of the boys' ill intentions. By 1999, when police arrested the four young men and the mayor said that we could now begin to heal, she might have come to believe she had a duty to help put them away. At both trials, she gave a partial description of the boy who'd sat with his back to her. He was, she said, older than the other one, with a broader, thicker physique.

But who knows, maybe her instincts were correct; maybe they *were* about to make trouble, perhaps even to tie up the girls and rob the store. Or possibly they were just fooling around, making pests of themselves, as bored young slackers often do, if only to attract notice. All Lusella Jones really knew was they weren't the kind of boys she was used to seeing at the yogurt shop and that they weren't *from around here,* either. After midnight, when police collected evidence, they found her check in a money bag inside the cash register drawer, right where Eliza had put it.

At about nine, Jennifer drove to Northcross to pick up Sarah and Amy. Back at Hillside, the two younger friends went to get takeout pizza before Mr. Gatti's closed at ten.

We are two hours and forty-two minutes away from the fire.

The gym had closed by the time Maria Thomas got there, so she drove on to the yogurt shop. When she arrived at about nine-thirty, Eliza was on the phone, trying to convince her little sister to ride her bike to the shop. But Sonora couldn't leave without her father's permission, so Eliza handed the phone to her mother and went back to work. Soon afterward, Sarah and Amy returned with their pizza, opening the box on the table between them. Other customers will have a vague recollection of two girls with long hair sharing a pizza, nothing more specific. This might've been because the girls were so wrapped up in each other that they were, in effect, absent. Maria ended her conversation with her younger daughter and went to the cash register to confer with Eliza. (This information comes from Maria's testimony, with backup from James Thomas and various other customers.) When the ICBY phone rang, Jennifer rushed to answer it, knowing it was Sammy calling to make breakfast plans for the next morning.

Later, once news of the murders spread, reports of suspicious persons and vehicles streamed into Homicide. One woman said she had been at the shop four days prior to the killings, at about four in the afternoon, when a tall, thin, young white man walked up to the counter but "did not act as though he wanted to order anything." About twenty-three years old, with wavy shoulder-length blond hair parted in the middle, he stood beside the freezer display, looking not at the frozen pies and cakes but at the door to the rear of the shop, which everybody knew, by the time this woman called, was where the murders had taken place. Anyway, he finally, "with much indecision," placed an order. Still, his skittish ambivalence had made the caller feel so jumpy that she decided to leave. Driving out of the parking lot, she saw him again, getting into a light-colored vehicle, either a big car—perhaps a Delta 88—or a small pickup. Another woman said that on the night of the murders, she'd seen several dubious-looking people outside the shop between six and nine o'clock, but she was unable to offer a description. A couple called in about a questionable van, and so did another man, who said the van was white. Somebody else saw a boy on a skateboard rolling around the parking lot, alone and late in the evening.

Between nine-thirty and ten, Dearl (pronounced Darrell) Croft— a fifty-two-year-old former military policeman and current owner of Longhorn Security Company—parked his company car, a tan Ford station wagon with a rack of blue warning lights across the roof, in front of the Party House. After dining at Fuddruckers, he and two female companions had gone to ICBY for dessert.

After the women told him what they'd like, Croft entered the shop alone and surveyed the place: the girls behind the counter, Maria by the cash register, two young people—a boy and a girl—sitting in a booth along the right-hand wall, another couple standing close to the counter, studying a wall menu, and, just behind them, a fidgety young man in a green jacket that might have come from a military-surplus store. In his early to mid-twenties—medium build, 155 to 170 pounds, maybe between five ten and six feet—he was white, like everybody else in the shop. Having spent most of his life in law enforcement of one kind or another, Croft prided himself on his ability to note aberrant behavior, and right away he thought (or *remembers* thinking) there was something odd, something *off*, about him.

Having made their decision, the couple studying the menu moved forward and ordered. The jittery young man was next.

Croft was a regular at the yogurt shop and, like Maria and Eliza Thomas, belonged to the HQ Fitness Center, where he'd once run into them in the coed steam room. "Hi," Eliza had said. "I'm your yogurt girl. Remember me?" Like most people who hold security jobs, he believed in order and his responsibility to enforce it upon a sometimes-resistant populace. When the fellow in the green jacket hesitated instead of moving to the counter, Croft took a step toward him. At that, the young man turned around.

Was that his car out there, he asked Croft, with the lights on top? When Croft said yes, he asked was he police? Security? "What are you?"

His voice was deep, clear and distinctive, which Croft found unusual for someone in his twenties. In interviews he will sometimes mention a long, pointy nose. He thought it odd that this screwball guy would've noticed his car in the first place—and who did he think he was, asking what *he* was? But he held his tongue, avoided confrontational eye contact and said only that he owned a security company, at which point the fellow turned back around, to find Jennifer urging him to come forward, so he moved up and asked for a 7UP. When Jennifer said they had only Sprite, he said okay, so she put the can in a paper sack and handed it to Eliza to ring up.

Croft moved to the counter and gave Jennifer his order. But before he got to the cash register to pay, the unpleasant youth had gone around the end of the counter and through the door to the back room. Unaware that customers were allowed back there, Croft asked Eliza where he was going. When she said the bathroom, he told her he didn't know they had one, and Eliza laughed. The bathrooms weren't really open to the public, she explained, but the guy said he had to go, so she let him.

It's not clear why Eliza said that, or even if she did, because, as she well knew, the ICBY shop had two bathrooms—as required by city regulations—one for men and one for women, both open to the public. But that's what Croft remembered. Stalling for time, hoping to get another look at the nervous stranger, he initiated a conversation with Maria about the gym. Once he'd paid his tab and Jennifer set out his three cups of yogurt, however, he had no choice but to head toward the door.

Before he got there, Eliza stopped him. "Dearl?" she called. "Your yogurt?" Rattled, he went back, and they all laughed.

The next day, Croft drove to Houston for a football game. When he got home Sunday, he read about the four deaths and went immediately to the yogurt shop to tell a policeman about his experience and to sign an official APD incident report. Knowing that policemen generally regard the testimony of wannabe cops with suspicion, I asked Jones what he thought about Croft's account. Was it reliable? After hesitating a moment, all he was willing to say was, "He was okay. He didn't *hurt* the investigation."

Two years later, in an attempt to mine his memories for more specific details, Croft will undergo voluntary hypnosis, to no avail. In 1999, after the arrests, a homicide detective will show him a four-page photographic lineup of possible suspects, but he will not identify any of them as the snarky fellow he encountered.

A few minutes after Dearl Croft drove away, Maria Thomas left as well. Almost immediately afterward, James Thomas and his wife dropped by. Business had slowed again, giving Eliza an opportunity to tell her father and stepmother about an economics class she was taking. Thomas recalled seeing two girls in a booth with a Mr. Gatti's box on the table between them, but he hadn't ever met Jennifer's family and had no idea who they were. Neither he nor his wife remembered a young man in a green jacket. They stayed about fifteen minutes, maybe twenty.

During the next week or so, a number of others will call the special APD tips line to report having been to the yogurt shop between nine-thirty and ten-thirty: two African-American women in their late twenties, there for maybe half an hour; two male-female couples who lingered over their yogurt for some time; regular customers Joseph Sauter and Eva Reed, who entered the shop at about ten. Jennifer and Eliza talked with them about their FFA projects and both seemed to be in their usual good mood. At ten-thirty, a customer became uneasy when she saw a "white or Hispanic" man sitting in an older white vehicle in front of the shop, not doing anything, just sitting. When this customer went back out, the white car was gone. Another couple claimed to have seen a suspicious van in the lot between ten-thirty and eleven.

McCallum kids sneered at these nervous reports. They knew things their parents and other people didn't, like how high school boys hung out with armed skinheads down at the skanky field they called "the Fungus," many of them dropping acid and even doing heroin not just there but in the Northcross parking lot and all around Shoal Creek, Hillside and Allandale. Young kids, thirteen, fourteen. Girls, boys. So what if a kid rolled marbles around in a sack? Or even bullets? The neighborhood wasn't as white-bread predictable as folks thought.

"We did everything," says Kate Wallace McClung with a smile. "The streets were safe, so kids roamed around at all hours doing all kinds of things."

Once the four young men have been arrested, Dearl Croft's description will hew more closely to the appearance of the suspect thought to be the ringleader. Maybe that jittery guy was smaller than he thought, younger, no pointy nose or mature voice. In her testimony during the second trial, Maria Thomas will add to her memories a young man in a green jacket who was acting strange.

Working in his back room, Jorge Barney thought he might have heard something on the roof at about ten-thirty and halfway remembered that, worried about his Christmas decorations, he had gone outside to check. But later, he wasn't sure whether he really did or, for that matter, if he'd heard anything to begin with.

What do we actually know and how do we know it? Neuroscience teaches us that our brains are never still, even when we're asleep and have plunged into dreams. Neurons still continue to spark and fly, jumping synapses, digging up memories, creating new ones, adding, subtracting, removing, revising. Until the story feels right. Correct. What we want it to be.

At 10:42—eighteen minutes before closing time—Eliza will ring up the last real sale of the night. The couple who placed the order, Tim Stryker and Margaret Sheehan, had been to a movie and were stopping by for dessert before heading home. Entering the shop, they noticed only two other customers: large people in hooded jackets sitting across from each other in the last booth on the left, closest to the cash register.

Eliza—"the girl with the gorgeous eyes"—stood alone behind the counter, Jennifer having moved into the dining area to wipe down the tables, turn chairs upside down on top—two facing diagonally on the tables and one at the end of each booth—and refill the napkin holders. Sheehan ordered a small cup of vanilla with carob-chip topping and, once Eliza handed it to her, went to the booth next to the one already occupied to wait for Stryker, who hadn't yet made up his mind. For no important reason, she sat facing the front of the shop, so when looking up, she saw herself reflected in the plate-glass window and, behind her, the people in the next booth.

She couldn't really describe their facial features or even accurately pinpoint their gender, though because of their size she assumed they were men. The one sitting with his back toward hers was larger and his jacket, either khaki-colored or beige, was padded. The other had a thinner build and light brown hair. She sensed something odd about them, nothing she could articulate, but since they leaned across the table to huddle close together, she thought they might be homosexual.

Tim Stryker eventually ordered a large cup of vanilla with hot fudge topping and, after paying the $4.42 tab, sat down across from her. Neither of them noticed Sarah or Amy. Later, the pizza box will be found in the back room on a table adjacent to the big sink, where someone had begun washing utensils and topping containers. Presumably the girls had taken the box to the back and started doing dishes. There is no chance of knowing this absolutely.

Stryker thought they should take their yogurt and go, but Sheehan wanted to finish hers inside. When questioned, she remembered Jennifer and Eliza discussing the upcoming week's schedule and a friend they hadn't seen lately. She had a feeling the men in the hoods were listening as well. Something about their stillness. Neither she nor Stryker recalled seeing any food on their table and were pretty sure they weren't eating or drinking anything.

Minutes later, Stryker upped his argument. Since the girls were cleaning up, they should get out of their way. This time, Sheehan yielded, but as they left, she checked her watch, and it was 10:47. Out front, she noticed a green car, maybe Eliza's Karmann Ghia. Under hypnosis, she said she'd seen the same car when they arrived.

When asked by the APD about Eliza's temperament and habits, a coworker recalled her strictness about following Brice rules to the letter when she was in charge, especially when it came to cleaning up and closing. Therefore, soon after Sheehan and Stryker left, one of the girls—almost certainly Jennifer—must have locked the front door with a single key and turned the OPEN sign around to CLOSED. Because she'd already wiped off the tables, she then pulled a step stool close to the big silver swirl dispensers so she could remove the lids, drain the yogurt and bend into each can to clean and sanitize it. When the shop manager took stock of the dining area the next morning, she could tell investigators exactly how far the girls had proceeded before they were interrupted.

Jennifer's back was to the front door. Close to or behind the cash register, Eliza was running a rag over the counter when something happened.

An unexpected something.

She lifted her hand, left the rag on the stainless rim of the serving area and didn't pick it up again.

Early the next morning, once the bodies had been taken to the morgue, investigators took pictures of the rag—piled up unevenly, shaped by a hand—and the cash register tape and the open vanilla yogurt dispenser with the stool pulled up to it. The drawer of the register was open, but the till had been removed and was now lying on the storage room floor beside the place where Amy Ayers's shoulder had been, with coins scattered around her face.

At five or ten minutes past eleven on the night of the killings, Kate Wallace McClung had walked down Rockwood Lane on her way to Northcross Mall. Looking to her left, she'd noticed the lights were still on in the yogurt shop. Unusual, she thought, and then, not wanting to be late for her Rocky Show rehearsal, kept walking.

Though no one except Margaret Sheehan and Tim Stryker mentioned the people in hooded jackets, by then everybody else had left. While these were solid eyewitnesses, they could remember only so much. They will both provide signed APD incident reports yet won't be asked to testify in either trial, which defense attorney Carlos Garcia says was because what they had to say didn't match the confessions of the defendants, who said they'd parked in the alley and entered through the back door.

Maybe so, but why blame the prosecution? The oversight falls more heavily on both defense teams, who might have called Stryker and Sheehan to help them establish a plausible theory that didn't involve their clients. This they did not do.

Garcia readily accepts the accusation, citing his last-minute appointment to represent Michael Scott and the subsequent lack of time to properly prepare a defense. By 2009, when Scott's retrial was scheduled to begin, Garcia and his tireless intern, Amber Farrelly, were ready to put the Stryker-Sheehan testimony to good use. Then the case was dismissed. Mention of these two figures wearing hoodies won't surface in the press until 2011, during intense local coverage of the murders' twentieth anniversary, when reporter Jordan Smith, of the free weekly *Austin Chronicle,* asked Garcia what he thought really happened that night.

"It's the only explanation that makes sense," he told me, repeating what he'd said to the reporter. That the killers were already in the shop when it closed. Sitting at a table. Watching the girls clean up. Waiting. When one of them pulled a gun on Eliza, she rang up "No Sale" and handed over the cash drawer.

Reese Price has a different take. She thinks Eliza was simply closing out the register. Or maybe checking the till one last time.

As for John Jones, he brushed Garcia's theory aside. "Could be," he said, "but . . ."

I finished his sentence. "Can't prove it."

He nodded, shrugged; we moved on.

As for why this case had gone unsolved for so long and caused so much grief to so many people, Garcia had a simple answer: "Evil," he said. "Yogurt Shop was an act of pure evil. And when evil is let loose, it spreads. And doesn't stop."

TASK FORCE

John Jones has a wicked, often impertinent sense of humor. In the days ahead, he will be criticized by a superior for inappropriate wit. A black man in a white city might well decide to keep a low profile, but not Jones. Irony's his special gift; it gives him distance and keeps him sane.

Homicide, he has also said, is like being on an assembly line, watching as the bodies roll by. In his years as a cop, including accidental deaths and suicides, he figures his count comes to about 150, the last four being Eliza, Jennifer, Sarah and Amy.

As far as I can tell, police and prosecutors alike take murders personally, especially if they've been to the crime scene and viewed the butchery firsthand. Cops say they get used to it, but I'm not so sure. Ask them about a case, particularly one involving a child or a young person: They remember names, circumstances, smells, the pervasive sense of *wrongness* it is their job to correct. Assistant District Attorney Robert Smith visited the yogurt shop on Saturday, December 7. When the time comes to prosecute whoever is eventually accused of this unspeakable crime, he will devote all of his considerable intellectual and strategic energies to a conviction. Not that he wouldn't have anyway. But this one demanded payback. Including a trip to the execution chamber.

For his partner, Jones requested Sgt. Mike "Huck" Huckabay, a friend he'd worked with previously. Both were fathers, both had daughters; most important, they trusted each other. Working together, they would divvy up the responsibilities—Huck doing interviews and negotiations; Jones, the technical side. When Huckabay is interviewed, he'll admit that while homicide cops get used to seeing terrible things, the ICBY scene hit him hard and made him wonder where his own daughter was, especially since one girl owned a Mickey Mouse watch, just like his daughter did.

"I saw things in Vietnam," he told a reporter, "and I thought nothing will ever match that. Well, this matches that. Because it's in Austin, Texas, right down the street from where we live."

On Saturday, once they'd gotten the nod from Waters and Polanco to stay on as lead investigators, the two men made a private pact. This was, they agreed, an unusual case, and it called for unusual methods. To get an arrest warrant or an indictment, they were required to provide a pile of evidence solid enough to constitute what the DA's office considered probable cause. Both Huck and Jones were determined to do right by Yogurt Shop. They would not request an arrest warrant or an indictment form until they felt they had solved the crime to the furthest extent of the law: beyond a reasonable doubt. They didn't ask for permission to do that. They just did it.

A ustin is a city of white and brown people and not so many blacks, who make up about 8 percent of the population. Jones grew up in racially mixed Dallas, where his stepfather worked as a baker and his mother as a teacher's aide. When it was time for her eldest child and only son to enter first grade, she insisted on enrolling him at a Catholic school, where she thought the teachers were better.

"So," Jones told me, "I was a good Catholic boy five days a week, and on Sunday, I listened to the Baptist preacher rail against 'dem damn Catholics.' "

In sixth grade, he transferred to public school.

Those of us who live in Travis County, where the arts thrive and Democrats run the show, tend to think that because we're liberal we aren't racist. But when working undercover in narcotics, sporting a bushy beard, beat-up straw hat and baggy clothes, Jones regularly had to stave off the natural tendency of young cops who, when he showed up with a suspect, assumed he was the detainee. *Not me*, he'd have to tell them. *The white guy.*

"An ego the size of a washtub," a fellow officer anonymously quipped to a news reporter when describing Jones. Another cop once said "nigger" in his presence and afterward expressed surprise that Jones might have been offended. "I didn't mean *him*," he explained.

Jones is short and stocky, powerful in his trunk and legs. In 1972, he was attending the University of Texas as a music-education major—he sings bass and plays a couple of instruments—when his summer job waiting tables at a local country club ran out. Since the APD was advertising for cadets and Jones needed a job, he signed on for a temporary gig.

"I was black, a college kid; they snapped me up," he told me. He'd already looked ahead at career possibilities for a music-ed major. Church-choir director was at the top of the list; after that, high school teacher/director of the marching band. He thought maybe he needed a different line of work, one that paid better and offered solid benefits and advancement potential. After graduating from cadet training, he stayed on. He and his wife, Yolanda, raised four daughters on the salary of what he calls the "po-po." When he retired in 2004, he became security manager of Capital Metro, Austin's public transportation system, so he's still the po-po. During the heat of the ICBY investigation, he converted to Catholicism and now sings bass in the twenty-five-member St. Louis the King choir, acting as cantor and participating in oratorios and concerts not just in local churches and concert halls but also, every couple of years, in Europe. He has a snatch of Bach oratorios on his cell phone's voice mail. In his spare time, he referees amateur soccer matches.

He's a private man and, like a lot of cops, thin-skinned. He doesn't much keep up with the APD officers he knew back then. When I mention his musical education, lawyers and former colleagues are often surprised.

On that Friday night at ICBY, waiting for Lt. Andy Waters to give Jones and the others permission to proceed, Joe Pennington began taking measurements and drawing stick-figure pictures showing the exact position of the bodies relative to one another and to certain points of reference: the walls, shelves, doors, freezer, office. Having been trained to diagram vehicle crashes, he had exactly the expertise Jones needed.

Here, for example, are his written measurements for Amy Ayers:

Victim #1. Head: 15 Feet East of the West Wall 76 Inches from East Side of Office Wall. 72 Inches South from Bathroom Wall (North Side). Right Foot: 59 Inches East of Office Wall, 14 Inches South of Bathroom Wall. Left Foot: 22 Inches South of Bathroom Wall. Victim Was on Her Stomach or Right Side.

After sending out a mandatory dispatch to city departments and the media, Jones went back to his car and told the television reporters they could get out now and, incidentally, that they might not need to go to Houston after all. So by the time other press arrived—within three minutes—the KTBC duo were already videotaping firefighters on the roof, cops traipsing inside and out, the flashing lights, the store's sign, the Party House's red balloons.

Back inside, he conferred with the arson investigator, Stahl. They agreed that the situation required—"screamed for," Jones would write in a memo—processing and analysis far beyond the reach of the APD, which, along with many other small-city police forces at that time, had no forensic unit other than an old-fashioned fingerprint detail, useless in cases involving fire. The Texas Department of Public Safety did have a CSI lab and a criminalist trained in DNA collection. Although the lab was fairly new and its staff relatively inexperienced, calling them was really their only option (a decision both Jones and Huckabay will reiterate later when the work of DPS technicians comes in for lacerating criticism).

Jones also wanted to call Charles "Chuck" Meyer from the U.S. Department of the Treasury's Bureau of Alcohol, Tobacco and Firearm's National Response Team, who, along with Stahl, had worked with him on the other arson-homicide. Meyer had helped out enormously and both men trusted him utterly, but once Jones made the suggestion, Stahl hesitated, worried that summoning a federal agent might ruffle some feathers. Undaunted, Jones persisted. If they drew Meyer into the investigation, they'd gain access to federal wiretaps, search warrants and a trustworthy polygraph expert, as well as FBI behavioral analysts, ViCAP (the Violent Criminal Apprehension Program) and whatever else Quantico could offer. Stahl soon concurred.

The right to use federal resources in a local crime emerged during Ronald Reagan's war on drugs when, two years after Congress passed the Comprehensive Crime Control Act ordering mandatory sentencing for drug dealers and killers with previous felony convictions, BATF—often called simply ATF—developed its own program to ensure implementation of the stiffer penalties. Project Achilles allowed federal agents to work alongside local and state officers even when no state lines had been crossed.

After Andy Waters arrived and gave his approval, Jones called Chuck Meyer, then the DPS crime-lab manager, who, in turn, phoned the head of their DNA operation, Irma Rios. She agreed to meet her team at the DPS lab, where they would gather their equipment and aim to be at West Anderson Lane within two or two and a half hours. Waters himself called Huckabay. When he got there twenty minutes later, Homicide desk sergeant Jesse Vasquez was already on site, and Meyer soon followed. Attempting to identify the bodies, Waters began tracking down the store manager. Once he found her, he put in a request for crisis teams to notify the victims' families.

Heavy on the cops' minds was the issue of the medical examiner. For the most part, the APD and the ME's office had managed to establish a relatively cozy working relationship—except in homicide cases, and for good reason. "Dead body belongs to the ME," Jones says. "That's how it works. We call him 'the body snatcher.'"

But because of the water and fire damage and the potential loss of biological evidence when the bodies were lifted, the investigators—Jones, Stahl, Huckabay, Meyer and Waters—agreed that DNA swabbing and evidence processing should be performed *at the scene*. Jones had hoped to wait a while before calling the ME's office, but Jesse Vasquez, following APD rules, had already done so and been informed that since Roberto Bayardo, the chief medical examiner, was out of town, his deputy, Les Carpenter—a known tight-ass when it came to protocol—was en route, accompanied by his "transporters"—the men who would zip the bodies into bags and drive them, one by one, to the morgue.

Taking photos, Stahl noted the large amount of blood on the floor. He could see and smell it. This meant the girls were almost certainly dead from gunshot wounds when the fire was lit. Noting that containers on the steel shelves were more heavily damaged at the top, he took careful pictures of anything that might indicate the origin, progress and temperature of the flames: burn patterns on the walls, the distorted shelves, the melted aluminum ladder, the charred mop handle, products stored on the kitchen shelving that had burst, sending streams and puddles of sticky, combustible material across the floor. The disappearance of the ladder's *top* two steps was of particular interest since it indicated a very hot fire—at least 1,221 degrees Fahrenheit—that had originated above the floor level, swept across the ceiling and then moved down.

When Reese Price arrived and couldn't make any positive identifications, she opened the ICBY office to check the schedule for her employees. At about the same time, APD officers were unlocking the only two privately owned vehicles in the parking lot. Inside the S-10 there were purses and Amy's overnight tote bag; in both glove compartments, DMV registration papers. Eliza's Karmann Ghia was registered in her name; Jennifer's truck in her father's.

Because James Thomas lived nearby and his address was on Eliza's car registration, the crisis team went there first and then to Maria's house. By then, the girls had been dead for about four hours. Barbara Suraci said when somebody knocked at her door at three-thirty or so in the morning and she and Skip went to see who was there in the middle of the night, she felt so certain of her daughters' well-being that when asked where they were, she said, "In bed, sleeping." And when they were given the terrible news, they wanted to shut the door in the strangers' faces so that they could go on with their lives and wait for Jennifer and Sarah to get home. When the time came to tell the girls' father in New Boston, Barbara dialed his number but couldn't say the words, and so the job fell to Skip. Standing there with the phone in his hand, he went blank. "Am I saying the right thing here?" he asked his wife. "Jennifer and Sarah were *murdered*? *Burned*?" When he finally managed to explain the unthinkable truth, Harbison hung up the phone, and his wife had to call back to find out why he was weeping and screaming.

"And Amy?" Barbara had to ask. Was little Amy dead, too?

As for Les Carpenter, he showed up long before the DPS team did, and when Huckabay and Jones told him of their decision to have the bodies processed at the scene, the deputy ME went into a professional snit. The bodies were his. He could do whatever he wanted with them. Huckabay, who had seniority and was a better negotiator than Jones, said he knew that but hoped Carpenter would bear with them "because if we don't solve this in a few days, we are going to be in so much trouble."

After the autopsies, Assistant DA Terry Keel asked Jones to write a memo explaining the disagreement between Homicide and Les Carpenter. The wrangling, Jones admitted, was not pretty. And he listed the reasons he and Huckabay felt the DPS needed to act before the bodies were removed. One, the likelihood of trace evidence being lost during transport. Two, the likelihood of trace evidence being washed away by water from broken overhead pipes and firefighters' hoses. Three, lack of trace evidence due to body-temperature changes between there and the ME's office. And four, evidence being added or subtracted due to contact with sheets and plastic containers the personnel used there.

Carpenter's response? "Les was unimpressed."

Perhaps feeling outgunned, Carpenter eventually backed down and told his team to wait. But he spent all night at the ICBY shop and was, Jones reported, a source of constant irritation, threatening to load the bodies on his own and making nonstop disparaging remarks about the skills and methodology of the DPS and the APD.

If a homicide ever needed a thorough crime-scene investigation, it was this one. Considering the multiple victims, the fire and water damage and the lack of any obvious motive, evidence should have been examined in excruciating detail. There should have been a log signed by everyone who set foot inside, with time in and time out down to the second. DPS staff and everyone else should have worn booties. The bathrooms should have been dusted for latent fingerprints and the trash bags combed through. The metal shelves, the mop with the charred handle and the lock on the open back door should have been preserved. The list of "should haves" grew longer and longer.

In her entire career, Irma Rios had previously processed— "maybe," she would tell a defense attorney when he questioned her— one other case of arson-homicide. And while she did acknowledge that the DPS indeed had compiled a handbook of proper procedures, she wasn't all that familiar with the guidelines. And Rachel Riffe, the latent-fingerprint expert, thought of her job as mostly visual: If she saw a fingerprint, she examined and recorded it.

No one knows what happened to the metal shelving. Rios testified that she and her team used the shelves as a convenient place to store potential evidence. In a Polaroid photo taken by Hillside fire insurers over the weekend, the shelves have been wrapped in crime-scene tape and moved into the alley, along with the truncated aluminum ladder, the charred mop and the mop bucket. At some point, all of these things disappeared, and although one of Rios's responsibilities was to maintain custody of evidence collected at the scene, nobody has ever owned up to knowing who took them, where they went or why nobody went wherever that was—dump, landfill—to find them. The next day, the lock on the back door—crucial in determining the entrance and exit routes of the killers—was replaced with a new one purchased by Jesse Vasquez from a local locksmith and charged to APD Homicide; the original has never been found. The melted body of the wall telephone ended up at an AFD training location.

That Austin wasn't ready for a crime like this seems obvious; even the lead prosecutor in both trials said as much in his opening statements. But in fact, what city would have gotten it right? When you look at other big murders, the shocking cases that land on page one of the local paper and stay there, you start to understand what are called "botched investigations." JonBenét Ramsey, Nicole Simpson, the children in West Memphis, the Central Park Jogger, Sharon Tate, Rosemary LaBianca . . . Politics often interfere. Cops get testy. Newspapers, television stations and Internet news-media sites all scramble to tell the hottest story. Professional rumormongers feast on cooked-up outrage. People talk. Information spreads, much of it inaccurate. Things quickly get out of hand.

Certainly the processing team could have done better, especially Irma Rios, who never took full responsibility for her errors and misjudgments. But Jones thinks she's been unfairly maligned, and years from now, her "scene swabs" will prove crucial to the eventual dismissal of the state's case against the two boys—now men—who'd been convicted.

Just after seven o'clock on Saturday morning, Les Carpenter instructed his crew to zip the body of Amy Ayers into a body bag and transport it to the morgue. Because a homicide officer had to be present at the autopsy, Huckabay and Waters accompanied the van in a police vehicle. Jones would soon show up with Vasquez. Once Amy's body had been delivered, Carpenter's team went back for Eliza's. The autopsy of Amy Leigh Ayers began that morning at seven-fifteen; Eliza Hope Thomas at nine-thirty; Sarah Louise Harbison, noon; Jennifer Ann Harbison, one-thirty that afternoon.

All four autopsies were conducted by Dr. Tommy J. Brown, from the Harris County Medical Examiner's Office in Houston, who had signed on to do the occasional weekend stint in Travis County. In his memo to the DA's office, Jones reported that Les Carpenter groused throughout the morning, directly influencing Brown's attitude toward Homicide, the DPS and everybody else involved. As Jones put it, "By the time we got down to the ME's office, the air was cooler than it normally is in there . . . and it took a while for Dr. Tommy Brown to warm up."

Among the routine procedures conducted at any morgue after an arson-homicide is the swabbing of bodies for the presence of an accelerant—generally, lighter fluid or gasoline. But in this case, that didn't happen, a mistake both Huckabay and Jones blamed on Carpenter, who had so poisoned the air that Dr. Brown might have done his job more quickly than usual. At the crime scene itself, there hadn't seemed to be any reason to conduct this test. Everybody there—APD, ATF, AFD—agreed that the sharp, enduring smell they all were familiar with simply was not present: on the bodies, on the painted floor where they'd lain or on any of the ligatures that bound them. Nobody could have known that the possibility of an accelerant would become a major issue in the pursuit of certain suspects, leading Jones—who by then had been taken off the case—to wish they'd performed an exhumation.

THE FIRST WEEK: INNOCENCE

On the morning of December 7, the *Austin American-Statesman* ran a small, error-ridden story in the "Metro-State" section, getting the number of bodies right but much else wrong. Based on Jones's middle-of-the-night dispatch and testimony from an EMS shift commander, it described the victims as two white females, one white male, a fourth of unidentifiable race and gender, all "ranging in age from 18 to 30," and quoted Jones as having said he was handling the incident as a homicide because one of them had been struck on the head.

But word had gotten out fast, and many Austinites already knew far more than was in the paper: that the victims were four young girls, two of them sisters, were naked and bound and had been shot point-blank in the back of the head, then burned, with at least two of the bodies stacked up. What they didn't know was that one girl had been hit in a sideways trajectory, didn't die right away and had been shot again with a larger-caliber gun, a fatal shot that was known as a "through-and-through"—a round that pierced and then exited her body.

Early on the morning of December 7, Kate Wallace McClung's mother heard about the ice scoop when a lawyer friend called. *Don't say anything about this. I'm not supposed to tell you. . . .* But one of the EMS guys had told him. Or maybe a cop. And maybe he said an ice-*cream* scoop.

Jones doesn't think the killers put the ice scoop between Sarah's thighs. "No telling how it got there," he says. "Probably fell off a shelf." Others blame the high-intensity spray of the fire hoses. But, whatever the truth, for many people the most hellish version of this story is the one that remained fixed in their minds.

In the autopsy reports submitted on Saturday, the cause of death was listed as "shot by another person," but two days later District Judge Jon Wisser ordered the reports sealed, "because the details [are] essential to [APD's] investigation." And, he added, "whenever you arrest someone and they decide to give a confession, you have to have stuff that no one other than the one confessing knows about." In accordance with this ruling, the DA's office released a sanitized version to the press, despite knowing full well that in Travis County autopsies are public documents and by law cannot be sealed.

This case was huge, however, the manner of death grisly in the extreme, the victims young white girls. Wisser's decision harkens back to the days when the names of rape victims, whether girls or boys, were omitted to protect them from shame and ruin. In years to come, Roberto Bayardo will say that in his fourteen years as a medical examiner he'd never heard of a sealed autopsy report. But at the time he remained silent, like everybody else.

By that afternoon, Jones and his colleagues had created a list of thirteen pieces of evidence to be *held back*, in police terminology, from public notice:

1. How and where the fire was started
2. The key in the front door
3. How much money was taken
4. How the girls' bodies were arranged
5. What was used to bind the girls
6. That the office was not entered
7. That the office key was still under the cash register
8. The caliber of the weapons [a .22 and a .380]
9. That two pairs of the victims' underpants were missing
10. Amy's missing leather bomber jacket
11. Amy's bruise under her chin from a blow of some kind

12. That Amy was strangled and what she was strangled with
13. That Amy was shot twice with two different-caliber guns

This list will have to be revised several times.

Because the APD had no public information officer, Jones himself issued a press release stating that the bodies of four young women had been found "in an area near the back door to the ICBY shop at 2949 West Anderson Lane" and that "each of the victims suffered gunshot wounds to the head and severe burns as a result of the fire." Half an hour later, with Huckabay and other APD representatives, he met with the girls' immediate families at the main police station downtown.

After Jones gave a preliminary outline of what they knew so far, the families wanted to know if their daughters had died fast (yes) and if they had been raped (to be determined). Barbara Suraci also wanted to know if her daughters were close to each other when they were killed and if there was any part of their bodies that hadn't burned. Jones was straight with them. He hoped the vaginal and rectal swabs would preclude sexual assault but could make no promises. And, no, he regretted to say, there was no part of Jennifer, Sarah or Eliza that was unburned, only Amy.

CEO Bill Brice flew in from Dallas to meet with the families and to announce that Brice Foods was offering a $25,000 reward for evidence leading to a conviction. After declaring the company's outrage, Buddy Harvey, a vice president based in Austin, turned defensive. Yes, the girls had been alone in the shop after closing, but Brice had two other shops here and hundreds more in other states and countries and these were the first killings in the firm's fourteen-year history. When asked if Brice would reopen the Hillside shop, Harvey said possibly not, but that they were always on the lookout for new locations.

That Sunday, the *Statesman* was all Yogurt Shop, featuring photographs of the four girls accompanying a front-page story that began, "Austin police, calling the killings of four teen-age girls in a Northwest Austin yogurt shop among the worst they had ever seen, said Saturday that robbery was the apparent motive."

As APD spokesman, Mike Huckabay speculated about motive and cause. "The first thing that comes to mind," he was quoted as saying, "is crack cocaine. I've been in homicide a pretty good time and this is the worst one I've seen considering it involved four young ladies at the same time." He also disclosed that firefighters had found the back doors unlocked and that the girls were apparently closing the shop when "I would say they were killed one after another . . ." and that they probably were left "where they were shot, in the rear of the store." After giving two call-in numbers, he issued a general plea, asking people who'd been in the store that evening to come forward.

There were interviews with Lanier students and teachers. By that afternoon, flowers and potted plants had been piled on the sidewalk in front of the ICBY shop, festooned with teddy bears and scribbled notes proclaiming love for the victims. Young people carrying candles paraded in front of the crime-scene tape. Girls screamed and cried. Even weather did its part, winter darkness setting in early as El Niño rolled closer.

On Monday, the APD sent out a nationwide dispatch asking other police departments to contact them about similar crimes in their jurisdictions. This described the weapon used as a "small-caliber gun" and noted that the store was set on fire "to cover the crime." Also revealed was that materials found at the store were used to bind the girls and to set the fire, and that there was no evidence of forced entry. Another front-page *Statesman* story quoted investigators as saying that some of the victims were tied up and that when firefighters arrived, the front door was locked but the back door was not.

That night, St. Louis the King held a Rosary for Sarah, Jennifer and Eliza, all Catholics. Skip Suraci asked that, in lieu of flowers, contributions be made to either the Lanier chapter of FFA or the Jennifer and Sarah Harbison FFA Scholarship Fund. An Amy Ayers FFA Fund would soon be established, as well.

Searching through the lingering muck, a DPS agent found the spent shell casing from the .380 pistol used to shoot Amy the second time in a clogged drain under the main sink, not far from her body. By then, Chuck Meyer had been in touch with ViCAP, which, after a thorough analysis, had discovered nothing on their database that matched a crime involving four young girls stripped, bound, gagged, arranged and burned. "It's all yours," an FBI agent told Jones, adding that if the APD hadn't solved it in two to three weeks, well, good luck.

On Tuesday, Andy Waters told the *Statesman* that more than one person was involved in the killings and issued a warning to the perpetrators that while they might have believed that torching the shop would obliterate the evidence, "they were not successful," a ploy used by all police departments to lure criminals and accomplices out of the woodwork. He also revealed that Amy Ayers had been shot twice; the other girls once, in the back of the head. And that the APD assumed the motive was robbery.

So, little by little, information seeped out and rumors spread, providing those who yearned for notoriety a credible base for a detailed confession and forcing the APD to modify the hold-back list.

Also on Tuesday, Mayor Bruce Todd attended the girls' funeral, as did Chief of Police Jim Everett and a number of school officials. Speaking from behind four matching white caskets, the Reverend Kirby Garner officiated before an estimated one thousand people inside St. Louis the King, with another five hundred on the lawn outside. "It's not just Austin," he declared. "This is happening all over the country. . . . When we point the finger at the culprit, three fingers are pointing back at us . . . the individual, the community and the society."

Barbara Suraci—who had worked with Child Inc., an organization that focuses on early childhood education and care—agreed. Whoever did this, she suggested in a remarkable display of compassion, had not been loved enough. "We have to love our children from the first day."

The funeral procession to Capital Memorial Gardens was said to extend for five miles. Three of the girls were buried side by side. When grief rendered Maria Thomas unable to make a decision, her ex-husband made it for her, and Eliza was buried in Austin Memorial Park Cemetery, closer to where her parents lived. Brice had covered the funeral expenses, but some years later, when Maria expressed regret at not having had her daughter buried with the other girls, Barbara Ayres-Wilson looked into the cost of exhuming Eliza's body and moving it. But Maria still couldn't decide, and the idea soon lost immediacy.

The APD videotaped the funeral services in case the criminals showed up, whether out of curiosity, pride or remorse. They also planted a still watch—cops doing surveillance—at the graves.

Within days, the city had gone even crazier, spouting rumors, theories and surefire clues. It seemed everybody knew somebody who'd been acting weird, a kid who came home with blood on his shirt, a boy who liked to set fires, another creepy-looking person at the yogurt shop. A teenage girl came in and explained that her boyfriend had left their apartment at ten-thirty on the night of the killings and didn't come back until one in the morning, sweating and nervous and anxious to change his clothes. Young people sat around imagining how the thing had gone down. When some boasted how *they* would've done it if they'd had a mind to, others made mental notes and some called the tips line to report the conversation. And when Mike Huckabay made the comment about crack cocaine, everybody knew what that meant—the black man's drug. To score in Austin, you went to the east side, around Chicon and Twelfth streets, miles away from West Anderson Lane and the ICBY shop.

On Wednesday, a theme was born in another front-page *Statesman* story: "Austin buried a part of its innocence Tuesday." The mayor quickly seized upon it. "We think of it," he told the *St. Petersburg Times*, "as innocence lost for Austin. Not that we haven't had violent crimes before, but this took out four young girls in their prime." And then he rolled out a larger premise: "I think people realized more than anything else that it could happen to them. It could happen in the most innocent place to the most innocent people."

The battle was between innocent and weird, familiar and suspicious, certainty and mystery. After being hauled in for questioning, one young member of the so-called people in black said, "It was a bizarre crime and so they questioned the most bizarre-looking people in town and I was one."

On Thursday, December 12, in a telephone survey, the *Statesman* asked its readers to answer two questions: "Have you changed your habits or lifestyle out of concern about crime?" and "Have you or has someone you know in Austin been a victim of a crime during the last two years?" Participants could help construct a theory, not about *who* they thought the murderers were but on what effect the killings were having on the city.

To some, the concept of innocence seemed a little too convenient. In Austin in 1983 in the early-morning hours, somebody had doused opposite corners of the first floor of a boardinghouse with an accelerant, probably gasoline, and flicked a match. Four people were killed, all Latinos, as were the other residents. Nobody spoke much English. This happened on the east side, in what was considered the Mexican part of town. The only Spanish-speaking policeman in APD Homicide at the time, Juan Gonzalez, was overwhelmed and eventually gave up looking for the perpetrator. Besides, he said, no families came forward pushing for the case to be solved. "Nobody knew them," said a neighbor of the victims.

This article had run in the B section of the *Statesman,* with only one follow-up until a 1993 story contrasted the lack of interest in this arson-murder to the nonstop focus on Yogurt Shop. The boardinghouse was torn down and replaced by an apartment building; the original address no longer exists, and the arsonist has never been found.

As Jones says, "Yogurt Shop wasn't about innocence. It was about crime comes to West Austin."

DARK DAYS, BLACK NIGHTS

The bad news kept coming. On December 14, APD Homicide was called out again when a father and son were found stabbed to death in their South Austin apartment, each knifed more than a dozen times—savagery that led detectives to look for Yogurt Shop connections. But the killer, an unemployed chemist and their house-mate, was quickly apprehended when, during the investigation of a bank robbery committed that same day, his license plate number was discovered. He still had the knife on him but also had a solid alibi for December 6.

Two days later, the *Statesman*'s front-page story, "The Spark of Fear," reported on the telephone surveys. Callers said Austin wasn't the place it used to be. Not long ago, girls could go anywhere without fear. Now you couldn't trust anybody. A lot of people blamed drugs, especially crack cocaine. Some said it wasn't just Austin, that murder could happen anywhere. Look at Killeen just two months ago, when George Hennard crashed his pickup truck into the front window of a Luby's Cafeteria and opened fire with a Glock and a Ruger, stalking and killing twenty-three people and injuring another twenty before shooting himself in the head. The owner of the Cutting Edge gun shop said that since Yogurt Shop he was getting fifteen to twenty calls a day asking about the legality of carrying a gun or arming employees. People were putting burglar bars on their windows and alarms in their cars. According to realtors, women were requesting second-floor apartments. One mother said she was worried for her child. "What has happened to our little city?" she'd asked her own reflection in the bathroom mirror. An angry young man said he was taking his family and leaving. "We want to get the hell out of this town," he said. "We moved here twelve years ago. Austin was beautiful. You didn't worry about gangs or anything."

Gangs? many citizens wondered.

Statistically, with a population of 465,622, Austin was still among the safest in the country among cities of comparable size. In 1991, Fort Worth homicides totaled 180, Cleveland 183, and New Orleans topped the list with 313. By the middle of December, Austin had fifty-two.

Much of the self-protection rush wouldn't last, nor would the emphasis on workplace safety. But the mood of the city had shifted, and more dark surprises were in store before the end of the year: another murder and a shocking abduction at a downtown car wash.

As if in kinship with these dark events, El Niño disproved the predictions. On Wednesday, December 18, the day Jones ordered the removal of the ICBY crime-scene tape, a thundering Pacific system dumped an inch and a half of rain into the region's saturated river basin. Rainstorms that fill rocky-bottomed creek beds and cause flash floods are not uncommon in central Texas, especially along the Balcones Escarpment, but they usually hit in late spring. The Christmas Flood of 1991 shattered all records.

On Friday the twentieth, the father and son knifed to death by the chemist were buried at Travis County International Cemetery in paupers' graves. A newspaper article began, "The rain was unrelenting, the gray skies somber, as a dozen friends huddled beneath umbrellas. . . ." No relatives of the two men—who, it turned out, were using pseudonyms—had been located. Friends from the neighborhood insisted on having a graveside ceremony despite the weather, but the matching metal caskets were wrapped in plastic and left in the hearses. One man offered to give a eulogy he'd written, but he couldn't read it because the words smeared and ran "like the tears on the friends' faces."

Five inches fell on that day. By Christmas Eve, more than fourteen inches had fallen, breaking the previous monthlong record of 5.91 inches, set in 1944. Lake Travis crested at 710 feet. Ten people died, most in flash-flood accidents, some sitting in their cars at a low-water crossing despite the frequent EMS warnings to "Turn Around.

Don't Drown." The governor called for federal disaster relief, and the National Weather Service deemed the storms "catastrophic." And when Shoal Creek overran its banks, the APD lost any opportunity of finding a gun or any other evidence left along its banks.

Between his office and his home in northwest Austin, John Jones had to drive through pounding rain, flooded streets and wild jabs of lightning, sometimes in the dark hours of very early morning.

On the morning of Sunday, December 29, as church bells rang and Austin looked toward the end of a troubled year, its fifty-third murder arrived when twenty-two-year-old Brenda Lee Anderson was shot three times at the Studio M massage parlor, where she worked. The killer—said to be a big man wearing a cowboy hat—was seen fleeing in a white pickup truck, and that was the end of it. Her killer was never found.

That afternoon, Jones—now concentrating exclusively on Yogurt Shop—followed a hot tip about a black man named Cornelius, who, friends said, had been bragging about killing white girls. Given his history as a reputed drug dealer and former member of the L.A. Crips, Jones had him brought in. But Cornelius, too, had a solid alibi, which the APD confirmed.

And just when it seemed things couldn't get any worse, they did.

On that same Sunday, the rain let up, but the night was unpleasant and cold, the air heavy with dampness. At about nine-fifteen, Colleen Reed, a twenty-eight-year-old accountant, pulled her small black Mazda into a popular twenty-four-hour self-service car wash on West Fifth Street. She'd done volunteer work at the Lower Colorado River Authority phone bank that morning, taking emergency calls from people whose houses were flooded out or without power. Afterward, she attended Mass, had lunch with her boyfriend and went home to take a nap. That evening, she'd driven downtown to make a deposit at an ATM and shop at Whole Foods Market on North Lamar. Then she decided her car needed a wash. After parking in the third bay, she stepped out, slid coins into the water and soap dispensers and unhooked a wand from the appropriate canister, leaving her purse and groceries on the front seat. There were no other customers.

That area was especially well lit, since one of the city's moonlight towers stood 165 feet above it, casting a silvery white light over a radius of about seven blocks. Such towers were popular across the country during the mid- to late 1800s, but only Austin still uses them. According to local historians, they were erected downtown in 1894, after a number of maids and servants had been raped, disfigured and murdered nearby, and it was hoped they would discourage the killer, who was never apprehended. But in 1991, fifteen of these "moon towers," as they were popularly called, remained standing, and this one, on Sixth Street at West Lynn, was within two blocks of the car wash.

On a nearby front porch, four people saw a tan Thunderbird driving west on Fifth Street and yelled, "One way!" But the car kept going. From their position, they could see the vacuum canisters at the car wash but little else. They heard a scream and a car door slamming shut. Then the Thunderbird reappeared, going the wrong way—east—on Sixth. The witnesses were slack-jawed. What the hell?

When the police arrived, Colleen Reed's car was still sitting in the third bay with the driver's door open. On the front seat, her purse, groceries and an ATM receipt were covered in soapsuds. Her identity was easily established. But she herself was gone.

In certain respects, this abduction was almost as shocking as Yogurt Shop. What did the abductors want if they didn't take her money or her car?

Austin closed out 1991 with Colleen Reed's whereabouts and status still unknown. On New Year's Day, when the *Statesman* asked John Jones about prospects for 1992, his response echoed the pessimism of a lot of residents. "It ain't looking good. . . . The light at the end of the tunnel? It's the headlights of a train. [Nineteen ninety-one's] been a bad year. A real bad year."

Was this *Austin*?

UNTIL THIS CASE IS SOLVED

On January 3, Jones wrote Police Chief Jim Everett a long, forth-right memo. It began: "The investigation of the I.C.B.Y. Murder has been in progress now for 3 days shy of 1 month. The volume of phone tips has slowed to approximately 10 per day, down from a high of 50 to 75 per day the first two weeks of the investigation. Homicide is in the process of re-verifying all the call-ins, making sure no lead has slipped through unchecked." Three promising leads, he explained, had already fizzled under scrutiny, none able to go beyond what was common knowledge about the crime scene.

To date, he continued, the team had interviewed all merchants in the shopping center, all customers who were at the shop between eight o'clock and closing, all area bus operators from Cap Metro, the victims' families and boyfriends. They had also inspected area phone calls within a thirty-day period as well as traffic tickets from that night and videotapes of the girls' funeral service. Most important, information about the crime had been submitted to the FBI's Behavioral Science Unit, which had created a "personality profile" of the offenders. Led by nationally acclaimed Judson Ray, members of the unit had arrived in Austin that very day to discuss their findings and suggest how to use the press to draw out one or more of the offenders. Pending those discussions, plans to spotlight the crime on *Unsolved Mysteries* and *America's Most Wanted* were on hold. As a side note, Jones further advised the chief that although he spoke with the families of the girls twice a week and so far they had the utmost confidence in the APD, their frustration was growing.

That was the catch-up part of the memo. Then Jones got down to it. Manpower, he declared, was his biggest single problem. While the four uniformed patrolmen assigned to the investigation had been invaluable, it was Jones's understanding that they'd leave the team that day. "Now we are in trouble. It is a simple matter of numbers, we (Homicide) start out with only 6 investigators, 2 are on nights which leaves 4 investigators to continue this case and still handle the other murders, suicides and deceased persons continuing to come in. I need at least 4 investigators totally dedicated to this case and this case only for at least 60 days or until 'it is solved,' whichever comes first. I appreciated the patrolmen, but they are patrolmen. What this case needs now is experienced investigators to continue follow-ups and interrogations of suspects and witnesses."

He summed up:

1. The F.B.I. will be assisting us with bringing an extreme amount of psychological pressure to bear on the suspect. It is therefore important that an experienced investigator screen all calls from here out and personally handle the call-ins.
2. An experienced investigator will be better able to evaluate a potential witness as to whether or not he has useful information or just hearsay.
3. The F.B.I. will be providing us with a list of 14 to 18 questions for any suspect that will tell whether or not he has information pertinent to the case or not.
4. D.P.S. lab was able to narrow down one of the guns used to an exact brand name. The pawn shops were searched for this gun and need to be searched again, then sellers/purchasers interviewed.

The manpower issue was something both the FBI and DPS had urged him to address immediately. As they saw it, the case needed at least five investigators: Jones as case agent to keep up with paperwork and act as liaison between the three agencies; the other four to handle the actual investigation. For a pro, clearing a suspect took up to eight hours. The three mentioned earlier had required between thirty-six and seventy-two.

In response, Chief Everett made an official announcement that, to bring the Yogurt Shop case to a close, he was giving Sgt. John Jones the opportunity to create an officially sanctioned task force, made up of an alphabet soup of representatives from APD, AFD, BATF, FBI, Texas DPS Intelligence, TCSO (Travis County Sheriff's Office) and the Travis County DA's office. Its goal: to identify, arrest and prosecute those responsible for the murders of the four girls by developing a "major crime assessment based on an in-depth examination of the details of the crime," as well as to provide the expertise of the FBI Behavioral Science Unit, which would filter crime scene details through its database of ten thousand murders nationwide and create the personality profile. The press would play its part by presenting this profile to the public.

Jones referred to the group from Quantico as "the *Silence of the Lambs* folks," after the best-selling 1988 thriller. Within a month of the FBI's arrival in Austin, the film version would open as a huge box-office hit, enabling moviegoers to toss profiling terms into a conversation as casually as if they had the expertise down pat.

For most of us, profiling seems a stretch. How predictable *is* behavior? Can we pin particular acts of violence on certain life experiences? The idea is thrillingly seductive: figure out what kind of person would or would not commit a specific crime, exclude the latter—even those who'd confessed—and eventually you'd zero in on the perpetrator. When I asked Jones if this really works, his answer was a simple "Hell, yes." One of the lead defense attorneys told me the same thing.

The meeting with the FBI team lasted all day. Late that afternoon, having been prepped by the experts, Jones talked to *Statesman* reporter Enrique Gonzales.

The Behavioral Science people, he told Gonzales, "helped us focus, sift through and evaluate" the case. Things were "real positive" now, he said, and he didn't think the current situation would drag on much longer. "It would be safe to say an apprehension is imminent. We are confident about what happened today." The APD had even scheduled a news conference for the following Monday, the one-month anniversary, at which time Police Chief Everett would reveal the FBI's official findings. And, further, "we may have some names to name."

Gonzales's story ran on the front page the next day, headlined, INVESTIGATOR SAYS ARRESTS IMMINENT IN TEEN KILLING.

At Monday's press conference, after assuring the public that the police department was doing everything possible, Everett issued a curt apology. John Jones must have been misquoted and would not have said "imminent." The information they'd received had helped them eliminate several suspects, nothing more.

Gonzales insisted the quote was accurate, that he had called Jones and read it back to him before the story ran. The chief made no further comment. Embarrassed, Jones stepped to the microphone and gave details of the FBI profile:

1. More than one person was involved, one of them with a dominant personality.
2. The assailants are probably white, in their late teens to mid-20's.
3. The one with the dominant personality in all probability did not finish high school. In school would have been considered an underachiever with less than average grades. Resents discipline, would have been a discipline problem for school officials and parents. Has an explosive personality, angers easily especially when drinking alcohol or using drugs. An impulsive person who acts without considering the consequences. Will engage in physical confrontation only when he has the advantage. Will not engage in any confrontation with adult male without friends present. Probably unemployed or working in a menial job. Will have a history of changing jobs, is not dependable as an employee with high degree of absenteeism. Lives in dependent relationship with older person, possibly a parent. Frequents the area of the ICBY shop. Familiar with the streets and stores in the area, probably a resident of neighborhood. Probably has a criminal record, may be abusive to women, may seek out women who are younger and "less

adequate" than himself. Has no remorse about killing the victims but is under tremendous stress from fear of apprehension because crime may not have gone as planned. Also very concerned about loyalty of his accomplices because they may be feeling regret. Disharmony may be developing between the offenders as stress level rises as well as increased paranoia, because of which they may maintain close contact with each other in order to keep a close watch. In time this may change into a falling-out leading to violence.

4. Immediately after leaving the crime scene, offenders would have gone to a secure location to clean up or change clothes, although the crime scene does not indicate they would have had a lot of blood on them.

5. Offenders may have returned to the area that night to watch police and fire departments. Or they may have left town. May have missed some work days.

That's it, and of course this could describe a lot of aimless young men. As for *apprehension is imminent,* Jones swore years later that the FBI gave him the line as a strategy meant to encourage an informant or accomplice to come forward. "I did what the FBI told me to do," he said, "and got slammed for it."

The FBI profile appeared in all Austin news outlets. The *Statesman* donated a full page to it, with MANY PEOPLE KNOW THIS KILLER, DO YOU? in blaring letters above it.

What Jones didn't tell his chief or the public was that, like ViCAP, the profilers had declared the Austin crime unique. The one that came the closest, they suggested, was the Atlanta child murders, and they weren't that similar. Which meant their database had come up empty and the psychological profile was based on supposition.

The Sunday before, January 5, *The Washington Post* ran a long front-page story by biographer David Maraniss entitled "Parent, Child and Death's Dominion; Texas Family's Dreadful Pain Began with a Knock on the Door." It began, "This is the saddest story any parent could ever tell." Primarily an interview with Barbara and Skip Suraci—their first—it emphasized lyrics from Jennifer Harbison's favorite Garth Brooks song, "The Dance": "Yes, my life is worth the chance. I could have missed the pain but I'd have had to miss the dance." It ended with a quote from Barbara Suraci: "Our house was a total disaster most of the time. We were never living up to our expectations of what life was supposed to be. We were noisy and always talking and doing things and arguing and going and going, and I never had enough time. And, damn, I miss that. I miss never having enough time. Now I have so much."

Two days later, the *Post* ran a follow-up that covered the FBI profile and Everett's press conference. Over the next few months, there will be stories and photos in the *Christian Science Monitor, USA Today* and *People*. Later in the spring, *The New York Times* will quote an Austin public school counselor as saying, "It's been very hard on some kids to accept the idea that a place like a yogurt shop or a cafeteria can suddenly become a scene of violence. It makes them aware not just of death but of danger. It produces both grief and anxiety . . . and can push them to self-destructive or violent behavior."

Locally, there was no stopping the repercussions. Cashing in on Yogurt Shop and Colleen Reed's kidnapping, a suspended Austin lawyer running for Travis County sheriff promised that if elected, he would form a people's posse to "get together and attempt to find out who these killers are." When the city manager was asked about the local crime rate, she flatly stated that Austin's number-one enemy was drugs, and crack cocaine an epidemic. Mayor Todd declared the 7 percent rise in murders "disturbing," something that "sort of shatters the myth that Austin is a small community where violent crime doesn't occur."

Toward the end of the month, Jones composed another long memo, on the one hand thanking Chief Everett for the additional personnel and on the other wondering how fifteen investigative and support personnel were supposed to operate in a "space designed to hold 9 on a good day," sharing desks, phones, files, computers and storage space. And there was also the issue of curtailed overtime pay—an economic measure put into effect by the city council, about which Jones pulled no punches. "Attempting to hold us to 20 hours a week overtime is paramount to answering 'No' to the question, 'Do you really want to solve this case?' "

Eight weeks in, they were still interviewing customers and employees. Jones continued to maintain solid rapport with the families, as a result of which they'd cooperated in every way he'd asked them to, including not speaking to the press or filing a civil lawsuit against Brice. But he hadn't had time to take affidavits regarding their daughters' clothing and daily routines. He and his assistant were able to keep up with paperwork—managing a six-hundred-name database, looking for suspects, tips, witnesses, customers, family, not to mention additional law-enforcement personnel—thanks to equipment donated by IBM and CompuAdd. But there were still approximately fifty potential witnesses they hadn't had time to interview. For this investigative unit to evolve into a true task force, he needed a separate work space with enough offices for investigators, supervisors and the case agent, as well as conference and interview rooms, furniture, mainframe terminals, ten telephone lines, a fax line, a tips line . . . the list went on and on.

By February 1, he'd been given everything he'd asked for.

In years to come, when offered the opportunity to criticize his supervisors, Jones refuses. "The chief, the mayor, the DA? They gave us whatever we needed," he'll say again and again. "A task force? We got it. Equipment? Offices? Yes. Everybody wanted to see this case solved and *nobody* wanted to go on record as the one who stood in the way."

In the meantime, Chuck Meyer exploited his access to federal agencies and their information, including the newly created (1989) CODIS database (Combined DNA Index System), to check out leads from all over the country: from Waco, where he interviewed a convicted serial killer, to Florida, to talk to another one, to San Marcos, to speak to a young man whose violent episodes included raping his little sister. He also traveled to Las Cruces, New Mexico, where in 1990 two people carrying small-caliber pistols had herded seven others into an office at a bowling alley and restaurant, made them all lie facedown and shot them one by one in the back of the head; after robbing the business of five thousand dollars, the killers set the building on fire. While acknowledging the similarities between the two cases, federal agents couldn't see how to connect them. Whenever a Crime

Stoppers bulletin prompted calls—from Michigan (Kalamazoo), Virginia (Roanoke and Manassas) and elsewhere in Texas (Killeen), one of which involved a man who'd been in Austin on December 6 and had threatened a female with a small silver gun—Meyer set off again, often accompanied by FBI polygrapher Jack Barnett. They went everywhere and got only garbage possibilities.

BILLBOARDS

Later in February, a local sign company donated twelve public-service billboards for three months. People driving to work looked up and there they were, as familiar as family. Lined up across the top of the sign were black-and-white yearbook photographs: on the far left, dark-eyed Eliza, head dipped fetchingly to one side, long hair falling down the side of her face; next to her, young Amy with a formal straight-on smile, chin resting in her cupped palm, a big watch on her left wrist; then serious Sarah, her big eyes lit up with that skeptical "Oh yeah?" expression; and on the far right, tiny, electric Jennifer, pretty as a fairy-tale heroine, long hair rolling down her face in springy curls.

Beneath the photos, an angry slash of red spanned the sign, within it a stark question in white: WHO KILLED THESE GIRLS? Below that, Brice's $25,000 reward and the number of the tips line. There was no need to give the girls' names or say anything else. Everybody already knew.

On Amy Ayers's birthday, Burnet Middle School planted a fifteen-foot crepe myrtle in her memory. The Lanier High School FFA voted in a new president to take Jennifer Harbison's place. Friends of Amy and the Harbison sisters volunteered to show their animals at the livestock show; Eliza's sister, Sonora, would show Stony. A psychic from California called to say that the main offender was afraid of roller coasters but rode them all the time. More hold-back information was leaked, which, according to one defense attorney, should have come as no surprise, since so many people were in and out of the crime scene that night, "chock-full of what they know or think they know." Jones tracked down three of the leaks, including one that involved a woman who'd heard about the ice scoop and the arrangement of the bodies from her hairdresser, who also did the hair of someone in the ME's office, and who herself was the mother of a suspect who'd subsequently included that information in his "confession."

The first two homicides of 1992 occurred during crack-cocaine transactions, one in the backyard of a rumored dope house, the other after an argument in the street. The next two were less predictable: the shooting deaths of two brothers, ages eight and twelve, while their mother was in the shower. Hearing the shots, she stepped from the bathroom to find her boys dead and the seventeen-year-old killer still in the room. She wrestled him to the floor. After telling her he'd been feeling like killing somebody since December, he broke loose but was quickly captured a few houses away. Huckabay talked to the culprit but found no connection with Yogurt Shop.

End of February, into March. As the three-month anniversary approached, Jones assured the chief that "EVERYTHING THAT CAN BE TRIED IS, INCLUDING SOME THINGS THAT HAVE NEVER BEEN TRIED AND THAT GO AGAINST THE PREVIOUS CONVENTIONAL WISDOM OF HOMICIDE INVESTIGATION IN THIS DEPARTMENT" (his caps and underlining).

When I asked him about possible motive, he said he wasn't interested in *why*, just *who*. The hope was, the FBI profile as well as its interview guide with its "Indicators of Innocence vs. Others" would help, if not locate the actual killers, at least narrow the field.

Soon after the signs went up, Jones heard from CBS News producer Jon Klein, who wanted to shoot a *48 Hours* episode about the "yogurt murders" and "the community and the fears triggered by a few sensational cases." He sent a videotape of the show they'd done on the Luby's massacre so that the APD could get an idea of the kind of access they needed. Within a week, Klein had visited Austin and persuaded Chief Everett and the mayor to allow police participation during two to three days of taping. The city also provided the CBS crew not just with an office but with full access to the department's Homicide Unit, which was extremely unusual in an open investigation.

In late March, CBS aired "Who Killed These Girls?" the first of three *48 Hours* episodes featuring Yogurt Shop. As the opening credits ran, the voice of veteran newscaster Dan Rather introduced that night's theme: "Four all-American teens, executed. A crack police squad desperate to solve the case. And a city on edge, frightened by a new reality: *it can happen here.*" Rather himself then appeared, sitting at a glass-topped table and surrounded by photographs taken at several different crime scenes as well as by the billboard portraits of the ICBY girls.

"Are you safe," he asked, looking square into the camera lens, "sitting where you are right now? The people of Austin thought they were, until one horrifying night brought home the truth: there is no safe haven anymore." And he went on to cite an FBI report from the previous year indicating an "alarming" rise in violent crime in the suburbs, "the very place Americans have sought sanctuary from big-city fears." Tonight, he told viewers, they'd be joining the investigation into the murders of four innocent girls, "to see what crime in America is doing to families, communities, even the tough cops who live with it every day."

Reporter Erin Moriarty, who will host each of the ICBY episodes, then appears on-screen. "It started out," she begins, "as just another night in Austin, Texas, for homicide sergeant John Jones . . . when a call came in that would change his life." A strain of dramatic music is interrupted by the crackle of Jones's mobile and a video of his car flashing its rooftop warning lights. Then there he is at the wheel, filmed from the backseat by the KTBC videographer, talking to the reporter over his shoulder as his siren wails and I-35 exit signs flash by. Suddenly, his mobile, clamped to the dash, lights up.

"Jonesy," a voice calls out. "Make that four."

Falling back on the "sleepy town" stereotype, Moriarty echoes Rather's warning: Although Austin was known as a place people moved to so they could feel safe, they might well discover that beneath what seemed like the placid surface of everyday life there roiled an "undercurrent of violence." To illustrate this, Moriarty runs through the chronology—Troy Gay's discovery of the smoke, the fire department, the water, the discovery of one body and then another, the call to Jones—while video clips show firefighters and cops in black slickers moving in and out of the shop and, eventually, the money shot: two people from the morgue struggling to heave a body bag onto a stretcher.

The scene then shifts to the new task-force offices, where we see Jones at work, Huckabay taking a call ("Whadd'ya got?"), Chuck Meyer pacing nervously behind the others, Hector Polanco at a table overrun with incident reports and printouts from the database Jones has created. When interviewed, Huckabay acknowledges that Homicide is taking this crime particularly seriously because of the age of the girls, and because "if we don't catch the guy, he wins." Barbara Suraci, Maria Thomas, Bob and Pamela Ayers make brief appearances. There are heartbreaking home videos of the girls, tussling, laughing, tending livestock. We see Jones at his desk in earbuds and hear what he's listening to—an operatic aria.

At the time, Homicide's focus was on the Satanists, a circumstance that fed directly into the show's undercurrent-of-violence theme. In one scene, Moriarty and a cameraman accompany Jones, Huckabay and other cops in a raid on the small home of a reputed high priestess of darkness who called herself Claire Lavaye, after the founder of the Church of Satan, Anton LaVey. But the raid proved a bust and a public embarrassment for the cops when the woman was discovered naked and alone in her bed—taking a battery-powered time-out from the rigors of life—and the skull on her mantel turned out to be a clay doodad. Other bones in her collection were in fact real but came from rats and squirrels. Although nobody said so, the obvious conclusion was that the APD was very wide of the mark, and that while this woman might have been involved in some offbeat graveyard capers, she was no murderer.

The show also touched on Colleen Reed. There were clips of the Fifth Street car wash and an interview with her sister, who had repeatedly accused the APD of ineptitude and a halfhearted investigation. Other segments dealt with a drug deal gone wrong as well as the unsolved murder of Harold Carter, who'd been robbed and killed only four months before Yogurt Shop as he walked from his car to the furniture store where he'd worked for twenty-eight years.

Local CBS affiliate KTBC-TV also ran studio interviews with Barbara Suraci and the Ayerses, who said there were things they thought they'd put behind them which got stirred up again. "It is just a reality," Bob Ayers went on, "and you've got to face it." Suraci said when they saw the girls' pictures hanging in the APD offices, it touched her heart, "because I know those people are working so hard to help us find the murderers of our babies." Maria Thomas watched at home with Sonora. "Like pouring salt in the wound," she later commented.

Overnight ratings ranked the undercurrent-of-violence episode among the ten most watched in the show's four-year history. Hundreds of new tips rolled in, many focusing on the occult, which by the time the show aired had become pretty much a moot point, and local teenager Maggie Halliday remembers being called from her junior high class to talk to an FBI agent—in her view, a big joke. She and her black-garbed friends buckled on spiky dog collars, dyed their hair blue and colored their lips black because they wanted to be different. They never, she added, called themselves PIBs. They thought of themselves as part of the Austin party scene and a force to counteract the "We're so liberal and love everybody" Austin bullshit. But their difference had made them vulnerable. "Little Dracula hippies walking down the street are pretty easy to spot," said another girl.

Jones defends the Satanist push. They'd received some 230 calls implicating the devil worshippers, so his job was to check them out. And indeed, a good many unconventional folks were out there pulling off weird stunts, but they were mostly interested in creating theater and raising a ruckus, not committing murder. The only offense a person in black was charged with was "burglary of a mausoleum."

There would be two more *48 Hours* featuring Yogurt Shop, one in 2000, after the arrests, and another in 2010, once the cases were dismissed. But the first gave the case its official title. Previously also called the ICBY killings or slayings or murders, it was now and forever indelibly known as "The Yogurt Shop Murders."

In late March, a man left a message saying he'd seen the killers put yogurt in the girls' vaginas. "I know who did it," he whispered, "but I need protection. We'll talk later." After TrapTrace located the call, Jones and a partner paid him a visit. He denied having left the message until they played the tape, then said he was only joking. A young woman phoned in to report that her boyfriend told her he did it. A man said a friend of his had witnessed the girls being cut up in pieces. A late-night downtown regular described the girls being sliced open and chickens put inside them. Somebody blamed the KKK, while another swore he'd heard at a party that the girls' heads were cut off and dropped in a well; the man who told him had smelled the putrid water and seen their hair.

Around that same time, lawmen working on the Colleen Reed investigation put together information that placed paroled serial killer Kenneth McDuff in Austin when she was abducted. A group of ATF agents, U.S. marshals, a DPS criminal investigator and several McClennan County deputies zeroed in on one of McDuff's closest running buddies. Haunted by the memory of December 29, Alva Hank Worley quickly broke down and admitted he'd driven from Waco to Austin with McDuff that night, planning to score weed and meth or cocaine. But before Worley knew it, they were headed into the car wash and the hulking six-foot-four McDuff was grabbing Reed by the throat and carrying her—screaming "Not me! Not me!"—to their car. She was so small, Worley remembered, her feet didn't even touch the ground. After throwing her in the backseat, McDuff told Worley to keep her under control.

He confessed to having forced oral sex on Colleen Reed and then raping her vaginally while McDuff drove. Once they got back to Waco, McDuff burned Reed with cigarettes and raped her repeatedly, until at one point she laid her head on Worley's shoulder and begged him to please not let McDuff hurt her anymore. After driving to an open field, McDuff told Worley he was going to "use her up," a line he'd used before when he was ready to kill a woman, usually by stretching her out on the ground, laying a broomstick across her neck and pressing down until it snapped. Worley said he didn't know how McDuff had killed Reed, but he'd buried her in a field somewhere up near Waco; and he didn't know where McDuff was now, though he didn't think in Waco. Once incarcerated, Worley admitted that he'd actually watched McDuff break Colleen Reed's neck, this time without the broomstick.

When I suggested to Jones that of all the suspects they investigated, McDuff was the one most likely to have committed the Yogurt Shop Murders, he agreed. "No question," he replied. McDuff was capable. There was only one problem.

He paused. Waited.

"It wasn't him?" I asked.

He shook his head. McDuff had alibis. He told Chuck Meyer if he'd done the yogurt girls, he'd be proud to say so. Anyway, these weren't his kind of murders.

Capable of was a long way from *did it.*

After a number of people claimed to have seen a Latino man sitting in an older light-colored American car in the yogurt shop parking lot at closing time, the APD had a composite sketch drawn. Another "Have you seen this man?" notice ran in the *Statesman* and on local television news programs. And then, in his April report to the BATF, Chuck Meyer mentioned a search for "three Hispanic males" who—on November 17, 1991, only two and a half weeks before Yogurt Shop—had raped a woman at gunpoint in a car parked outside a heavy-metal bar called the Cavity Club, just off Sixth Street, then driven her to San Antonio and dumped her. The suspects were soon identified as Mexican nationals: Alberto Jimenez Cortez, aka El Brujo (the Warlock), who had allegedly fled to Mexico; Ricardo Hernandez, aka Dienton (Big Teeth), who was missing but thought to be in California; and Porfirio Villa Saavedra, aka the Terminator, who might still be in Austin. They belonged to a sixty-member motorcycle gang called the Mierdas Punks, specializing in drug trafficking and car theft. Several people called in to say they knew Alberto Cortez and that he resembled the composite sketch.

A day later, Jones sent out a dispatch about another man whose resemblance to the sketch had been noted. Armando Razo also fit aspects of the FBI profile: He had a penchant for physical violence, carried a pistol under the front seat of his white 1977 Pontiac and had bragged about a drive-by shooting he'd gotten away with in San Antonio. After the sketch appeared, the nineteen-year-old Razo quit his job at the Sonic Drive-In and told friends he was going into hiding. As a suspect, he looked promising. But before the APD could locate him, the *Statesman* got wind of Jones's in-house memo. When a reporter called, Jones emphasized that while Razo was wanted for questioning, he was not a suspect and that putting his name in print would be a disservice both to the families of the victims and to the wanted man.

Early the next morning, Pam Ayers called. Some of her friends had heard on the radio that a suspect had been arrested. Within minutes, Skip Suraci called to say the same thing. Jones made a general statement to the press, saying that Razo only *looked* like the composite, which meant only that he *might* have been in the parking lot on the night of the murders. He was *not* a suspect. Later, Jones arrived at his office and saw the *Statesman*'s headline: TEEN ARRESTED IN YOGURT SHOP MURDER.

In his opinion, media one-upmanship caused many of their biggest problems. Nobody wanted to come up short, so they all rushed to break a story. That afternoon, Jones interviewed Razo, who offered to bring in three solid alibi witnesses. All of them checked out. He'd been in some trouble with the law and was wanted for forfeiture of a bond. But he wasn't a killer.

In April, Eliza's 254-pound pig won the 1992 Grand Champion prize of the Austin–Travis County Livestock Show. At auction, Stony fetched six thousand dollars. Amy's light-heavyweight hog, weighing in at 235 pounds, won fourth in his class. Sarah Harbison's lamb got sixth, Jennifer's ninth. Stony's life was spared when he was given back to the Thomas family, who sent him to Crowe's Nest Farm, a pretty place north of town where unwanted animals lived long, quiet lives, being petted and pampered by schoolchildren on field trips. In a front-page *Statesman* story entitled "In the Shadow of Death," Maria Thomas described her feelings. "It doesn't seem like it can possibly be true. I've been out of my mind since Eliza's been gone. *I wish she would come back and end this terrible nightmare*." She'd been able to work only a few days at her job, and was having dark thoughts. "You live one more day when you don't really want to."

Mayor Todd proclaimed April 6, the four-month anniversary of the murders, "Let Your Lights Shine for Them Day," and encouraged motorists to drive with their headlights on.

When Hector Polanco was investigated by Internal Affairs for questionable practices during an arrest, he was taken off Yogurt Shop and replaced by Senior Sgt. Ron Smith, who had never worked in Homicide and, further, had had a checkered career, having shot and killed an unarmed seventeen-year-old boy and once participated in the smothering death of a handcuffed Nigerian by sitting on his head and forcing his face into a water bed. Smith had been cleared in both cases. And despite his inexperience, Jones liked him.

"He was a good administrator," he says now. "A street guy who wasn't afraid to take heat. He didn't insert himself unnecessarily into an investigation and provided us with a measure of stability."

Unlike Polanco?

Jones declined to comment.

By then, 485 tips had rolled in and the database had rocketed to 2,200 records, of which 800 were suspects. Twenty more WHO KILLED THESE GIRLS? billboards went up, this time with a reward of $100,000, the increase donated by local businesses. Jones was given office space and equipment for another six months. By the middle of the month, sealed indictments had been obtained for the three Mexican nationals whom the Sex Crimes Unit had identified as the men who had raped the woman outside the Cavity Club.

The rains continued, and water stood in pastures from South Austin to San Antonio, nearly eighty miles to the south. Livestock were sheltered on high ground, and to feed them, ranchers had to paddle out in rowboats.

When no Yogurt Shop news was forthcoming, the *Statesman* ran more stories about crime and fear. Gun shops reported that sales were up some 10 to 15 percent, especially among women. To take advantage of the trend, Nova Technologies advertised a half-price sale of a stun gun for $49.95. Alarm companies and shooting ranges reported increased business. One story about the changes in the city borrowed its lead from Dan Rather: "Four girls die in a yogurt shop murder and months later, the killers remain free. A woman is abducted from a car wash and . . ."

For backup, reporters found residents who no longer drove anywhere after dark but stayed home instead and watched videos. Others considered moving somewhere else. Even Ronnie Earle, the Travis County DA, contributed. "The world," he said, "is turning upside down on us here. This is not the way we thought we'd be living, with hostilities walking among us. They don't wear uniforms and it's hard to tell who they are. . . . And it is the most disturbing thing that can happen to a community because it makes us distrust each other."

Two days later, fifty-five-year-old Police Chief Jim Everett shocked the APD and the city by announcing his retirement. Asked if this had anything to do with low morale on the force, he said no, that he'd been planning for a while to live a peaceful life in the hills of western Arkansas. In a leaden response, DA Earle said it was "a hard time to be head of a law enforcement agency. . . . The problems will not diminish with the next chief."

A career cop, George Phifer, was named acting chief. Addressing the recent incidents and internal uproar, Phifer transferred six experienced homicide detectives, including Andy Waters and Bruce Boardman, to other units. During the move, Boardman might have misplaced a number of files, including unsigned, handwritten notes taken during interviews with future suspects Robert Springsteen and Michael Scott.

As it turned out, Jim Everett had no intention of retiring. He'd already applied for a chief's job in Aurora, Colorado. After he won the job seven months later, he paid off his mortgages in Austin and Arkansas and moved to a town that, until the 2012 *Dark Knight Rises* massacre, seemed the safe sort of place that others were now looking for.

In early May, Kenneth McDuff was arrested in Kansas City, Missouri, working as a city garbage collector under a name he took from a stolen Social Security card. Worley was convicted and given a life sentence for the rape charge, but he never confessed to Reed's murder, and neither did McDuff, who in 1993 would be sentenced to death for the 1992 murder of a pregnant twenty-two-year-old store clerk at a Waco Quik-Pak. Chuck Meyer immediately went after him about Yogurt Shop, and also talked to associates who said McDuff made regular trips to Austin because he couldn't get resale-weight cocaine in Waco.

Colleen Reed's body would not be found until 1998, when McDuff agreed, a few weeks before his execution, to give up the location in exchange for a reduced sentence for his nephew, in federal prison on a meth charge. He also provided directions to the burial spots of two other women he'd raped and murdered. A low estimate of his total assaults amounts to fourteen. After his execution, *Texas Monthly* published a story about him called "Free to Kill," and ran his mug shot on the cover with the word MONSTER across his forehead. People still shiver a little whenever McDuff's name comes up—even cops, lawyers and at least one judge—and serial-killer lists dub him "the Broomstick Killer." To this day, some people still believe he either killed the Yogurt Shop girls or had sent two or more of his coked-up wannabes to Austin to perform a rite of initiation.

Confessions, tips and accusations came and went. An incarcerated man named Steve Sharber spoke of strangling the girls, defecating on them, scooping out their left eyeballs and having sex through the empty sockets. The Iowa Department of Corrections called to report that a former inmate named Darrell Duane Ochs might be of interest. A violent criminal, paroled in November 1991 after kidnapping and sexual-assault convictions, Ochs had ties to San Antonio, and during his exit interview he'd told a social worker he was going to commit a crime that would put him on death row. The Des Moines ATF agent who—at Chuck Meyer's request—interviewed him reported that while Ochs bore a startling resemblance to the composite sketch, he could find no evidence that he had been in Texas in 1991. Meyer and Jones also followed tips from all over the state, driving to Midland and Lubbock in pursuit of a confidential informant called "Mike-Mike"; to Taylor, north of Austin, to interview a boy who told his sister he knew *exactly* who had killed the Yogurt Shop girls; to Temple, Belton and Waco to question McDuff's cronies. Meyer also fielded out-of-state calls, one from an ATF agent in Westmoreland County, Pennsylvania, about two drug dealers who'd been in Austin that weekend to purchase narcotics; another from the Arcadia Parish, Louisiana, jail about an inmate who'd made incriminating comments.

Governor Ann Richards declared June 6, the six-month anniversary, "We Will Not Forget Day," and local musicians wrote and performed a song about the girls, also called "We Will Not Forget." To mark the occasion, Austin was awash in WWNF buttons, T-shirts and coffee mugs, and white ribbons adorned clothes, trees and cars.

A parade of an estimated twelve hundred people marched from the Congress Avenue bridge to the capitol, carrying white candles and WWNF banners. In a speech on the capitol steps, Ronnie Earle declared, "These four girls belong to all of us; they are all of our responsibility." At eleven o'clock that night, at a candlelight vigil held at the empty, dark, boarded-up yogurt shop, people brought flowers and letters to the dead girls. There wasn't much to do there except sing the song and say the same things over and over again.

That summer, *America's Most Wanted* ran the composite sketch and a brief story about Yogurt Shop. Afterward, Barbara Suraci exulted, "Getting those pictures out there, we'll find them. Everybody watches *America's Most Wanted*." The following week, the sketch ran again and new tips streamed in. The task force figured only 10 to 15 percent were useful, but a familiar name resurfaced a couple of times. One caller said the man in the composite was absolutely Alberto Cortez, and that if El Brujo was involved, so were Saavedra and Hernandez. They were probably together somewhere outside of Mexico City, where they'd grown up.

Everybody liked having suspects like these—brown-skinned noncitizens, out-and-out bad guys known for brutality, drug trafficking and crimes against women. After informing the families, Jones again warned them not to get their hopes up, but Chuck Meyer requested advance permission to travel to Mexico City with Jack Barnett and a bilingual ATF agent once the men were located. Jones wanted to go as well, but Ron Smith wouldn't let him. If the lead cop went down there, he reasoned, people would jump to overblown conclusions. Jones should send Huckabay and direct proceedings from Austin.

In August, Ronnie Earle's office conferred with the Mexican consulate in San Antonio and agreed to turn the Cavity Club kidnapping and rape case over to the Mexican government, in return for which he would be allowed to file an order of detention—in effect, enabling him to interrogate the three of them about a different crime. This was risky, and APD Homicide didn't like it, but once Earle had made the deal, they had to live with it.

That same month, APD morale hit a new low when city manager Camille Barnett announced that Jim Everett's replacement would be Elizabeth "Betsy" Watson, formerly Houston's chief of police, and Mayor Todd stood behind Barnett's choice. "Watson," he said, had "big-city experience" and that "certainly some of the things we're going through now have happened in Houston." He set the swearing-in ceremony for December.

Watson was considered a New Age believer in the evolving law-enforcement philosophy known as "community policing," or some-times, the "broken windows" theory. This settled cops into their precincts, not as outsiders come to enforce the law, but as mem-bers of the community. The neighborhood cop, its advocates held, would notice when broken windows weren't replaced. The depart-ment could then pinpoint the area as one in which the breakdown of standards might foreshadow the onset of failing ethical values that often led to criminal behavior. This would bring residents into a "shared relationship" with the police, in which both recognized the obligation to do what was necessary to maintain order and peace. It also matched Ronnie Earle's beliefs about his duties as the district attorney. Moreover, he had ambitions to run for statewide office and needed fresh ideas for his campaign.

Nothing about Watson appealed to Austin's cops. Like many others, they generally believed there were bad guys they were duty-bound to go out and round up, regardless of broken windows or community togetherness. Besides, by hiring Watson in secret, the city manager had disrespected the force by ignoring protocol, which demanded that the Austin Police Association (APA) be consulted before a new chief was appointed.

John Jones, however, has a simpler explanation for the hostility. "Sexism," he believes. "Pure and simple."

In October, prior to Watson's arrival, Porfirio Villa Saavedra and Alberto Jimenez Cortez were arrested on suspicion of the Yogurt Shop Murders. Both were flown to Mexico City, where they were also charged with the Cavity Club kidnapping and sexual assault, as well as drug trafficking and gun smuggling. The third suspect, Ricardo Hernandez, had not yet been found. In a prepared statement, Ronnie

Earle expressed gratitude to the Mexican government for its police work. "Not only the people of Texas but the entire United States have grieved with us over our loss," he said. "This case represents an unprecedented level of cooperation and we look forward to continuing to work with the Mexican officials."

But in Mexico, Deputy Attorney General José Luis Romero Apis stood firmly against extradition. Texas had the highest rate of executions in the United States, while in Mexico the maximum murder-rape penalty was fifty years, with a possible good-time reduction of one-third, even if there were multiple victims. Even if the men were convicted of all the Yogurt Shop charges, they could be out in thirty-five years.

When brought before reporters, handcuffed and without representation, Saavedra admitted to killing the girls. When asked why, he shook his head and then was quickly led away.

Jones called the families. There was, he warned, no telling what that confession would establish, exactly, so they should hold off believing anything they might hear. That same day, in a televised announcement, a Mexican official did exactly what Jones had feared by announcing that Saavedra had "forced the girls to submit, then he raped them, tied them up and shot them."

Jones heard about this statement from the local news, but Huckabay, who was already in Mexico City, didn't know about it until he called the home office. The APD had been careful not to mention rape, or the DNA found inside the girls' vaginas, so for Homicide, this development was another setback.

"A feeling of helplessness went over us," Jones recalled, deeming October 22 "Black Thursday." Barbara Suraci described being sick to her stomach when she heard the statement. "You want to feel good about it, but it brings the reality back. . . ."

When asked for an official response, the APD maintained a wait-and-see attitude. Meantime, Huckabay asked Chuck Meyer to join him in Mexico City to help out with the questioning, and Jones sent two Spanish-speaking detectives, Ociel Nava and Hector Reveles. At first they felt optimistic, Reveles testified during the Scott trial, and were hoping that this would be a "satisfactory conclusion to the case." To speed up the process, he urged Jones to honor the Mexican request for full, uncensored autopsy reports.

But Jones refused. "If we'd have done that," he reasoned, "they'd have had every piece of information they needed to charge them, try them, find them guilty, put them away for life. And we weren't convinced they were even there."

In his first interview with Huckabay and Reveles, Saavedra seemed to have little knowledge of the crime. Yes, he'd said, they'd killed girls at an ice-cream shop, but he didn't know how many—three? And yes, they'd "mutilated the girls, cut up their breasts, arms and vaginas, tied them up with rope . . ."

By the end of the first day, Reveles was convinced "these persons were not responsible for the murders."

Within three days of his confession, Saavedra recanted, repeatedly saying, "I didn't do this." Both he and Cortez, who was interviewed separately, claimed to have been tortured during the flight to Mexico City, with plastic bags pulled over their heads, threats to attack their families and violate their wives, daughters and sisters.

But nobody wanted to give up on these perfect suspects. By then Barnett had arrived, and he and Meyer kept scheduling polygraph tests, which were either postponed or canceled. And when they finally did manage to prep Cortez, he told them he would say nothing against his friend, that they'd shared a cell for weeks and had been in the same gang for much, much longer. "We are," Saavedra informed the federal agents, "united as one." Barnett unhooked the machine.

This calamitous investigation would continue for years, with no further progress. Cortez and Saavedra were eventually tried and convicted of the Cavity Club charges, but nobody in Austin seems to have heard about the outcome. Ricardo Hernandez was never apprehended.

We can't always trust what suspects say, for obvious reasons, but in hindsight these two men sound convincing. When Huckabay and Reveles confronted Cortez with the testimony of a woman who said she'd seen him sitting in a car in the Hillside parking lot only minutes before the girls were killed, his (translated) answer was, "I wasn't there. I didn't see who did it. . . . Perhaps you will find me guilty. I'm going to tell you this, I was never there and I never did any of that. . . . It could have been someone that looked like me; I am not the only one who has long hair or the only car. Does she have a license plate?

She should have given a license plate. . . . They are going to dispose of my life . . . my time and my thoughts . . . and do you know what, you can give me the death penalty and . . . I am going to die telling the truth because I didn't do anything."

As for Saavedra, he simply said, "Just because I [am] a criminal . . . doesn't mean I killed them. That's not what that means. I know you are going to take me, but I will never say that I did something I did not do. This is a total waste. . . . Since I am a criminal, then no one believes me."

A year from now, Jones will ask the Mexican government to provide information on the status of the charges against these two. He will also ask about Ricardo Hernandez. More often than not, his requests will be ignored. The suspects and the cases were, as the Mexican attorney general had declared, their own business.

But Skip Suraci and other family members held on to their certainty: Those three thugs had killed their daughters. Some people still agree. "But didn't the Mexicans do it?" they say to me. "Didn't they have the real guys back at the beginning?"

ANNIVERSARY

All initial optimism had fallen away before long. More confessions and more tips, a bigger reward, even Barbara and Skip Suraci talking on *Geraldo* about establishing a new reward for information leading to Ricardo Hernandez's arrest.

Homicide came in for more trouble, and even humiliation, when Ronnie Earle, Mayor Bruce Todd and incoming chief Elizabeth Watson held a joint press conference. Flanked by the two men, Watson stood there looking small but confident. At forty-three, she had short, curly hair and wore button earrings, a double-breasted suit jacket and a dark blouse with a bow at the neck. After a brief introduction, she handed things over to the DA, who announced from a prepared statement that because of recent incidents suggesting possible misconduct among investigators, all ninety pending homicide cases would be reviewed. This process, Earle assured the public, was not about one bad cop, but a general attitude throughout the unit that "the end justifies the means" and "anything goes."

When it was her turn to speak, Watson—who hadn't yet been sworn in—took the high road. "It is *shocking* to me," she said, "that there could be this breach of ethics. . . . I cannot fathom it." That seemed quite a stretch, since she'd spent twenty years on the force in Houston, from street cop to chief, and must have seen and fathomed plenty of disagreeable things.

The reaction was immediate. Hector Reveles described the announcement as "demoralizing," a "bombshell" and a "blanket indictment of the entire unit." Since the APD divided its Crimes Against

Persons Division into four components—Sex Crimes, Child Abuse, Homicide and Robbery—singling out *one* detail seemed particularly vexing. In addition to which, because cops were regularly transferred from one unit to another, which one were Earle and Watson referring to? The one handling Yogurt Shop?

For Earle, this was especially risky, given that prosecutors and cops are on the same team. He'd turned against his own players, some think because this might help establish him as hard-nosed if he ran for state attorney general.

The next day, the soon-to-be chief tried to cover her tracks by assuring the public and the APD that the current Homicide Unit wasn't the problem, and, in fact, had been improved back in April when "certain individuals"—mentioning no names—had been transferred out. She also announced two new requirements, the first being *mandatory* supplemental narratives. These reports filled in the basic incident report with details: how many cops were there, who made the arrest, who did the interview, what happened next. Supplements were already part of the process, but because of funding cuts and reduced overtime pay, investigators often sloughed off the duty as the least important part of their job. Second, and perhaps more significant, Watson ordered that all interrogations be recorded *in their entirety,* by video or audiotape, to keep tabs on the unit's tactics and to make everything as transparent as possible. Because the state's case against Robert Springsteen and Michael Scott will rely almost exclusively on videotaped confessions, this new development will eventually play a crucial part in their arrests, indictments and trials.

In December, homicide cops received an administrative questionnaire divided into five sections: "Training," "Inadequate Resources," "Case Preparation and Review," "Management/Personnel Deficiencies" and "Malfeasance." Comprehensive answers to the questions posed in each were to be submitted by early January. A few cops like paperwork, but most despise it, and Watson was becoming more unpopular by the minute. The following day, she was sworn in as the first female police chief in Austin's history. Introducing her, the mayor extolled her long stint in the Houston department and boasted that she came from a family of cops and was, he declared, a "cop's cop." Dressed in policeman's blues, Watson said she was "fiercely proud" to serve Austin.

———

The months following the arrest of the Mexican nationals did not, of course, seem flat at the time, especially not to Jones, Huckabay and Meyer—and certainly not to the families. But looking back from some twenty-odd years out, the repetition and frustrations of the fall of 1992 into the winter of 1993 seem to have a predictable refrain: *And then . . . nothing.* Every time a promising possibility showed up—phone call, visit, scribbled note, hopeful message—it quickly evaporated. *Nothing again.*

There were still more than four thousand entries in the database. Daily, John Jones chose one to explore; when it didn't pan out, he picked another. "The investigators in the yogurt case have lived with that case every day," George Phifer, now the assistant chief, told a reporter. "They go to bed with it and wake up trying to solve [it]." Mike Huckabay's twelve-year-old son asked him most every night, "Daddy, did you solve the yogurt case?" Then, in his dreams, he saw the dead girls again. Sometimes Jones couldn't look the girls' parents in the eye. Sorting through leads, he drifted into an "ozone layer," where time blurred but the names and faces still jumped out at him. And he would ask himself the same questions again and again: What have I missed here? What is it I'm not getting? *Huck, remember so-and-so? Did we clear him too soon? What about . . .*

Jones's supervisor, Ron Smith, tried to be upbeat. "Being a cop," he said, "you can become pretty cynical. You see the worst side of people. But in this case, the community support has been overwhelming. . . . When you've got twenty years of cynicism it helps bring you back to earth, that there is a good grain in humanity."

But in Homicide, clearing a case is everything. What cops can't bear is the possibility of a case never going to trial. "The only way you can face this," Lt. David Parkinson commented, "is by thinking that someday, somewhere, you'll find information that leads to solving it."

Jones wasn't sleeping. His marriage was falling apart. He paid little attention to his daughters. He was starting to withdraw into a small, dark shell.

———

On December 6, 1992, the *Statesman* ran a front-page story on the status of the year-old case, as well as a feature about the families, what it was like when Victims' Services came to their door and what their lives had been like since then. They commented on the warmth and generosity of the police department and people from all over the city. They said how much they missed their daughters. When asked how he planned to get through the anniversary, Jones said he intended to sleep all day. And then he unearthed a previously unspoken fear. "What I dread," he said, "is the trials. When I testify about how those girls died, for the families it'll be December sixth all over again."

Two days later, three Austin cops on a domestic-disturbance call fired twenty-eight shots at a twenty-three-year-old when, during a drunken fight with a girlfriend, he turned a pellet pistol in their direction. Seventeen shots hit home. The dead man's relatives admitted that he'd made a mistake, but couldn't they have shot him just once? Within a week, Betsy Watson voiced her support for the cops, who were not indicted. The APA reluctantly congratulated her for doing the right thing, but its gratitude didn't last long. Within two months, Watson fired a ten-year veteran for use of excessive force in the beating of a fourteen-year-old suspect with a nightstick. This case had, in fact, preceded her. When the incident occurred in July, acting chief Phifer recommended a five-day suspension, but the cop's attorney quickly said that five days was unwarranted. Obviously, Watson disagreed.

If the Yogurt Shop case had stalled, no wonder. The APD lacked leadership, constancy, solidarity. Homicide detectives were spending precious time answering the new chief's questionnaire. By March, as the publisher of *Texas Monthly* conducted a tireless campaign against Elizabeth Watson, the APA had raised $21,000 with which to investigate her background. Within two years of her swearing-in, people were buying bumper stickers and T-shirts saying LIFE IS A BITCH . . . THEN YOU GET ONE FOR A POLICE CHIEF.

Austin Chronicle reporter Jordan Smith dubbed this the era of cop wars. Which continued for years.

FATHER CONFESSOR

It is time now to go back to February 1992 and the man who played an important role in those wars, Senior Sgt. Hector Polanco. As one local attorney declared, "If you want to know about APD Homicide in the eighties and nineties, you have to know about Polanco . . . the father figure of all the detectives who came in his stead . . . with the same 'convict-at-any-cost' mentality." As Jones says, "Everybody had a Hector story. *Everybody.*"

Dark-eyed, handsome, supremely self-assured, Polanco was known for his sexual appeal and his interrogation skills, assets that aren't unrelated. Beloved by Ronnie Earle for his record—100 percent clearance rate during his tenure—he had a special knack for obtaining confessions, often without evidence and almost always without producing any incriminating weapons.

According to some jailhouse and courtroom insiders, Polanco believed he'd been endowed with mystical powers that enabled him to pluck guilt from a suspect's heart, especially when he was Latino. Mexican-American boys revered their mothers (*Don't shame her! Tell the truth!*) and the Virgin Mary (*She wants you to confess!*) and were terrified of prison rape (*You're young, you're new, they'll have you.*) and the enforced deportation of undocumented relatives (*I can make it happen!*). These characteristics gave Polanco the leverage he needed. In his community, he was known as "the Bogeyman" or "El Diablo." Lawyers and cops called him "the Cobra."

One defense attorney told me he loved calling Polanco to the stand, not so much for his testimony as how he delivered it, looking straight at the jury and focusing particularly on the females. "You could see the women melting under his gaze."

Polanco was loved, hated, respected, distrusted and often feared. Everybody I talked to said Jones didn't like him and that the hostility was returned, but when Jones was asked about this by APD Internal Affairs officers investigating a perjury charge against Polanco, he dodged the question.

APD: Do you like him?
JJ: Do I *like* him? I don't understand that question.
APD: Do you like Hector as a person?
JJ: Yeah. I mean. Yeah.
APD: Do you respect him?
JJ: He's my supervisor.

And when that question was repeated, Jones elaborated: "I've always done what Hector said because he's supervisor."

As a community, cops value solidarity beyond personal opinion, and Jones is no exception. He calls *Thou shalt not speak ill of thy fellow officer* the Eleventh Commandment.

Boys are important to this story. Many will come into it, some to lie through their teeth about where they were that night and who they were with—not to escape detection, but to attract it. Using leaked, rumored or reported information, they show up at the police station, declaring, *I'm the one you're looking for,* and, when interviewed, go to great lengths to create a grisly description—*drove a stake through her heart, gouged out her eyeballs, stuffed yogurt in her vagina, nailed her breast to the wall*—that, while often wildly inaccurate, usually includes at least a few precise details. And because it's a big part of their job, the cops listen.

Criminalists, social scientists and those who study aberrant behavior define false confession as an "admission to a criminal act that the confessor did not commit, usually followed by a narrative of how and why the crime occurred." They divide these phony unburdenings into three categories, the first of which they call "voluntary."

To no one's surprise, the APD heard a lot of these. After a splashy murder, people go haywire. Craving the spotlight, they will simply lie, passionately and with conviction. More often than not, they retract their statement once the polygraph machine appears.

The second kind, called "coercive-compliant," usually occurs after an intense, often lengthy application of what to the suspect feels like intolerable pressure from an exterior source—an interrogating officer, for example. Most people who fall into this group say the same thing: *I thought if I could just get out of that room and away from those guys pounding away at me, I could take a lie-detector test and give a DNA sample and prove I didn't do it.* This happens more often than you might imagine. People convince themselves that giving the examiner what he's asking for is the most rational response they can come up with—a notion cited throughout recorded history. *Tell me what you want me to say,* victims plead, *and I'll say it.*

In the third category, the suspect becomes so thoroughly persuaded of his guilt that he actually begins to hear and see himself in the act of committing an offense he previously had no memory of. This one, called "coerced-internalized," is the rarest of the three and can be invoked only by an investigator with special gifts.

Like Hector Polanco.

In 1988, during one of his best-known cases, he questioned Christopher Ochoa, a twenty-two-year-old intelligent Mexican-American boy who, along with his friend Richard Danziger, was a suspect in the brutal, high-profile rape and murder of Nancy DePriest, a young woman working at a local Pizza Hut. Polanco invited Ochoa into the interview room; somebody else took the other boy. That was before Betsy Watson became chief, so the interrogations weren't taped.

At first (according to Ochoa) hoping to "get this Chicano bond thing," Polanco spoke to him in Spanish. Danziger was about to talk, he told him, and when he did, he'd be the one to "get the deal." But when Ochoa answered in English, his interrogator switched.

Hispanics like us, he assured him, always get shafted; the white guy gets the deal. When Ochoa said he didn't know what he was talking about, Polanco showed him the autopsy photos. And when Ochoa still denied having taken part, Polanco told him he was tired of the bullshit and was going to go ahead and book him, that he was young and fresh and the other inmates were going to "have" him. Then he pointed his finger into the crook of his own arm and said, "Right there. That's where they'll put the needle."

Years later, Ochoa described what that moment was like for him. "You're just like shaking because you don't know. If you knew, you'd tell him because you don't want to die. . . . You're thinking, I don't want to die; I got to think of something."

He signed a statement. Then he signed another, implicating Danziger. The last step was to convince him to take the stand, which Polanco and his colleagues accomplished by telling Ochoa they didn't think he was the main guy, just the lookout, and that if he agreed to finger Danziger, he wouldn't get the death penalty. "Okay," he told the cops, "yeah, I was the lookout." There was no evidence tying either boy to the crime, but Ochoa's lawyer pleaded him out, swapping his testimony for a life sentence. Danziger, on the other hand, maintained his innocence throughout his interrogation and trial, though after Ochoa testified against him in excruciating detail, even his own lawyer considered him guilty. Danziger also received a life sentence.

Six years later, a Texas inmate decided to clear his conscience by writing letters to the APD and the *Austin American-Statesman,* confessing that he had raped and shot DePriest. Achim Josef Marino backed up his statement with details that included the whereabouts of the stolen Pizza Hut money bag, the handcuffs he'd forced on the young woman and the gun he'd used to shoot her. But because of ingrained prosecutorial reluctance to back down from a conviction, nothing happened. A year later, Marino sent another letter, this one addressed to Governor George W. Bush, Travis County DA Ronnie Earle and the APD. This time, a cop and a Texas Ranger were sent to interview Christopher Ochoa.

Fearing a trick, the distrustful young inmate refused to retreat from his confession until a lawyer convinced him to ask for a DNA test. Results were definite: Both he and Danziger were excluded as suspects and, in 2001, released after twelve years in prison. Achim Marino's DNA was a match, and the items he mentioned were found in his mother's house in El Paso, exactly where he said they'd be. But by then Danziger had been attacked by a fellow inmate who came at him while he was watching television, threw him to the floor and kicked him repeatedly in the head with the pointed ends of his steel-toed boots. Parts of Danziger's brain had to be removed, leaving him permanently damaged. The convict with those boots offered a lame excuse: He'd gone after the wrong guy.

Attempting to explain why he confessed to a heinous crime he didn't commit, Christopher Ochoa has said, "It's like you don't have a choice. Life sentence, death penalty. Life sentence in prison . . . you're going to die a slow death at an old age—or you're going to die in the death chamber. It was no choice. You're twenty-two years old. What do you do?"

John Jones provided the cop's perspective: "People say they'd never confess to something they didn't do. Until you get put into a six-by-six room with no windows and two armed guys going at you, you don't know what you'd do."

According to the Innocence Project, between 1989—when DNA testing was first used in this country in a postconviction appeal—and 2013, some 308 men and women have been set free, 29 of whom had served time on death row. Most of the convictions were based on false or improper forensic evidence, prosecutorial misconduct, incorrect eyewitness accounts or false confessions.

As a homicide supervisor and a member of Jones's team, Polanco had considerable influence on the Yogurt Shop case, and by early February of 1992, he'd already come up with a credible confession. He'd been on early-morning duty when a tip came in from the Del Valle jail, where an inmate had reported overhearing a fellow prisoner, Shawn "Buddha" Smith, brag about having "done" the yogurt girls. Polanco had Smith brought downtown and then interrogated him alone, in a room with no recording device. Six hours later, he emerged with a signed statement.

He called Jones and Jones called Jack Barnett, who prepared to fly in from Quantico, and soon everybody was thinking this nightmare was, by God, about to get *solved*. Jones even asked ADA Terry Keel to initiate indictment procedures to take to the grand jury. Later that day, Barnett hooked Buddha Smith up to a polygraph machine.

As the test was about to begin, Smith backed down. What if he'd made it all up? Still suspicious, Jones had the polygraph run anyway, and it showed discrepancies, holes, deception. Barnett flew back to Virginia. But the confession had a good many details right, which confirmed Homicide's worry that leaks had spread so widely that there was no chance of differentiating between what any single person knew and what he merely had heard about.

Why did Shawn Smith sign this document? After six hours with Polanco, he *believed* what the detective had told him. He could actually see himself and his friends at the yogurt shop, raping and killing.

A month later, in March, another young man—Alex Briones, previously arrested but not yet tried for tying a sixty-year-old woman to a chair, then raping her and burning her to death—also confessed to the Yogurt Shop Murders, once again during an interview conducted by Polanco without witnesses or a recording device. He then called Jones and Huckabay, and Huck got there first. This time, they definitely had their man, Polanco told him, but there was one small problem: Briones wouldn't talk to anyone except him. Ignoring Polanco's seniority, Huckabay stood his ground: If somebody else didn't hear the statement, it wouldn't stand up in court.

Polanco was forced to relent. By now, Jones had arrived.

Ten years later, during the Michael Scott trial, Huckabay described his own interview technique. "What I do is just . . . continue to talk with them, and just by the grace of God . . . every one of them will eventually say something that, bam, strikes a nerve and . . . once you get that, then you can just start attacking another way."

The first thing he asked Briones was about the four girls. "Four?" Briones said. "I thought there were three." Jones says Huckabay came out in a state. "Hector?" he said. "This guy don't know jack." And that Polanco resisted. "Wait right here," he said. Then he went back in, came out and said, "Okay, he's ready now." So Huckabay gave it another try, but Briones wouldn't sign a statement until he talked to Polanco one more time.

By then, Barnett was on the scene and had begun setting up the polygraph test, when suddenly Briones coughed up the truth: He'd been threatened and told what to say. When pressed, he fingered Polanco. But he wondered, since he *had* committed another crime, couldn't his family—who'd turned him in—still get the reward money for these killings? He had a brother who was dying of AIDS and they could use the cash.

Within ten days of the Briones interrogation, Hector Polanco was taken off Yogurt Shop and in September would be fired on grounds of suspicion of perjury, misuse of authority and witness tampering during a different arrest. In retaliation, he immediately sued the city for racism and was reinstated by acting chief Phifer, who, allegedly, was hoping this might help him win the job that soon went to Betsy Watson.

Over the years, Polanco will get promotions and eventually retire with full benefits and pension. Magic Man. Teflon Man. The Cobra. *He cleared his cases.* Looking back at the Yogurt Shop files and time lines, we need to consider Polanco and his shining record as an indication of how things were done in the APD during those long years of cop wars.

Jones again, to the Internal Affairs investigators: "If there's any kind of problem with Hector, it's never understanding where he's coming from. . . . I've told Hector this. I never know what song book we're singing out of, what song we're singing, what verse we're on, what key we're singing in, and that kind of stuff is important to me."

PTSD

On May 10, 1993, Senior Sgt. Ron Smith announced the disbanding of the Yogurt Shop task force and its attendant focus group as of May 21. John Jones would work exclusively on the case, but only between 8:00 a.m. and 4:00 p.m., Monday through Friday. He heard about this when everybody else did and blew a gasket. From home at 3:15 the next morning, Jones composed an emotionally charged eight-page memo, which began, "I'm tired of this case. Everyone is. The difference is, Jones, John W., #839 [his city of Austin employee number], is at the bottom. J. Jones #839 will be the Task Force after May 21."

After listing the seven major suspects and some of the numerous tips as yet unexplored, he went on: "This case controls us, we don't control it. We can't control it because we have never had the resources to control it. When we were getting 700 tips a month we had to 'triage' them, work on the ones that 'sounded' good because we only had 5 full-time investigators. That situation forced us to be in the predicament we're in now, still working tips that are over a year old. . . . Is this case a priority or isn't it?"

The memo was the cry of an exhausted man who'd become an insomniac and was considering converting to Catholicism, in part to have someone to talk to. Two months earlier, in early March, six patrolmen had been assigned to the case for ninety days. Chosen not for their investigative skills but for high scores on a promotions exam—most of them rookies—they were supposed to dispose of all remaining tips, one way or the other. "There simply comes a time when you spend so much time on a case without results and you have to move on," the assigning officer had drily commented.

Concerning the patrolmen, Jones wrote, "We found out early on last year that it takes about a month for anyone coming into this case to get enough of a feel for it to where they are both comfortable and productive. I addressed this last year by asking for four patrol officers that had already been assigned to the case and knew the routine . . . request denied. Is this case a priority as the families have been led to believe or what? The six patrolmen have been great. Given another month or two, we could probably whittle those 250–300 tips down to less than 100. But no. June 1st was always someone's deadline. . . . The members of this Task Force want to end this case much more than anyone else in the department. You would think our input would be appreciated; apparently it is not. . . . Who's kidding who here? This case is being shoved in a corner with me along with it. Worst, the families have been lied to. I've been lied to. Is this how a Priority Case is treated, is this how the department treats its investigators who have been thoroughly used up by this case?"

Toward the end of the memo, he answered a question his superiors never asked: "Why am I depressed? I'm depressed because I will no doubt have to sit down at the computer and punch out another memo detailing why it's important to travel out of town to interview suspects. . . . I'm depressed because I'm being told this case is a priority but in reality it's being treated as just another unsolved case. . . . I'm depressed at the thought of a return to the crowded conditions we fought so hard to leave . . . depressed because this is definitely a 'Take Home' case yet I must fight for a 'Take Home' car I might not get. . . ."

He went on, ending with the memo's theme and the question he'd repeatedly asked his superiors: "Is this case a priority or isn't it?"

Although there was no written response to Jones's memo, certainly Homicide supervisors took it into consideration when they changed their minds and gave him permission to work full-time on the case—including overtime hours, if necessary—for another ninety days. Huckabay and others would assist when they could. After that, another lead investigator should be appointed, giving #839 a break from burnout, exhaustion, stress and depression.

Without telling anybody, Jones had begun seeing a psychotherapist, who was helping him feel somewhat less lonely, especially now that his marriage was in shambles. On his own and sometimes with the help of Chuck Meyer—who would continue working on the case until after the 1999 arrests—he combed the database and followed phone tips, including one from an anonymous caller who'd picked up a hitchhiker who told him Eliza Thomas was a dope dealer and that her mother's boyfriend was the murderer. A Tennessee detective suggested Jones might want to interrogate a convicted serial killer who liked to kill women in ice-cream shops and set fires afterward. Meyer went to check him out, and again . . . *nothing*. Somebody called about a guy who didn't work, smoked pot, carried around a jar of peanut butter and had the billboard photographs of the girls on his wall. Texas Crime Stoppers—a state program that invites citizens to provide anonymous information about unsolved crimes—planned a closed-circuit interview with Jones to show inmates in the state prison system. "They know more about what goes on than we do," a spokesman there said.

Ronnie Earle still thought McDuff had done it, or one of his buddies. So did Chuck Meyer, who spent a great deal of his time driving up and down I-35 between Austin and Waco, following up leads there. Back in April, he'd participated in Operation Trojan Horse, the attack on David Koresh's Branch Davidian compound. Because four ATF agents had been killed in the February shoot-out and Meyer's wife hadn't heard from him in several days, Jones and other APD cops had driven up to Mount Carmel to make sure he was okay, and they found Meyer—a helicopter pilot in Vietnam—safely hunkered down in a ditch. A federal agent there asked Jones to create the kind of database for this debacle that he'd designed to handle information on Yogurt Shop. Grateful for the praise, he agreed to do it.

The DA's office issued a report summarizing Chief Watson's Homicide inquiry, which cited a vacuum of leadership, undertrained officers and unethical practices leading to dismissals and lawsuits, as well as detectives writing reports that omitted information they felt was either untrue or "not good for our side." Also noted was their use of the phrase "misdemeanor murders" when referring to cases that might receive little media attention.

The APD's confident response stated that all these problems had been addressed. Video and audio equipment had been purchased and would be installed in Homicide's three interrogation rooms during the next week. Lt. David Parkinson praised this development as a benefit for both sides, protecting the investigator from false accusations and eliminating any confusion about what was said during interviews. "We will record everything in its entirety," he said. "You leave yourself open to question if you try to edit."

The families of the girls erected a memorial to their daughters in the Hillside parking lot; made of pink Austin stone, it was set beneath a scrub oak and inscribed, *In Loving Memory of Amy Ayers, Jennifer Harbison, Sarah Harbison, Eliza Thomas. Forever in Our Hearts.* There's no grass around the stone, just white landscaping pebbles that cover the ground between gnarled, runty trees. By now, the glass facade of the ICBY had been bricked over, leaving the shop a dark splotch between Suzanne's Dress Shop and the Party House.

By this time, Jones had become friendly with Bob Ayers, the two sometimes going to Spurs games in San Antonio. On one outing, Ayers told Jones he wasn't looking well; maybe he should take a break. Struck by the fact that a grieving parent was saying that *he* looked bad, Jones asked for a fifteen-day administrative leave, suggesting that the time off would allow him to return with a better attitude, renewed energy and a fresh commitment to "winding down the case" by January. Chief Watson refused to approve the request but authorized a sick leave that required medical approval before he could return to work. Clearly, she wanted him to just step aside, but Jones refused. And then he made a mistake.

Mexican officials still claimed to be trying to arrange a time when Austin cops, federal agents and a Travis County prosecutor could again talk to Saavedra and Cortez. Impatient with the endless to-ing and fro-ing, the families, led by Skip Suraci, asked Jones if *they* could do anything to help speed up the process. When Jones said this was doubtful, Suraci took it upon himself to call the Mexican consul in San Antonio. After receiving a response that sounded positive—at least to him—Suraci organized the families to write a joint letter that this attaché could forward to his attorney general's office.

Improvidently—and fully aware he was disobeying departmental rules—Jones faxed the letter to San Antonio, which his superiors viewed as both grandstanding and evidence that he'd grown too close to the families, giving them information that only the APD should be privy to; he was even accused of soliciting them to write this letter. On October 20, Jones received a Record of Sub-Standard Performance, with Parkinson citing "conduct or work habits which conflict with departmental policy or orders."

This was a low blow. And by his own admission, Jones cratered on the spot, right there in Homicide. When he'd calmed down, he told Parkinson, "I did what I thought I had to." Two days later, his psychologist wrote the APD to say that after carrying sole responsibility for Yogurt Shop for six months and as a result of a "critical memo from a superior officer," Jones was exhibiting more than 90 percent of the symptoms of post-traumatic stress disorder (PTSD), including recurrent dreams of the event and intense distress at exposure to things—such as anniversaries—that symbolized the original trauma, feelings of detachment from others (including his family), insomnia, irritability, difficulties in concentrating, jumpiness and hypervigilance.

She recommended a one-month leave, which was granted, but by mid-November he was back on the job. Despite the damage that Parkinson's report might have done to his reputation, he felt no animosity toward him. "I'd have done the same thing," he says now.

As for his relationship with the families, he admits that by department standards, he might have gotten too close to them. But at the time, it felt right. "We were all crazed and obsessed, so for us that was normal. Nobody seemed crazy. Because we all were."

Four days before the second anniversary of the murders, Jones received a subpoena from attorneys for five of the family members to appear in a pretrial hearing in civil court, where he would be asked to produce his complete investigation file as well as the unedited autopsy reports from the ME's office. The families—with the exception of James Thomas—were revving up to sue Brice Foods and Morrison Properties, owner of the Hillside Center, for damages. *Barbara Suraci and Michael Harbison, Pamela and Robert Ayers and Marcia [Maria] Thomas v. Brice Foods, Inc., I Can't Believe It's*

Yogurt, LTD, Rockwood Plaza Associates, LTD and Charles Morrison Individually and D/B/A Morrison Properties charged that lax security contributed to the likelihood of assault at the yogurt shop and other stores. The suit also noted how late the ICBY stayed open and that teenage girls ran it alone. When, in response, the city filed a motion to keep the autopsy reports sealed, Mike Harbison called Jones to lambaste him for thwarting their intentions. Bill Brice, he claimed, was as guilty of his daughters' murder as the men who shot them.

On December 6, 1993, the St. Albert the Great Catholic Church held a Mass in memory of the girls. At ten o'clock that evening, friends again participated in a vigil at the yogurt shop, which the *Statesman* called a "shrine to innocence lost."

A month later, in January, Brice Foods and Morrison Properties escaped the embarrassing publicity of a trial by agreeing to pay the victims' families twelve million dollars in a civil-suit settlement. Having formed a nonprofit organization called We Will Not Forget SAJE (an acronym of the girls' first names), the families intended to use some of the money to teach teenagers about workplace safety. The lawsuit was sealed, but rumor suggests they had information about the lock on the back doors—faulty, possibly unlocked, now missing—which left the workers at risk. But by now, the families have closed ranks. "Hush-hush," one parent called their pact. "Blood money," said Doug Tash from the nearby pet store.

Later that month, Jones traveled to FBI headquarters in Quantico with Chuck Meyer and Mike Huckabay to discuss their difficulties with the Mexican attorney general's office. Foremost among the topics to be covered was the ongoing DOJ request to interview and polygraph Saavedra and Cortez in the United States under the provisions of the Mutual Legal Assistance Treaty with Mexico, established in 1991; this created an opportunity for cooperation between the two countries, but each new instance had to be negotiated by both Justice Departments—therefore slow going.

As Austin lost faith and Yogurt Shop's immediacy faded, other crimes moved into the spotlight. In northeastern Travis County, near Pflugerville, a baby-sitter named Cathy Lynn Henderson either accidentally dropped three-month-old Brandon Baugh on a concrete floor or delivered the infant a killing blow with a blunt object. Instead of calling 911, she wrapped the dead baby in a blanket, taped him up in a wine-cooler box and absconded up I-35 North, burying him beside the interstate in a shallow grave near Temple. The search for Henderson took over front-page news until she was located in Independence, Missouri, with dyed hair and a changed name, a month's rent paid in advance. To some, this incident was as disturbing as the Yogurt Shop Murders. After Henderson's lawyer was forced to give Travis County officials the map her client had drawn, showing where she'd buried the baby, his body was dug up and brought home for a funeral. In 1995, after Medical Examiner Roberto Bayardo testified that the injuries could not have resulted from an accident, Henderson was found guilty of capital murder and sentenced to death by lethal injection. After Bayardo changed his testimony in 2012, stating that new scientific procedures suggested that the baby's death might well have been an accident, her conviction was overturned and a new trial ordered. But the ailing fifty-eight-year-old Henderson waived that right and, after pleading guilty to first-degree murder, agreed to a twenty-five-year sentence with credit for time served— which meant she'd have been released in four years. But two months later, she had a stroke and, while in the prison hospital, developed pneumonia. When she died, Brandon Baugh's parents said now they could move on.

On Friday, May 6, his day off, John Jones received a call from Bruce Mills, whom Watson had appointed deputy chief, telling him he was being replaced. Four days later, Mills announced that Jones and Doug Dukes, of APD's Child Abuse detail, would trade positions. The transfer, he told the press, was mainly at Jones's request, because of burnout and a recent promotion. "John Jones is not being thrown off the case. He will continue to act as a consultant."

The next day, Jones publicly begged to differ. He'd asked for a 50 percent reduction, not a transfer. "I'd always expected to be a part of any decision," he told a *Statesman* reporter. "I expected to be sat down and asked what do you think is best here." Instead, he said, they "called me and said you got a week and goodbye."

Pam Ayers spoke for the families. "We want him to stay. . . . This is a complex case. It can't just be handed off." She also complained that they weren't told about the change from the APD, but "heard it through the grapevine."

No matter, Jones was out. And once again, Yogurt Shop slipped off the front pages. In June, O. J. Simpson was arrested for the murder of his ex-wife, Nicole. Four months later, Susan Smith confessed she'd lied when she reported that a black man had carjacked her Mazda Protegé with her two little sons inside, when in fact she herself had rolled the car into a lake. Even as the national crime rate fell, random crime in Texas was reportedly on the rise, partially due to the popularity of home-cooked meth. In Austin, people interviewed by the *Statesman* still cited Yogurt Shop and the abduction of Colleen Reed as the chief reasons to be fearful.

The Yogurt Shop families used the money from the settlement to buy new homes. The Ayerses moved out of Austin onto acreage outside of Blanco, where Bob could fulfill his dream—and Amy's—of being a rancher. Maria Thomas purchased a house in Oregon. Barbara and Skip Suraci sold their house on Tamarack Lane and bought one in a new suburban development slightly closer to Capital Memorial Gardens, where Sarah, Jennifer and Amy were buried. After the murders, their daughters' friends had often come to Tamarack Lane, asking to sit in the girls' rooms and look through their stuff, perhaps spend the night in their beds. Barbara always said yes. The new home was bigger, more formal, but she turned one of the bedrooms into a kind of shrine, with twin beds and a display of cheerleader uniforms, teddy bears, FFA jackets and certificates, toys and Jennifer's *The Boots, the Jeans, the Dream* collage. The girls' friends still visited.

Bored with management and computers, Skip enrolled in law school at the University of Tulsa. For a while, he and his wife shared a commuting marriage and spent a lot of time on the road. They hired an attorney to conduct their own investigation, concentrating on the two imprisoned Mexicans and the one still on the loose. But once again Barbara found herself in a familiar role, adjusting her own life to accommodate a husband reinventing his, and she began to feel edgy, impatient.

When John Jones was transferred to Child Abuse, he hotly protested. *Child Abuse? Really?* So the APD changed his assignment to Assault and Family Violence. He'd been taking instruction at St. Louis the King, which might seem more dramatic than it was.

Having spent those years in Catholic school, he was familiar with the ritualism and formalities. His wife and daughters were Catholic. Once he converted, he joined the choir.

But he was still a cop, working for the APD. And failure was a bitter pill to swallow.

II

THE PAUL JOHNSON SHOW

THE NEW GUY

Cop wars continued. In October 1995, Chief Watson enrolled Austin in a task force code-named Mala Sangre, a federally funded initiative designed to attack organized drug trafficking and money laundering. But the local chapter quickly imploded when undercover informants accused APD officers of protecting the dealers the task force had already put under surveillance, in exchange for cocaine, sexual favors and, for some, an expense-paid trip to the Super Bowl. This discovery led to prolonged allegations, denials, reassignments, lawsuits and whistle-blower complaints, along with further attacks on Watson. She then, possibly hoping to save face, focused on the best-known unsolved homicide in Austin's history.

The following January, she announced a "fresh take from within" on the ICBY murders. When she selected homicide detective Paul Johnson to reorganize existing files and search for evidence of leads, tips, suspects and statements that might have been insufficiently investigated or unjustifiably cleared, nobody was surprised. Known as meticulous and persistent, a bottled-up guy who didn't much care whether colleagues liked him or what he did or how he did it, he'd been with the APD for some twenty years, serving nine on patrol duty, a year in general assignment, five in Sex Crimes and five in Homicide, during which time he'd won awards for public service and commendations from within the department. Most important, he liked to work alone.

In its early stages, cold-case work is archival. You sit in a room to see what's already been done. You read incident reports, witness interviews and supplemental narratives many times over, looking for careless processing, missed opportunities, the palm print not taken, the question not asked, the gun not properly tested, the tip overlooked or taken too lightly. You reorganize information, examine crime-scene photographs and create a time line that reaches back to the beginning, then study the drift of events and reports for coincidences and patterns. A lot of cops go stir-crazy, just sitting there. Not Paul Johnson, whose cell phone's ringtone, I'm told, was the overture to *William Tell,* popularly known as the *Lone Ranger* theme song.

As his partner, Watson assigned Sgt. J. W. Thompson, who had worked on Yogurt Shop with Jones and Huckabay. He was pretty much Johnson's opposite—outgoing, talkative, likable—and the two would divide the work similarly: Johnson the hard files and computer database; Thompson the fieldwork and active investigation, the kind of shoe-leather beat he preferred. Instead of being given leave to work exclusively on the case, each would remain in regular Homicide rotation. When asked, both of them would play down their new assignment, saying that Yogurt Shop was just one of many cases they were working on.

Johnson soon became as obsessed as Jones, but with a difference. In the four years since the murders, the ardent confessions had ceased and the special tips line had been disconnected. Discouraged, the families had retreated. Reporters weren't jamming microphones in Johnson's face. He could work when he liked, at quiet times in the office and at home nights and on days off. As a kind of cop-ascetic, he became a scholar of Yogurt Shop, not as it had happened but as it had been defined and refined and reframed.

Yet many refer to the case from here on out, through the initial arrests and trials, as "the Paul Johnson Show."

In March, Watson set up a meeting with Chuck Meyer and representatives from the APD, the FBI, the AFD, the DPS and the DA's office. Having still received no response from the Mexican attorney general's office, she wanted a reassessment of the Yogurt Shop strategy, from not only the lead cops but *all* the relevant agencies.

Some people thought a reappraisal *from within* guaranteed a rehash, and in some respects this was correct. The same things kept happening. Meyer took more trips; Ronnie Earle's office made lists; Paul Johnson kept analyzing. Despite persistent attempts at editing it down, the Jones database still held some five thousand entries, in addition to four four-drawer cabinets jammed with hard files. In the years to come, Johnson would heavily criticize the operational strategy he had inherited as being obscure, wrongheaded and even—despite Jones's reputation—unmanageable.

The two men were destined never to become friends. A retired cop I know said that given Johnson's inscrutability and Jones's ego, he wasn't surprised. They were both thin-skinned and irascible, and each was known to hold a grudge.

In August, when Crime Stoppers ran its interview with Jones on its closed-circuit prison network, some 130,000 prisoners watched, but nobody came forward with information, despite a sizable reward. Governor Bush offered to write a letter to the Mexican government, as did State Attorney General Dan Morales, but for one reason or another, the letters were never sent.

Forging through Jones's list of major suspects, Johnson soon came to the Maurice Pierce file but, finding no reason to pursue these tips, moved on. He would work on the ICBY files through 1996 and seven months into 1997; in that time, he reduced the database to some 2,080 reports. In 1999, he explained his methodology: "We started generating offense reports for each tip. . . . A tip would be a particular suspect or group of suspects. . . . All the searchable fields, names, descriptions, vehicles, anything that's searchable would be set out and locate-able. And then a file of actual paper and any other evidence would be kept by that number for each tip." When asked who did most of the work, he said, "As I was making each of these [supplements and tips] into offense reports, which we classify as open or closed . . . if it appeared that a group of suspects had not been cleared appropriately or if it wasn't clear why they were cleared, I kept that open. And then the open tips were assigned to Sgt. Thompson," who would go out and conduct interviews.

By this time, Jones and his wife were "divorced in place," sleeping in separate bedrooms, leading separate lives. His older daughters were in their last two years of high school, the younger ones entering first and second grade. "I'd never believed people who said they stayed together for the children," he says now. "But that's what we did." Every time he reread the symptoms of PTSD, he felt like he was looking in a mirror.

He and his wife and daughters lived in a ranch-style home in the Quail Creek subdivision, where he "was the only guy in the house." He pauses. "Except for the dog." When he flashes a bemused smile, you know a sardonic wisecrack is forthcoming. "And he ran away." Then he thinks of an addendum. "Oh, and there was a fish. But the fish didn't care."

He was now in the process of failing, not just as a cop but as a husband and father.

Johnson's part-time assignment continued until July 31, 1997, by which time the embattled Elizabeth Watson had left Austin for a job with the Department of Justice in Washington, D.C., and Bruce Mills had been appointed the interim chief. Popular on the force, Mills had begun his APD career at nineteen as a dispatcher and been steadily promoted. Like every cop, he knew full well that police chiefs never come from within the ranks. But while he was interim chief, he decided to give Paul Johnson a different team. And if this helped solve Yogurt Shop, he might well have a shot at the job.

Because the planning meetings were held in Attorney General Dan Morales's office, cops called Mills's new team "the AG task force." There were five representatives from Morales's office, one from the U.S. attorney's office, Chuck Meyer from BATF and several prosecutors from the DA's office, including Robert Smith. Nobody from the DPS. Nobody from the AFD. Mostly lawyers.

In an official statement, an APD assistant chief cautioned the public against undue optimism. The team was purely investigative, he said, not a task force. Chief Mills's action didn't imply the possibility of new leads, only that they wanted to take "a fresh look at the existing evidence." Ronnie Earle lent lukewarm support. A lot of hard work had been done on the case, he said, and "it helps to get the whole team together from time to time." A spokesperson for Morales gave a rather muddled explanation. They hoped, he said, "to make use of persons and a perspective that has not yet seen the evidence, seen the information, that may not have any preconceived ideas about the case and may not be influenced in any particular direction."

Homicide was incensed, feeling that Yogurt Shop belonged to them. When asked for a comment, Lt. David Parkinson had none.

Johnson and Thompson were given permission to work exclusively on the case for five months. During that time, Johnson returned once again to the early tips files and the parameters of the original FBI profile. Rereading the Maurice Pierce file, even though the suspect was too young to match either the profile or any eyewitness description, he found the tip "did not appear to have been closed justifiably." They began actively to pursue Pierce and his friends—Forrest Welborn, Robert Springsteen and Michael Scott.

Jones hotly objects to this assessment. His people didn't *close* the Pierce file; neither did they clear it. They came to a dead end and felt that without additional information, they could go no further. Had they found more evidence, they would've *revisited* it.

But Johnson thought he might be onto something, and in September he sent Pierce's 1991 lie-detector test results to APD polygrapher Bruce Stevenson, who reported that while the suspect had "scored out truthful" back then, those particular tests were no longer used and the best score he personally would give was "inconclusive." Although most APD cops didn't have a lot of confidence in Stevenson's abilities, and Johnson didn't much like polygraph tests anyway, he chose to interpret this response as an encouragement.

NORTHCROSS

The initial incident report was dated Saturday, December 14, 1991, eight days after the murders. At about six o'clock that evening, sixteen-year-old Maurice Pierce tucked a loaded .22 pistol into his left-hand jeans pocket and jammed sixteen extra rounds into the other one. An energetically imaginative boy with flashing blue eyes and spiked hair, Maurice had taken the gun off thirteen-year-old Johnny Holder, who'd lifted it from his father's gun collection. Satisfied with his attire—shirttail out to hide the weapon—he picked up his dad's car keys and left their apartment, followed by his disciple, fifteen-year-old Forrest Welborn.

Both were enrolled at McCallum High, but Maurice almost never went. Nobody in his family seemed to mind. And when his father wasn't using his car—a sky blue, pristine 1985 Ford LTD—he allowed his son to drive it.

Maurice drove with Forrest to Northcross Mall. Inside, he strolled around the concourse, the pistol warm against his skin. It didn't take long for another kid to notice it. Maurice might've lifted his shirt to show him.

This kid reported what he'd seen to Malcolm Wilson, the moonlighting off-duty cop whose name we remember from the night of the murders. When Wilson found Maurice and Forrest wandering around in a store, he took possession of the pistol and ammunition and escorted the boys to the security office. The .22 had three rounds in the chamber. When asked why he would bring a loaded gun to a shopping mall, Maurice shrugged.

"Just to be carrying it," he said.

Of all the statements he would make on this day and over the next ten years, perhaps *Just to be carrying it* rings the truest. Texas is well known for its avid gun culture, and Maurice's father was a gun guy. What better way for a small, quick-tempered boy to take on tough-guy status than to pack a loaded pistol and show it off in a public place, not for any particular reason, not to *shoot* anybody, just to be carrying it.

Wilson called the APD to arrange for their transfer to the juvenile detention center. Within minutes, a policeman arrived at Northcross and, after charging Maurice with unlawful possession of a weapon, took both boys in. When Hector Polanco heard about the arrest, he wanted to interview them himself. The confiscated weapon and ammunition were put in APD custody, where they remain to this day.

So this is how it began, with the brainless antics of a hotshot, smart-alecky kid.

By the next morning, Maurice had announced to Polanco that his .22 was probably the gun used to kill the yogurt girls and that Forrest might be the one who had done it. On the night in question, he said, he and Forrest had gone down to the Fungus at ten or ten-thirty and hung out with a skinhead group led by a guy named Mace. At some point, Forrest borrowed the .22 and went off with the skinheads. When he came back, the gun had been shot six times. There was a scratch on Forrest's neck and he smelled of hair spray.

Hair spray? There was that thing you could do—spray it in the air, apply a lighter flame and WHOOSH! That was how they'd started the fire. Forrest told Maurice he'd done something bad and wanted to do it again. To kill more girls.

Maurice was quick on his feet, but the story made little sense. Nobody'd ever heard of anybody called Mace. And hair spray? To start a fire hot enough to melt aluminum?

When Polanco asked who he'd been with earlier that night, Maurice told him that except for the hours he spent baby-sitting for his sister, he'd been with Rob Springsteen and Mike Scott, who lived together in a condo on some little street on the other side of MoPac.

Polanco called Jones, who had Springsteen and Scott picked up. The two boys went willingly, having no idea that at the very same moment their friend Maurice was being wired up by a BATF specialist.

There was more. In the early-morning hours of December 8, 1991, Maurice had taken those same three friends on a wild ride to San Antonio in a Nissan Pathfinder he'd stolen from a car lot. He hadn't been caught, but when Polanco started questioning him, it seemed likely the Pathfinder would soon come up. And it did.

ROB

Seventeen-year-old Robert Burns Springsteen IV had lived in Austin less than four months. Born in Chicago and raised by his mother and grandparents in Cross Lanes, West Virginia, after his parents divorced, he'd called his father late that August to ask if he could live with him for a while; he was having trouble getting along with his new stepfather. Robert Burns Springsteen III didn't immediately concur. He had to talk with his girlfriend first, especially since the two condos they lived in were in her name.

Known in West Virginia as "Robby," the boy had dark, darting eyes, a notable widow's peak, devilish eyebrows and a habit of carrying his chin cocked to one side, as if to indicate his readiness to take on all comers. Quick-tempered and boastful, he seemed too swaggery for his own good. In junior high he'd been characterized by teachers and school administrators as a misfit who wore out his welcome in a hurry wherever he went. Because of his temper, his absences and an attitude of unearned and unapologetic entitlement, he'd been assigned to an alternative-learning center with other disruptive students. Counselors also singled him out for sporting weird clothes to get attention—a Nehru jacket one day, a bandanna around his head the next—though this complaint might say more about the town than the boy. Nobody called him bad, exactly. He had roots in Cross Lanes, and his mother worked hard and was respected. He was just one of those boys.

When his father and his partner agreed to convert the second condo, which they'd been using as a guest and family room, into temporary quarters for Rob, he traveled to Austin and moved in. The condos were small—maybe 750 square feet—but Rob would have his privacy, and his father agreed to give him some slack when it came to discipline. His plan was to see what the boy could handle and then start applying some rules.

A week or so later, Rob registered for the fall semester at McCallum High, and since he needed to repeat a grade, he'd be a sophomore. Tall and somewhat athletic, he turned out for football but in no time got into a squabble with the coach and quit before making a down. "Me and him," he said later, "didn't see eye-to-eye." Not long after that, he became involved in a lunchtime scrap at a nearby McDonald's. When words were exchanged, Rob pulled a knife.

Because of this incident and his poor attendance record, teachers and counselors wanted to send him to their own alternative school, but the McCallum principal overrode them. He was a new student, Penny Miller explained to her staff, the semester had barely begun, and he'd written a letter of apology about the knife, which he said belonged to somebody else. She executed this decision with stipulations: Rob had to be where he was supposed to be—in class—and follow administrative rules and show signs of academic progress.

When he quickly resumed his habits, Miller ordered him to the alternative-learning center. In December, when an APD cop asked how long it was since he'd been to class, Rob drew a blank. "A week? Two weeks? I don't know . . . probably at least a month. Maybe a month and a half or two months. . . . Because they sent me [there] and that's when I just quit. I was like, *Screw this.*"

In late November, shortly after his seventeenth birthday, when Rob asked if his friend Mike Scott could move in with him, his father was skeptical. But Rob assured him that Mike was a good guy and would be no trouble at all; besides, he had a *situation* at home.

Robert Burns Springsteen III decided to trust his son's judgment, and his girlfriend agreed to go along on one condition: If the boys quit school, they had to get jobs. Both of them agreed. The truth is, they'd probably already stopped attending class. In 1999, Mike Scott will say that by December of that year, he hadn't attended class once since September 30. He will contradict this statement a number of times, however, and in the end, when it comes to Springsteen *père et fils* and Mike Scott, there is so much *Who knows?* to their stories we have to take it as a given that whatever has been said or attested to, whatever has been vowed, promised or testified under oath, might or might not be actual fact. This goes for cops as well, who in the interest of collaring the boys will tell them they know things they don't and warn them of consequences that will never occur. We have to swing with that and depend to some extent on what in the detective business is called "heuristics": rule of thumb, instinct, a hunch, likelihoods based on given assumptions.

Located about three miles from McCallum and seven from the ICBY shop and Northcross Mall, the condominiums where the Springsteens and Mike Scott lived are well maintained and attractive. Two-story, built of local stone, with landscaped surroundings and carefully placed rocks and boulders, they are shaded and quiet, far enough from the university to lack the beer-party atmosphere that often rules in many apartment complexes in Austin.

When he called Teleserve, on the morning of December 6, to report that his son was missing, the elder Springsteen, a contract computer programmer, was between jobs and therefore was at home a good bit of the time, and he might've noticed if the boys weren't going to school. When called to the stand, he will testify that he has no memory of making the call. And when the chief prosecutor hands him the incident report taken by Teleserve officer Mary Ann Hueske, he will sit there looking at it and still claim not to remember.

When, in 2010, I visited Rob in West Virginia and asked where he'd been those nights his father claimed he was missing, he waved the question away. "Oh," he said, "my dad. My dad and I don't get along too well."

But if he *had* been gone for two nights, where might he have been?

He shrugged. On some friend's couch, maybe playing video games all night. He did that a lot. Maybe . . . oh, who knows? He stayed away from home quite a lot in those days and had no idea why his father had made the report.

"I may have been gone," he concluded. "But I wasn't *missing*."

MIKE

Michael Scott also had no idea why Rob's father had made the report, because, as he told an APD detective, he and Rob had spent that Thursday night at the condo and the next morning had gotten up early and, after smoking weed by the swimming pool, left as if they were off to school. Like many young and not-so-young people in Austin, Rob and Mike smoked pot pretty much on a daily basis. They also dropped acid, ate psilocybin mushrooms and drank endless cans of beer. Mike will one day describe himself as the "Mushroom King" of Austin, while Rob, a follower of the Grateful Dead, recalls dropping acid in seven states.

Born in Micronesia, where his family had gone to live after his grandfather served in Guam during World War II, Mike had moved around a lot as a child, but during most of his school years he lived in Austin and struggled, having received an early diagnosis of severe dyslexia. But in his freshman year at McCallum, 1989–90, he made the freshman football team, joined the drama department's Royal Court Players and played viola in the school orchestra. He was also active enough in Boy Scouts to become a Life Scout at sixteen. A photograph in that year's school yearbook shows him with a short haircut, wearing a white dress shirt and tie, smiling faintly. He looks tense, shy, cautiously hopeful and very young.

But the dyslexia balled up his mind and he didn't do well academically. "School was boring, really," he told cops, as if having hit on a new idea. "Very boring."

By his sophomore year, his parents were divorced and his mother was suffering from serious emotional disorders. Mike grew his hair long and quit orchestra, football and the Royal Court. He began to dress, according to a friend, "like he didn't care much about his appearance." When required to repeat his sophomore year, he began skipping school, shuttling between his parents' homes and often spending nights with friends. A classmate of all these boys described Mike as the one who was "always trying to cheer everybody up," but socially awkward and, like Forrest Welborn, a follower.

He was handsome, tall, with straight light brown hair and a wide smile. There's a blandness about him, in his eyes a soft, sweet look of perpetual questioning, as if he's lost and can't find his way home. By the time he moved in with Rob, he'd become one of many do-nothing boys forever hanging around, with no plans beyond figuring out what to do that night. *Lookin' for some trouble to get into,* he often said, describing their aimless itineraries. *Being a general pest.* Mostly what they did was wait.

Unlike the others, Mike had interests. At the time of the murders, he was involved in a branch of the Explorer Scouts devoted to the study of the dress and culture of pre-1840 Native Americans. There are photos of him in Indian dance attire he made himself, having been mentored by an Explorer leader who taught him how to tan leather for leggings and breeches. Mike's hair flowed unbound behind him when he performed. A few years later, he'll wear different costumes when he joins a medieval reenactment group.

Although in 1999 Michael Scott would apologize for having a "piss-poor memory," he supplied a good many interesting, if wobbly, details about his and his roommate's actions on December 6, rattling them off in a kind of verbal shorthand: "Got up, got high, screwed around, made some phone calls, smoked a joint by the condo pool, rode the city bus to McCallum to see what was going on." In the big fields around the school where students gathered during lunchtime, there was a girl who'd caught Mike's eye. *Went there,* he said. *Saw Amber.*

From the condos, McCallum was a straight shot east. Built in 1953, an assortment of low-slung redbrick buildings and temporary classrooms surrounded by fields, parking lots and chain-link fencing, it closely resembled a prison. When asked how he got to school that day, Rob Springsteen made one thing clear: "I guarantee you," he said, "I didn't walk." Three miles isn't very far, but in a car-and-pickup culture a boy wanting to man up and attract girls didn't ride the school bus or walk.

In a later statement, Mike Scott came up with an entirely new and different account: "Went up to school Friday morning, eight a.m. Talked to Rob in front of school. I don't know how he got there. I told him I would be at the bowling alley at lunch. Left school at lunch with Rob and Maurice and Forrest around two-thirty. Went to Capital Bowl, had lunch, then left thirty minutes later. Amber was at the bowling alley. From the bowling alley went to Northcross, a little after three."

In an interrogation, cops look for inconsistencies and discrepancies. While a practical tool, this omits many possible influences: drugs, alcohol, a braggadocio temperament and the inborn tendency, for boys like this, when faced with trouble, to serve up what they figure the authorities want to hear. People misremember or re-create, think they remember things that never happened, then back up their memories with reasons dreamed up on the spot. Sometimes, for one reason or another, they just lie.

Cops start with that assumption: *Everybody lies.*

FORREST

However Rob and Mike got to McCallum, they seem to have arrived around lunchtime, about when Forrest Welborn emerged from class. Known as the "quiet one," Forrest had once been musical, too, playing stand-up bass in the Lamar Middle School orchestra. Also like Rob and Mike, he had moved between parents and stepparents for much of his life, his mother and father having gotten divorced when he was in the first grade. His mother currently lived in Lockhart, twenty or so miles from Austin, while Forrest lived with his father in Austin. Elementary school teachers commented on his lack of attention in class. He liked to draw—superheroes, weapons, gun blasts, villains. He would sit in the back of the room and sketch one picture after another, never lifting his head, never hearing anything that went on in class.

Forrest had a long face, deep-set eyes and a lean, loping frame. A tall boy, six one, in years to come he would grow his dark brown hair long and let it hang loose down his back. By the time of Yogurt Shop, he was beginning to let go of ambition and, perhaps, hope . . . except when he was with Maurice, who fired him up. Maurice explained his appeal straightforwardly: "I was the one with the car, so he came with me a lot." Rob Springsteen put it differently: Forrest would do anything Maurice told him to.

A soft-edged boy who drank too much beer and couldn't quite pull himself out of the morass his life had tumbled into, Forrest didn't do well with girls and once got arrested while just sitting in the car waiting for a friend who went into a convenience store and stole a twelve-pack. And later, when his driving tickets mounted up, instead of coming up with a way to pay them off, he decamped to Lubbock and lived in an abandoned family trailer. He was good at one thing: fixing cars.

Rob couldn't remember how he and Mike met up with Forrest that day. "Sometime," he said, "somehow, I ran into Forrest and Maurice. Or I had gone over to Forrest's house and Maurice came by. Or—I don't know. . . . Some days I was with so-and-so and some days I was sitting at the house by myself for eons. . . . Sometimes I get things in my head I can't get out."

If the three guys—Mike, Rob and Forrest—actually went to the bowling alley, they didn't stay long. A sign posted there said that kids under eighteen had to bowl, order food or leave. Forrest lived right across the street from the school. Maybe they went there or to a field to smoke a joint; nobody quite remembers. What they all recall, however, is that at about two or maybe two-thirty—just before the end of lunch period, when Forrest had to go back to class—Maurice showed up in his dad's LTD with the mag wheels and razor rims and the handcuffs hanging from the rearview mirror, and from then on everything was different. Better. Filled with possibilities.

RINGLEADER

Small guy. Built low. Glittery blue eyes. Spiky haircut. Wired, nervous. That's Action Man. And there was the car, immaculate as always. No smoking, nobody else could drive, no trash on the floor or seats. Mike said Maurice cared more about his car than anything, including girls and booze. A female friend agreed. What Maurice was about, she said, was cars, just like his father, who was always selling or trading one in for another. Cars and guns, guns and cars, that was really it.

Of the four boys, Maurice was the only one who'd been in serious trouble with the law. In 1990, age fifteen, he was picked up for unauthorized use of a motor vehicle (UUMV) *twice*, once after he drove off in a car whose owner had left the key in the ignition, then after his own father reported him. Maurice, his dad told the police, had driven his car to Houston; and though he'd brought it back, he shouldn't have taken it in the first place. That same year, he was suspended from school for fighting and for having a knife and then arrested for stealing fire extinguishers. Earlier in 1991, he'd been charged with criminal trespass, having jumped the fence of an apartment complex with a double-edged knife in his belt, and then for possession of a stereo believed to be stolen, and for criminal trespass in a schoolyard after allegedly threatening to cause bodily harm to a student, somebody said with a bomb, and *finally* for assault.

The mix was perfect: three aimless dudes, one troublemaker with firepower and wheels.

As for the guns, Mike said on the day or maybe two days before the murders—he wasn't exactly sure of the date—they'd all been together in the LTD when Maurice pulled over and hollered at some Mexicans to come over to the car—Mike suspected to buy some grass. But Maurice bought a gun instead, a .38, Mike thought, shiny black. They went up to Lake Travis that afternoon and shot at trees. Maurice, he remembered, couldn't shoot worth shit. As for the .22, he'd gotten it from Johnny Holder and didn't plan on paying the hundred-dollar asking price.

After Forrest went back to class, Rob and Mike had a conversation with Rob's girlfriend, Kelly Hanna, in the parking lot, next to her brown pickup. She said she'd be hanging out with a few girlfriends that night, and after Rob said they might swing by if they got a ride, Kelly returned to class.

At about two-thirty, Maurice had to run an errand, so more than likely he dropped his buddies off at Northcross, close to the video arcade. Mike remembered drinking beer while driving over, even though they were underage and couldn't buy it. He couldn't remember where the beer had come from, maybe a guy named Larry, maybe somebody else. What he did know was that the three of them scored a twelve-pack of Bud and polished it off before arriving at the mall, and by then they were, in his words, "buzzing pretty good." He and Rob went straight to the food court to sit at a table and sober up a little.

Then what? Mostly nothing, killing time until Maurice came back. Play games, smoke cigarettes, watch the ice-skaters, wait, dick around. Mike said the only reason they went to Northcross was to watch girls, play video games and look for trouble to get into. Some boys they knew came by their table. Mike marveled when a fat Mexican kid drank a whole bottle of ketchup. Asked if it was just the three of them at the table after Forrest got there, Rob said it was never just them, that other people came and went. Nobody cared about last names or made any plans; they were happy to sit bullshitting and pestering the shoppers and mall walkers. After sunset they went outside to watch the Hooters girls come in to work. *Dudes without dates,* John Jones called boys who didn't bathe enough, had little ambition, clustered in video arcades, drank ketchup straight from the bottle and ogled girls.

Sometime after four o'clock—after Jennifer Harbison had left in the S-10 to go see her boyfriend and just before Barbara Suraci arrived home from work and found her younger daughter, Sarah, sitting on the couch, peeling an orange—Forrest showed up and, soon afterward, so did Maurice, but not for long. He had to baby-sit for his sister, Renee Reyna, and he wanted Forrest to go with him. When Rob and Mike protested, Maurice concocted a story about some dangerous Mexicans who might be after them and then left with his sidekick, promising to return. So Mike and Rob were stuck. And without wheels, there was no hope of swinging by Kelly Hanna's.

When asked about the crucial hours between eleven and midnight, Rob, Maurice and Mike told different stories (and Forrest none at all).

Rob said he sneaked in to see the midnight *Rocky Horror Picture Show,* as he always did on weekend nights, and that Mike failed to get in and had to wait in the lobby until the show was over, around 2:00 a.m. They were hoping to go to a cast party Rob had heard about, but when they couldn't find it, some dude dropped them off at Mike's mother's place because it was close.

Mike, however, said Maurice took them down to Sixth Street and they partied like everybody else; then he dropped them back off at the condo by ten-thirty or so—early for them on a weekend. They turned on cable TV and watched that Robin Hood flick with Kevin Costner before falling asleep, Rob first.

Messed around, Maurice reported, partied, went down to the Fungus; Forrest borrowed his gun, went off with skinheads, came back smelling of hair spray. Got home, crashed.

After being picked up with Maurice at Northcross, Forrest wasn't questioned by Polanco or any other cop. Homicide had another plan in mind for him.

PATHFINDER

When Polanco asked Maurice what he and the others had done between late Friday night and Sunday, the eighth, the boy sighed. Here it came.

December 7, everybody slept late: Rob and Mike at the condo, Forrest and Maurice at Renee's until one o'clock that afternoon, when they had to baby-sit her three kids until she got off work at nine-thirty, when they had to go pick her up. Renee worked close to Northcross and, getting in the car, she said everybody was talking about the murders at the ICBY shop. Whatever Rob did the rest of the day was nothing he could exactly remember, maybe video games or Dungeons and Dragons at a friend's house, normal stuff, same as any other Saturday. Mike, on the other hand, had a schedule. Early that afternoon, a Scout leader drove him to Round Rock, north of Austin, for a craft session. There, he and other Scouts spent all afternoon sewing turkey feathers together to create sweeping garments to attach to the back of their leather breeches. To the leaders, Mike seemed like his regular self, good-humored, easy. While the boys worked, the adults talked in the kitchen about the murders, careful to speak quietly.

When Mike returned to Dry Creek, Rob was there. They waited around, did nothing. Maurice picked up his dad from work at ten, after which he was allowed to use the LTD. Forrest was with him. They headed down MoPac to grab the other guys and drive to Sixth Street, where they hung out until the bars and music joints closed at two. In Rob's words: *We, you know, whoopied.* After dropping Rob and Mike off, Maurice and Forrest left the car at Maurice's dad's and started walking toward Renee's, taking a shortcut through the Town North Nissan lot. In no time, Maurice spotted a gold Pathfinder with keys in the ignition.

They jumped in and Maurice rammed the SUV through a low chain blocking the exit and returned to the condo, where Rob and Mike piled in. Wild boys. Roaring west up Farm-to-Market Road 2222 to the rocky back roads, four-wheeling, acting wild. Maurice still had Johnny Holder's .22 on him, so they stopped at a lake and shot at light posts. Pitch-black out there, all curvy roads, no other cars or signs. Maurice got lost and drove in circles for a while, so by the time they made it back to the highway, they were low on gas. Maurice pulled into a Stop 'n Go and Rob went inside to buy the Sunday paper and a soda. When he came out, Mike was filling the tank. After Rob got in, Mike dropped the hose and jumped in after him. Go, he told Maurice. *Just go.*

That early on a Sunday morning, four kids in a big gold car? Of course the manager was watching. He took down the plate number and called the cops, and the APD tracked the car to the dealership. But the officer on the line recorded the time and date of the incident as early morning on December 7—Saturday—a minor mistake under ordinary circumstances.

With a full tank and time to burn, the boys wanted to keep going. Mike offhandedly suggested San Antonio, because he wanted to break up with a girl who lived a little northwest of the city, in the suburb of Helotes. Rob had never been to San Antonio, and Forrest and Maurice figured why not, so in no time they were heading south down I-35. Delayed by a blowout after Maurice more than likely nodded off and skimmed a median, they didn't make Helotes until nine or nine-thirty. In the meantime, Mike had changed the tire—he told the cops Maurice didn't know how—and in Helotes he called the girl, who agreed to meet him, but not at her house. She was alone; her parents were at church and wouldn't like it if she let somebody in. The other boys waited in the Pathfinder while Mike took her for a walk. To pass the time, somebody, probably Rob, opened the Sunday *Statesman* and read the story about the murders at the ICBY shop out loud. All three remembered that.

Mike came back, saying the girl had burst into tears, and they all cheered. Maurice dropped Rob and Mike off at a little past one that afternoon. Town North Nissan was open by then, so he parked the Pathfinder in a remote corner of the lot and returned to Renee's with Forrest. Once he copped to the theft, the APD charged him with unauthorized use again. He had to pay for the damaged tire rim.

Ordinarily, a joyride in a stolen car is no big deal, not unless you get hauled in for something else and law enforcement wants to know precisely where you were that day and who was with you and what you did and why you bought a Sunday paper if you didn't read much. Close to eight years from now, when a new APD team develops a plan to investigate Maurice Pierce, this caper will become a narrative chink in the prosecutorial time line of a crime spree that began with boys on the loose, as reported at 8:44 a.m. on December 6, when Rob's father called Teleserve to report his son missing, continuing with an afternoon of drink and weed, rolling into a night of murdering four girls and lighting a fire to cover their tracks, ending in car theft the next morning, the joyride to Helotes, gas theft and a suspicious newspaper purchase before they drove back to town. That the cop who wrote up the gas theft got the date wrong won't be noticed by the APD until after the arrests.

Back home in Austin, the four boys crashed and did the usual: sleep, drink, smoke, work the video knobs, drink, sleep, smoke, go whoopying, sleep, wait.

WIRED

After Maurice signed a statement saying that Forrest probably used his .22 to kill the yogurt girls, John Jones and several other cops took him to the apartment where he lived with his father. There, he and his dad, William "Bill" Pierce, showed them other guns, shells and bullets, then Maurice led them to the Fungus, where he said a communal .22 pistol was either buried or stored in a drainpipe, but nothing turned up. Later that day, under the guidance of Jones and Chuck Meyer, and with the permission of Bill Pierce, Maurice agreed to interrogate his young friend. After the specialist wired him up, he drove to Forrest's house and knocked, but nobody was there, so he went next door. The girl who answered said she'd seen Forrest earlier but that he'd gone somewhere, so Maurice drove around the neighborhood, looking for him, tailed by the cops, who sent frequent instructions: "Don't drive so fast. Don't look around. Act normal."

Two hours later, Forrest finally strolled down Koenig Lane toward Woodrow, and when Maurice called to him and asked him to get in the car, the unsuspecting Forrest complied. Maurice then drove into the parking lot of a nearby Laundromat and general hangout spot called Woodrow Washateria, and the two went inside.

"Where's your hair?" was Maurice's first question.

"Huh?"

"What happened to your hair?"

The newly shorn Forrest said his dad had it cut off, apparently in an attempt to disguise his identity.

Maurice then began pounding away. "What did you actually do that night, that Friday?"

Forrest: Pardon?
Maurice: That Friday when the girls were dead.
Forrest: Huh?
Maurice: And you said you wanted to use a gun.
Forrest: When I wanted to use a gun?

This went on until, a few minutes later, Maurice made a direct accusation: "You said that you wanted to use the gun. And that you had killed the girls."

But Forrest said he was only playing; he was joking; he never *killed* anybody. And when Maurice lost his temper—"Don't play that game, Forrest. . . . Don't jack with me"—he became even more confused, and wondered why Maurice was getting so mad.

Polanco had finished with Maurice at six that morning; Jones took down his signed statement at two-thirty. It was now around 6:00 p.m., and Maurice was frazzled, fearful and exhausted. He started to cry a little. "You know *I* ain't got the guts to kill them girls," he said. But the gun was *his* and the cops had him in their clutches and barely let him go, and if anybody was going down for those murders, it was *him*. And so he was scared.

Well, Forrest said, he was scared, too.

They argued about who was more scared and then got back in the LTD and Maurice drove Forrest home.

J ones, Meyer and the other cops considered the interview a complete bust. Forrest clearly had no idea what Maurice was talking about, and after several hours face-to-face with Polanco, the panicky Maurice had simply lied to save his own skin. Convinced that their case against the four boys had come to a dead end, Jones inactivated them as suspects and filed their names separately from those they'd either cleared or were aggressively pursuing.

When asked if he thought Maurice Pierce was a hothead, Jones shrugged. "He was a kid. A kid."

And that was that for a while. The boys went on with their lives.

In late February, Rob would move back to West Virginia. Mike hit the road, taking whatever odd jobs he could find. Forrest moved to Lockhart. Maurice kept on being Maurice. The APD filed the reports away. But here's the dumb-luck thing: *If Maurice Pierce hadn't shoved the loaded pistol in his jeans just to strut around Northcross like a movie badass, if he hadn't implicated Forrest or brought Rob Springsteen, Mike Scott and the Pathfinder into the picture* . . . if none of that had happened, there's no reason to think anybody working on the case would've ever paid them any attention at all.

THE BOYS, 1997

They're now twenty-one (Forrest Welborn), twenty-two (Maurice Pierce) and twenty-three (Robert Springsteen and Michael Scott).

They no longer hang out together. They aren't friends. They lead separate lives in different towns and cities. The strongest friendship, between Forrest and Maurice, has been permanently poisoned by the older boy's accusations. Although one of them earned his GED, when arrested they will all be labeled high school dropouts.

By that summer, Maurice has married his high school sweetheart, Kimberli, and is living in Lewisville, Texas, not far from Dallas. They have one daughter, Marisa, who is five. He has worked at construction, car-detailing and in the shipping and receiving department of a local wholesaler, loading trucks. He still drives fast cars, currently a Mustang.

Forrest is working in a car-repair and body shop in Lockhart. He has one daughter with a girlfriend he hasn't married. He was caught driving with a suspended license but will soon open his own shop.

Mike has been on the move again, having worked near Austin at an adult video store and as a roofer in Dallas. He drove to Evansville, Indiana, when a friend needed company, then back to Texas, doing automobile repair in San Antonio. Married to a computer technician, Jeannine Marie Stark, he has assumed fatherly responsibility for her four-year-old daughter, Jasmine. In 1999, when Jeannine is given a promotion at UniSys Corporation's Austin office, they will house-sit a friend's trailer near Buda until they find their own place.

Rob is in West Virginia, working for minimum wage, flipping

burgers, selling newspaper subscriptions door-to-door, living with his mother. By the end of 1998, he will be married, working double shifts at two jobs, renovating a cabin his wife has inherited and living in a small two-story house set on a hillside, taking prescription drugs for ADD and seeing a doctor for chemical imbalances.

If they're waiting for something to happen, they won't have to much longer.

NOT A TASK FORCE

In October 1997, Stan Knee—formerly chief of police in Garden Grove, California—was sworn in as head of the Austin force. After the Betsy Watson debacle, he seemed a safe choice, being a longtime rank-and-file cop and a Vietnam vet. But because of Mala Sangre and continuing budget cuts, the APD hostilities lingered on.

Later that month, after reactivating the tips files and changing Maurice's ranking from "major" to "likely," Paul Johnson began looking for accomplices, friends and witnesses. In early November, he called Pierce, arranged for a meeting and drove north to Lewisville, where he and a fellow detective sat with the suspect in his living room.

Friendly and helpful, Maurice signed a sworn statement that began, "Me and my friends always used to hang out at Northcross Mall. I am having trouble remembering the exact day of the yogurt shop murders but I can remember the night that me and some of my friends went out and shot a gun that I had. . . ." On the night of the murders, he thought he either went to the mall with Forrest or met up with him there.

He then repeated the story about Forrest borrowing the .22, but this time he changed the location from the Fungus to a video arcade. He mentioned Rob Springsteen and a longhaired guy whose name he couldn't remember. He said when Forrest returned the gun and told him he'd done something bad, he seemed to be joking, but when he then asked to use the gun again to kill more girls, Maurice had to wonder.

He summed up: "I know I made a statement when I was arrested that said that Forrest told me other details about the murders. I don't remember any of that now. I know I was very nervous and I was trying to say things to help me get out of the police interview and they were twisting my story up."

Johnson next drove to Lockhart, only to discover that Forrest Welborn was on the lam for unpaid driving tickets. When police found him in Lubbock, Johnson interviewed him there. Forrest didn't specifically remember the night of the murders—once, when detectives asked him, he had the date wrong—but he thought he was probably at Northcross, because that's where he hung out, and probably with Maurice, because that's who he hung out with. After denying any involvement in the crime, he was given a polygraph test that registered him as truthful. In his report, Johnson noted that Forrest was helpful, credible and cooperative, and that he now had doubts about his participation. He also made phone calls to Springsteen and Scott, but neither offered anything new or of interest. Rob talked about sneaking into the Rocky Show, hanging out with somebody named Travis, looking for a friend who never showed up. Mike rambled on in his usual scattered fashion.

In February 1998, Johnson again called Mike, Rob and Maurice, who gave him nothing useful. In March, twenty months after its formation, the AG Task Force was disbanded. Hoping to shine a positive light on yet another failure, a spokesman praised the team for its work clearing leads and making the caseload more manageable. Paul Johnson was transferred out to work the streets, but he couldn't let go. In September, he sent Maurice Pierce's .22 and ammunition to ballistics to be checked again. The result was the same: This was not a gun used at the ICBY.

Looking for a new tack, he moved his attention from the weapon to the fire. The original arson investigator, Melvin Stahl, had retired. And even though Chuck Meyer had agreed with Stahl about the origin of the fire, Johnson decided to get in touch with former APD officer Marshall Littleton, who for the past ten years had been living in San Antonio and working for the BATF as fire investigator for Central Texas. In Austin, Littleton and Johnson had worked as partners for a year and a half, sometimes taking late-night shifts together, a duty that inevitably created trust and loyalty.

Meyer met with Littleton first and asked if the fire at the yogurt shop could be "modeled," scientifically re-created on computer software that could be run backward, from extinguishment to origin. Littleton advised against it, as fire modeling might "eliminate a possible suspect." When defense lawyers later questioned the ethics of that, Littleton quickly shifted the topic of discussion. But when asked again if he'd made the statement, he answered without hesitation: "That's correct."

In late fall, Johnson once again drove to Lewisville, where Maurice agreed to undergo hypnosis, against his lawyer's advice, but even that yielded nothing new. A few days later, Forrest provided a written statement echoing Pierce's account. Undeterred, Johnson asked DPS for more gun and blood tests.

In December, former ICBY manager Reese Price called. Now a Travis County deputy, she wondered if Johnson had been told that in the months prior to the murders, both she and Jennifer Harbison had received harassing phone calls at home and at work, and that her apartment had been burglarized. The intruder had left behind valuables, including a television set and jewelry, but had taken the time to arrange some of her underwear in a neat pile on her bed with a kitchen knife on top. When she heard there'd been clean cuts in the collars of Jennifer's and Eliza's shirts, she remembered the weird feeling she'd had when she saw the knife. She and Jennifer Harbison resembled each other, both tiny, with long light brown hair. Might there be a connection?

Intrigued, Johnson asked Price to come to the station. During her visit, she told him about the crawl space above the ceiling connecting one Hillside shop to the next; she and the other girls had heard noises up there. And then there was the night when, checking out the bathrooms, she found shoe prints on the toilet seat in the men's room and noticed that a ceiling tile above it had been moved. She used a broom handle to shift the tile back in place.

She and Johnson also talked about Brice protocol, the shop layout and the metal shelves. Afterward, writing up the interview, he described the shelves as where the "fire had been concentrated" and listed the items Price said they'd kept there: paper cups, cans of toppings, cleaning supplies, bug spray, oven cleaner, paint for the concrete floors, a gallon can of a gelatin-based product they used to clean the waffle maker. As for the back doors, she thought maybe they'd once used a padlock, but as she recalled, they couldn't keep track of the key, so they switched to a double-cylinder dead bolt or else a single-cylinder with a knob on the inside—she couldn't say which. A couple of other girls also had keys. Maybe one of them knew for sure.

Concerning the photograph of the unopened Coke can sitting next to the cash register and the Styrofoam cup beside it, Price said one of the girls might have been buying a soft drink for herself, but since the purchase didn't appear on the register tape, it seemed clear there hadn't been time to ring it up. And when Eliza rang up "No Sale," Price thought she might have been simply closing down the register for the night.

A few days later, Johnson asked Amy Dreiss to come in. Having worked with Eliza a few nights before the murders, she confirmed Price's report that Eliza Thomas had been upset about breaking up with her boyfriend, and said she thought the back-door lock had a "knob" on the inside but wasn't certain. Dreiss also described Eliza as a fair and thorough coworker, especially concerning Brice protocol, which she insisted on following to the letter. Jennifer, on the other hand, was always anxious to skim through the necessities and get home. Ordinarily, Dreiss told Johnson, Friday nights were hers, but the week before the murders she'd asked to take December 6 off. Eliza had volunteered to work her shift.

One thing to note here is that during the investigation, no one described the lock on the back door as a "thumb latch," always referring to it as a "knob" or a "twist lock." But once one of the arrested suspects used the term, "thumb latch" stuck. Prosecutors called it that and so did witnesses, including former ICBY employees. This is the kind of stealth trial lawyers often use, knowing that casual repetition can draw disparate testimonies together and give an impression of unanimity.

Marshall Littleton finally met with Paul Johnson early in 1999 and again advised against fire modeling. There were too many oddities, and too many grievous consequences for screwups. If the aluminum ladder and metal shelving were available, they might yield important clues, but they weren't. For the time being, they should just wait.

POWERPOINT

After nine months on the job, Chief Stan Knee offered Paul Johnson yet another opportunity to organize a Yogurt Shop team, this one focused primarily within Homicide and known generally, if not formally, as the Cold Case Task Force. Senior Sgt. John Neff would serve as unit supervisor, Johnson as case agent, with six homicide detectives working under him—Ron Lara, J. W. Thompson, Robert Merrill, John Hardesty, Doug Skolaut and Manuel Fuentes—along with Texas Ranger Sal Abreo and the tireless Chuck Meyer. The team would work out of the Twin Towers, two reflective gold buildings, north of the main offices, where the APD undercover division was based.

Having been transferred to Homicide in May, Ron Lara had been working with Johnson for two months, tasked "to go out and interview any individuals that may not have been spoken to" and, more important, "to re-evaluate the Maurice Pierce tips." Lean and tightly wound, perfectly coiffed, with black eyes and high cheekbones, Lara was one of the growing number of Latino officers in the APD and, like Johnson, known for his knife-edge tenacity; together, they made for a power couple in the land of cold-case work. Within a month, Lara had organized and distributed a detailed briefing "about the Maurice Pierce tip, the times that he was arrested, some of the people he hung out with. . . . The profile that was established back during that time frame [and] primarily updated everybody to where we were at now."

Other active suspects included Kenneth McDuff, the Mexican

nationals, a few Satanists and others. But one name attracted the most heat.

"Maurice Pierce," Lara would explain, "was an individual that we were trying to either pursue or eliminate."

On August 6, at the Twin Towers, the task force held its first formal meeting. Johnson gave a four-hour PowerPoint presentation with some 205 slides he and Lara had pulled together. Once the room had been darkened, the computer screen flashed electric blue and then the title came up, in jagged yellow and white letters: *The Investigative Plan to Pursue Maurice Pierce*. Clearly, pursuit had won out over elimination.

Computerized presentations can be teacherly and static, but Johnson's had narrative suspense and front-loaded drive. There were color photos of the yogurt shop on the night of the crime; the billboard portraits of the murdered girls, followed by photos of their burned bodies; mug shots of various suspects, jazzy graphics, time lines, charts, even sound effects—a drumroll to introduce particularly important items, the sound of hands clapping when an officer's name appeared. To no one's surprise, John Jones's name rarely came up.

Johnson had made his choice.

Jones himself remained skeptical. "The fact is," he said later, "whoever was charged in this case was going down."

Using FBI profiling and DPS crime-scene conclusions as background and backup, Johnson's presentation created a story line of unraveling possibilities, often featuring a photo of the spiky-haired Maurice at the center of the screen. Like rays of the sun drawn by a child, straight lines led from Maurice to other suspects or possible witnesses—friends, running buddies, family members, girlfriends—and then to scenes where, at one time or another, he'd claimed to have been on the night of the murders, including the area behind Hillside where he said he'd met up with the skinheads. Forrest Welborn's photo was one from school days, when his hair was cropped; underneath it, a caption described the Northcross incident. Rob Springsteen's yearbook photo showed an unkempt boy, wired and alert. For some reason, Mike Scott's picture was noticeably absent, perhaps because the last time cops had talked to Pierce, he couldn't even remember Scott's name.

One slide featured Officer Joe Pennington's diagrams. The stick figures had blossomed into more realistic, computerized representations of the girls' bodies arranged as they had been found, with their names written across the bodies. The layout of the shop was pretty complete, down to chairs on the tables in the front room and an outline of the office in the back. On a long rectangle representing the steel shelving along the south wall of the storage room was an italicized notation: *Origin of the Fire.*

However promising Pierce looked, so far he'd given them nothing to work with. They needed somebody else, a second-tier associate, friend or girlfriend, somebody attached to any of them who could be persuaded to tag the foursome's weak link, the one who'd be most likely to burn Maurice. Somebody wondered if Rob Springsteen's girlfriend was still around. Maybe Kelly Hanna knew something she'd be willing to tell them.

Paul Johnson had called Hanna in 1998. She'd acknowledged then that, yes, she and Springsteen had dated for about three weeks in November and early December of 1991, and that on December 6 Rob had told her he might swing by that evening with Mike and Maurice. But when he didn't show, she wasn't all that surprised. And no, she hadn't been at Northcross that afternoon or night, nor had she gone to San Antonio. They'd come by her house and asked her to, but she wasn't interested and, once she found out the Pathfinder was stolen, she'd said absolutely not. So whatever they'd told the police, she hadn't gone joyriding with them.

That wasn't much, but she did know all four guys. Maybe she'd overheard Maurice say something. Or maybe Rob and Mike had witnessed what happened at the yogurt shop and Rob had bragged to Kelly about what he'd seen. The girl still lived right there in Austin. Ron Lara and John Hardesty were assigned to talk to her, while other members of the task force were given other duties. But Johnson had a feeling they were on the right track.

On August 26, when Lara and Hardesty knocked at her door, Kelly Hanna was twenty-four and in the third trimester of her third pregnancy. The detectives politely introduced themselves and said they had a few questions they wanted to ask about Rob Springsteen and his friends, some inconsistencies they needed to clear up about the night the girls were killed at the yogurt shop. Hanna had an honest, open face and a straightforward manner and didn't seem mindless or drug-sodden like so many of the others. They talked with her at home for fifteen or twenty minutes, then wondered if she'd be willing to go down to the police station the next day to help them out. They could talk there in a private, quiet place, say at three-thirty the next afternoon?

Kelly said she would, of course. She had nothing to hide, but they should understand, Rob had been a part of her life for only about a month and she hadn't seen him since he left Austin in late December of that year. She was raising two kids now, with a third coming, so high school wasn't something she thought much about anymore. Still, she considered herself a good citizen, a person who trusted the police, so of course she'd do what she could to help.

THE PURSUIT OF MAURICE PIERCE, ROUND ONE

Government agencies aside, Carlos Garcia has become keeper of the Yogurt Shop archives. Transcripts, crime-scene diagrams and photographs, DVDs, Paul Johnson's PowerPoint presentation . . . he has pretty much everything. Sometimes he thinks about burning the folders and files just to get them out of his life. But he doesn't. Because even if he did, he'd still have the digitized copies. And the memories.

It's unlikely he'll ever use his collection in court. Not long after preparing for Mike Scott's canceled retrial, Garcia abandoned private practice to become a senior staff attorney for the Texas Defender Services, a nonprofit watchdog organization that aims "to improve the quality of representation afforded to those facing a death sentence and to expose and eradicate the systemic flaws plaguing the Texas death penalty." For ten years he traveled all over the state teaching defensive strategies, from plea bargaining to jury selection to final argument.

Yogurt Shop, he says, changed him and everybody else who had anything to do with it.

His bookshelves are crammed with tomes purchased during *Scott,* including books on the art of persuasion, the mind-set of serial killers and the Reid Technique of police interrogation. When I asked him if the questioning of Kelly Hanna had been videotaped, he said yes and that he had the DVD, but why was I interested in it? He'd already given me the Scott and Springsteen discs. Honestly, I said, I didn't know why. Maybe it was because without her, the APD might not have gone after Mike Scott when they did, and also because it wasn't shown in court. He burned me a copy.

My son and daughter-in-law were living with me during the weeks it took me to watch her interrogation, along with Mike Scott's and Rob Springsteen's. Anytime one of them walked past my door and heard the thin, wavery voice of a young person under fire, their footsteps quickened and they hastened past, not wanting to hear. I, on the other hand, was transfixed: zooming back to catch a muffled phrase and then forward again to stay on track. My own life fell away and I was so much in the present with the person being questioned that it might as well have been me getting hounded in the hot seat, contradicted and lied to, videotaped without either knowledge or consent. *Our job is to get the bad guys,* I know the questioners would say to this, *and this is how we do it. You do want us to get the bad guys, don't you?*

Of course the answer to that is obvious. But in this and many other cases, it's not always clear it's bad guys who are getting the third degree.

APD headquarters are located in a pale stone building downtown at the corner of East Eighth Street and the I-35 access road. Driving south down the freeway past the UT football stadium and the capitol, you can see the Main, as it's called, rising up ahead, a hunkering five-story structure with an attached garage. Built in the early eighties, it's far too small for Austin now and has been for many years. Inside are holding cells, a county jail and the offices of various police units.

Held up by traffic and a confusing maze of one-way streets, Kelly Hanna arrived a few minutes late for her appointment and was sent up to the second floor, where Lara and Hardesty escorted her past the Homicide offices to a narrow hall containing three interview rooms.

When I insert the "Hanna-1" DVD, the screen fills with jumpy geometric shapes that quickly yield a bird's-eye view of a small windowless room furnished with a round white table that takes up most of the space. Around it are four government-issue chairs; on top, an open computer with its screen facing away from the camera. When the door opens, we hear Kelly's voice, light and girlish, a musical burble.

Hardesty enters first and, after ushering her in, moves briskly to his left. "Have a seat," he says, pointing, "in this chair right here."

Wearing a dark, long-sleeved V-neck top and light-colored pants, her hair pulled back loosely from her face, Kelly sidles around the table and sits in the indicated chair, having no idea that—thanks to the Elizabeth Watson directive—she has been seated squarely in front of a video camera attached to a light fixture hanging high on the opposite wall. Looking relaxed and unbothered, she straightens the APD access badge pinned to her shirt and then, after she and Lara exchange small talk about downtown traffic, moves right to the topic at hand. There's something, she says, she needs to tell them.

Lara responds brightly. "That's what we like to hear," he says. Hardesty's beside him, setting up the computer, both men facing her.

Kelly tells the detectives that when she saw them the day before, she'd said Springsteen had left Austin in late December, but afterward she recalled seeing him at a party in January, so she'd gotten that date wrong. . . .

Hardesty interrupts to ask if the rest of what she'd said was accurate.

"Yes, sir."

Fingers on the keyboard, he moves on. "Date of birth?"

In the black-and-white tape made that day, Kelly's face will be the only one we can see, and only, of course, from above. The image isn't sharp, but her features are pretty clear. Of Lara and Hardesty, we see only their scalps, shoulders, arms, hands, torsos. Of considerable importance is the dance they perform, moving from one chair to another, leaning back or forward, coming close or pulling away, clasping their hands—elbows out—behind their heads or cupping them between their knees as if in prayer. Occasionally one of them walks abruptly out the door without explanation, then returns. The table—so white, it seems to glow—takes center stage; they have to move sideways to get around it. And although the chairs look wildly uncomfortable, Kelly sits politely for the whole two and a half hours they keep her there, despite the pull of her swollen belly.

Hardesty asks for the basics: phone number, full name, place of employment. . . .

He and Lara are trim, fit. Hardesty's blond, with close-cropped hair, pale blue eyes, a square jaw and direct gaze and rock-hard, no-nonsense handsomeness. A former Marine paratrooper, he wears light-colored clothes, with the shirt tucked in and a pager attached to his belt. Lara's in a dark shirt, dark tie, dark pants. Both sit straight and tall, rarely relaxing into their chairs. On the walls are floor-to-ceiling panels of a ruglike material that absorbs sound and reduces echoes and reverberations for better acoustics.

Hardesty glances up. "Is that the Subway shop on Burnet Road?"

Kelly nods and gives him the address.

In a monitor room just down the hall, police officers and Texas Rangers and ATF agents and representatives from the DA's office can watch the proceedings on a video screen and even page one of the interrogating detectives. But because Kelly Hanna is a nobody—at best a conduit to information that might or might not lead anywhere—that room is empty today.

Hardesty's a slow, assertive typist. The laptop keys clack like an old-fashioned typewriter's when he punches them, keeping his head down. When answering, Kelly sometimes leans forward, occasionally resting her chin in cupped palms or laying a forearm across her belly or rubbing it with curious fingers. Otherwise, she remains still, waiting, unafraid.

Homicide doesn't think Kelly Hanna killed anybody or even went joyriding in the Pathfinder. Compared to everybody else in Maurice Pierce's world, she's a straight arrow who works a steady job, has children and makes eye contact when she answers questions—which, according to the BAI Scale of Innocence, scores her as "probably truthful." It's possible she might come up with something unexpected, but what they're really after is the answer to one crucial question.

Kelly Hanna, of course, doesn't have a clue about any of this.

I know a man who ran a little wild in Austin in the late eighties and early nineties, and he told me that the APD knew everything about him and his friends. Cops would regularly show up at their doors. "We know what you have," they'd say. "Hand it over." And whoever answered the knock would come up with the bag of tabs or weed they'd hidden in the closet or under the bed, thinking that was that. A little later, the cops would be back: "We know that's not all; now give us the rest." And they'd hand over the pillowcase with guns in it, then close the door and wonder, *How the fuck did they know?*

During those years, the police came in for a lot of criticism, but this man held them in high respect. He's in his forties now, married, with kids, a manager at a big computer company. He wasn't in Austin when the ICBY murders occurred. Having watched his friends getting into deeper and deeper trouble, fearing he was about to find himself in the same trap, he called a Marine recruiter. "How fast," he asked, "can you get me out of here?" He was gone in a week.

But back before he enlisted, he and his friends had agreed that if anybody got hauled in for questioning, the key was to say nothing. Don't ask for a lawyer; don't acknowledge a single thing they say. Especially don't believe it when cops get friendly and say they only want to ask a few questions and then everybody can go home. Or, worse, that they know you're innocent but your friends are scapegoating you. The cops were always after something different from what they were saying.

O nce Hardesty has entered Hanna's basic information, he says, "Go ahead, Ron," and Lara takes over. They'd like to work chronologically, he tells Kelly; is that okay with her? Yes. Was Rob Springsteen her boyfriend in December 1991? Yes, she and Rob went out for three or four weeks, starting in November of that year, maybe a month. Yes, she knew Maurice and Mike a little and had met Forrest in junior high. And yes, on the afternoon of December 6, Rob had told her he "might swing by" that night. No, he didn't say who might be with him, but she thought possibly Mike and almost certainly Maurice, since he had a car, but she really "never knew exactly who was going to be in the group" or even if they'd turn up, because they all smoked weed and drank a lot of beer and everything was loose. Nobody had "dates" or "plans." But she'd thought that if Rob *did* show, it would be around eight. She and two of her girlfriends—

Amber and Janet—sat outside on the tailgate of her father's pickup and waited until about ten, when they gave up and went inside. The next day, Rob came by, and she asked him where they'd been. "Driving around," he told her.

Did Kelly suspect anything when he said that?

Well, by then she'd heard about what happened at the yogurt shop, and when she asked if they'd seen fire trucks or anything and he said no, she did think *that* was odd.

Odd? Both men jump on it, but she doesn't notice. The thing was, she says, they always drove around in the same part of town and it *seemed like* they would've *seen something*, that was all. It was just . . . *odd* they hadn't.

The detectives push harder. Hardesty—the more forthright of the two—asks if by "seeing" something, doesn't she really mean "involved in"?

Kelly frowns and doesn't answer. Noting her uncertainty, they keep hacking away about this point. During Michael Scott's trial, she will tell a defense lawyer that she felt pressured and somewhat intimidated by the two officers, that every time she quoted Rob as having said they "might swing by," either Hardesty or Lara would suggest that "they were supposed to be there" or that she and Rob had made "plans" for the night. And whenever she offered a correction, they'd slide right by it "over and over again."

The detectives dial the pressure up a notch. Kelly's friend Amber was interested in Maurice, right? Right. Did Kelly know if they were having sexual relations? Clearly embarrassed, Kelly says she's pretty sure they weren't, or Amber would have told her. Was Amber dating Mike? No. The officers don't mention that Mike had claimed to have met up with an "Amber" at the bowling alley.

When they move on to the stolen Pathfinder, Kelly—still talking openly, lightly, sweetly—says yes, the boys had asked her to go with them, but she thought maybe it was the *next* weekend, not the weekend of the murders. Or maybe even the weekend before? Whenever it was, she didn't go.

But, Hardesty says, she'd told them the day before that the Pathfinder adventure happened on the *same* weekend as the murders, hadn't she? Not that he's accusing her of *lying;* he's just wondering why she's changed her story.

One of his favorite instructions is to "think real hard," as if the hidden thought he's looking for will, if she really concentrates, fly up into her consciousness. But it's *lying* that gets to her. She's trying to remember things that happened seven years ago, to be precise and careful. Why would they bring up *lying*?

Interrogators like to use abrupt shifts in tone and subject matter. A sucker-punch question can sometimes throw a person off. At about forty-six minutes in, this is what happens when Lara asks if Kelly considered Rob Springsteen a liar. A bit tentatively, she says no. Would he, Lara wonders, his voice turning slightly edgier, have any *reason* to be a liar? She doesn't think so . . . but maybe about *some* things.

Some things? He pauses. Would he lie about *her*?

The implication stings, and Kelly squirms. All she can come up with is that she "would hope not," but she doesn't *know*. And was Rob suggesting things about her, that she knew something? Or more than that? Her voice breaks. Lara moves closer.

Other people, he says, have told them that she went along to San Antonio. When Kelly again insists she didn't, he ignores her. "Kelly," he says, "there are other people putting you in that Nissan. *I'm* not accusing you of anything. But why would people be saying that, Kelly?" Was there somebody who didn't like her?

She turns her hands palms-up and says she doesn't know why anybody would say that. All she knows is that she was the weenie of the group, didn't like guns, didn't drink or smoke pot, and everybody knew it. And once she asked and the guys finally admitted they'd swiped the car off a lot, she *knew* she didn't want to go with them. In fact, her mom was standing there in the doorway, watching, when this happened.

Lara doesn't let up. "Several people" were willing to make sworn statements in court "in reference to" putting her in the Pathfinder. This isn't true, of course, but Lara's tactics are perfectly legal within the U.S. Supreme Court's definition of reasonable deception.

Hardesty: "We couldn't care less if you were in that Nissan, Kelly. It's not a crime."

When Kelly starts to cry, she's the one who apologizes and says that pregnancy's hormones are making her emotional. At that, Lara leans forward, elbows on his knees, his face only inches from hers; in court, when asked why he did this, Lara will say it was to comfort her.

"Nobody," he assures her, "is here to try to upset you, but there are some inconsistencies with you and what people are telling me." He wants the truth and hopes she realizes that consequences are always worse when people lie. Without explaining the implications of that, he reminds her that it's clear the joyride to San Antonio happened on the weekend of the murders. And if she doesn't come clean about that, they'll find out. She's still crying, and he lowers his voice. "I feel you're holding back on some of your answers."

She says she's *trying* to remember. Maybe she gets some things wrong, but she's not lying, and it's upsetting to be accused of something she didn't do.

Hardesty: "Nobody's accusing you, Kelly."

"Yes," she says, "but even if somebody *else* is . . ."

Kelly Hanna does pretty well and evades most of their traps. Toward the end of the session, when Lara again suggests that she's been lying, she pulls herself together: "I'm not stupid," she tells him. "I have kids. I make good decisions. I'm trying to give you honest answers."

After two and a half hours, the detectives at last ask the crucial question, posed as a hypothetical they're only slightly curious about. If she had to choose between Mike Scott, Forrest Welborn and Rob Springsteen, who did she think would be most likely to talk to them about Maurice Pierce without too much of a problem?

Kelly chooses Mike Scott.

Once again, it's hard not to wonder what would've happened if she'd said she had no opinion about that. If she'd belonged to the group who knew to say nothing. If she'd said she didn't know Mike Scott very well or simply didn't want to answer. What if she'd chosen Rob Springsteen instead?

Wondering doesn't help. She said what she said. Like others, she thought she was doing the right thing. Plus, she was scared and her feelings were hurt at the thought of people lying about her, especially Rob.

It's close to six when she leaves, accompanied by Ron Lara. Hardesty remains at the computer, punching away. Alone, fearing he might've accidentally deleted the interview, he curses the screen, until Lara returns to help him retrieve the file.

Then, standing in the doorway, Lara asks his partner what he thinks about "this girl."

> Hardesty: I still think she's holding back on something, but I
>   don't know what.
> Lara, inaudibly, and then: . . . hate to be too rough on her.
> Hardesty: If she fucking starts bleeding in here, that's our ass.
> Lara: Let me turn this thing off.

He walks out into the hall, and the screen goes blank.

When asked if he thought they were too rough on Hanna, Lara will say no. As to why she cried, he'll claim it was because she was putting things together and realizing that her former boyfriend had been involved in a terrible crime. His written report will state that on the basis of their conversation, he and Hardesty had reassessed Scott's importance, that possibly he was the "weak link" who might help them land Maurice Pierce.

But before talking to Scott, they decided to bring Forrest Welborn to Austin and give him one more chance to finger his friends. According to Hardesty, this wasn't something they decided the day before, that "he was a focal point in the investigation." To this day, Hardesty believes Forrest knows more than most people think, but in 1999, he offered nothing new. When they asked him about buying the newspaper at the convenience store, he *knew* he hadn't done that because he couldn't even read very well then. "I was dumb," he told the detectives.

THE PURSUIT OF MAURICE PIERCE, ROUND TWO

Having located Mike Scott at a rural address just west of Buda, Lara and Hardesty drove down there. There were no street addresses, just roadside mailboxes, isolated double-wides, gravel roads, scrub oaks and flat fields—and the Scott name didn't appear on any mailbox, so they asked a neighbor if they were at the right place. When told they were but that nobody was home, they hung around for a while and finally drove to South Austin, where Mike's wife worked. At the UniSys reception desk, they asked to speak to her. When she appeared, Lara introduced himself and asked if she'd mind stepping outside so they could speak privately.

Jeannine Scott is a tall, forceful woman who walks with a wide stride and speaks with deliberation and intent. Her eyes are set far apart, her mouth is firm and her straight light brown hair reaches past her waist. Inflexible in her opinions—against the death penalty and in support of Mike—and resolute in her actions, she's the polar opposite of her husband. Having been raised in the Midwest, she's forthright and plainspoken, and it's hard to imagine her backing down under pressure or answering any question she didn't want asked of her.

In the parking lot, Lara went straight to the point. They were investigating some inconsistencies in a case and would like to talk to her husband. Could she arrange for Mike to be at her office the next morning, say at eight-thirty? Although Jeannine describes herself as a cynic, she agreed to his request and even tried to call Mike then and there. But the line was busy—probably, she said, because he was playing an Internet game. And that was that. After giving Lara their home phone number, she went back to work.

Lara tried Mike forty-five minutes later, and this time he picked up. Lara explained who he was and asked if he'd be willing to talk to him about a case he was struggling with.

At that, Lara says, Mike "got real quiet" and wanted to know what was wrong. What was going on? Nothing, the detective assured him, he was just working on a case and had already talked to Jeannine, who'd agreed to set up a meeting the next morning. Mike said okay.

This happened on Wednesday, September 8, 1999. Lara and Hardesty had no idea what the following week would bring, and neither, of course, did Michael Scott.

Lara drove alone to UniSys the next morning. The Scotts arrived soon after. Once Jeannine had gone inside, he introduced himself and asked if Mike was ready to go, and did he want to follow him in his car? Mike said no and got in the unmarked APD sedan.

He hadn't been frisked, arrested or handcuffed and could have refused to go anywhere. All according to plan: If a suspect isn't in custody, interrogating officers don't have to issue a Miranda warning; they can all just sit around and talk . . . for hours, if the suspect's willing.

A couple of minutes into the drive, Mike spoke first. "Let me guess," he said, "about eight years ago?"

This according to Ron Lara's written report and his testimony in court, an important *according to,* because no one else was in the car and the conversation wasn't recorded, neither of these facts particularly surprising, since nobody expected Scott to blurt anything out right off the bat.

Out of the blue is how Lara described the moment, as if to say—addressing police chief, judge, jury, history itself—Why would Mike Scott have known what we wanted to talk about if he wasn't involved or hadn't seen something?

In 1999, driving to the station took, in morning traffic, maybe twelve or fifteen minutes, and Lara says that before they got there, Mike asked, "So, you guys looking for Rob?"

Lara looked over at him. Was this it? Already? "Should we be?"

When Scott didn't answer, he changed the subject. But Mike's a naturally chatty guy, desperate to be liked, and right before they arrived, he again set himself up for a longer discussion with Homicide than he—or they—had expected. "So," he began, as if in mid-conversation, "you guys don't really have anything new on this investigation, do you?" When Lara refused to respond, Scott gave his own wrist a playful slap. "Oh well," he reportedly said, "that was a dumb question for me to ask, wasn't it?"

They parked on the second floor of the APD garage and passed through a controlled access door into Homicide, where Mike was offered a seat while Lara and Hardesty set up an interview room. When asked why, if he'd played no part in the crime, Scott had immediately guessed what they wanted to talk to him about, Carlos Garcia has a quick answer. "Sure he knew. Why wouldn't he? They'd picked him up a week after the murders. There were all those phone calls from Paul Johnson. Of course it was Yogurt Shop. There was nothing else it could be."

The "Mike Scott-1" DVD opens pretty much the same as Kelly's, but this time the computer screen faces the door and the video camera's more centrally positioned, its lens aimed at the back wall.

Lara enters alone—hair perfectly groomed, dressed again in a dark shirt and tie—and leaves the door open while he leans down and types on the laptop. After a few seconds he goes out and closes the door behind him.

Within minutes he escorts Mike inside and asks him to sit in a chair behind the table against the back wall, then leaves again. Mike's long hair is pulled back in a ponytail that falls halfway down his back. He's wearing dark jeans and a loose, collared shirt and is holding a pack of cigarettes. He hangs his sunglasses from the neck of his shirt in an attempt at hipsterism that doesn't work. Alone, he slouches and looks around. After a short wait, he stands up and moves around the table to peer at the computer screen, reads what's there and then sits back down in his chair, glancing upward once toward the camera lens. But there's no indication he suspects he's being recorded. He's loose, easy and altogether aimless . . . and this will cost him. A life lived day by day proceeds without punctuation, making it difficult to remember what happened when and who he was with and what they got up to, exactly. When grilled about December 6 on a later occasion, Mike will say, "I don't remember anything special about that night other than another night of going out, getting fucked up, going to the mall, going home and going to sleep."

Whether or not he participated in a murder, this statement seems altogether credible. Mike Scott—it's fair to say—didn't know what day it was most of the time.

The detectives have undoubtedly been in the monitor room, watching him, taking in his body language and gauging his temperament. After about ten minutes, Lara returns with Hardesty, who shakes Mike's hand and sits at the computer. When Mike asks him about the age and make of the laptop, Hardesty says it's new. While they chat about lithium ion batteries, Lara waits, tilts his chair back and, once more assuming the position, joins his hands in a basket on top of his head, elbows splayed out.

It is 9:15 a.m. on Thursday, September 9. Mike Scott will not speak to his wife for ten hours, when the detectives finally come up with a mobile phone they previously claimed couldn't be found anywhere in the unit. By then he will have become convinced that he more than likely had some involvement in the ICBY murders, if only as a witness, despite the fact that he still has no memory of anything happening that night.

"Dear," he'll say to Jeannine at 7:04 p.m., "I know more about this case than I thought I knew." When she presses him for details, he'll change the subject, and when she complains about a migraine, he'll tell her where the Vicodin is and then mention the big can of "raviolis" in the cupboard that she and the little girl could have for dinner. After that he'll hang up and turn back to the detectives.

You have to wonder how in a day's time this man came to believe he knew more about an incident than he thought he did. Was he led to believe this supposition, or did he suddenly remember something? Who persuaded whom and of *what*?

In the 1930s, after the Wickersham Commission, appointed by President Herbert Hoover, reported that police in more than half the states in the nation habitually used "physical brutality or other forms of cruelty" to extort confessions from people under suspicion or arrest, physical torture—"the third degree" of brass knuckles, rubber hoses, telephone books to the kidneys—was gradually outlawed throughout the country. Anxious police departments searched for other methods of inducement. In the mid-1940s, former Chicago cop and polygrapher John E. Reid came up with an alternative. Having had enough experience with the earlier methods to know that a physically tormented person could hold out only so long before confessing to whatever he'd been accused of, Reid developed a highly structured psychological approach to persuasion and confession. His five-hundred-page *Criminal Interrogation and Confessions* was published in 1962 and is still in print. He died in 1982, but the Reid Technique is registered and copyrighted, and his company offers weeklong seminars all over the nation, mostly for cops and prosecutors.

To identify a criminal and establish his potential participation in a crime, the technique broadly divides the investigative process into two stages: the interview and the interrogation. Nonaccusatory, friendly and conversational, an interview can take place anywhere—in a home, the backseat of a squad car, a restaurant—and its stated purpose is to search for the truth—what really happened?—and, most important, to determine whether or not there is reason to believe someone's guilty. To comfort the interviewee and make him feel important and smart, investigators are encouraged to take notes.

The process should move on to the next stage only if the investigator—through close observation of behavior, a pattern of inconsistencies in testimony and physical or circumstantial evidence—has become "reasonably certain of the suspect's guilt." At which point, interview becomes interrogation. Those of us who watch cop shows on TV are familiar with this switch and can readily pinpoint the exact moment when it occurs—for instance, when Kyra Sedgwick (as Brenda Leigh Johnson in *The Closer*) changes from sweet southern nice girl to a lying, devilish, two-faced cop.

Interrogations are accusatory and should be conducted in a controlled environment, free from distraction. No more note-taking. By then you want your suspect to feel trapped and edgy. Recording his comments might alert him to the incriminating consequences of his words and thus inhibit further admissions.

"Be sure you have the right person," the reader is warned in the preface to Reid's book. Because you *will* get a confession.

If Mike Scott can be called a *weak link,* it's not because he's willing to rat out his friends, but simply because his capacity for submission—his compliance and uncertainty and, most of all, his eagerness to be liked and believed—sabotage his own best interests and perhaps even his ability to separate truth from suggestion. He doesn't say that if he knew what happened he'd tell them, but that "if I knew what I *needed* to tell you . . ." These small slipups and the gradual accretion of doubt in the suspect's own mind enable an interrogating officer to bore in more deeply, to fill an untethered mind with dreamlike possibilities until doubt becomes certainty and a person can start to believe he committed the crime they're asking him about and that he'd better confess to it.

When police use the Reid Technique, they're usually seeking confirmation, not truth. Having decided in advance he's their man, they need to persuade him to agree with their version of what happened. The question of *Why?* doesn't even come into it. That's for the punishment stage of a trial, which will determine whether a convicted party acted with intent, is a continuing threat to society, feels remorse and so on. After creating a possible narrative, cops don't mess with motivation; they just need to find somebody who either committed the crime or fits the bill.

"Confession," John Jones insists, "is a beginning. We had fifty." When he was the ICBY case agent, he searched for solid physical evidence, hoping to build *toward* a confession. Paul Johnson's task force, on the other hand, relied on what Jones calls "the pyramid theory of investigation": get the confession, secure it at the top and then build a case to support it. And if the evidence doesn't agree, figure out how to make it match up.

This might well be true, but in terms of support and approval from the APD, the Travis County DA's office, the mayor, the families of the murdered girls and most Austin citizens, there's a big problem: Johnson got arrests and Jones didn't.

The way Jones sees it, Johnson then took advantage of his success and turned the families against him. That was the worst part. "I could've handled everything else," he says now.

O nce again, Hardesty asks basic questions about Scott's personal life and painstakingly records his answers. In response, Mike is expansive. He and Jeannine have been back in Austin for less than a month, since UniSys offered her a ten-thousand-dollar raise to move from their San Antonio office to the one here. Not a bad deal, and this is a cool city. It's where they met, at a party around 1990. Although she wasn't born or raised here, Jeannine considers Austin home. Mike's father still lives here, and the extra money will help fund Mike's pursuit of a GED, and when that enables him to find a better-paying job, he can repay Jeannine. They don't particularly like living in somebody's trailer but figure they can manage until they find their own place.

After Hardesty completes his debriefing, Lara leans forward and identifies the case they're investigating, as per Reid protocol: *Let the suspect know what he's there for.* And even though the detectives don't necessarily consider Scott a suspect, they want him to know how much they appreciate his cooperation.

"No problem," Mike says.

What they're going to be doing, Lara says, is taking Mike back nearly eight years, to 1991. A long time ago, he acknowledges, but "it's an incident that sticks in people's minds," which makes it easier to remember.

Mike pulls back a little. "I'll be honest with you guys," he says. "I have a piss-poor memory."

That's what they're there for, Lara counters, to help him remember.

N euroscience claims that memory might be a matter of chemistry and that someday we'll be able to pluck a particular recollection from the mind like a grapefruit seed. What's clear in the case of Mike Scott is that if he has a piss-poor memory (or even thinks he does), his interrogators can make use of this. They can suggest and assert and imply things he doesn't remember but cannot firmly contradict or deny. After a while, he may come to think he remembers things they have persuaded him to accept as true. *Okay,* he'll say. *I guess you're right. I don't remember, but maybe you know.* And then, once he's settled into being a compliant confessor, he might even begin to internalize his accusers' version of what happened.

What we know can be evasive and become, over time, what we *think we* know or *thought* we did, which, in turn, might be contradicted by data that documents what really did happen. What we know. How memory connects to facts and the truth, or fails to. How memory actually works. Lara explains to Mike that they're planning to "plug away" at him to get a better feel for where he was that afternoon and evening, who he was with and what happened on the following days. They want to narrow down some time periods, hoping that something they ask or he says might act as a trigger to something else he thought he didn't remember.

Mike says he's okay with that.

This is classic interrogation technique: start slow, ask broad questions, make vague, nonthreatening inquiries, adopt a convincingly honest demeanor. Insist you're there to help. Mike nods, answering with "Yeah" or "Okay." In a quick reversal, once Lara has provided the setup, Hardesty switches back to basic questions, some of which Mike can't answer—for instance, his address, zip code and phone number. But he's lived in Buda for only a month and they're house-sitting, so why should he know the zip code? In addition to which, Jeannine says his memory's like Swiss cheese. What the detectives realize immediately is that they've made the right choice; he is definitely the weak link if he doesn't even know his own phone number.

From a file box, Lara removes photocopied portraits of the dead girls and places them faceup on the table. These, he says, are the people they'll be talking about. Does Mike remember those girls? He straightens the photographs one by one, watching for a reaction with, as instructed, his powers of "behavioral observation." Of course Mike remembers. He didn't know the girls personally but knew them "by face" from newspapers and TV—and, boy, they "flogged the crap out of that one, didn't they?"

Bad start. Sometimes a person who's overly trusting or not clever enough to dope out what's really going on will assume a casual, knowing attitude. In the interest of appearing knowledgeable, he might make comments—a wisecrack—he'll come to regret. Sometimes, perhaps even often, it's hard to tell whether or not Mike recognizes a mistake when he's made one. *I'm with you* is what he means to imply. *We're the kind of guys who can make sharp comments about dark and terrible events. We can laugh at what others call tragedy. We have the wit to do that. Flog the crap . . . Joke's on the media clowns, right?*

The detectives ignore this and once again take Mike back to December 6. Where did he live then and with whom? How long had he known Rob Springsteen? "About three years," Mike says. Three years? Yes, he says, even though when Mike moved in with Springsteen and his father, Rob had been in Austin a total of three *months*.

They take it minute by minute. Who was with him that day? Did they smoke dope, take acid or drink beer? How did they get to McCallum and whom did they see there? When did they meet up with Maurice Pierce, and did Mike say Maurice had purchased a gun only the day before the murders? If so, what kind? Mike is almost positive it was a blue-black .38, because they'd all gone out to the woods around the lake to shoot it. Yes, he was pretty positive it was a .38 with a black handle, and maybe Forrest was with them and maybe not—he didn't know Forrest that well—he wasn't even sure if Forrest was his first name or last. And there was another guy—he can't remember his name—kind of preppy, short blond hair, with a stud earring in one ear, drove a red truck, didn't drink or smoke, a kind of my-body-is-a-temple guy. Bowling alley, beer, maybe smoked a bowl, went to Northcross, maybe Maurice drove them, maybe they took the bus. . . .

Which bus, what route?

He reminds them of the piss-poor memory.

No, he is told, he has a good memory; he's remembering very specific things.

Okay. He's pretty sure Maurice drove them.

In what kind of car? A light blue Ford LTD, a former police cruiser belonging to his dad. Maurice cared about that car more than girls or friends or anything. Mike's pretty sure now that, yes, Maurice drove Rob and him to get more beer, then to the mall; by then they were buzzing pretty good. Then Maurice left to go run errands for his sister or baby-sit her kids; Forrest went back to school. And he and Rob sat in the food court or where the video games were and they did the usual. Hang out. Let the buzz settle. Walk around looking at T and A. T and A? Tits and Ass. Hooters? Right.

He'd broken off with Rob a couple weeks after the murders, when he stole four free Metallica tickets Mike had gotten from his father, who worked at the Erwin Center. What a prick to do that to his closest friend, right? And the cops agree with him, because their sympathy adds to the narrative context they are creating, of a nice guy like Mike being railroaded by punks like Rob, Maurice and perhaps Forrest.

To avoid charges of misconduct and coercion and yet still manage to redirect the suspect's ordinary decision-making processes, police must set up a situation in which the subject believes he's answering a question in the same spirit in which it was asked, which is to say truthfully, honestly, with no underlying implications or intentions. In 1969, the Supreme Court ruled that while investigators shouldn't threaten possible consequences—grand jury investigation, prison time, execution—or make promises of leniency, they can use tactics of "reasonable deception" and duplicity to solve crimes. Another reason neither to believe what cops say nor to answer their questions.

To keep the suspect off balance, the questioning zigzags. At one point, Lara focuses on the day Maurice bought the .38 from the Mexican boys, when Mike thought maybe he was looking for grass. (Scott begins using TV-cop lingo—"firearm," "vehicle," "accelerant"— while the cops adopt street talk, like "the get-fucked list," "bullshit," "fuckin' penitentiary.") Knowing it's the wrong-caliber gun, Lara jumps from the .38 to the Pathfinder and the newspaper somebody bought and the question of who read it aloud to the others, then back to Northcross and ahead to the questioning on December 15, after Maurice got picked up with the .22, then back to the sixth, then again to Helotes, the girlfriend. . . .

Mike rubs his face and yawns before staggering through another rambling account of the hours he and Rob spent at Northcross: food court, basket of fries, fat Mexican drinking the ketchup, more beer in the parking lot, saw a red Jeep, dropped off at home by Maurice at ten-thirty, cable movie, asleep by maybe 1:00 a.m. Early night. He remembers things, then doesn't, then apologizes. The detectives assure him it's all there, that it'll come back. If he just keeps thinking real hard—the same instruction Hardesty had doled out to Kelly Hanna.

After an hour and a half, they take a break. Does Mike want a Coke? He prefers Dr Pepper. When the two cops return with the soft drink, Lara begins amiably enough. But when he asks what Mike told Paul Johnson in 1998 about hanging out in the Northcross parking lot at the time of the murders, his voice takes on a slightly sharper edge. It seems that during the break, the detectives decided that the so-called weak link might know more than they'd imagined and so it was time to start grinding.

Moving away from the laptop, Hardesty pushes his chair closer to Mike.

"Do you understand, you *have* to help us out?" Then, in order to establish "voluntariness" and emphasize that Mike's will wasn't "overborne," he pulls back. Mike should understand he's not under arrest, not even in trouble; they just want to talk. But, Lara steps in to remind him, he needs to know that "this *is* going forward" and they want him to help. In the meantime, however, he should remember they're only talking, he can walk out that door anytime he wants to and . . . would he like to take a smoke break?

All three leave. Eight minutes later, the session gets back on track and the detectives sit even closer to him, both leaning forward.

"Mike," Hardesty says, "you seem real wound up, [like] there's something you're not telling us. You're acting real nervous." When Mike says it's because he's scared, Hardesty wonders what he has to be scared of. Something he hasn't told them? Well, Mike says, he's sorry for seeming wound up, but he's really told them everything he remembers. Hardesty tells him he doesn't have to apologize, they're just talking. And Mike relaxes a little, thinking everything's okay. They like him, after all; they're on the same team.

By noon the tone has changed again. "Michael," Hardesty says, "we've been working on this a *long* time; we've talked to everybody— Maurice, Robert, Forrest—and we *know* what happened." And now it's time for him to do the right thing, too, and clear up the inconsistencies. "We know more than you think we do, Michael. You're covering something up." When Mike says he isn't, the cop groans in disgust and turns away.

None of this is unusual. Police interrogators always say they know more than the suspect thinks, that other people have confessed and implicated him and they're 100 percent certain about what happened. And although the routine isn't necessarily good cop/bad cop, skillful partners will differ in tone and style. In this case, Hardesty's tense, profane and threatening, a dark cloud that might suddenly turn into a killer storm; Lara's steadily intense, kind of nonchalant and disinterested . . . until the moment comes to strike.

Pulling one knee toward his chest, cupping his hands around it, he cuts to the chase. "Do you know who shot those girls?" he asks, and then, realizing he'd mistakenly given Mike information, quickly corrects himself: "Do you know who *killed* them?" When Mike emphatically says no, Lara reminds him that when they sat down together that morning, the first statement he'd made was, "I remember the night of December 6, 1991, the night the four girls were murdered."

Mike didn't ever say that, of course, and Lara knows it; but Mike himself isn't sure, so the statement stands.

Soon afterward, the detectives create a scenario in which confession would work to his advantage. The police have talked to the other people involved and this thing is snowballing; there are going to be arrests. They don't think *he* killed any of the girls (right out of the Reid playbook), but they do believe he has knowledge of who did, and that the other guys are the assholes, while he's the scapegoat, the one the others are dropping the dime on, who was forced to do things he didn't want to. If he tells them everything he knows, he'll be in a better position vis-à-vis the grand jury.

Mike stiffens, frowns.

Does he know what a grand jury is?

Voice trembling, Mike says he has a pretty good idea.

I asked John Jones why suspects turn to jelly whenever the grand jury is invoked. "TV," he said. "*Law and Order* uses it as a scare tactic. Against the law to lie to the grand jury and all."

Garcia has a different take. "Mike had no idea what the grand jury was," he states. "For him it was like threatening the Spanish Inquisition."

Hardesty: "Let's go back to the trip to San Antonio. Think real hard. You're getting real close. . . . Those others, they're covering their ass, how do you think they're doing that?"

Mike comes up with what he seems to think is a smart conclusion: "Either lying or pinning it on somebody else."

"There you go. There you go."

Mike: "And let me guess. I'm it."

"There you go."

He's starting to get it.

They tell him he's in a hole. Inconsistencies are digging it even deeper, putting him on the top of the "get-fucked list." They've talked to Rob, who's done the right thing and told them everything, and Mike has to realize they now have all the answers and this thing's going to end really soon. Whatever he's holding back, they already know what it is. He's in this up to his ass, but if he'll just tell them what happened, they'll type it up and that will be that. Then they can all go home.

Without realizing it, Mike begins using their language. "I think," he says, "I've dug myself a hole and don't know how to get out."

By this time, news has spread throughout the APD that Lara and Hardesty might have cracked Yogurt Shop. Many task-force members, including Paul Johnson, are watching from the monitor room. En route to a call from North Austin, Chuck Meyer made a U-turn toward downtown and will take part in the interrogation later today. Manuel Fuentes will soon escort Mike on smoke breaks while the others confer. In the monitor room, the men crowd around the television screen and occasionally page Hardesty to offer suggestions.

As if on cue, Lara jumps in: "Did Robert kill those girls?"

Mike doesn't think so.

Well, then, was *he* the one who killed them?

No.

Ten minutes later, just after noon, Hardesty asks Mike what he's scared of.

Mike: "I'm not scared."

Hardesty: "You're scared. Michael, look at me. You're scared because you've had this information all these years."

At that, Mike's thinking turns creepy. "I'm scared I have information and don't know I have information."

One more step and he's entering the zone of no return, where fear feeds imagination and changes to speculations that seem like memories and even belief. *I did it. If I have this memory of it, then I must've done it.* Once he acknowledges that what they're telling him *might* have happened, he opens himself to the possibility that maybe he did tie up a girl, rape, smack, strangle and shoot her, then burn her up.

The full confession won't be made for many hours, but the detectives are scoring points fast now, and they know it's coming. They just have to keep pushing to get him to directly involve Maurice Pierce and the others. They need him to "visualize" himself inside the yogurt shop, not as witness, but as participant, and they especially need his version of events to match the evidence John Jones and the others found at the crime scene. Later this afternoon, they'll ask him to stand in his chair and imagine he's on the ceiling of the yogurt shop, looking down on himself and the other guys doing unspeakable things to the girls, just as the hidden video camera's watching him now.

When the ceiling trick doesn't give them what they want, Hardesty comes at him fast and furious. That "information he doesn't know he has" line is bullshit. He shouldn't fog things up by saying he doesn't remember, because, he says, "You remember that night. You remembered the date. You understand that when you first sat down here you volunteered the date. We didn't bring it up. You brought it up."

This time, Mike's thrown. "I did?"

The detective says yes.

"Okay," Mike says. "If you say so."

Cashing in on his growing uncertainty, Hardesty orders him to stop playing games and tell them what happened and what he knows, and to haul himself "out of this fuckin' hole." Why is he covering for these assholes?

He says he isn't.

But Hardesty persists: Knowing what he's known all these years without ever volunteering anything, *now* he's scared that knowledge is going to jam him up? And if he doesn't clear this up and tell them what he knows, isn't *that* going to jam his ass up? Lara chimes in: "No doubt." Hardesty echoes him: "No doubt." They sincerely do *not* want that to happen. They like him and respect the fact that he has a family now, a wife with a good job, plus the desire to earn a high school diploma. He's the one in the whole bunch they'd like to see get out of this.

Mike comes up with something. Okay, he did see the fire trucks and whatnot, and he lied to the officer about seeing the red Jeep in the Northcross parking lot when he didn't, though he doesn't know why. Hardesty supplies the reason: He was covering up something he's afraid to reveal because it might jam *him* up.

When he tries to deny that, they roll right over him. They know he was involved, they listen to people day and night and recognize deception when they see it, they know he was there, so now he needs to clear out the crap he's been living with for eight years, and once he does that, they'll work with him. They've told him what the consequences will be if he lies to them, but they're giving him this opportunity to tell them what he knows and go on with his life. And when Mike says he doesn't know what he's supposed to tell them, they go at him harder.

When asked if he might be willing to take a lie-detector test, Mike's all for it. Maybe he thinks the machine will help him remember. The detectives take a break, as if to go find the polygrapher, but when they come back, they don't mention him. Minutes later, Hardesty switches directions and out of left field asks Mike how old he was that December. Startled, he doesn't answer. After the officers have left him alone again, he gets a pen and writes on his palm, perhaps figuring out his age in 1991. Then, still loose as rubber, he leans back and stretches, folds his arms and hands together like a pillow, rests them on the table and puts his head down for a moment before, as if having had a sudden thought, he sits up and reaches across the table for some papers Lara had been consulting. He flips through them, returns them to their proper place, sits there with his arms across his chest and sips his Dr Pepper, as blank as a white page.

———

What I'm looking for here is a clear turning point, the moment after which nothing will be the same, but there are several. Certainly 12:40 isn't *the* turning point, though it *is* one of them. That's when the first DVD ends. Making notes in the margin of the transcript, I wrote, *He's theirs. Whether he did it or not, he belongs to the APD.*

Was Mike Scott's will overborne? Yes. Did Lara and Hardesty use illegal methods of coercion, promises and threats? Almost certainly. Can we trust Scott's confession to be honest and true? Not under the circumstances, even if he *did* participate in the crime. And if he didn't? We hit a snag on that one. The idea of a false confession simply won't compute; it confounds our sensibilities. *We'd* never confess to something we didn't do, so why would he? After all, they didn't beat him with a rubber hose or rip out his fingernails.

APD polygrapher Bruce Stevenson—a big guy with breathing problems and a heavy Texas accent—comes in, sits down, looks Mike in the eye and explains how a polygraph test works. He also declares that not only is he a polygraph expert; he is the APD's forensic hypnotist. Does Mike know what that means? "It means I know how the mind works."

Mike nods.

Stevenson then explains what he calls the VCR theory of memory. In our minds, there's something called "revivification," which means Mike has a VCR in his head that records everything that ever happened to him. He didn't know that? Well, it's there. All he has to do is insert the tape and push PLAY. The memory will be there like a movie inside his eyes. Revivification's real; everything else is bullshit. Mike nods again. Stevenson says his claims of not remembering are also bullshit because the information's already there. Mike repeatedly protests that he's being honest and doesn't recall being there and doesn't think he was, but Stevenson and Lara ignore him and ask if what's causing his memory lapse is his own involvement. When Mike says, "No, sir," Lara cocks his head. Is he positive? "Yes, sir." Well, the detective points out, he doesn't *look* positive.

Mike yields. "I'm not sure about everything now."

Stevenson's ready to go forward with the lie-detector test, but Lara and his colleagues in the monitor room have decided not to run it after all. Their guy's on a roll that they don't want to interrupt.

For Mike, this is a sharp disappointment; he'd been hoping that once he'd either passed or failed the test, he'd know what had really happened. And then he could go home.

It's about now that he starts rocking in his chair and holding his head in his hands, as if trying to swirl up memories they insist are inside. He tells them he doesn't want to hinder this investigation or be the patsy while the other guys cover their asses; he wants to cut through and push PLAY on his VCR memory so he can visualize the event and watch the pictures roll by. He wants to do what they're asking him to, and they say they understand, that they simply want him to realize how important this is for *him,* his future, his family, his life.

A little more than four hours into the questioning, Lara points to the pictures of the dead girls again and asks Mike to look at them. "That's it for them," he says, "and for what?"

"For twelve or fourteen bucks," Mike says. "Something like that."

Lara: Was it worth it?
Mike: Not for four lives.
Lara: No. It wasn't worth it. Whose idea was it to go there?
Mike: Huh?
Lara: Here we go again, getting into that nonresponsive mode
    of yours. How long do you think you can keep this up?
Mike: Wait a minute.
Lara: You need some time to think real hard, buddy. Because
    the next phase—
Mike, head down, as if defeated: Yeah.
Lara: —is coming really quick. Real quick. And your
    opportunities are slowly diminishing. But you realize that,
    don't you?

Lara moves in closer, hands wide on the table.

Mike rocks back and thinks, mumbles, seems to generate a thought, then shakes his head, still rocking.

Hardesty: Whose idea was it?
Mike, point-blank: Maurice's.
Hardesty: Right.

Done deal, then. At 1:30, two men get what they wanted; another has no idea what he just got himself into.

The Texas Court of Criminal Appeals does not like overturning convictions or granting appeals. This, after all, is the court whose presiding judge, Sharon Keller, will—on September 25, 2007—refuse to answer a lawyer's call on the afternoon of his client's execution because the phone rang a few minutes past the five o'clock deadline: So, guilty or not, the man was put to death. But on June 6 of that same year, having already reversed Robert Springsteen's conviction and ordered a new trial, the TCCA will vote five to four to overturn Mike Scott's conviction.

Both appeals were based on the abrogation of the Confrontation Clause of the Sixth Amendment, guaranteeing the right of every citizen to confront his or her accuser. Although the justices weren't asked to rule on possible investigative misconduct, the court's majority opinion in *Scott*—written by Judge Tom Price, a moderate Republican from Dallas—cited many instances of improper questioning, in which the accused was fed implications and suggestions that led him to make self-incriminating statements and to supply accurate crime-scene details he'd previously either misstated or denied knowing. Judge Price refers to the moment when Mike said the idea was Maurice's and then writes:

> At first he [Scott] insisted he had not gone into the yogurt shop himself and that Pierce and Springsteen had gone in through the front door. Asked whether they had carried guns, the appellant initially asserted that he could not remember but that Pierce might have. He eventually described Pierce's gun as a .38 caliber revolver. When the detectives asked him if a second gun had been used, the appellant first could not remember whether Springsteen had a gun. Later he said he had seen the handle of a pistol in Springsteen's waistband. He volunteered that it had had a wood or "wood facsimile" handle but when they inquired whether he knew what an automatic looked like, he suddenly changed his story and claimed it had been, in fact,

an automatic. He could not tell them the caliber of the second gun, and soon after stated that he was not really positive Springsteen had had a gun at all.

And when one of the detectives asked whether they had "cased" the yogurt shop, the appellant acknowledged that they had. First he said they had noticed that the back door of the yogurt shop had been "propped open" but he later abandoned this assertion. The appellant continued to insist he had not gone in, even though the detectives accused him of "minimizing" his involvement, to his eventual detriment. He even alluded at one point to the fact that "we" came back out of the shop and drove off but immediately insisted he had misspoken.

The videotape shows Lara, at this point, bolting out of his chair and heading toward the door and saying Scott didn't want to talk anymore. It was time to "just take him to the grand jury."

Mike's reaction is immediate. Covering his face with his hands, he breaks down into tears. "I don't remember going inside the . . ."

They tell him yes, he does, and should be a man and tell the truth; all he has to do is open the doors in his mind. And he says he's trying to be a man and to tell the truth, but honestly, he doesn't think he went inside that store and—

Hardesty: Michael, Michael.
Mike: Are you telling me I went inside?
Hardesty: I *know* you went inside. *You* know you went inside.
Mike: I don't remember going inside.
Hardesty: Come on, Michael, you went inside. Earlier you said, "*We* ran back out to the car," meaning you, Maurice and Robert. You said "we." Well, "we" did. Michael, you went with them inside that store.
Mike: Okay.

"Okay" isn't perfect, but it's a start.

———

The TCCA opinion continues:

The detectives falsely assured the appellant that they knew "all about those two guns," even before the use of a second gun had been acknowledged, thereby feeding him important information. They told him that they did not believe he had shot the girls. The appellant asked, "Look, can I tell you all what I keep seeing in my head? I keep seeing these girls get shot." He followed this almost immediately with the disclaimer, "I don't know if this is real or not or if this is—" at which point one of the detectives interrupted him to assure him, "Michael, it's real." Even as the appellant began to describe events inside the yogurt shop, he continued periodically to claim, *e.g.,* "I don't honestly remember going in the building. . . ."

After a break, the appellant returned with fresh memories. He remembered the girls had been tied up, but could not remember with what. He thought they were wearing their uniforms when it happened. The detectives accused him of "starting to go off in this other tangent and bullshit with us again." The appellant replied, "I can't even remember going inside the place, guys. I don't remember walking through the doors."

It's 4:30 when Hardesty asks Mike what the girls were tied up with.

Mike, hopeful, looks up: I want to say [long pause] extension
    cords?
Hardesty, slightly sarcastic: Really. Why do you want to say that?
Mike, getting the implication: I remember it being white.
    Napkins?
Hardesty, in utter, if feigned, disbelief: Not *napkins*. You can't tie
    her up in napkins. Give me a break. Something white. Tell
    us what it was.

Mike is thinking hard, just like they're always telling him to. He wonders aloud if they might have used a T-shirt and an electrical cord? Hardesty says no and tells him to think harder about a T-shirt and something else and that he's not going to tell Mike what that is, because he *knows*. Struggling, Mike says he's trying to remember;

Hardesty repeats *"something else,"* then asks if he helped Rob tie the girls up, and Mike says he thinks—no, he *guesses*—he did. But Hardesty answers the question more definitively: "Yeah, you did," and he also wants to know what the girls were wearing by the time they were tied up. When Mike doesn't answer, Hardesty repeats the question then says, "Michael, that's a gimme. That's an easy one."

"Not a whole lot."

"Not a whole lot." A flat statement, then waiting.

"Used their own clothes to tie them up." He's getting it now.

"Used their own clothes to tie them up. You and Rob. And by the time you were done, what were they wearing? *Say it.*"

"Nothing."

"Right."

That done, Hardesty takes the next step: "What did the other boys make you *do* to those girls?"

Mike thinks he sees girls getting hit in the back of the head with the butt of a gun, was that it? No. Did they make him kick them? Hardesty brushes past that one and returns to his original question: "They made you do something, what did they make you do?"

Mike thinks maybe one of the girls was strangled to death. "I didn't choke one with a garrote, did I?" Hardesty waits. Mike keeps trying. Did they make him bludgeon them, even *rape* one of them? He answers that one for himself. No, he didn't rape anybody, "that's not me." But he did have a pocketknife on him, was that it?

Hardesty, stepping in: That's four. Kicking, strangling,
  bludgeoning, knifing. No.
Mike, fearfully: They didn't make me shoot them, did they?
Hardesty: Well, did they? Tell us. I want to hear it. Did they?
  Say it, Michael, is that what happened?
Mike: I think so.
Hardesty: You think so?

He does.

The TCCA opinion noted a significant number of other errors in Mike's confession. For one thing, in the interrogation room, he repeatedly insisted that the girls were shot one by one behind the counter. In a crude, haphazard drawing, he drew four vertical lines behind the horizontal line that represented the counter. Girl, girl, girl, girl. But he later stated for the record that the girls were taken to the back of the shop, where they were sexually assaulted and then shot. And after his assertion that he shot a girl in the face gained no traction with the detectives, he altered that to the forehead and finally—after they again waited for him to get it right—to the back of the head. Which was a bingo.

Judge Tom Price was elected to the court in 1996 and remained on the bench until his retirement in 2015. He is particularly remembered for publicly taking an eloquent stand against the death penalty—a distinctly unpopular opinion in Texas—and for quietly wondering, in a *Texas Monthly* interview, "How far to the right is this court going to be?" Even Republicans, he added, "want there to be fair trials." The dissenting opinion on Mike Scott's appeal was written by Presiding Judge Sharon Keller.

At 5:35 that afternoon, Mike will wonder if maybe he should get a lawyer. At that, the detectives quickly suggest another break, and when they come back, Hardesty says they need to clear up this thing about a lawyer, at which point Mike backs down. What do *they* think he ought to do? Dodging the question, Lara encourages Mike not to do anything until he remembers everything and can go on with his life and be a good husband and father, not a dirtbag like the others.

Other members of the Cold Case Task Force will join the interrogation that evening, including tall, lean, self-assured BATF agent Chuck Meyer and, from Homicide, Sgt. Manuel Fuentes and burly, seasoned Detective Robert Merrill, whose folksy manner and country-boy humor will charm Scott and give him the confidence to share some embarrassing details—for one, that Rob called him a "pussy" that night and bullied him into raping one of the girls. Merrill does a real man-to-man about the shame of being called a pussy. Mike says it didn't matter much; he couldn't get an erection anyway.

But Rob? He raped the shit out of one of those girls, the girl he spun around in the front room.

The questioning shifts gears again and the detectives turn to the fire. Mike first says Maurice piled Styrofoam cups and napkins *close* to the girls, then changes that to on *top* of the girls, and started the fire with a Zippo. Then he insists he was in the car and didn't see the fire and, a little later, that actually Maurice instructed *him* to spread cups and napkins on the girls' piled-up bodies, then go to the car and get a can of lighter fluid and pour it all over them. And then use the Zippo. Which, he says, he did.

At about eight o'clock, Lara and Merrill take Mike to the yogurt shop, which by now has become a check-cashing and quick-loan operation. They've arranged to have a video camera there to catch any significant information he might come up with, but he just walks around, saying little. On the drive back to the station, they buy him a burger and another soft drink.

It's 10:22 when Lara opens the door to the interview room the final time, and past eleven when Mike gets home. By then, his step-daughter's asleep and Jeannine's still suffering from a migraine. To keep the peace—and abide by the detectives' instructions—Mike won't divulge anything to her about his ordeal. Tomorrow, he'll tell the detectives he didn't sleep much the night before, and it isn't difficult to picture him lying in bed beside his wife in the small hours, jabbing at his mind and memory, trying to piece together the facts and possibilities the cops have hammered into him, insinuations and suggestions, as well as his own attempts to remember what really happened all those years ago.

Maybe the Buda trailer finally goes dark. Perhaps Mike sleeps. Early the next morning, as if spellbound, he'll walk the half mile from the trailer to the highway in time to meet Ron Lara, who arrives at a little before eight and is surprised to find Mike standing at the top of the gravel road, alone, waiting for him.

THE PURSUIT OF MAURICE PIERCE, ROUND THREE

In the car, Mike again speaks first, but this time Lara has brought a tape recorder. Last night, he says, when he tried to replay what he'd told them, all he could really remember about the yogurt shop was that the walls and hallway were white, nothing else; but then, he doesn't even remember what happened last week and the only way he knows today is Friday is because his wife is wearing jeans for dress-down day.

When Lara doesn't respond, he keeps talking.

"What scares me the most is, I can't recall a lot of the specific details of what happened that night. I'm scared I'm going to prison. I'm scared I'm going to get the death penalty. . . . I'm scared what's going to happen to me and how my wife is going to take this. And I'm scared when this is all over I'll be walking down the street and somebody will have seen me on TV or read my name in the news-paper and shoot me."

When Lara congratulates him for facing up to what he's done, Mike says he just wants to put it all behind him, to open the doors to his head and "fucking talk to y'all and finish this." And he wishes he had a photographic mind or could plug into one of those machines like the one they had in the movie *Total Recall;* then he'd know everything.

He remains silent for a bit, then continues: "I keep asking myself do I want a lawyer and I keep telling myself no. . . . But, man, I still don't believe I did this."

Lara, driving, says, "What's that?" As if he hadn't been listening.

In the interview room, Mike wraps himself in a blanket they've provided and sits hunched over, bundled up to his chin. He's been thinking, he tells Lara and Manuel Fuentes, that maybe he lied yesterday, because his heart tells him he didn't kill the girls, rob the store, set it on fire. But his brain tells him something different. On TV, he heard about something called "hypnotic regression," which would put him under and let him float while the memory tape played. Maybe they could help get him into that. Then he'd know.

But when the detectives ignore that and press for further details, he suddenly remembers having seen the keys in the front door of the shop, and when Lara assures him that he definitely was inside and "pulled the trigger," Mike craters, saying he "probably" shot one of the girls, although he's not quite sure which one. And when the detective then accuses him of having shot all four, he says, "I can't remember shooting *any*body. You all are telling me that I did. I was telling you all what you wanted to hear."

Later in the day, Merrill returns. Alone with Mike, he takes out a pistol and puts it to the back of Mike's head. A clip from the video showing that scene will later surface on its way to the Internet and cause something of a scandal. When a story by Michael Hall appears in the January 2001 issue of *Texas Monthly*, it will open with:

It's a gun, all right, and Detective Robert Merrill is holding it to the back of Mike Scott's head. The detective is standing as if braced for action; the suspect is sitting at a small, round table, his left hand resting on the white surface. From the camera's angle, up high in the cramped interrogation room, you can see Scott's receding hairline. His body language says he is sitting perfectly still. This is his second day of interrogation, and Merrill and a series of other Austin policemen have been yelling and cursing at him for hours. Their frustration is, perhaps, understandable. This is no ordinary interrogation. Scott, they believe, has details about the biggest and most horrific case in the Austin Police Department's history, the slaughter of four teenage girls at an I Can't Believe It's Yogurt! store on December 6, 1991.

———

Merrill had been given the gun by Paul Johnson, who thought it might scare Mike into talking. Instead, as Merrill will acknowledge during Mike's trial, it shut him down.

By the time Texas Ranger Sal Abreo enters, it's two o'clock and Mike is exhausted. But the soft-spoken Latino detective has a gift for intimacy and, like Hector Polanco, knows how and when to put it to good use. Alone with Mike, he places a comforting hand on his shoulder and, sitting close, practically whispers in his ear. He's there to help get the girls' screams out of his head; it's okay; he only wants to help. And he describes the "little girls" tied up on the floor and they're squirming and he's raping them—was it from the front or back?—and then they're lying on top of one another and he's squirting lighter fluid on their little bodies. "It's all right to tell us, it's important, Michael. It's all right."

Mike is weeping and all but gone, but, like a preacher pushing the Gospel, Abreo presses on. Think about it, he says. "Up to that point you could hear them screaming, crying, begging not to be killed, but at some point they stopped screaming, didn't they?"

Mike: Yes, sir.
Abreo: Why? Lean your head back and think about it. Why did they stop screaming, why did that happen?

Abreo keeps repeating the question, until Mike finally gives him what he's after: They were gagged.

Abreo: Yes.
Mike: But I don't know with what.

Yes, he does, Abreo tells him. And again he reminds him of the little girls squirming while he was raping them, but was something stuffed in their mouths? Can he see what it is? And can he see the face of the girl he's raping?

When Mike says he doesn't, Abreo says that's because he's found a way to take her face away and now must put it back on.

By the time Merrill reenters and asks if he got his "wanger" up that night, Mike's bent over with his head between his legs and he's sobbing.

At 2:45, Merrill calls for a break. Half an hour later he returns with a diagram of the shop, which Mike wants to take home and study, but Merrill says no; they're going to take him home now, and he should get things in order over the weekend, on his own.

The following day, Saturday, Lara will call Mike at home and tell him he doesn't sound so good—as if to say, No wonder, now that you've remembered killing those girls. On Sunday, Lara and Fuentes tape a session at Mike and Jeannine's home, using a battery Mike takes from his wall clock when their audiocassette recorder goes dead. In his living room, Mike strokes a stuffed cat while fielding questions. He likes cats, he tells them. They can't have a real one because his wife's allergic, but this one's okay. The detectives have already had a run-in with Jeannine in which she called them names and accused them of turning her husband into a liar. After she leaves, they ask Mike if they can call him on a mobile phone, so they can avoid his wife from that day forward. Mike says no. She's pissed at them and won't let up.

On Sunday, Mike wants to visit high bridges in the vicinity of the yogurt shop, thinking maybe he'll recognize the one they drove to after the murders, where he supposedly threw up over the railing and tossed a set of ICBY keys into the lake. Lara and Fuentes drive him around for hours, but Austin is ringed by five lakes and none of the bridges resembles the one he remembers—"that rust extension bridge with that big shit over the top." And anyway, no keys were reported missing from the yogurt shop. And neither was the bottom half of a blender he mentioned for the first time that day.

They then take him back to the scene of the crime, but nothing much happens. Mike just looks around, saying nothing. During both trials, however, Lara and Fuentes will each note a moment when the three of them were sitting on a fallen tree limb, taking a break, and Lara asked Scott point-blank if he still had the .22 pistol used in the murders. Both officers say that Mike looked Lara straight in the eye and said, "It's no longer in my possession." Though none of this was recorded, that statement confirmed the detectives' gathering belief that they had the right man—not just a link to Maurice Pierce but a participant.

In Mike's final, brief interview—Monday, September 13—he remembers gagging one of the girls with a paper towel and seeing Maurice with another one in a separate room that might have been an office. He's still saying they tied the girls' feet together, which the detectives—rather than question how they were able to rape them then—choose to ignore. And he thinks the gun he'd used came from Rob, not Maurice, and was a .22. As for the caliber of the second gun, he thinks it was a semiautomatic .38. Getting nothing but contradictions and discrepancies, the detectives take him home.

On Tuesday, at Ron Lara's request, Manuel Fuentes drives to Uni-Sys and finds Mike sitting on the curb in front of a Grandy's restaurant, across the street from Jeannine's office. Mike tells Fuentes he called a lawyer his family knows, Betty Blackwell, who wasn't inclined to represent him, or even offer much advice, but did strongly suggest that he quit talking to the police and find a criminal attorney to represent him, because otherwise he might well be looking at a prison sentence or even the death penalty.

So why is he sitting there waiting to be picked up?

The last thing he needs, Scott tells Fuentes, is a lawyer.

So does he want to go to APD with Fuentes or not? It's up to him. Scott gets in the car. When asked why, he just shrugs.

On his own, Fuentes has decided to take a written statement, just because nobody had done it yet. Mike agrees to comply, but only if Sal Abreo is present. By phone, Abreo agrees to join them but will need a good twenty minutes to get there.

At Fuentes's office on the second floor of the Twin Towers, at 10:39, after issuing a Miranda warning, Fuentes sits at his computer and brings up a blank APD statement page, asking Mike to stand behind him as he types. Abreo takes his place at the end of the desk.

Five hours later, at 3:45, the officers locate two civilians in the building—statistics and computer guys—to serve as witnesses when Michael Scott signs the fourteen-page written document admitting his participation in the Yogurt Shop Murders and implicating Robert Springsteen, Maurice Pierce and, to some extent, Forrest Welborn. The signing wasn't videotaped. When asked why it took so long,

Fuentes will say Mike talked slowly and kept excusing himself to go outside and smoke a cigarette.

Neither Lara nor Hardesty was there at the signing. Lara had already left on a flight to Charleston, West Virginia, to question Robert Springsteen, and his partner was tending to other Yogurt Shop business. When Mike's statement veered significantly from his videotaped confession, Fuentes didn't correct or question him. He knew only scraps of what the interrogation had produced, just what Lara had told him. (See Appendix 1 for Michael Scott written statement.)

Although Mike won't be arrested for several weeks, the task force is certain he knows the location of at least one of the murder weapons, so they keep him under surveillance. When he's officially charged, he'll be at his and Jeannine's storage locker on South Congress. Hearing cars drive up, he'll look around and see two cars and a slew of cops. They tell him he's under arrest for capital murder, for killing Amy Ayers, and for robbing the ICBY shop. Then they cuff him and take him in.

Mike Scott will remain incarcerated from that day in September 1999 until the summer of 2009, when he's released on a personal recognizance bond.

THE PURSUIT OF MAURICE PIERCE, ROUND FOUR

The first mistake Robert Springsteen IV made on the Monday afternoon of September 13, 1999, was to answer his phone; the second, to accept a free cell phone offer made by an anonymous caller; but it was the third mistake that sank him. When the caller asked for the lucky recipient's name and address, promising to call back later with details, Springsteen complied.

Chuck Meyer made the call. Right guy, right number. Let's go.

On Tuesday, while Manuel Fuentes was at the Twin Towers taking Michael Scott's statement, the big guns—Lara, Merrill, Meyer and task-force supervisor John Neff—left for Charleston. With Scott a sure thing and Springsteen directly implicated, they could skip the friendly overtures and jump to the accusations. Although on the stand Merrill will say they went to West Virginia to find out what Springsteen had to say about Mike Scott's declarations, their behavior hardly confirms this. They were after another killer. Once they linked Springsteen's account with Scott's, they could go after Pierce and Welborn. And if those two continued to stonewall, they'd go back to the first two and make a deal.

Legal advice from the DA's office supported their basic strategy, which was once again to bypass Miranda requirements by assuring Springsteen he wasn't in custody, not charged, that they just needed his help to clear up a few inconsistencies.

The four-man posse flew commercial. By the time they checked into a Charleston motel that evening, Mike Scott had signed his statement in Austin and gone home. Springsteen was at work, filling in as a short-order cook for the local Fraternal Order of the Eagles.

Though still working mindless jobs for minimum wage, Rob hadn't done badly since leaving Austin. There had been a couple of scrapes with the law, but he'd gotten his GED, after a drunk-driving arrest, when the judge offered him the option of finishing his degree instead of doing time. He'd married a woman twenty-two years his senior who had two nearly grown children and a grandchild, was restoring an 1890 log cabin she'd inherited and held a regular job as a graveyard-shift stock boy at Kroger. He'd also worked at chemical plants and been assistant manager of a burger joint. He was looking for more meaningful work but thus far hadn't been offered anything close to what he thought he deserved. His wife, Robin Moss, was a banker, which helped. As for Austin, once his father moved away, he'd lost all connection to it.

Because the Charleston PD interview rooms weren't equipped with recording devices, the APD audiovisual lab had provided the detectives with a clock containing a hidden video camera that could wirelessly transmit a signal to a television set with a VCR. Before leaving town, Merrill had tested the clock-camera, which worked as promised; nonetheless, Meyer suggested that for backup they use a hidden Nagra reel-to-reel audiotape recorder.

When I asked an audio specialist what he thought of Nagras, he laughed. "Remember those?" he said to a colleague. "Tape maxed out at three hours?"

On the morning of September 15, with the help of Charleston police officer Eric Hodges, Merrill hung the clock-camera at about eye level on the wall of a windowless seven-by-nine interview room. Then, testing the device, they discovered that a persistent hum was fuzzing up the audio, often rendering speech indecipherable. There were also inexplicable bursts of static and "explosions on the screen of some sort," perhaps from interfering radio traffic. The screen would distort before coming back into focus, then go bonkers again. They fiddled with the wires, but nothing worked. The room was furnished with a large desk and three chairs. After loading the Nagra and hiding it in a drawer, they taped a microphone underneath the desk and pointed it toward the chair Springsteen would sit in. By the time they finished the setup, it was close to noon. As for the hum and the static, they'd done the best they could.

When Merrill and Hodges knocked on his door sometime after twelve-thirty, Rob had been asleep for maybe an hour, having worked from five until ten the night before cooking for the Eagles, and then from midnight until eight at Kroger. Before that, he'd worked all afternoon on the cabin. After arriving home that morning, he'd spent a couple hours on his PlayStation before going to bed. He figured he'd slept maybe six hours in the past three days.

When the policemen knocked, Rob staggered to the door. Two men stood there in regular clothes, wearing sidearms. *Cops,* he thought, and opened the door. After Hodges introduced himself and Detective Merrill, he said they'd like to ask him a few questions. Rob invited them in, but they declined to engage in conversation. There were others, Hodges explained, who wanted to talk to him; they'd all come in from Austin. Would he mind going downtown with them?

Rob offered them chairs while he went upstairs to dress, but the policemen chose to stand, and then heard him phoning someone from the kitchen—his wife, they assumed—to explain where he was going. After a few minutes, he returned wearing black jeans, a dark knit shirt and a ball cap pulled low. He grabbed a pack of his wife's cigarettes—a brand, Eve, made especially for women—and a lighter. On the drive to the police station, he told the cops about the cabin he'd been working on, and they feigned interest.

By the time Robert Burns Springsteen IV was escorted into a Charleston PD interview room at about two o'clock, his wife had called his stepfather, Brett Thompson, to tell him that Rob had gone downtown with two policemen to answer questions about something that had happened in Austin. More than slightly alarmed, Thompson set off for the station himself.

The videotape of Rob's questioning begins with the usual glitchy lines, though this time they're accompanied by the background hum, as persistently annoying as a leaf blower in the distance. Lara comes in—wearing a lighter-colored shirt this time—and lays some papers on the desk, then leaves. Rob enters with the husky, frowning Merrill, who quickly vanishes from view when he sits with his back to the camera. Rob's attitude, like Mike Scott's, is one of unworried ease, but he lacks his former friend's affability. He sits where he's been directed to, in an old-fashioned wooden office chair with arms. When Lara returns, Rob stands and politely extends his hand. They shake and exchange names. When Lara suggests they sit down, Rob reaches in his belt pouch and says, "I'm just going to get me a cigarette," and when Lara says there's no smoking, he points toward the desk and says that, well, he saw the ashtray and figured it was all right.

Lara stands firm. They can go out for a smoke later. Rob takes his chair and says, "No problem." And he waits. He's even chewing gum.

Four girls, I remind myself. Stripped, bound, molested, shot dead, burned to the bone. This is how cops get the bad guys. Do not automatically sympathize with this man. He might have been there, might've done what Mike Scott said he did and "raped the shit out of" one of those girls. But what I see on my computer screen is a tall, thin young man answering questions with "Yes, sir" and "No, sir," happily engaging in what he thinks is a consensual conversation about a crime that happened in another city almost eight years ago, when he was seventeen and had pretty much dropped out of high school. But as with the other two who sat in a similar hot seat—Kelly, then Mike—it's hard not to have feelings for someone who's trapped and doesn't know it yet. In a narrative sense, blind ignorance turns him into a protagonist.

Again, following Reid protocol, Lara establishes the reason for their presence, citing issues that need clearing up from interviews that weren't done all that well the first time around, and then he yields to Merrill, who asks for the usual personal information: date of birth, address and the rest. The interrogation will last only five hours, but because Springsteen doesn't request bathroom or food breaks and Lara changes his mind and lets him smoke in the room, the three-hour Nagra tape will run out with two hours to go. By then the police are too close to getting what they came for to risk interrupting the proceedings; and since they don't want Springsteen to know he's being recorded, they can't replace the tape and thus have to depend on the faulty clock-camera for sound.

It's an odd mistake, especially given Lara's repeated suggestions to Mike Scott that he get a soft drink, use the restroom, have a smoke . . . not because he thought Mike needed time to think but because they did. Maybe the detectives have become overconfident and impatient and simply don't realize how bad the clock-camera's reception really is. This will prove to be an extremely costly error.

Rob's voice is pinched but unwavering. When Lara inquires how he's feeling this morning, he answers with a flat-out "Tired," then relates the story of his jobs and lack of sleep and how he'd been in bed for only an hour when—*boom boom boom*, he hammers at the air with his fist—somebody knocked and he wondered, Who in the world?

Lara nods as if to say, I'm with you, brother; I know how that is. And he asks Rob to tell them a little about himself, what he's up to, how he likes living "out over here." Talking with his hands, waving toward some lake or town he's describing, Rob complies. His family history elicits a "Wow" from Lara when he lists the professional positions his father, grandfather and an uncle have held. His accent is softly southern. When he asks Lara how long they think this will take, since he has a job to get to, the detective says they just need to clarify a few things and they'll get him out of there as quickly as possible.

This seems positive to Rob. But in about half an hour, Lara makes a sharp turn toward the night in question, in response to which Rob recites a list of his activities that afternoon and evening, at the school and the mall, including the midnight Rocky Show and the cast party he didn't get to. He shakes his head when Lara asks him about casing the yogurt shop that afternoon and swears he's never been in the store in his life, and no matter what they've heard, he had nothing to do with killing those girls. Foolishly cocksure, he remains unconcerned. By this time he's smoking—Eves are thinner and longer than a regular cigarette—and sitting with his chin defiantly high, awaiting the next question.

The inquiry continues, pointed but not aggressive, for two hours or so, until Lara abruptly launches into a series of "Would you be surprised to know" questions, the first of which he backs up with statements from "five or six different people" who have sworn that Rob was with Maurice, Mike and Forrest not just for a few hours, as he'd claimed, but for the entire night.

Would Rob find that to be a surprise?

Springsteen says yes, a complete and total surprise. But it's the next question that gets him.

"Would you be surprised," Lara asks, "if I told you that the 'Rocky Horror Show' wasn't even showing at Northcross on Friday, December 6, 1991?"

The effect of this is not reflected in the written transcript. To understand the damage, you have to watch the tape. Of course, Lara didn't *exactly* say the movie hadn't played that night, but the inference hits home. Rob's head pops up and his voice tightens as, clearly, the worm of doubt begins to uncurl. And within the next quarter of an hour, Lara tells Rob it's no coincidence they came to West Virginia after all these years. It's because of a new technology "called DNA" that's tremendously important, and Rob gets it. The cops are talking science. They're saying they found his DNA at the scene, aren't they?

At about this same time, the Charleston cop Eric Hodges is refusing to allow Brett Thompson into the station to talk to his stepson, even after Thompson says he doesn't think Rob's capable of making a legal decision on his own. Hodges assures him that Rob has been afforded his full rights and issued a Miranda statement, which he has waived. But Thompson's not convinced and suspects Hodges doesn't really know what the Austin cops are up to or if what he just said is true. Perhaps Rob's stepfather sniffs this out, because he goes home and calls David Bungard, a local attorney whose offices are directly across the street from the police station. Bungard strolls over and, right at the moment when Rob's starting to crack, he's in the reception area, telling Hodges that he's been hired by Robert Springsteen's family to represent him and would like for the interrogation of his client to come to an immediate halt. Hodges tries soothing him with the same lies he told to Thompson, adding what the Austin detectives had instructed him to, that because a third party had arranged for the lawyer, not the suspect himself, they don't have to let him talk to Robert. Bungard gives Hodges his business card and leaves.

The Charleston Police Department will close for the day at four-thirty: lights off, doors locked, one officer to stand patrol, everybody else gone. Half an hour later, Eric Hodges drives to the mall for dinner. Anyone hoping to enter the CPD offices is out of luck until he returns. But in the interrogation room, the lights burn on. The Nagra tape has run out. The APD is nailing Rob Springsteen to the wall.

Pretty much all of us maintain belief in a sense of self that defines us and what we think we might or might not be capable of. Many friends of the four men arrested for the ICBY murders refused to believe they were involved. *He's not that kind of guy*, they'd say. At his home in West Virginia in 2010, Springsteen characterized himself to me as a "normal guy" who would never "do anything like kill somebody" because "that's not me." As for prosecutors, cops and Austinites, "They don't know anything about me." Like a psychiatrist, the interrogator has to figure out how to break through the armor of a suspect's self-characterization and drive him to the point of thinking he isn't who he'd always thought, dreamed or hoped he was; that he is—or may be—somebody else altogether, a stranger to himself, perhaps even a killer. At about five o'clock, just after he plants the seed of doubt in Rob's mind about the Rocky Show, Lara pulls this off.

He's still hammering at Rob's time line, employing a repetitive "What happened next?" series of questions focusing on the crucial hours from ten until midnight. "Okay," he says after Rob describes driving around in Maurice's car on what he *thinks* was that night, although he can't be sure; it might've been the weekend before or the one after. They were always driving around in Maurice's car. "What happened then?"

Rob says he *thinks* they went to the movie, though given what Lara told him, he guesses they didn't. And if they didn't go to the Rocky Show, he doesn't know what they did. "Or anyway," he says, "I don't remember." But he does know one thing: "I was never in that yogurt shop. Never."

Lara ignores that, presses on. And so now Rob's sure there wasn't a movie, "Now that I've told you?"

Rob says no, he's not sure of that. He said he doesn't *remember* one way or the other, but he wants the detectives—"you guys"—to believe him. "I believe that to be the truth."

"So what then? Do you remember *seeing* the movie?"

"Not that night, precisely. Maybe I did and maybe I didn't."

So what Rob told Lara was a white lie, wasn't it? Because he wasn't really there. "We know that," Lara declares. Can he at least admit he wasn't there?

"Well," Rob says, "we were definitely *outside* the movie."

Okay. But outside's a whole lot different than inside, right?

"Maybe we didn't go in," Rob concedes.

Lara takes on the tone of a disappointed father: "Rob," he says. "Rob." But when he continues to insist he doesn't remember, the detective becomes streetwise. "I wasn't born yesterday, brother." Does Springsteen get that?

Yes.

"Okay. You weren't actually in the movies as you told us earlier."

Springsteen says no.

Got him.

Lara pushes for specifics. Was he inside, or outside in the parking lot, or somewhere else? What exactly was he doing? Isn't it *reasonable* to think he was *next* to the theater but not *inside* it?

Rob agrees that's a very reasonable thing to say. He doesn't really *remember* being outside, but it's probably *reasonable* to think he was.

At this point, the overconfident Rob might have convinced himself he was asserting his proficiency as a gamer and quite adept at engaging in hypotheticals. That he has a chance to outsmart this wise guy Latino by seconding the *reasonableness* of a statement without specifically acknowledging the truth of it.

Lara knots the two strands of conjecture into one: Okay, so he's down with Rob's suggestion of a reasonable possibility. Is Rob comfortable with it?

Although Rob hadn't said "reasonable possibility," he says he'll go with it.

No, Lara says, he can't just go with it. Is he *comfortable* with it?

Springsteen says yes, he is.

"Is it the truth?"

"It's possible."

"It's possible," Lara says, echoing him. "Anything's possible, right?"

Rob's into the wordplay. "Well," he says, "yes."

But Lara's not. "Is it possible," he asks calmly and without obvious ill intent, "you killed those girls?" After all, Lara reminds him, that's what he said, that anything's possible.

Rob guesses it's possible.

After another couple of minutes, Lara rolls from possibilities to likelihoods and the logical reason why the others involved in the murders—Maurice, Mike and Forrest—have all included him in the picture, and in no time Rob's powers of strategic banter fail him. Possible is possible, and what was once flatly denied begins to yield to the realm of imagination, of endlessly evolving conjecture. The gamer has crashed belly-up in a real-world match.

What we have, then, are two confessions obtained by some of the same interrogators relating to the same crime and yet in each case the result of a different process, strategy and breakdown. When Mike Scott was asked to stand on a chair and picture himself at the crime scene, he began to do exactly that: to envision the scene below with himself in it. Then with a little help, he seems to have created a memory of an event that might or might not have occurred, what neuroscientists call a *false* or *illusory memory*. Like Shawn "Buddha" Smith, who said while under Polanco's spell that he actually *saw* the blood and the raping, in false-confession terms Mike Scott *internalized* his custodians' suggestions until they turned into what seemed like memories.

Rob, on the other hand, appears to have tricked himself into playing what he thought was an intellectual match against the big guys, without understanding the enormity of the mistake he'd made about the game itself, which had no rules other than those prescribed by Reid, where possibilities morph into certainties and cops make incriminating statements they assign to the suspect.

That they were the smart ones never occurred to him.

———

The edges of what Robert Springsteen IV considers his *self*—a normal guy doing normal things—begin to blur. He starts to think like the two men hammering at him, to imagine himself as he's being told he is. This is the turning point of many interrogations, when the subject accepts the definition of himself that his persecutors have created and labeled authentic and unbiased. Imagination rules. Taking the blame becomes, weirdly, an escape. Rob accepts the detectives' version of the night, describing what happened as a "total cluster fuck." He gives details of the rapes, the murders, very little about the fire. He lays his head on his bent arm to re-create the position Amy Ayers was in when they left her. Prosecutors will describe his pose as a perfect replication of Amy's death posture, even though it isn't.

The detectives are close to having what they came for. And then, just after seven o'clock, Merrill makes what from the police point of view is an unfathomable mistake by issuing a precipitous Miranda warning.

Rob comes to, as if from a swoon. Having seen the TV shows, he knows what happens next. They're not just talking; he's in custody. He refuses to sign. He needs to talk to his wife. And to an attorney. He's not saying anything bad about the officers; he just needs to go home and "clean up my mess."

"There's the door," says the flustered, abashed Merrill. Springsteen hasn't implicated Mike Scott or the other two, and they barely touched on the fire. But if he won't sign the Miranda, they have to let him go. They even give him a ride.

By eight that night, some twelve hours after he finished restocking shelves at Kroger, Rob is at home with his family, having given the Austin cops a verbal statement describing his participation in the Yogurt Shop Murders. Some of the details he provided match Scott's, but many do not. Some match the crime scene, yet, again, many do not.

In the years to come, Rob will recant. During his trial, when his attorney asks him to tell the jury why he confessed to something he didn't do, he says, "I guess I gave up on myself." He had assumed that once he got out of that room, he could take a lie-detector test—in West Virginia, not Texas—and that eventually forensic tests—fingerprints, DNA, blood, hair, whatever—would prove he hadn't been in the ICBY shop. There is, however, one thing he said that might be more important than he'd realized. In the final hour of his interrogation, Lara had pushed him to admit what he did to thirteen-year-old Amy Ayers sexually. *Just admit it,* he kept saying. *Say it, Rob, just say it.*

Eventually, Rob yielded. Yes, he said. Yes, okay, he did it.

Lara demanded the words.

"Okay," Rob said. "I put my dick in her pussy and I raped her." And, still wearing the ball cap low on his forehead, he looked up through those devilish eyebrows as if to say, Is that enough?

Game over.

Before being extradited to Texas, Rob will take a polygraph test in which he tests out as truthful when he says he didn't commit the murders and doesn't know who did. Although the results of the original rape-kit test performed on Amy Ayers were negative, and even when more sophisticated DNA tests exclude Robert Springsteen IV from having left bodily fluid anywhere at the scene, the "dick in her pussy" statement will, according to his lead lawyer, seal his fate. Once the jury heard it, Jim Sawyer believes, his client was a dead man.

Lara, Neff, Merrill and Meyer fly back to Austin. Merrill works for three days on a transcript of the interrogation, as all three of them struggle to recall words and phrases lost due to the clock-camera's malfunction. Still not satisfied, Merrill sends the video and the Nagra tape to the Houston crime lab, and then to the BATF lab in Washington. Both work to enhance the videotape by merging sound from the Nagra into it, a kind of jerry-rigged voice-over they hope will create the *semblance* of an authentic recording. On the stand, Merrill will say that maybe 85 percent of the audio was accurate. There are also eight or nine minutes in the processed audiotape that don't appear on the video at all. But Springsteen said he did it. And he said he'd raped Amy Ayers. Next to that, everything else seemed pale and stingy.

ARRESTS

Paul Johnson called in the task force. Though they had confessions, there were holes, contradictions, inconsistencies. Above all, they needed the weapons, and for Maurice to confess. A few days later, Johnson himself teamed up with APD cop Douglas Skolaut and drove to Irving to interview Pierce in his lawyer's office. There, they told him he was about to be arrested, but if he confessed, he could at least prove he wasn't the ringleader like the other guys said. But Pierce again denied any involvement in the murders, and the detectives came back empty-handed. Fuentes and Hardesty then drove to Lockhart to pick up Welborn and transport him to APD headquarters, where Fuentes produced the first and last pages of Mike's statement. Rob had also confessed, he told Forrest; both men had implicated him, and so had Maurice. Brilliant at keeping his mouth shut, Forrest also gave them nothing.

So Skolaut and Meyer drove him to the former site of the yogurt shop for a surprise meeting with Mike Scott, who walked straight up to Welborn and said, "Hey, Forrest. Remember me? I'm Mike Scott. I told the police everything," and suggested that he do the same. Clearly shocked, Forrest said he had no idea what the fuck Mike was talking about or why he'd signed that statement, then turned away and just stood there gazing toward Shoal Creek. So Lara and Hardesty took Mike home, and Skolaut drove Forrest back to headquarters, where he conducted a wildly inept interrogation, going on far too long himself, describing the girls' screams and telling him over and over again that he was there when they were killed, and even if he didn't kill any of them, he could've stopped what was going on—giving Forrest little time to offer anything other than the occasional "I don't believe I was there." But he came to when the cop informed him that no matter what he said or didn't say, he was going to be arrested. That being the case, Forrest said, he was ready to go home right now. "There's the goddamn door," Skolaut told him, and Forrest left. The interview had lasted twenty-five minutes.

A friend of mine who lived in Lockhart for a while used to take her car, a beater in constant need of repair, to Forrest Welborn's shop. She said he was a sweet guy and often refused to charge her. In the second of three Yogurt Shop episodes on *48 Hours,* aired in April 2000, after the arrests, Erin Moriarty interviewed Forrest on the front porch of a small frame house he was hoping to buy. The floorboards of the porch sagged and skipped; the support beams leaned; the place seemed little more than a shack. Obviously, he couldn't afford to work for anybody for free, but my friend was nice to him and he liked her, so he had. Like others, she couldn't imagine his being involved in any kind of violence. Some people to this day believe that Forrest Welborn was seriously damaged by this case, ruining whatever shot he had at a better life.

Knowing that photos of all four suspects would soon appear in local newspapers, the APD sent officers to interview some of the original eyewitnesses. Dearl Croft was shown three photo sheets with head shots of six young men, including Scott at seventeen, Springsteen at fifteen and Pierce at sixteen. While most of the other pictures were in black and white, Maurice's was in color. Croft couldn't make an identification.

When Lusella Jones was shown the same photos, she, too, was unable to positively finger anybody. But when asked which one looked *"most"* like the young man she'd seen in the yogurt shop on December 6, 1991, she chose photo number five—Maurice Pierce—on the first sheet. Not a bad response to take to the grand jury, although far less conclusive than what the APD and the DA's office were hoping for.

There was also the matter of Maurice's eyes, which were a memorable icy blue. In the lineup photo, his eyes are dark and dull and his photo has been cropped close to his face, leaving his hair color a mystery. A dark band around his forehead is presumably from a cap, but it might seem like his hair. When questioned on the witness stand, Lusella Jones will say that for her skin coloring was the best way to determine identity. During her original report in 1992, she thought that one boy might be Latino, but maybe not. Dark, at any rate.

Out of respect, John Neff called John Jones before the story broke. Assuming that the arrests were the natural follow-up to the work he'd done, Jones congratulated him.

Friday, October 1, the *Statesman*'s page-one headline made it official: ARRESTS LIKELY IN YOGURT SHOP KILLINGS: POLICE HAVE SUSPECTS IN 1991 DEATHS OF 4 TEENS. No names were given, but it was reported that two of the four had confessed, that another had been questioned shortly after the murders, that none currently lived in Austin. According to a "high-ranking law enforcement official" who spoke to the paper on condition of anonymity, they hadn't made arrests before now because "you don't want to solve just part of the case. We knew if we had arrested two of them right away, the other two would clam up. We have to bring all four to justice." As for the suspect who'd been questioned in 1991, that tip "wasn't taken as far as it could have been."

Jones's mood darkened. He couldn't help but take personally the implication that he'd somehow let Maurice Pierce off the hook.

Four days later, on October 5, Paul Johnson wrote up separate affidavits, in which he swore he had good reason to believe and did believe that each of these four men had committed the offense of felony and capital murder. He took the documents to 167th District Court judge Mike Lynch, who read his brief descriptions of the suspects' involvement in the crimes and decided there indeed was sufficient probable cause to issue arrest warrants to Robert Burns Springsteen IV, Michael James Scott, Maurice Earl Pierce and Forrest Brook Welborn on four counts of capital murder during the commission of a robbery. Under Texas law, prosecutors aren't required to offer bail to adults accused of a capital crime, so none was set for Springsteen and Scott. To ensure their legal rights, Lynch appointed attorneys to represent them.

As for Pierce and Welborn, because they were sixteen and fifteen at the time of the murders, their affidavits were delivered to 98th District Court judge Jeanne Meurer, who specialized in juvenile and family law. She would appoint counsel as well as set bail and the starting date of a certification hearing to determine whether probable cause existed to justify waiving her jurisdiction in this juvenile case, thus sending these two into the adult system. The "cert" hearing would include witness testimony and arguments by both sides, at the end of which the judge herself would decide what would happen next.

O n Wednesday, October 6, the four men were arrested in a coordinated sweep: Scott just after he arrived at his storage space in South Austin; Springsteen at his home in Charleston; Pierce on his way to work; Welborn at the auto-repair shop. That afternoon, local television stations interrupted regular programming to show live footage of the four men being transported to jail. The coverage began, as usual, with the WHO KILLED THESE GIRLS? billboard. In a brief press conference, Ronnie Earle announced the arrests and Chief Stan Knee praised the persistence of the investigators who had brought to justice "four individuals for the brutal murder of four little girls." When his turn came, Mayor Kirk Watson appealed to a familiar sentiment. "On December 6, 1991," he said, "we, as a city, lost our innocence. Today, we regain our confidence." This prompted Jim Sawyer to call him later that day. "What happened," Sawyer asked, "to innocent until proven guilty?"

All of them handcuffed and shackled, Scott was taken to the Travis County jail, Springsteen to the South Central Regional Detention Center just outside Charleston, Welborn and Pierce to the Gardner-Betts Juvenile Detention Center. The names of the two younger defendants weren't released, but when they arrived that afternoon, the courtroom was packed.

Welborn sported a droopy mustache, his brown hair hanging to his shoulders, his blue eyes brimming. His sister, mother and father were there. When Forrest heard the state ask the judge to set bail at five million dollars, he covered his face with a towel and wept. Maurice Pierce wore jeans and a white T-shirt, his light brown hair gelled in spikes. A muscle in his jaw twitched as he listened to the proceedings, and his bright eyes sometimes closed momentarily; otherwise, he let nothing show.

Described as a "diminutive woman" whose "reconnaissance eyes can lock into a target and search the soul," no-nonsense Judge Jeanne Meurer altered the bail prices: one and a half million for Pierce, one million for Welborn. When transferred from the Juvenile Detention Center to jail, each covered his head. After making dark remarks about suicide, Welborn was put on immediate "fire watch." To be on the safe side, Meurer also ordered psychiatric examinations for both.

Barbara Suraci, now Barbara Ayres-Wilson, attended the hearing with her new husband, Manley Wilson; so did Pam and Bob Ayers. Having sold her house and moved to Oregon, Maria Thomas didn't make it back to Austin in time, but Eliza's father was there. In a statement to Erin Moriarty, Pam Ayers expressed her surprise and radiant pleasure at this development, "the last thing on earth we were expecting." Bob Ayers said he hoped they had the right guys. Barbara Ayres-Wilson dreaded revisiting December 6, 1991, and discovering exactly how horrible the girls' ordeal had been. The questions she'd been asking herself—Were they afraid? Did they know they were going to die? Were Jennifer and Sarah close to each other when they were killed?—would now be answered, and she wondered if she was ready. So did the other parents.

The front page of the October 7 *Statesman* was top-to-bottom Yogurt Shop. One story featured profiles of the four "unremarkable" young men who'd been arrested; and people who'd known them in high school expressed shock. In newspaper and television reports, all four were characterized as dropouts and their lives chronicled from childhood through broken families, failed classes, minor crimes, marriages, low-paying jobs. Yearbook photos accompanied the stories. Austinites read the details and studied the faces, then read the stories again. A former McCallum student, a young woman who gave her name as Janet, said the boys did do a lot of roaming and hanging out back then but were never violent. Mike was the clown, the cutup, always trying to make people laugh. Rob was an oddball who insisted on speaking his mind. Maurice had the car. Forrest was the quiet one.

A week after the arrests, twenty-two-year-old Amanda Statham would show up at the APD headquarters to inform Homicide that back in 1991 or '92 her friend Mike Scott had not only told her he'd committed the murders but also showed her, her sister Sarah Adair and her mom the gun he'd used. Although Mike was the sweetest guy she knew, he'd said they'd shot the girls and chopped off their heads and feet and left them on the counter. Neither she nor her sister had gone to the police back then because their mother had told them not to, but now that Mike was under arrest . . .

When Maggie Halliday (the former PIB) heard the news, she walked off her waitressing job and didn't go back. You mean the guy who'd kept her from slashing her wrists in the backyard of that house on Woodrow when they'd all hung out back then? *That* Mike?

Although the state of West Virginia had never granted a defendant's case against extradition except on grounds of mistaken identity, David Bungard fought against sending Springsteen to Texas, arguing that because West Virginia wasn't a death-penalty state, the harshest penalty he should have to face was life without possibility of parole. But the Kanawha County prosecuting attorney had other ideas. "If I can't kill them here," he joked, "maybe I can help kill them in Texas." After a couple days' consideration, Circuit Court Judge Charles King ruled against Springsteen, and on November 18—handcuffed, shackled, still dressed in his own clothes—he was flown by chartered jet to Austin, along with an APD officer, a Travis County ADA and, of course, Chuck Meyer.

All four boys were home again and nobody but nobody was not noticing. Among those paying attention was Will Sheff, lead singer of an Austin rock band called Okkervil River. Sheff had a day job back then, doing clerical work. Hearing about the arrests, somebody had switched on an office television set.

"The people at work," he recalled, "were watching the suspects of the Yogurt Shop Murders and they were just straining to see the evil in their faces. But evil don't look like anything."

A year or so later, Sheff wrote "Westfall," a mandolin-driven song about a boy who murdered a girl, which became known for its refrain:

> *Evil don't look like anything.*
> *Evil don't look like anything.*
> *Evil don't look like anything.*

It became Okkervil's most popular tune.

In a different context, W. H. Auden said something similar:

> *Evil is unspectacular and always human,*
> *And shares our bed and eats at our own table . . .*

III

THE COURTS: LAW, SCIENCE, BLUNDERS AND LUCK

CERTIFICATION

Once Judge Meurer had read the Pierce and Welborn affidavits, she picked up her phone.

"I didn't live in Texas in 1991," says criminal defense attorney Guillermo Gonzalez. "I knew nothing about the Yogurt Shop Murders." Without providing a reason, the judge told Gonzalez she needed him. And when he said he already had too many commitments, "all she said was, 'Be in my chambers this afternoon at three.' And that"—he shrugs—"was that."

In the landmark, unanimous 1963 decision *Gideon v. Wainwright,* the Supreme Court ruled that state courts were required under the Fourteenth Amendment to provide counsel in criminal cases for defendants who couldn't afford their own attorneys, but the implementation of this ruling was left to the states. In Texas, some counties employ public defenders, while most, including Travis, use attorneys chosen by the judge and paid, if modestly, by the county. In splashy cases, judges often appoint hotshot lawyers because of the inevitable press coverage and notoriety, but it's an iffy deal for popular attorneys. For a capital case—which can take years—in Travis County, the maximum pay for a lead defense attorney is fifty thousand dollars. "If you want to know the value Travis County places on a life," one anti-death-penalty lawyer says, "it's fifty grand."

When Gonzalez and another defense attorney, Robert Icenhauer-Ramirez, arrived in Meurer's office, she held out two affidavits, one in each hand. "Choose," she said.

Gonzalez got Pierce, and Icenhauer-Ramirez landed Welborn.

For the prosecution, Yogurt Shop belonged unreservedly to Ronnie Earle's favorite death-penalty prosecutor, ADA Robert Smith, but he was busily involved with another capital case and therefore his colleague Howard "Buddy" Meyer would work the juvenile courtroom.

Within days of the appointments, Meurer granted the attorneys' request for a bail-reduction hearing, at which Ron Lara argued against lowering the amount because the defendants were flight risks. In rebuttal, Welborn's mother described her son's attachment to home and his job, his plan to buy a house for himself and his child and his family's desire to raise the one million dollars to bond him out. Kimberli Pierce then spoke of Maurice's strong family ties and pointed out that even after the police warned him he would be arrested, he stayed put. "Innocent people don't run," she insisted. In closing, defense attorneys cited two other capital cases with bail set at $250,000.

After a brief break, the judge agreed to reduce Pierce's bond to $750,000 and Welborn's to $375,000. The cert hearing itself would begin within thirty to sixty days and would last between ten days and three weeks. Sessions would not be held on the anniversary of the murders or the day after. In a bold move, Meurer ordered the state to make available to both defense teams the thirty-three boxes of evidentiary material the APD had gathered over the past eight years, a decision the DA's office ardently opposed. Prosecutors everywhere fight like crazy to hold on to whatever they can, dishing out to the defense only what they must. But they can't keep everything. The Supreme Court's 1963 *Brady v. Maryland* decision ruled that to satisfy the Fourteenth Amendment due-process mandate, the state was required to hand over to the defense any evidence that might prove exculpatory to its client. And a year later, in 2000, federal courts authorized a pretrial period of what's called "discovery," in which prosecution and defense exchange raw evidence, including witness lists, crime-scene evidence, autopsies, DNA and ballistics reports.

Once the judge banged her gavel, bailiffs escorted Pierce and Welborn back to jail.

Five weeks later, Judge Meurer called the cert hearing to order and stated its purpose: to decide if she should waive her jurisdiction and allow the case to be reassigned to the adult system for trial. Since both defendants were minors at the time of the murders and hadn't been indicted by the time they turned eighteen, Texas law limited her to two options: certify them as adults or set them free. This was not a trial. Meurer's job was to respond to a single question: Is it more likely than not that the young men committed the crime they were accused of?

Buddy Meyer opened the state's case, citing the confessions by Michael Scott and Robert Springsteen, in which Pierce and Welborn had been named as coconspirators. The families of the girls sat side by side across the front row on the prosecution side, often holding hands, sometimes linking arms. *48 Hours* had sent a cameraman and reporter. During a break, Bob Ayers told the press he didn't think victims' families should have to go through a certification hearing at all. "If you're grown-up enough to pull the trigger," he said, "you're grown-up enough to stand trial."

The Ayerses liked to dress in costume: Bob in cowboy gear, complete with aviator sunglasses, large hat, tight jeans, boots, wide western belt and pearl-snap shirt. Pam often went western as well, but for opening day she'd chosen a cropped, wide-shouldered red jacket with braided gold frogs across the front that wrapped around shiny brass buttons, drum major–style. Now that arrests had been made, the Ayerses were moving closer to Austin from their place near Blanco. The trials would be lengthy, and they intended to miss nothing.

Barbara Ayres-Wilson looked snazzy as ever, meticulously coiffed and made-up. She says she's a little embarrassed about her behavior back then, dressing for the camera and rehearsing sound bites before leaving the house. But the girls needed a spokesperson, and if she was going to take on that responsibility, she wanted to be ready.

Maria Thomas's wildly shorn hair looked barely combed, and behind dark-rimmed granny glasses her expression was clamped and tight, giving her a madwoman aspect, furious on the one hand, fragile and crumbling on the other. Eliza's little sister, Sonora, previously always in the background, had accompanied her from Oregon.

On the opposite side of the aisle, the Welborn and Pierce families sat apart.

In their opening statements, Gonzalez and Icenhauer-Ramirez accused the APD of conducting a witch hunt in pursuit of Mike Scott and Rob Springsteen and then linking the statements they'd wrung from them to their clients. Aside from that, the state's case depended on testimony from "undependable sources," with no forensic evidence. Icenhauer-Ramirez said that, as a result of poor police work, sitting next to him was an innocent man who risked having his very life and liberty stolen away.

The downside for the state was that in order to get what it wanted, it had to reveal a healthy chunk of its case to the defense, the families, the city and the media. Pieces of the videotaped confessions would be shown to the public for the first time. Hold-back information would become common knowledge. If the APD didn't, in fact, have the right guys, the prosecution was obviously cooked.

Hoping to seal the fate of all four men, Detective Paul Johnson resubmitted Pierce's .22 to the ATF ballistics lab without telling the DA.

As his first witness, Meyer called Manuel Fuentes to read Mike Scott's written statement, after which Gonzalez—on cross-examination—asked why the witness had failed to ask Scott about the discrepancies between this and his videotaped confession. He actually hadn't seen the tapes, Fuentes had to admit, and knew little about what the accused had said other than what Johnson and Lara had told him.

Other witnesses for the prosecution—Merrill, Lara, Hardesty, Johnson—provided narration for the tapes, which a technician played in stop-and-start fashion. Between the clips, each one lasting ten or fifteen minutes, a cop would testify. Merrill—who sat in the box like a bull about to charge, all readiness and forward motion, his white shirt strained against his thick belly—proved to be a good witness. Calm, patient, he didn't fluster or turn snarky. If as tetchy as most cops, he knew how to hide it. When asked why Scott's first statements conflicted with ones he gave later, Merrill simply said the early ones weren't the truth and that to get the real story they'd had to prod him to dig deeper inside himself. For instance, Scott said he'd seen Robert Springsteen raping a girl in the ICBY office, though everybody knew firefighters had found the office locked and undisturbed, the keys in place on the cash register. Leading Mike to the truth took time. But what he and the other cops were sure of was that both Scott and Springsteen *knew* what happened, *knew* they were there, *knew* what they'd done. They'd buried the memories, which sometimes happened. A suspect comes up with inaccuracies and maybe isn't exactly *lying,* but definitely isn't telling the truth. When Gonzalez asked if Maurice Pierce was the main target of their investigation even though he'd confessed to nothing, Merrill simply said, "Correct." From the get-go? Yes.

After watching the first run of video clips, Bob Ayers told a television reporter, "I thought I had prepared for the worst. I didn't come close." Barbara Ayres-Wilson called the experience a kind of persecution. At the end of the first day, she thought, "My God, it's only day one and we're not even in trial yet." Ayers also spoke of the years they'd waited: "We've put this out of our minds for so long. Now we need to get through the certification and get some indictments. We're ready to go to trial."

On cross, Icenhauer-Ramirez grilled Hardesty for hours, ripping into the APD's willingness to accept only the admissions that fit its conjectures. Paul Johnson testified about reopening the Maurice Pierce tips file. When asked by the state about Maurice's .22, he neglected to mention the ballistics tests he'd just run, which had come back from the lab with the same findings: probably not the murder weapon.

On December 1, the state rested its case.

Defense re-called Hardesty and then Merrill. During a long, sometimes tedious direct examination, they dismantled the prosecutorial theory of the boys' Friday-night rape and murder spree, capped off with a Saturday-morning theft of a Pathfinder and a victory-lap ride to San Antonio, producing evidence that the car had been stolen sometime after Town North Nissan closed at eight o'clock on *Saturday* night, almost twenty-four hours after the murders. When faced with this mistake, the intransigent Hardesty refused to back down.

In one significant moment, when the defense played undecipherable clips from the Springsteen video and Merrill started to read from the transcript they'd put together, Meurer stopped him to say she was "deeply concerned with having a transcript based on somebody typing out what they *think* they heard." She also scolded the state for continually withholding exculpatory material from the defense, violating rules of discovery. Her opinions on these matters varied considerably from District Court Judge Mike Lynch's.

On December 8, when the state was asked to present its closing argument, Buddy Meyer reminded the judge that evidence from the crime scene indicated that the gun found on Maurice Pierce at Northcross Mall was "the .22-caliber weapon that had been used in the offenses." This, of course, had never been confirmed by any firearms analysis, and there had been quite a few, but even ADA Meyer hadn't been told about the most recent one.

On December 9, as the families of the murdered girls stood holding hands across the front row, Judge Meurer announced that she had found probable cause to believe that Maurice Pierce and Forrest Welborn had committed the offenses alleged by the state. She would therefore remand them to the adult system, where the charges against them—four counts of capital murder—would be sent to the grand jury for possible indictment. Because they were minors at the time of the crime, they would not be eligible for the death penalty. With a 10 percent deposit of the total bail amount, she would allow the defendants to be released into the custody of their families.

Maurice Pierce's eyes rolled up, Welborn hung his head and wept. Court was adjourned.

"We've crossed one hurdle," said a beaming Pam Ayers. "Now we're getting ready to step over another one." Her husband, who alone among the victims' families occasionally entertained the possibility of doubt, said he just hoped the system worked. Sonora Thomas talked about the eight years they'd waited. In her mind, she said, it was almost like it hadn't happened. "I mean, if there's no criminal then there's no crime, right?"

Forrest Welborn's mother said if this was all the evidence the APD had, she couldn't imagine her son would be convicted. The next day, Welborn's aunt emptied out her pension fund to come up with the $37,500 required to bond him out. Escorted by his father and his sister, India, a tearful Forrest left the jail. "It was hard for him," India told the press, "being in there and being innocent." But she was glad he was certified as an adult so he could now clear his name. Gonzalez—who in his closing statement said he had no doubt that Springsteen and Scott were guilty and had sought to help themselves by fingering his client as the ringleader—had an unpleasant task ahead: If Pierce was indicted along with the other two, he'd have to make some apologies to their attorneys for casting blame on their clients.

The DA's office wasn't happy with Meurer about the 10 percent allowance, and ADA Rosemary Lehmberg said they preferred that both young men remain in jail.

Judge Meurer had the file boxes of evidence shipped from her jury room to Judge Lynch. Because his chambers were small and somewhat accessible, he then had the files sent to his court reporter Jim King's office, where thirty-three brown cardboard boxes marked "YSM" in black Sharpie were stacked against a wall.

O n November 24, Rob Springsteen's appointed attorney, Berkley "Berk" Bettis, had asked for an "examining trial" for his client on December 1, but ADA Robert Smith quickly requested a thirty-day postponement due to his schedule. In an examining trial, a jailed but unindicted suspect comes before a magistrate, who, after hearing accusatory evidence, decides whether or not to release the suspect pending the grand jury's decision. Bettis's move was strategic: If his request was granted, the DA's office would be forced to reveal much more of its case than it wanted to. The county official compromised, setting the procedure for December 15. In the meantime, Bettis told the press, "Mr. Springsteen is not guilty and you may quote me on that. The sooner we get this case into court and ready for trial, the better."

On December 14—remembering the 1966 Supreme Court decision in *Sam Sheppard v. Maxwell,* which temporarily set aside Sheppard's conviction for the murder of his wife because of the "carnival atmosphere of the trial"—Mike Lynch signed a gag order prohibiting comment on Yogurt Shop by anyone associated with the case or the trial. A few hours later, Ronnie Earle, flanked by the victims' families, announced the grand jury indictment of Robert Burns Springsteen IV for capital murder, thus jumping the examining trial by one day. Two weeks later, the same grand jury indicted Michael James Scott and Maurice Earl Pierce on the same charge but refused to indict Forrest Brook Welborn. Determined to reel in his youngest suspect, Earle received permission to extend the grand jury term by another ninety days so it could reconsider this decision. In response, Robert Icenhauer-Ramirez invited prosecutors to his office to question Welborn. After three hours they left, apparently having learned nothing useful. Erin Moriarty was also given permission to interview Welborn. Shackled, wearing a dark blue prison jumpsuit, his dark hair streaming around his face and reaching well below his shoulders, he looked straight into the camera and protested his innocence. He wasn't there, he said, he knew nothing about those murders, and as for his friends, "I can't see them doing anything like that."

When Mike Scott's family learned the identity of the attorney Lynch had appointed, they protested. So the judge came up with another name, and when that one didn't meet with their approval, yet another. In the end, the family put some money together and called a lawyer they'd heard about—Pedro Antonio "Tony" Diaz from South Texas, who, having been suspended from the bar, was extremely available. The family couldn't pay much, but Diaz was known primarily as a civil rights litigator and Yogurt Shop was his shot at big-time redemption and fame, so he quickly signed on.

Separated in county jail, each living in holding tanks that housed four to eight inmates, Springsteen, Pierce and Scott made friends, ate bad food, shooed off rats. The DA's office had planted audio-recording devices in case they said anything incriminating. Pierce, for instance, would stand in line many times a day to make phone calls home, all of which were duly taped. Meanwhile, Welborn—now the father of two small children—went back to fixing cars. Awaiting the grand jury's decision, he got a tattoo, and then another. In the coming years he would become a ready canvas for the skin artist's needle.

Indicted first, Springsteen would be tried first, which makes sense. But the defense lawyers had other ideas. Garcia and Diaz think that because Scott's confession was problematic, Robert Smith thought Springsteen would be easier to prosecute and that once they'd gotten the verdict they were after, the next jury would be more likely to cave as well. Sawyer, on the other hand, thinks Smith knew from the beginning he'd offer a sweet deal to the first defendant to come to trial and that Springsteen's lawyers were more likely than Scott's to convince him to take it. In any case, Garcia was surprised by the decision, Diaz was disappointed, Sawyer liked the idea and Robert Smith isn't saying. Although the codefendants would be tried separately, defense attorneys for the three young men began working together immediately, discussing expert witnesses and preparing to push for speedy trials.

In late December, when Jim Sawyer asked to be on the Springsteen team, Berk Bettis welcomed the help. He knew Sawyer well and he couldn't really afford to devote the kind of time a capital case demanded, especially this one. In addition, the Texas criminal code required that in a capital case, an indigent defendant should receive counsel from two attorneys; Lynch authorized the funds and approved the appointment.

As for Tony Diaz, it didn't take him long to realize how unqualified he was to run a death-sentence defense, so within a year he would convince the Scott family to dig up enough money to hire Dexter Gilford, a respected criminal defense attorney, as cocounsel.

Christmas came and went. The families of the murdered girls made plans, as did the arrested boys' families. None of them could have predicted how many tedious and painful months would pass before Judge Lynch gaveled the court to order in the first of many pretrials. The *Statesman* and the *Austin Chronicle* often commented on the thinness of the state's case, the lack of evidence, the bungled investigation, while the general consensus among citizens remained constant: *They confessed, so let's get on with it.*

As the twentieth century came to an end and the world awaited apocalyptic technological snafus, Austin defense lawyers and prosecutors readied themselves for what was about to happen. And in the jury trials, four men will play leading roles: the judge, the lead defense attorneys and the lead prosecutor. Many others participated, but these extravagantly dissimilar men worked the main controls, called the shots and created the inevitable theater at the heart of every criminal trial, often as powerful an influence on a jury as the evidence itself. As Jim Sawyer once commented, "A trial is stagecraft, pure and simple."

THE JUDGE

During *Scott,* for the first time in his nine years on the bench, Mike Lynch kept a journal. "I am sitting in court in the trial of State v. Michael Scott," he began, "a capital murder case where the state is seeking the death penalty. . . . This makes the fifth death penalty case I've been involved in over the last five years. . . ." And he chronicled the prior four, ending with *Saldana,* which had commenced four months *after* he was asked to sign arrest warrants for Pierce, Springsteen and Scott. After detailing the crime in a few lines, calling it "one of Austin's most infamous and heinous crimes," he mentioned the all-out press coverage and some of the reasons the case had remained unsolved for so many years. Then he jumped to the arrests. "The three suspects," he wrote, "were indicted in late December of 1999, officially beginning an arduous and painful, not to mention lengthy, trip through the criminal justice system for everyone involved. Over 2½ years into the process, we are in trial on the second suspect, and there is no end in sight when remaining trials and appeals, etc. are considered." He ended that paragraph with a blunt statement: "No physical evidence has ever connected these defendants to the crime."

Fifty-two when he signed those affidavits, Mike Lynch kept fiercely fit by playing racquetball, tennis, softball and basketball, and also by working out at a boxing gym. "I used to play racquetball with him," one lawyer told me. "I'd look back when he was about to serve and he had this furious look on his face. We were friends, but for him winning was everything."

When he could get away, Lynch traveled widely to hunt fowl not found in Texas, and like fellow Arkansan Bill Clinton, he preferred to go by the short version of his given name. Nobody had ever called him Michael until he went to the first grade and the teacher asked him to spell his proper name, but he got it wrong—an embarrassment he has never forgotten. When he ran for the judgeship, he used the name everybody knew. On the bench and off, he's plain Mike.

His career had traveled a restless path. A National Merit Scholar, after graduating from Amherst, he taught high school history and government in East Texas for a year and then, to avoid military service, went to law school at UT Austin. By 1974, during the era longtime residents consider the city's salad days, he was interning for a group of left-leaning defense lawyers. When his apprenticeship ended, he teamed up with four friends in a criminal law firm and stayed there off and on for nine years, until twitchiness hit him again and he sold his share of the partnership and zoomed off on his motorcycle for a solo cross-country trip. Returning to the law after a couple of years, Lynch switched his field of advocacy, working for the state in the attorney general's office and then in the Travis County DA's office, where he headed up a team investigating government corruption and white-collar crime. During those years, he became a colleague of Assistant DA Robert Smith, who would act as chief prosecutor in every capital case tried in his courtroom, including *Springsteen* and *Scott*. Lynch swears their connection was not close, though others think differently. Nobody has ever accused him of collusion, but some say their friendship—for God's sake, they played on the same basketball team, a lawyer told me—might have clouded his judgment.

In a hand closer to print than cursive, Lynch wrote in his journal during breaks and the showing of interrogation videotapes—which he'd already seen—or at lunch and on weekends, filling most of every schoolboy-lined page with general observations about the law, his jurors, the death penalty and the challenges of judgeship. On the death penalty, which he upheld, as the law required, he wrote that once the state gets into the "killing business," the decisions it has to make—execute minors but not mentally retarded defendants, or the other way around?—are of necessity arbitrary and sometimes even capricious and discriminatory. In the end, he wrote, capital punishment doesn't work.

He'd never kept a journal before and isn't sure why he did during Yogurt Shop. Maybe simply age, the need to reflect. There was also his longtime connection to the case: He had read about the murders on the very day he put the finishing touches on a speech announcing his candidacy for district judge. (When asked if, considering that coincidence, he believed in fate, he will only say, "I didn't used to.") And there was its size and thrilling complexity, and the long list of rulings he'd have to make, some of which had a shot at eventually reaching the U.S. Supreme Court. If that were to happen, he'd be glad he'd written things down. If anything becomes clear from reading these pages, it's that he wasn't keeping notes just for himself.

Describing the emotionally intense atmosphere that infected any death-penalty case and the stress that ran higher on both sides than "during your normal robbery, rape or even murder case," he admitted that while trying to "maintain a calm, steady demeanor both on and off the bench," he'd be lying if he said he didn't feel pressure "fueled by the fear of a mistake, a gaffe or a forgotten requirement that might jeopardize the process." This stress resulted in a "compulsive need to prepare, prepare, anticipate, anticipate . . . the need to constantly deal with the problems, real and imagined, of the trial lawyers as their intensity and animosity for each other grows as the trial nears; the difficult and time-consuming process of researching, analyzing and producing written or oral orders on a myriad of legal issues, from simple to extremely complex."

Within courthouse circles, Lynch was considered by most insiders—not all—to be fair and compassionate. He was also known for his ability to move his docket along, one of many reasons the lengthiness of Yogurt Shop especially aggravated him. Taken at face value, the journal does much to rescue Lynch's reputation from legal and journalistic criticism.

"Don't get me wrong," Carlos Garcia told me. "Lynch is a good judge. But he fucked up on Yogurt Shop. No question."

SAWYER

Springsteen's lead attorney, Joe James Sawyer, was born in England and is proud of his immigrant status—his father from Mexico, his mother a Brit. He grew up in San Antonio, the eldest of four boys. After serving in Vietnam as a Green Beret paratrooper, he thought he might like either to write for the movies or to go to law school, and though the movies lost out, he still thinks about writing screenplays.

When asked to describe himself, Jim Sawyer does so with a big smile, flashing his perfect teeth: arrogant, demanding, determined to win. Known as the kind of attorney who will resort to whatever courtroom theatrics he thinks might help his client, he attracted a good bit of notice when in a shaken-baby case he banged a doll's head against the railing of the jury box to demonstrate how hard it is to dislodge a brain. Bettis, now his cocounsel, was better at preparation but less articulate on his feet and far less willing to engage in high jinks. "Berk doesn't have the ego I do," Sawyer proclaims with unabashed glee. As a courtroom performer, he's a natural. Literate, nicely tanned, he reads poetry, has a sexy burr in his voice and a movie-star smile, can quote Shakespeare, the Bible or Thorstein Veblen at will. A female prosecutor describes him as likable in "a sleazy, gangsterish kind of way." What you have to understand about Sawyer is that he knows *exactly* who he is and what he's up to and how to construct a narrative and then play it out to the hilt. Self-knowledge, a visceral love for the game and an especially keen memory partially explain his courtroom success. Plus, he's really smart, and so is his chief advisor, researcher and passionate life partner, lawyer Deirdre Darrouzet. When asked about his sources and strategy, Sawyer always gives Deirdre fulsome credit.

GARCIA

Carlos Garcia came late to Yogurt Shop. In early September 2001, after Springsteen had been convicted but before Lynch could get the next trial under way, the Texas legislature approved a statute requiring that in a capital case, one of the two attorneys assigned to represent an indigent defendant must be drawn from the short list of certified capital counsel—lawyers with substantial experience in defending clients who face a possible death sentence. Through no fault of the judge, Mike Scott was represented by Tony Diaz, a civil litigator with scant criminal experience, and Dexter Gilford, an attorney who was respected and articulate but hadn't made that list. But because his family was paying them, Scott didn't qualify as indigent, so the rule didn't apply. On the other hand, allowing Diaz to lead the defense all but guaranteed an appeal on grounds of ineffective counsel, and a potential reversal. Despite objections from the prosecution, Lynch chose to honor the statute anyway. "I never understood why he did it," Carlos Garcia told me many years later. "He didn't have to."

Forty-two at the time, a former prosecutor from a small town on the Texas-Mexico border, Garcia was so busy working on his third capital case that he hadn't paid much attention to Yogurt Shop. And he wasn't particularly interested in the job, given the stakes, the late start and his penchant for fastidious preparation. But he was a true believer when it came to the death penalty, and like all trial lawyers, he liked the hands-on tussle of adversarial law, so he agreed to take the case *if* the other two men yielded the lead position to him. To give him time to catch up, Lynch postponed the next hearing for two months; when they were used up and Carlos asked for more time, the judge postponed again. *Not ready* will become Carlos's mantra during the entirety of *Scott*—a motion for a 120-day continuance his most insistently recurring request.

In his early career, Garcia had focused on the pursuit of child sexual offenders. A round man with short legs and curly, prematurely gray hair, full-blooming cheeks and sparkling eyes, he seems—and is—authentically warm and engaging, but on the job he's all-out. "He may look like the Pillsbury Doughboy," a cop told me, "but Carlos can be tough. He can rile people up." When he took on *Scott,* he figured he'd be finished in no time. After all, his client had confessed; he'd plead him out, get a shorter sentence and dodge the death penalty. But after he talked to Gilford, read police reports, studied evidence photos, watched the videotapes and got hold of Johnson's PowerPoint presentation, he turned a corner. "Those boys had nothing to do with it," he says now, flipping his hand upward as if brushing an absurd idea away. "They were kids. Those girls would've laughed at them if they tried anything. Even if they *did* have a gun."

Garcia's an excellent attorney and a prodigious researcher, but if he's brought to trial before he's ready, his arguments can be diffuse and wordy. When Mike Lynch referred to Scott's lawyers as "anal-retentive on the law," he was mostly talking about Garcia, whose linguistic bypasses, intense attention to detail and curlicued style of questioning explain why the trial carried on for so long.

After the guilty verdict, Garcia kept working on Yogurt Shop. In 2009, after Scott's conviction had been overturned, a colleague sat in the courtroom of the 167th District Court and listened to him practice a new opening statement. Perfect, she called it, moving and precise, organized and finely tuned; perhaps the best she'd ever heard. Too bad nobody else got to hear it. *Scott* was dismissed before he had a chance to present it.

THE STILETTO

In contrast to both defense attorneys, the tall, lean, camera- and interview-shy Robert Smith seems to have channeled the actor Jimmy Stewart as he appeared in *Anatomy of a Murder:* calm, quiet, low-key, with a cutthroat intelligence he keeps under wraps, preferring to come across as your everyday ordinary citizen, just like the jurors he's addressing. In truth, insiders call him "the Stiletto" for his ability to anticipate defensive moves and quietly slice them to shreds. Outside the courtroom, he's a different guy entirely. A man of contradictory pleasures, he likes to skydive from airplanes in his spare time, doing cartwheels in the air at 180 miles an hour. There's also an unverified rumor that he has sometimes engaged in parkour, the practice of jumping from high places in free fall to the ground, using momentum and the redistribution of body weight to perform impossible body maneuvers and land unharmed. It's hard to know which version of Smith is authentic, especially when one defense lawyer describes him as "emotional" while a female colleague sums him up as hypocritical and delusional. Wears sunglasses all the time, she snaps. "Struts around as if women were falling over all around him." Mike Lynch calls his trial work "lethal." His partner in both Yogurt Shop trials, Darla Davis, will be his favorite death-penalty teammate, the tall and attractive, dark-haired, sharp-tongued woman whom detractors call simply "the Darla." Together, they are fierce. A third ADA, Efrain de la Fuente, will soon join them; when both cases are reversed, he will be the only one of the three to stay on.

From January through March of 2000, the lawyers continued to prepare. Trial dates would soon be set for Springsteen and Scott. Awaiting his turn, Pierce would spend the next three years in the county jail, despite his constitutional right to a speedy trial. Welborn kept busy at his shop.

Disappointment dogs us, however adamantly we demand answers. When a jury comes in with a guilty verdict, all we really know is that's how twelve people voted. As for not guilty, this might mean a lack of evidence or simply, as the British put it, "not proven." But for the families of murdered children, ambivalence is unacceptable. Once a guilty verdict has been reached, they inevitably speak of their relief, not just because a painful process has ended but also because the truth has been discovered, the perpetrator identified and justice finally served.

Trials matter, of course. Studying them gives us a better sense not necessarily of what happened but of what various intelligent, determined, passionate and committed men and women made of whatever evidence and relevant speculation they'd come up with. They don't, however, always provide what we really want. Yogurt Shop jurors did their job; so did the lawyers and the judge. But in the end, nobody was satisfied with how things turned out. Nobody at all.

PRETRIAL

Pretrial is discovery time, when prosecutors and defense counsel exchange information and the judge decides which evidence he'll allow to come before the jury and which he'll exclude. Since it sets the stage for what's to come, in many ways it's the most important part of a criminal trial. Because everything's on the line—strategy, tactics, overriding arguments and narrative line—the attorneys go for broke. To gain admittance of whatever evidence the police have gathered, a prosecutor will overload his stash to maximize his percentage and use any tricks he can think of to win the judge's approval. Mike Lynch says he usually allows about half of the state's grisly photographs into a murder trial. On their end, defense lawyers request witness lists, exculpatory material, raw evidence and money to call in expert witnesses; perhaps most important, they file motions to suppress at least some of the state's evidence and even—if for no other reason than to get the request on the record—the case itself.

Between March 30, 2000, and January 11, 2001, thirteen Yogurt Shop pretrials were held jointly, with all three indicted defendants and their counsel present. Within days of the first one, at least five issues of dispute had been established: the defense's access to evidentiary materials; forensics, including DNA testing, crime-scene processing and ballistics; the admission of confessions; alleged police and prosecutorial misconduct; the scientific analysis of fire. Rancorous arguments—"squabbles," Lynch will call them—will continue long after two of the defendants have been convicted and carted off to prison. Most remain unresolved.

The first major obstacle had to do with the matter of the file boxes. When Guillermo Gonzalez reminded the court that Judge Meurer had ruled that *all* documents should be copied for discovery use by *each* defense team, Lynch seemed to agree, until prosecutor Darla Davis informed him that the boxes contained some 55,000 pages of records, of which by the state's estimate only 12,000 were the "Brady" material—potentially exculpatory—they were required to hand over; everything else was their "case in chief"—the story they planned to sell to the jury—and not to be shared. Even the lower number gave Lynch pause, and he postponed his decision.

Springsteen's attorneys then filed a motion to suppress the state's only real evidence against their client: the audio- and videotapes of the "extended conversation" conducted by APD officers "within the bowels of the police department in Charleston, West Virginia." In his motion, Sawyer cited underhandedness and lies, the poor quality of the audiotape and the actions of both Charleston and Austin police to deliberately thwart the attempts by Springsteen's attorney to meet with him and advise him of his rights. David Bungard, the lawyer, and Eric Hodges, the policeman, were flown in from Charleston—the latter to testify that he'd said Rob had been given a Miranda warning when he hadn't, the former to describe his travails in the police station. The prosecution did score a point on cross-examination when Bungard was forced to admit he didn't know about the 1966 U.S. Supreme Court ruling that police weren't constitutionally required to inform a suspect that his lawyer was trying to see him.

Citing the Texas Code of Criminal Procedures, which states that confessions should be "freely and voluntarily made, without compulsion or persuasion" and without the respondent's will having become "overborne," Mike Scott's attorneys also filed a motion to suppress all statements made by their client, written, recorded or otherwise presented. Once he's on the case in January 2001, Garcia will cite lies, coercion, improprieties, misuse of the Reid Technique and wanton disregard for the truth. He will also display a prescription for Baclofen, a drug Mike was taking for back pain, which might have weakened his ability to effectively defend himself from their grilling.

Neither Sawyer nor Garcia expected their clients to be cut loose. They made these requests only to place them on the record as grounds for a future appeal and, possibly, outright dismissal. Judges get cranky when that happens, but lawyers do it anyway; they have to. As Sawyer explained, part of his job was "to remember that this record may be reviewed someday, beyond the scope and time of a jury trial." Gonzalez also asked for dismissal of the case against Maurice Pierce, citing a total lack of admissible evidence—an argument he would eventually win.

Lynch postponed these decisions as well, knowing that once he allowed Springsteen's and Scott's statements into their own trials, their attorneys would then ask for suppression of accusatory testimony by any nontestifying codefendant, no matter how it had been recorded, whether on videotape, on audiotape or by transcription. A far trickier matter.

To avoid hearsay allegations from a nontestifying witness, the Sixth Amendment of the U.S. Constitution guarantees its citizens the right to confront—cross-examine—an accuser in court. In a 1999 ruling (*Lilly v. Virginia*), the Supreme Court showed its preference for a strict interpretation of this clause by ruling in favor of the petitioner, whose brother's incriminating statement to the police had been read at his trial. The vote wasn't unanimous, but the powerhouse justice Antonin Scalia—who'd turned this issue into a pet cause from which he would never back down—marshaled his troops and snagged the victory.

But lead prosecutor Smith had come up with a risky strategy that, if allowed, would enable him and his team to skirt the ruling. If they edited a codefendant's statement so it corroborated the defendant's confession without accusing him of anything, couldn't the jury then compare the two versions and determine on its own whether there were enough points of similarity to warrant a conviction? To accomplish this, they would omit—redact, in legal terminology—the defendant's name and all significant pronouns from the statement.

Again, Lynch postponed his decision.

Next up, murder weapons. As would soon become apparent, since early 1999, Paul Johnson had subjected Maurice Pierce's gun to ballistics testing at least three times—once that January, then in early November and again in May 2000. While DPS test results deemed the projectiles too damaged to be compared, ATF agents offered a more conclusive report: When fired into a telephone book, the bullets from Pierce's pistol retained impressions *distinctly different* from those recovered from the girls' bodies. In other words, this .22 was almost certainly *not* the murder weapon. Because of the difficulty of correctly analyzing the spiral grooves inside the barrel of a particular gun, "almost certainly not" is the most positive statement a ballistics expert will make. Other weaponry gurus would simply say it just ain't the right gun.

After Johnson acknowledged his mistake in failing to inform the DA's office of the most recent tests, Gonzalez went before Lynch to demand bail reduction for Maurice Pierce on the grounds that when Meurer set his bail, she didn't know about those tests; further, in his closing statement Buddy Meyer had unconditionally claimed evidence had *proved* that Maurice's gun was used on the girls. When asked on cross-examination why he hadn't shared the test results with the DA, Johnson again admitted his mistake and said he guessed he somehow forgot to mention it.

"Forgot?" Gonzalez repeated. But wasn't he known as an especially meticulous investigator?

"Honest mistake," said Buddy Meyer, stepping in.

Lynch cut Pierce's bail by less than 10 percent, to $700,000. The next day, on May 11, 2000, a local television station cited the DPS and ATF ballistics reports on its six o'clock and late-night broadcasts. Three days later, the same story ran in the *Statesman* with a direct quote from the federal agent who'd conducted the tests. How did the press get the information? Obviously, the prosecution hotly charged, Lynch's gag order had been violated, and they promptly studied how to turn this allegation to their advantage.

Meanwhile, to draw attention from Johnson's gaffe, the DA's office asked for and received permission from the city to hire, at taxpayers' expense, speedboats equipped with side-scan sonar so the DPS Dive Recovery Team could search under the Loop 360 bridge over Lake Austin for the missing second gun, which Mike Scott *thought* Rob Springsteen *might* have tossed into a lake from one high bridge or another. Of course, Mike thought the gun was a .38, not a .380, and even if somebody definitively identified *which* bridge, the chance of actually finding the weapon ran from slim to none. During the 1991 Christmas Flood, five sluices had been opened three times a day, moving enough silty water through Lake Austin to make it flow like the Mississippi. Since then, five more storms had flushed it out as well.

After hauling up bed frames, grocery carts, shoes and car parts, the boats were trailered back to Florida, where they'd come from, and all ballistics reports were handed over to the defense.

Those lawyers also requested recordings or transcripts of all other Yogurt Shop confessions, as well as audiotapes of their clients' jailhouse conversations. For this, they needed money for an investigator and for expert witnesses on fire, false confessions and memory, not to mention a ballistics guy and a crime-scene reconstructor. They wanted to submit the state's DNA findings to their own lab. Arguing for a change of venue, Mike Scott's attorneys exhibited the video clip of Robert Merrill holding the muzzle of a gun to the back of their client's head. This request was denied, but the next day the *Statesman* ran a story headlined VIDEO COULD DAMAGE YOGURT SHOP CASE.

By the middle of May, Texans had begun steeling themselves for a blistering summer, yet for most of the state, June was unusually cool and a cold front had brought five inches of rain, which made for a bountiful crop of tomatoes and peaches. By then the prosecution had figured out how to benefit from the ballistics fiasco.

"You," a steaming Darla Davis told Lynch on May 21, "put us on our honor not to disclose information to reporters or anybody else." But the defense, she claimed, had clearly ignored his order and leaked the "non-results" to the TV station and the newspaper. And since there was no way of knowing *which* lawyers were responsible, they *all* should pay. The state then requested limited access to the thirty-three boxes, and no xeroxing; the files should remain in the DA's office. Defense attorneys or their officially registered representatives could ask for a particular box and then sit and take notes, page by page. There were carrels in the lobby of the office where they could work, so what was wrong with that?

Lynch doesn't like to talk about loneliness on the bench; there's no use in it. Occasionally, after handing down a ruling, he'll lean forward and ask, "Anything else you want me to decide?" Access to the boxes was a big one. After a long pause, he told Davis he'd issue his decision . . . soon.

The prosecution lurched ahead. Paul Johnson ordered another test of Maurice Pierce's gun, with the same results. The DPS issued a lab report concluding once again that no DNA left at the crime scene matched any of these four men. When the grand jury finally and definitively refused to indict him, Forrest Welborn was freed of all charges. One of those jurors, Diana Castaneda, requested a meeting with Lynch to talk about the conduct of the DA's office, especially during the Yogurt Shop proceedings. They were stingy with evidence, she claimed, and didn't provide the items they'd asked for. There was a rush to judgment. After thanking her, the judge ushered her from his chambers.

In late August, Lynch issued his ruling on Sawyer's motion to suppress Springsteen's videotaped confession: denied. He saw no evidence of coercion, given that the defendant had gone willingly to the Charleston Police Department's offices and remained there after being given several opportunities to leave. As for his interrogators' duplicity, the Supreme Court had sanctioned the use of "reasonable deception" to pry the truth from a suspect and had also ruled that police officers were not legally bound to allow a lawyer hired by a third party access to the suspect, even if the third party was family—decisions that the *Statesman* called major victories for the prosecution, after many setbacks. Lynch would issue the same ruling during *Scott,* citing the suspect's willingness to travel to the police station day after day, as well as his lack of interest in hiring an attorney.

Unquestionably, the prosecution was scoring points, but those gains didn't mean much if they couldn't nail Pierce. Ronnie Earle visited the other three defense teams to offer a deal to any codefendant who would testify against him. But the young men all said pretty much the same thing: They wouldn't admit to doing something they didn't do and, furthermore, had no intention of implicating a friend.

Welborn, when asked if he'd considered confessing to get the cops off his back: "No. I'd never lie about something like that."

Springsteen: "I got myself into this mess. I'll have to get myself out."

Scott: "How stupid do they think I am, not to take a deal if it was true?"

Garcia: "We told them, 'Look. There is no deal on the table.'"

———

Near the end of October, more than a year after the arrests, Lynch issued his decision on those thirty-three boxes and once again sided with the prosecution. No xeroxing. He had arranged to pay a maximum of $7,200 a month—$20 an hour for up to 360 hours— for representatives of all three defense teams to sit in the DA's office and make notes by hand. Once the two sides started bickering about details, Lynch asked a member of the sheriff's department to lock them all in a room until they hashed out a workable plan; after several hours they emerged with a schedule of discovery that was mutually acceptable.

But the defense had lost a big one. Attorney Alexandra Gauthier would soon begin her long relationship with Yogurt Shop as a researcher and intern. She would spend many hours in a cramped carrel in the DA's lobby, sitting in a stiff chair, going through material line by line and page by page, copying quotes, reports and diagrams. Before long, she'd develop carpal tunnel syndrome, her wrists simply worn-out.

In November, Ronnie Earle was reelected to his seventh term as Travis County DA, despite an unusual all-out Republican push, including billboards showing a mock Monopoly board with his face on a "Get Out of Jail Free" card. As the year ended, the coldest weather in years swept the state. Sleet, rain and even a little snow made for a dark and forbidding Christmas.

Every year, Barbara Ayres-Wilson buys artificial poinsettias to put on the girls' graves. She takes rags and a spray bottle of liquid cleanser to shine up the stones and the bench behind them. As 2000 neared its end, she and the other parents felt cautiously hopeful, even about Forrest. Surely the APD and the DA's office would figure out how to bring him back in.

FIRE

While lawyers split hairs, Paul Johnson kept busy trying to solve some nagging problems, starting with the discrepancy between Mike Scott's description of how the fire started—those cups and napkins thrown on the girls' bodies, sprayed with lighter fluid and lit with a Zippo—and the general agreement among arson experts that no accelerant had been used and that the fire had been set by igniting combustibles stored on the stainless-steel shelves.

Once again, he called on Marshall Littleton. But his old friend still declined to get involved. In the first place, he didn't feel altogether qualified; there were more experienced BATF experts in D.C. In addition, the modeling software didn't work in every situation. You fed the program with specifics—burn marks, size of room, height of ceiling, presence of windows or doors, heat of flames, duration and patterns of fire, whatever input you had—and it came up with what it considered appropriate data concerning the origin and cause. But if the model contradicted the prosecution's position, then where would they be?

When Johnson insisted that his help was essential, Littleton soon relented and, after a few tries, found a model that worked. Johnson then called Melvin Stahl and asked him to meet with them. Initially, Stahl wouldn't budge from his original analysis, but after hearing Littleton out, he either changed his mind or simply agreed to go along. In court he would testify that after recently examining the crime-scene photos for the first time—even though he'd taken most of them—he'd decided he'd been wrong. Clearly, he said, the fire had originated not on the shelves, as he'd once thought, but on the girls' bodies, as Mike Scott had claimed.

Nobody can say who persuaded Stahl to reverse himself, though the most likely candidates are Paul Johnson and Robert Smith. Most favor the cop. At any rate, this solved the DA's fire problem. Even Barbara Ayres-Wilson, who knew Stahl, felt bad for him. His testimony from the witness box, she said, destroyed him. You could see his face crumbling.

JURY SELECTION

SPRINGSTEEN

Lynch's plan was to call three hundred panelists from which to select a jury, yet on this issue both prosecution and defense agreed: The case was so notorious locally that they wanted him to call twice that many. Lynch concurred but made a bet with the lawyers that his estimate would suffice. After saying he hated to take the judge's money, Bettis shook on it—and eventually had to pay up.

To each group of panelists, Lynch made a general statement explaining reasonable doubt, the Fifth Amendment, our adversarial judicial system and the rules governing issuance of the death penalty. Then, after both sides made their opening remarks, each took turns conducting interviews. Among those in the courtroom that day—April 16, 2001—was Springsteen's wife, Robin, who told the *Statesman* her husband felt isolated in jail and had gained weight. He was, she said, "gentle and good" and had confessed only because he'd been drinking the night before and hadn't slept. But she didn't stick around for the trial; after a day or so, she went back to West Virginia, never to return, Sawyer says because Rob didn't want his family to make the trip.

Within fifteen days, after some two-hundred-odd panelists had been screened, a jury of seven men—including two alternates—and seven women had been seated. Ranging in age from late teens to middle age, two were African-American, three were Latino, the rest white.

Afterward in Lynch's chambers, Sawyer again pressed him to

allow other Yogurt Shop confessions into evidence, especially since many of them offered accurate details about the crime scene, including APD hold-back evidence, and the judge grudgingly promised to come up with a decision soon. But he warned Sawyer that every Tom, Dick and Harry who'd seen little green men at the yogurt shop would not be filing into his courtroom.

Sawyer agreed. No little green men.

The next day, *Springsteen* moved into its final pretrial phase. Called *in limine,* or "at the threshold," it offers attorneys a final opportunity to present motions. Once again the defense argued for suppression of Mike Scott's statement on the twofold grounds of hearsay and Sixth Amendment guarantees, though Lynch refused to rule on it until he'd heard the evidence and arguments, after "context" had been established. In postponing, the judge hampered both sides' ability to create a case, especially the defense's. But since this would be one of the biggest decisions of his career, and because he had the right to wait, he did.

On May 8, 2001, before a packed courtroom, Lynch swore in the *Springsteen* jury and issued his standard instructions. Jurors were not to talk to anybody about anything that happened in the courtroom or to *mingle* with people connected to Yogurt Shop. They shouldn't consult articles about it or read up on any laws or rules they didn't understand. Until they were discharged, everything they knew about this case should come solely from evidence presented in the courtroom. He also banned note-taking in the jury box.

SCOTT

Fourteen months later, on the day voir dire was set to begin in the second Yogurt Shop trial, Dexter Gilford filed an objection. The "racial array" of the panel, he charged, did not represent a fair cross section of the community as the law required. Mike Scott, of course, is white, but his defense team comprised two Mexican-Americans—Garcia and Diaz—and one African-American—Gilford—and this might have encouraged them to argue the point. More than likely, however, they were simply stalling for time, and when Lynch found no basis for the complaint, the defense dropped the objection, and two and a half weeks later, on August 8, 2002, a jury was seated: nine women and five men, two of them alternates. In his journal, Lynch called the *Scott* jury perhaps the most intelligent he'd ever had in his courtroom.

But Tony Diaz's unproductive tenure as Scott's lead attorney had forced Garcia and Gilford to start from scratch, so they had to scramble by working together every night and well into the morning, and the toll on their personal lives included health and marital issues. When Lynch denied their motion to suppress a summarized printout of Springsteen's videotaped statement, defense and prosecution cooperated to create a mutually acceptable redaction. By then Garcia had uttered the words *not ready* at least nine times, and when the judge asked if anyone objected to a day's postponement, Gilford weighed in as well to say their only concern was that it came up short by 119 days.

When he talks about Yogurt Shop today, Garcia still gets angry. "I hate this fucking case," he'll growl. "I hate talking about it." I don't think his anger will ever diminish, for one reason because he feels he and the other two lawyers did no better than an adequate job for Mike Scott and, for another, if there had been a retrial, he thinks they could've gotten him off. But mostly his anger stems from his unflinching belief that in order to win the case, the DA's office, especially Robert Smith, threw justice out the window.

In the courtroom, frustration sometimes got the best of him. During one of Scott's final pretrials, when he requested transcripts of the grand jury hearings and Lynch turned snarky, lecturing him on protocol, Garcia's response was equally caustic and imprudent: "This is your courtroom, and you know what you're doing." To which the judge replied, "There's been some doubt cast on that today." And when Garcia made yet another motion for continuance, Lynch grew even more impatient. "This case," he curtly explained, as if to an outsider, "was indicted December of 1999. Shortly thereafter we started joint pretrial hearings. We have covered squabbles that sounded more like a bunch of chickens in a chicken yard than it did lawyers in a courtroom arguing back and forth. . . . We've had three lawyers now on the case, some combination thereof, or four if you count the discovery lawyer, for over two years. There comes a time when you *just have to try the case.*"

Garcia countered with a request for a standing motion for continuance, to run through the entire trial. And after Lynch's instructions to the jury, Garcia objected to the note-taking ban, which necessitated yet another lengthy explanation from the judge. Higher courts had ruled that jurors' written notes must be collected by the bailiff before every break and at the end of each day and could not be shared among themselves or used during final deliberations. As Lynch saw it, note-taking didn't fulfill its intended purpose, so the jury should instead listen carefully, take mental notes and *remember* what had happened and what they thought about it.

But by then, Garcia had come up with another reason for delay, mistrial or, even better, dismissal.

JURY TRIALS

SPRINGSTEEN

An opening statement, Lynch explained to the jury, was opinion, not evidence. It represented a kind of table of contents for what each side thought the evidence would show. Jurors should remember that the system was adversarial, one story versus another, and he asked the defendant to rise so the trial could commence.

Asked to read the indictment, Smith stood. The case against the defendant was based on the grand jury's opinion that "on or about the sixth day of December, 1991, Robert Springsteen IV did intentionally cause the death of an individual, namely Amy Ayers, by shooting her with a firearm, a deadly weapon, and by strangling her with a ligature, a deadly weapon, while in the course of committing or attempting to commit the offense of burglary. Against the peace and dignity of the state."

And how did the defendant plead? "Not guilty, Your Honor."

Lynch again spoke to the jury: Because the state bore the burden of proving every element of its case beyond a reasonable doubt, it had both the right and the duty to speak first.

The Stiletto rose once more to continue.

"On Friday night, December 6th, 1991, two high school senior girls were working at the I Can't Believe It's Yogurt shop on West Anderson Lane here in Austin, Travis County, Texas. That Friday night it was scheduled to be closed by Jennifer Harbison and Eliza Thomas. They worked there after school and they were supposed to close that shop that night at eleven o'clock."

Prosecutors don't beat around the bush; they present their story without *maybes* or *perhapses*. After placing Eliza, Jennifer, Sarah and Amy at the ICBY shop, Smith then piled Springsteen, Pierce, Scott and Welborn in Pierce's car, first to assess the prospects at the shop and later that night, after it had closed, to enter it through the back door "for the purpose of robbing it." Because the DA had asked for a death sentence, this was important. According to the Texas Penal Code, a capital crime is one in which an act of intentional murder has been committed in the course of other felonies, including sexual assault and robbery.

Smith described the boys' surprise at finding four girls in the shop instead of two, then moved on to the crime itself. "The evidence will show you, ladies and gentlemen, that these four girls were herded to the back of the shop and they were robbed at gunpoint. And in the small, small confines of that back room, they were forced to take off all their clothes. Then they were bound with their hands behind their backs and then they were gagged with their own socks. And three of these girls, Sarah, Jennifer and Eliza, were killed. Shot execution-style—contact wound to the back of the head with a .22-caliber revolver." He then went on to describe the struggles and murder of Amy Ayers. After about an hour of this, he ended with a boilerplate prediction: "There is going to be no question, when you hear all of this evidence, that you are sitting in the courtroom with the man that killed Amy Ayers."

If Springsteen's lawyers were clear about anything, it was that if they were to elicit any sympathy at all for their client, they had to underscore their unqualified sympathy for the families of the murdered girls. And so Sawyer's opening also led off with the girls. "Your Honor, may it please the Court, counsel. I will not say good morning to you. That would be obscene. There is nothing good about morning when we begin the process of discussing the deaths of four young girls in the presence of the family and loved ones. And maybe the only thing to say in regard to that is"—quoting the New Testament—"'sufficient unto the day is the evil of the day.'"

He then addressed the overriding question from the defense point of view: "What went wrong? How is it that Robert Springsteen sits here having confessed to crimes that I believe he did not commit?" He criticized the lack of protocol and accepted standards in the preservation of the crime scene, spent a long time talking about the importance of fire as evidence and finished up with a flourish, telling the jury that in the end he could offer only one absolute regarding this case, which was that "there is not one shred of physical evidence to connect Mr. Springsteen to the commission of this crime and there was not before he was interviewed. . . . We have to let the evidence tell the story," he insisted, "not tell the evidence what happened."

Sawyer didn't use notes and he didn't put on his reading glasses. He, too, spoke for about an hour.

The state opened its case by calling Bob Ayers, who described his daughter, her cowgirl dreams and FFA activities and provided details of her plans for the evening of December 6. He recalled the last moment he and his wife saw her alive, and confirmed that the photograph Smith showed him was indeed of Amy. Smith handed it to the jurors, who passed it around. He then asked what Amy was wearing that night, what kind of underpants, jeans, boots and jacket. And what about the heart-shaped buckle from the missing belt, and did Ayers recognize the Jiminy Cricket tote bag? When Smith passed his witness, Sawyer declined the opportunity to cross-examine. He would ask no questions of the girls' families.

The prosecution was following standard procedure in a murder case, establishing chronology and "humanizing the victims." When Barbara Ayres-Wilson was called to the stand by Darla Davis, she spoke of her daughters' love of animals, sports and country music, then described her after-school meeting with Sarah, Jennifer's arrival, the call to Amy and the two sisters heading off together in the S-10. Davis then presented photographs: Jennifer in her graduation gown, smiling radiantly; Sarah in a sweater, a cross around her neck, shrimp earrings, those big, wide-set, skeptical eyes. Maria Thomas, in turn, described Eliza's love for her pig and her beat-up green VW, their visit to the barn and hers to the yogurt shop that night. The photograph Davis showed the jury was of a lustrous, smiling Eliza in a friend's Texas A&M dorm room, wearing a fuzzy white sweater, her dark hair falling in deep swirls around her face. Smith then returned to question James Thomas, after which de la Fuente questioned the Harbison girls' boyfriends—Sammy Buchanan and

Mike McCathern—as well as former security guard Dearl Croft. Prompted by Davis, Lusella Jones told the court that, in the APD's photo lineup, Maurice Pierce "most resembled" the scary young man she'd seen that night.

And so, before moving to the closing of the shop and the discovery of the bodies, the prosecutors set the stage, establishing the innocent, hopeful nature of the four girls and their activities before turning to the crime itself, beginning with the testimony of Troy Gay, who explained DWI patrols and then how he had driven toward Anderson Lane and seen the smoke, then the flames, then Jorge Barney, and then called the fire department. Urged on by Smith's quiet questions, he covered his every move and thought, eventually arriving at the moment when a firefighter came outside and said there were naked dead girls lying inside, in the muck. When Robert Smith asked for permission to project color photos of the crime scene onto a large video screen, he apologized for the graphic horror of what jurors and spectators were about to see. As Sawyer says, it was time to wave the bloody flag.

When asked which girl they had seen first, Gay replied, "The one body that was by itself, Amy Ayers." And as Smith projected photos of Amy—head resting on the flowered blouse, right arm torqued oddly under her body, as if she were reaching beyond her left shoulder, head turned, chin almost resting on her upper arm, then a close-up of her face—Gay pointed out the cash drawer, the loose coins, her swollen bottom lip, the exit wound in her cheek, the red marks on her neck.

One juror crossed her arms over her chest as if in protection. The girls' families dropped their heads and sobbed. Barbara Ayres-Wilson, who had gone to the DA's office before the trial to study the photos, had told the other parents and grandparents to look down and close their eyes. *Just don't look.*

The state called firefighter Rene Hector Garza, who re-created how the AFD had entered, sprayed some five hundred gallons of water on the flames and discovered first Amy's body, then those of the others. The last photos Garza identified were of the shop's front door with the cardboard sign in the window flipped to CLOSED and pictures of the service area taken from the front doorway: the upside-down chairs, clean tables, everything still neat and carefully tended, despite the smoke and the chaos. During cross, Sawyer asked Gay and then Garza if by chance they'd moved the bodies, even accidentally. They couldn't answer absolutely, of course, but didn't think so. When Garza's testimony ended and Lynch called for an early recess, nobody minded.

Efrain de la Fuente was the prosecution's fire expert, and by noon the next day he and Smith had presented testimony from two other firefighters and the three police officers who'd arrived before the bodies were found. But they didn't summon John Jones, who, after all, was the first homicide detective on the scene and the investigation's original case agent. When asked why not, Jones just shrugs. "They didn't know what I'd say."

Instead, they depended on others, like Joe Pennington, whose diagrams established the positions of the bodies, and Irma Rios, whom Smith walked carefully through the crime scene, asking her what she was seeing now . . . and now . . . as they continued together from the dining area into the storage room, past the melted telephone, the bucket, the mop, the sink, the door to the walk-in cooler, past the body of Amy and the table where the girls often counted up the day's receipts.

Irma Rios did not make life easy for Smith. When asked if she'd noticed any special marks on Amy, she said she hadn't, except for a "stain" on her cheek that, no, she hadn't recognized as an exit wound from a .380 cartridge; gunshot evidence was not her department. And no, she hadn't known the girls had been shot. She hadn't looked.

One photograph shows her in the storage room in white tennis shoes and a little red sweater, holding a flashlight and looking for all the world like a woman who has no idea what she's doing but is improvising nonetheless. Responding to a question about the debris, she said:

> The big items, we were just putting them up onto the shelves. So we removed those so we could find the bigger items. The other one was just going right through onto the ground. Again, it was like mush or ashes. Basically, that's all it was. It was not anything large, because we have sifters, it's almost like a chicken-type wire on there. . . . And we're just putting debris

in and we're sifting it and using the hose. The reason we're using the hose is because it's wet, and it's mush, so we can't sift it anymore. It's not dry.

Within two years of this trial, Irma Rios would be hired by the Houston Police Department to run its discredited crime lab when thousands of pieces of forensic evidence—including swabs for DNA tests, rape kits and articles of clothing—had been discovered on its shelves, untested and in many instances gone stale and useless. After shutting down the lab and firing its director, HPD had farmed out that work for a while and then hired Rios. But within five years of her arrival, another inspection revealed some four thousand untested rape kits. The city had to close the lab again, though Rios managed to hold on to her job.

On cross, Sawyer went to town on her. Had she kept a log of who came and went? No. Was there a manual of protocols? Not really. Had they examined the contents of the dumpsters in the alley? They'd looked at what was on top. Sawyer reserved the right to re-call her on direct.

Reese Price provided Brice's rules regarding the closing of the shop and the handling of the night's take. A dependably strong witness for the state, when asked to describe the back-door lock, she stuck to her original response. She couldn't remember.

The next day, a well-rehearsed Melvin Stahl described his arrival at the scene and acknowledged that, yes, he and Mike Huckabay and Chuck Meyer had all agreed that the fire originated on one of the melted storage shelves near the back doors; however, he said, after recently examining photographs taken that night, he'd revised his opinion. Again, Jones wasn't mentioned, nor was the fact that Stahl himself had taken the photographs. But when questioned by Sawyer on cross, he had to concede that, yes, his change of mind about the fire's origin came *after* the four boys' arrest, *after* Mike Scott's confession and *after* Marshall Littleton had come up with a theory that agreed with it. Littleton himself then took several hours to explain how he'd come by the new analysis. Under cross, he admitted that, yes, he had fed the wrong ceiling height into his computer, but that all he'd had to do was go to the shop and count the cement blocks to correct it. He'd then gone back to his office and rebooted his software. By the next day, using a higher estimate for the ceiling, he'd made his theory work.

Outside the presence of the jury, Sawyer took a last-ditch stand against the use of the enhanced videotape of his client's confession. "I think," he said, "we have increasingly become a culture that ascribes greater reality to broadcast video images than things we hear or read," and that because a transcription had been added to what was *already* enhanced, it delivered a more immediate suggestion of "trustworthiness" than freestanding images alone would convey and therefore stacked the deck in the state's favor. And he wondered why, in a courtroom setting when a man's life was at stake, the printout—in essence, a version of the Springsteen interrogation that the cops had transcribed as best they could remember—should be admissible.

The plea was interesting and not entirely fruitless. Lynch agreed to instruct the jury that while the videotape was evidence, the transcript—having been prepared by the state of Texas *for its own use*—was not. If jurors noted any variance between the two, they should trust the videotape. At the end of each day, they would return the transcriptions the court had given them and would not be allowed to review them during final deliberations.

So the jury would listen to a sometimes undecipherable audio recording superimposed on a murky videotape, accompanied by a guesswork transcription that was possibly biased. Appropriation artists and folklorists call this kind of media stew "a recontextualization," while musicians and computer techies prefer either the term *mixtape* or *mashup*. In any case, the DA's gamble was that jurors tend to trust policemen's memories more than those of indicted suspects.

During a criminal trial, the defendant sits with his back to the spectators, and unless he turns toward them, they don't see much beyond the occasional glimpse of his profile. Lynch sometimes allowed an officially appointed press photographer to snap a few photos before the jury came in. Entering the courtroom, Springsteen carried himself high, swinging his arms in a wide, confident arc, his chin lifted and cocked to one side. Most defendants dress for the occasion as if for an office job—dress shirt, tie, sport coat—but Rob wore either a long-sleeved button-down shirt or a dark short-sleeved one, along with khaki pants. Still ashen and slightly heavy, he'd had his hair cut in a defiant buzz that emphasized the deep V's of his widow's peak, his bad skin and receding hairline, those wispy side-burns and lifted, know-it-all eyebrows. Except when whispering to his attorneys, he'd been silent as a rock since entering his plea.

Once the videotape had been loaded, the state called Robert Mer-rill, and Smith opened his direct examination with some standard setup questions. Had he worn a gun in the interview room? No, left it in his fanny pack in an office somewhere. Why hadn't he immediately issued a Miranda warning? The suspect was not in custody. Had the billboard photos of the four girls been shown to the defendant when he was questioned back in 1991? Yes. After Lynch reminded the jury that statements by officers conducting the interrogation were not to be considered the *truth* but were admitted to provide possible con-text for the defendant's statements, the bailiff handed out the tran-scripts and had the lights dimmed.

The videotape opened with the white room, then Lara and, in no time, Merrill and Rob, who stood loose-limbed and polite in front of his chair, looking around, saying "Yes, sir" and "Thank you," and when Lara reentered, he offered him his hand. Then came the moment with the cigarette and the "no smoking" conversation, and Springsteen saying, "Hey, no problem," and taking his seat. During the early, gum-chewing portion of the interview, he would place his right ankle on his left knee and swing his knees back and forth, not nervously, just out of habit.

Sawyer's earlier statement about the power of film and video made a valid point. When we see people on television or in a movie, we think we know them. On May 15, 2001, while the actual defen-dant remained mute and all but faceless to jurors and spectators, the unsuspecting Robby of nineteen months ago was about to appear before them as a virtual *presence:* alive, speaking, moving, animated, *real.* Years from now, onlookers might well remember the tape with more clarity than the sight of Springsteen himself. They might run the tape in their minds and, hearing his voice, wonder what it was like to sit at the defense table watching a younger version of himself dig his own grave.

While the videos ran, Lynch consulted his laptop, checking relevant laws and court decisions. Keeping an eye on his jury, he was careful to interrupt the proceedings regularly to give them long breaks. By the time Rob uttered the line about putting his dick in Amy Ayers's pussy, the Nagra tape had run out, and so his words were extremely difficult to make out, despite the enhancement, especially if you didn't know what was coming. But the jury had it spelled out right there on their laps. Minutes later, when he got it wrong about the guns, Merrill read him his rights and Rob finally left.

Lights up. Court adjourned. Families were hopeful, the prosecution pleased. When confronted by the press, Sawyer assured them that during cross, he would question the tape line by line. Springsteen returned to county jail thinking his goose was probably cooked.

B ut the state wasn't finished with Merrill or the taped confession, and the next day Smith re-called the detective and asked why interrogated suspects sometimes gave answers that minimized their participation and blamed others. Merrill said he didn't know why; it's just what happens. Often? Yes. Was this suspect under arrest? No, sir. Did the detectives tell him he was free to go? Yes, sir. Did any officer bring a gun into the interview room? No, sir. The prosecution then began playing repeated three- to ten-minute clips of the questioning, afterward asking Merrill to explain their significance. Here is an example:

> Q: Detective Merrill, we watched a clip here where you tell him that he is just as much a victim as anybody else. Do you recall that?
> A: Yes, I do.
> Q: In fact he indicates that Maurice went something like ape shit. Do you recall that?
> A: Yes, sir.
> Q: And at the end there, you say to him, "If you haven't figured it out, Maurice blames you." Do you recall that?
> A: Yes, sir.
> Q: Can you tell us what you're doing there during that portion of the interview?

A: I'm trying to make Maurice the bad guy, the real bad guy, and him as the victim. Let him be the victim here. Let him think we believe that, and start getting to what actually happened.

Q: Earlier in that clip he had said, when he was talking about being out in the parking lot, Maurice and Forrest ran in to get something and "something, something, something." Do you recall that phrase?

A: Yes, I do.

Q: And you saw him use that throughout the interview, this little "something, something, something" phrase?

A: That's correct.

Q: Is that significant to you?

A: We find that in an interview if they are using "something, something, something," you know, "yada, yada, yada," they know what they want to say or what's there; they just don't want to say it yet.

Q: Thank you. Next clip.

After two hours of this, Sawyer had had enough. If the prosecution wanted to replay the entire tape, they should do so, because at present "all we are doing is reemphasizing the state's greatest hits." Lynch overruled. If Sawyer wanted the jury to see the whole tape again, he could run it himself. Later that morning, in his cross-examination of Merrill, Sawyer touched on Reid and the deceptive practices of the APD. But as usual, the officer faced hostile questions head-on without trying to second-guess subtext or figure out what he *should* say. His answers were blunt and unapologetic, even when Sawyer called him a liar.

"Yes, sir," Merrill will say, he did do that. He lied. And yes, sir, Lara and Chuck Meyer also lied. "That is correct."

But when Sawyer asked why he'd ended the interview before getting everything they wanted, Merrill lost some of his usual composure. "It was time" was all he'd say, even though it clearly wasn't. When asked about the cop's slipup, other defense lawyers say they have no idea why it happened and neither, more than likely, did Merrill.

In preparation for a favorable decision allowing them to present Mike Scott's redacted statement, prosecutors spent the better part of two days placing the codefendants—along with Pierce and Welborn—together at McCallum, the bowling alley, Northcross and in the stolen Pathfinder. To accomplish this, they brought in friends of the boys, including the one Rob was supposed to have met up with at the Rocky Show and, later on, their star witness, Chandra Morgan, thirteen at the time, who acknowledged to Darla Davis that, yes, she'd dropped acid that night but nevertheless remembered the boys riding around in Maurice's "beat-up, dirty two-door gray Honda" and him doing acid in the parking lot and a gun poking from the waistband of Springsteen's jeans and . . . Her testimony went on and on, but, in Sawyer's words, her manner was that of a woman underwater and she got so many things wrong, her usefulness to the state was negligible.

Robert Smith next called Rob's father, who didn't remember making a call to report his missing son, even after the Teleserve officer took the stand to read her account aloud. And in the end, so what if he had reported his son missing or Maurice Pierce and his pals had gone to Northcross? And maybe they had been all messed up with drugs and beer and had taken a Pathfinder on a joyride to San Antonio and Maurice had packed a .22 revolver. So? The state had presented a story that *might* play. After the verdict, *Springsteen* jurors will say they were still on the fence at this time, even after watching the interrogation video.

Lynch was meeting regularly with Bettis, Sawyer and Smith in chambers, hacking out a decision on the Scott statement. When the state first told him it intended to offer a redacted version, the judge's immediate response was, "No way." But Smith kept pushing, and at one session, an incredulous defense lawyer has sworn to me, he told Lynch, "Dude. I need it." *Dude?* Really? We call the judge *Dude?* And was *I need it* enough to convince a sitting judge to yield?

In any case, Lynch began to soften. He reread relevant Supreme Court cases from 1895 to 1998, as well as rulings from the Texas Court of Criminal Appeals. And little by little, this seasoned, intelligent judge convinced himself that a statement that was "truly self-inculpatory to the declarant and not directly implicating the accused on trial, could be . . . admitted as an exception to the hearsay rule and not run afoul of the Sixth Amendment."

The night before delivering his ruling, he took to his thinking couch, a long, low sofa in his chambers.

Lynch's blue eyes turn slightly wistful when he remembers making the decision. "I thought it had a chance to go to the Supreme Court," he says now. "If *Crawford* hadn't come down when it did, it might have . . ." And later, with some regret, "I always said, if Scalia ever got in the majority . . ."

Lawyers in town simply say he shouldn't have done it. And when offered a "Yes, but . . ." explanation, they shake their heads. "Shouldn't have anyway."

After reading the state's edits, he made further cuts, omitting all first-person pronouns, changing "I believe that she was working in the back room when we entered" to the oddly impersonal "Believe that she was working in the back room." Early Friday morning, May 18, he gave the final draft to his assistant, who—because the Supreme Court had ruled that blacked-out names and phrases only made obvious what had been omitted—typed it up as if nothing had been left out. Lynch then met with the relevant lawyers to relay his decision, and after lunch he gave the jury a thirty-minute break and, in a rambling statement for the record, explained why he was overruling the defense's motion to suppress Scott's statement. He then took on the objections one by one: hearsay overruled because of a court-defined exception allowing for the admission of a statement that was entirely self-inculpatory and against penal interest (legalese for "against one's interest in staying out of prison"), with no mention of a codefendant as a participant—an omission that gave it the "necessary indicia" of reliability and trustworthiness. And if it acknowledged *only* Scott's participation in the murders without accusing Robert Springsteen, the Confrontation Clause would be satisfied. As for voluntariness, he noted Scott's willingness to meet with detectives time and again, even helping out with their recording equipment. Regarding relevance, when the judge placed Springsteen's statement side by side with Scott's, he found sixteen points of consistency and eight of actual evidence, satisfying that question as well.

Thus, objection overruled. State's Exhibit 377 allowed.

Sawyer, regarding Lynch's decision: "My heart sank."

Rob: "That was it for me."

John Jones: "I was shocked. I thought you couldn't do that."

Sawyer: "I told Lynch it would be overturned. Even without *Crawford*."

Garcia: "No way it was going to stand."

Other attorneys called it a ballsy move, but wrong. Ill-timed, even shocking. Mike Lynch's unfathomable mistake.

When the jury returned, Manuel Fuentes was called to read the edited version aloud.

A fter the verdict, a juror will call Scott's confession the key piece of evidence, the one that "struck a chord" with the jury. Another will say, "We knew things had gone really, really bad when the judge allowed that detective to get on the stand and read the statement. We felt some sort of fundamental shift in the atmosphere of the jury, the courtroom and everything else after they allowed that to come in."

They weren't aware, of course, that Judge Lynch had just taken the first step toward the reversal of *The State of Texas v. Robert Burns Springsteen IV*, or that in 2002, when he allowed a paraphrased version of Springsteen's taped confession to be read to the jury in the Michael Scott trial, he would set himself up to be overturned again. (See Appendix 2 for Michael Scott redacted statement.)

F ifteen years later, Sawyer's memory of that day remains vivid. "It was a Friday. After the Scott statement was read, Lynch excused the jury early and then asked to see Robert Smith and myself in his chambers. Nobody else."

He says that when he and the prosecutor arrived, Lynch was sitting with his feet up on his desk, smiling. " 'Gentlemen,' " he quotes the judge as having said, " 'this trial is about to be over.' "

Smith then offered Robert Springsteen a very tasty deal: If he'd agree to a plea of guilty and then give testimony against the others, they'd take the death penalty off the table and offer him a life sentence of no more than fourteen years, which, with time served and a state-supported early parole, meant about eight more years of imprisonment.

Sawyer was impressed. It was, indeed, a fine offer. He said he'd consult with his client. The next morning, he and Berk Bettis went to the county jail and presented the deal to Springsteen: He would, they told him, still be in his thirties when he got out, his whole life ahead of him. "The boss"—Sawyer often refers to his client that way, after the rock 'n' roll singer—"looked at me and said, 'Would I have to testify against the other guys?'"

Reliving the scene, Sawyer turns up the volume. "I said of *course* you will. What do you *think*?"

But Springsteen refused. Those guys, he said, didn't do anything wrong and he didn't, either, but he got himself into this mess, so he'll have to get himself out. And when Sawyer warned him that he thought the jury would likely find him guilty *and* send him to death row, Robert said, "Fine. Let them kill me. I won't do it."

If Sawyer and Bettis had lingering doubts about their client's innocence, they vanished that morning.

That's how Sawyer remembers it, and he thinks this was the state's plan all along, to use the reading of Scott's statement as leverage in order to end the trial. That way, they wouldn't have to argue in favor of executing a man without a sliver of evidence linking him to the crime.

Mike Lynch confirms some of Sawyer's account. Yes, he says, he did confer with the lawyers in chambers on occasion to discuss "non-substantive issues like logistics"; on the other hand, he doesn't specifically remember this particular meeting or making the comment about the trial coming to an end. And while he has a "vague memory" of an offer made by the state and says Sawyer could be right about how it came about, he's pretty sure he had no advance knowledge of it. But he certainly would have supported efforts to settle the case and, yes, would have had his feet up on the desk.

If Earle and Smith did pursue this plan to end *Springsteen,* they gave up on it. Michael Scott was not offered a deal after a paraphrased version of Rob Springsteen's confession was read during his trial.

Monday morning, Sawyer informed the judge and the prosecutor of Springsteen's decision. And the trial continued.

On the tenth day, after putting on a few more witnesses, the state rested its case.

S awyer began his defense by calling Hector Polanco. Why?

"Because," Sawyer declared without hesitation, "he's the most effective cop witness I've ever seen in a courtroom." He was handsome, dangerous, with black eyes, a fine mustache and a roguish burglar's charm, and he talked directly to the jury. Everything he did to convince a suspect to confess to a crime he hadn't committed could work just as persuasively—whether for the defense or the prosecution—on the witness stand.

After establishing the detective's credentials, Sawyer led him through a summary of his career that included such questions as: "You have never used coercion, threats, duress of any kind to achieve any of the hundreds of confessions you have developed during the time you were in Homicide, did you, ever?" Polanco: "I have been accused of it, but no." Sawyer then asked him to talk about contamination of a crime scene and what happened when too much information reached the streets. Sometimes innocent people who heard things actually confessed, didn't they? Polanco said it might seem incredible, but yes, it happened.

To drive the point home, Sawyer described an investigation some years ago when the husband of a woman who'd been reported missing was brought in for questioning. With the suspect's family present, Polanco shamed the man until he confessed to his wife's murder and agreed to lead APD officers with shovels and dogs to a field where he'd buried her. But before they started to dig, the wife called her husband's mobile number to ask why he'd said he'd killed her.

It's a fine story, and Polanco confirmed it. But Darla Davis objected on grounds of relevance, and after Lynch sustained the objection, he cautioned Sawyer not to bring any more dead fish into his courtroom. After agreeing to stay within the dead-fish limit, Sawyer asked Polanco what he thought about allowing television cameras to roam at will around the perimeter of the ICBY crime scene and, later, the decision to give *48 Hours* full access to an open investigation. Polanco said that personally he thought both decisions were inappropriate. And when Sawyer asked if John Jones had made them, Polanco said yes.

Since Lynch had ruled that the defense could bring in two additional Yogurt Shop confessions, Sawyer called on Mike Huckabay to describe the interrogation of Alex Briones and read his statement. Then he called on John Jones, who—though still enraged by Sawyer's implication that he'd botched the crime scene—did the same with regard to his questioning of Shawn "Buddha" Smith. When asked, he also agreed with Polanco that hold-back information had quickly begun "coming back at us at such a frequency to where we had to cross [things] off the list"—for instance, Amy having been shot twice and the other girls once; the ice scoop between Sarah's legs; front door locked, back door ajar; the dead girls bound and gagged, two of them stacked on top of each other. People knew.

Described by Lynch as an "explosive witness," Jones quickly exited the courtroom, still flaming. When I asked him to talk to Sawyer in 2014, he refused. "I'd rather talk to Hector," he said. "And you *know* how I feel about Hector."

Sawyer then moved on to Irma Rios.

Did she know that Rachel Riffe had not dusted either of the customer bathrooms for fingerprints and that DPS photographs showed that both of those doors were closed during the fire? No. Had she ordered an inventory of materials within the yogurt shop so that, for instance, if someone said he'd taken a knife from the shop, they would know if a knife was missing? No. Had anyone created a log that anybody who entered the shop had to sign? No. Could she tell the jury what had happened to the steel shelves against the wall? No. The aluminum ladder? No. The mop, the wooden ladder, the mop bucket, the melted telephone—had any of those items been gathered and stored as evidence? No. Had she laid out a grid, as she'd testified earlier, so she could use its coordinates as a reference? No. Did her handbook suggest that she do so? She wasn't sure. Had DPS examined the contents of the dumpster in the alley? They'd looked at what was on top.

The judge released the jury early. Having decided not to re-call Merrill, Sawyer promised to finish within forty-eight hours, by noon, Friday, May 25.

Expert witness Gerald Hurst might have been the most intriguing *Springsteen* witness to take the stand. Scientist, chemist, inventor, born and reared in Oklahoma, he'd been awarded a fellowship to study chemistry at Cambridge, where he'd gotten his Ph.D. Back in the United States, he focused on high-energy chemistry—explosives, incendiaries, propellants, napalm. Having begun his professional life as a rocket scientist, after the first successful moon landing he moved into corporate warfare. During the Vietnam War, his job was to show U.S. troops how to destroy infrastructure behind enemy lines—"legal arson," he calls it—by setting fires and making them look accidental. After founding his own company in Dallas, he turned out new kinds of explosives, created a second-generation version of Liquid Paper and invented the Mylar balloon, then moved on, selling his company and the rights to his inventions.

Eccentric and polite, Hurst lived with his wife in a many-windowed house built high in the rocky West Austin hills. Fourteen years after a liver transplant, he was ailing. But his mind still sliced through scientific data with alacrity and his eyes were alive with knowledge and opinions. Tall, thin, with pale skin and long white hair and beard, his appearance suggests a modern Merlin, a wizard of fire and a mesmerizing presence, though it's somewhat suspect in a courtroom setting. Why didn't he have a job? Why didn't he do fire investigations for ATF or some other agency? Did pure science even belong in the courtroom?

Hurst had begun testifying in criminal cases in the late seventies, when he realized how often what he calls "witchcraft" or "the black arts" were still being applied to arson investigations. It didn't take him long to become the go-to defense witness on fire science, receiving many more requests than he could handle. Fire investigators, he makes clear, are trained to search not for the possibility of accident but for indications of arson. "I could take almost any fire," he has said, "and, if I were so inclined, convince a jury it was arson. It's frighteningly simple." When Sawyer asked how much he charged for his services, Dr. Hurst said if he liked the case, nothing; if he didn't, he wouldn't take it.

For the Yogurt Shop jury—and anyone else who'd seen photos of the crime—fire was important not just for the horrendous injuries to the girls' bodies but also because of its emotional and imaginative weight. And with no forensic evidence to tie the defendants to this especially hideous aspect of the killings, the state needed to corroborate Mike Scott's version of how it had happened: those cups and napkins.

Hurst destroyed Marshall Littleton's analysis of fire dynamics. Not only had the ATF agent based his calculations on an incorrect ceiling height, but he'd used an inappropriate equation to support his revised conclusion. With scientific aplomb and sharp wit, Hurst spoke eloquently of plumes and the percentage of flame taken up by the "flicker range." Unlike Littleton, he'd actually visited the ICBY shop and, after taking measurements and photographs, agreed with Melvin Stahl's original theory, that the fire was set on the stainless-steel shelves and had burst into flames when the combustibles exploded, then quickly spread across the ceiling, growing hot enough to reach 1,200 degrees Fahrenheit and melt the top steps of the aluminum ladder and send a blast of hot gases down on the girls' bodies. Their burns were the result of radiant heat. And yes, certainly, radiation was capable of causing that much damage.

After calling two other forensic scientists—a pathologist and a DNA lab technician—Sawyer turned to Richard Ofshe, a renowned social psychologist from UC Berkeley. Author of many scholarly books and articles—including seminal works on the recovered-memory scandals of the 1980s—and probably the country's best-known expert on false confessions, he was there to explain how these happened. But Ofshe was a terrible witness—arrogant, preachy and long-winded—who clashed with Lynch almost immediately. Initially patient, the judge soon termed social psychology a "soft science" and warned him to be brief in his comments and answer only the questions asked of him. He also limited his testimony to a description of how police interrogations worked, *without* drawing conclusions. In Texas, Lynch said, conclusions were the responsibility of the jury. Barely concealing his disdain for the judge and how things were done in Texas, Ofshe agreed to comply.

An undergraduate psych major, Bettis conducted the direct, during which he repeatedly asked his witness for brevity. But like many academics, Ofshe couldn't resist the chance to lecture. When he wandered far afield, Smith objected and Lynch sustained. Bettis struggled to rein him in, and Smith's objection was again sustained. After an hour or so of this, Lynch sent the jury out and the two sides made a deal. Smith agreed to call off his cross-examination if the defense simply asked Ofshe to step down. The jury would go to lunch and return to find this aggravation gone. The defense had little choice but to agree, even though Ofshe had been expensive. "Disaster," says Sawyer.

That night, the resentful expert gave television and newspaper interviews. In his opinion, he said, Springsteen had been coerced, and he couldn't fathom why he was asked to step down. After all, he had testified in Texas trials before.

Conventional wisdom decrees that, guilt or innocence regardless, you never put a defendant on the stand—thereby leaving him open to an aggressive cross-examination—except perhaps during the punishment phase of a trial, following a conviction. So when Rob told his lawyers he wanted to tell his story himself, Sawyer and his colleagues debated the wisdom of this, especially since it hadn't gained him any positive traction in the past. But Rob insisted. This was his life, his mess. On Friday, May 25, against the advice of the others, Sawyer summoned his final witness: the defendant himself, Robert Burns Springsteen IV.

Lynch quickly called Sawyer to the bench. Surely he didn't want this to happen in front of the jury? Leaving his client at the mercy of *Robert Smith*? Sawyer told the judge he had no choice, that Springsteen had insisted. The prosecutors were stunned. In a private conversation, one of them told a victim's family member that they weren't prepared. Smith had to rustle up a plan.

Lynch asked Springsteen if he was sure he wished to testify. Yes, sir, he said, so he was sworn in. Wearing khaki pants and a dark blue, long-sleeved dress shirt buttoned to the neck, he took the stand. He looked terrible, his skin blemished, pale and puffy, his goatee unkempt and skimpy. When Sawyer reminded him of his Fifth Amendment rights, he said, Yes, sir, they'd informed him about that.

Under Sawyer's careful questioning, Rob did fairly well. When asked why he'd admitted having done something so terrible if he didn't, he said he guessed he'd given up on himself. He was exhausted from lack of sleep and really thought he *had* asked for a lawyer. And when things went on and on, he started to make stuff up, thinking they'd let him go home if he gave them what they wanted. And once they did, he'd hire a lawyer and take a lie-detector test in West Virginia to clear himself. Then he'd be fine.

That was the easy part. When Robert Smith went to work on him, Springsteen tried holding his own, but when asked if it was just a lucky guess that he knew all those details about the murders, and how he and Mike Scott had come up with the same story, Springsteen said only, "I wouldn't call it a lucky guess."

No more questions.

The defense rested.

This being a Friday, everybody got the weekend off. Lynch would deliver his charge to the jury for the lawyers' approval on Monday, May 28. On Tuesday, jurors should show up with a suitcase packed for an overnight stay and, after closing statements, would begin deliberations, which would probably extend into the next day.

Court adjourned.

Springsteen to Sawyer: "I'm a dead man, aren't I?" Sawyer to Springsteen: "Yes, son. I'm afraid you are."

Pretty much everybody thinks Sawyer did the wrong thing by failing to convince the defendant *not* to testify; some even point out that if a lawyer can't talk a client out of doing something stupid, he'd better find a new profession.

Sawyer says he was convinced the whole thing would be overturned anyway.

And was Springsteen glad he'd taken the stand?

"Honestly, no, I'm not. Back then at the time I thought there was no other way to win because I didn't want to go through the four- or five- or six- or whatever-year appeal process, so I was like, 'All right, we got to do what we got to do now,' and that was a bad decision. I mean it wasn't horrible, but it wasn't particularly in my favor, either."

We were sitting on the screened-in back porch of his mother's house in West Virginia. He was smoking a cigarette. My little dog, Walter, was curled at my feet. It was early spring and I'd arrived a little late, having driven from Baltimore to Cross Lanes through patches of dense mountain fog. The afternoon was gray, damp and misty, too cold to sit on the porch, but we had privacy there, and a big-screen television was on inside, with the sound up high. Somebody I wasn't introduced to was watching *Kill Bill*.

This was one of six identical two-story houses built on a hillside cul-de-sac. Through the back screen we could see a very wet green landscape, bushes, grass and other backyards. A small tree stood by the screen door. Robert said it was a flowering peach, that he'd planted it for his mother.

When asked if it was his decision to testify, he said, "Well, it was. The way things came down, or at least the way I understood that things came down, there was some miscommunication between all the different attorneys working on the case and I misunderstood, had a misconception or whatever it is I had. I thought, 'Okay look, this is the last chance we got, the ship's sinking, these people [the jurors] are definitely going to be like, 'Okay, you know what? Screw this guy unless we hear something from him'; and Robert [Smith] was smooth enough to make me look like a moron, honestly. And if it had been a different prosecuting attorney, maybe it would have been a different story. You know, I have a lot of respect for Robert Smith, he was a very good district-attorney officer and he was doing what he was ordered to do and everybody's like, 'Don't you hate the situation and hate the people?' Well, no. Some of them I don't have particularly kind feelings for, but I don't hate them, because they were doing what they thought was right or what they were ordered to do. It's like being in the military. Follow orders or you lose your job or your position. I tried to speak with him one day in court. Me and Jim talked about that after the fact. I was like, 'Good morning, Robert, how are you today?' and he turned around and looked at me and said, 'I'm not allowed to speak to you!' Right on, man! Whatever. Okay. And Jim was like, 'Yeah, he's really not supposed to,' but a non-anything 'Good morning, how are you doing today' kind of greeting? He reacted like that because he knows he's doing you wrong, he's screwing you over. It was his job. And he couldn't see me as a person; all he could see was what he was presenting me as and what the media wanted to see and what the public wanted to see. So I guess I became the infamous bad guy."

Just inside the front door of the house was a display of family photos, including one of Rob on his mother's lap at about two years old. Blond and chubby, he looked happy and sweet. To use his term, a "normal" baby.

"Those people don't know me," Rob had said many times. "I'm not a bad person. . . . I'm a normal guy. . . . I wouldn't do anything like that."

He was utterly polite to me, but when I ask myself if well-mannered people who characterize themselves as normal are capable of committing terrible acts of violence, I remind myself what Jones said about who *could* or *would* do such a thing: that, legally speaking, the question's irrelevant, and as for the answer, isn't it obvious, given the case of, say, Ted Bundy? And I know he's right, even though the standards we use to determine guilt—probable and without reasonable doubt—are subjective, shifty and sometimes speculative.

SPRINGSTEEN: CLOSING ARGUMENTS, VERDICT, PUNISHMENT

Sometimes a story feels like it's over long before the credits roll. Middle of the movie, halfway through a scene, we know.

On Tuesday, May 29, fourteen jurors showed up with suitcases and Lynch gave his charge. The state would make first and last closing arguments; defense, in between. Darla Davis would speak first, then Bettis and Sawyer. Robert Smith would have the last word.

If courtroom lawyers are in general agreement about any one thing, it's that you don't give your closing from notes and certainly not from a prepared text. You plan ahead, rehearse, revise, rehearse again and then extemporize, engaging jurors with your passionate certainty and moving a soulful gaze from one to the next. But this case broke the mold in many respects. Darla Davis read her statement, and Berk Bettis talked from notes for the first time in his twenty-five-year career. Sawyer, of course, spoke off the cuff, but when he strayed a few minutes over his time limit, Lynch cut him short—an unusual move when a man's life was on the line. Never happened to him before, Sawyer says. He drew his statement to an abrupt close, wondering, as if to himself, if people really wanted to find someone guilty of a crime with no real evidence to support the decision. Robert Smith described Amy Ayers crawling across the storeroom floor, hoping to save herself, as a merciless Robert Springsteen fired the shot that ended her life. "Ladies and gentlemen," he concluded, "you are sitting in the courtroom with the man who killed Amy Ayers . . . the man who will be sitting here when you return with your verdict."

Nobody was brilliant; everybody was good. Everything had already been said.

At a little before one o'clock, Lynch sent the jury off to elect a foreman and commence deliberations. He informed the two alternate jurors of their status—which they hadn't heard until that moment—then thanked them for their service and sent them home. At five, the jurors asked to review Chandra Morgan's testimony. After the court reporter read it to them, they returned to the jury room and remained there until seven, when Lynch called an end to their day's work. A shuttle van transported them to a local motel. The next morning, they gathered again. After a couple of hours, they asked for a read-back of Springsteen's testimony. In the middle of the afternoon, they sent word they were ready.

At 3:55, the court reconvened without Sawyer. He says he hadn't thought the jury would come in that day. Some think he had other reasons.

Before Rob entered the courtroom, Bettis paid him a visit. The jurors were crying, he told him, which wasn't a good sign. Spectators, victims' families and the press had gathered, but the row reserved for Springsteen remained empty except for his grandmother, Maryjane Roudebush, who had attended his trial regularly, always wearing a red or pink hairpiece. For the verdict, she'd switched to black.

At 4:05, Lynch read the verdict: guilty as charged. The foreman affirmed the unanimity of the vote. Relieved, families of the victims sobbed and held one another. Jurors wept. Springsteen looked straight ahead. Lynch adjourned the court until the next morning, when the punishment phase would begin. The bailiff escorted the inmate back to county jail as photos were snapped. Reporters rushed to file stories. Family members embraced detectives.

"One down," Merrill commented.

The next day, Austin attorney Joe Turner told the *Statesman* that "this case appeared from all angles to be a defense case," described Lynch's decision to let the jury hear Scott's confession as "pivotal" and said he thought that allowing Springsteen to take the stand was a desperate attempt to counter its admission. He attributed the outcome largely to the preparation and skills of Robert Smith.

Under Texas law, when considering punishment in a capital case, a jury has to respond to three special issues. First, is there a probability that the defendant will commit future acts of violence that would constitute a continuing threat to society, including within a prison setting? Second, taking into consideration the circumstances of the offense and the defendant's character and background, are there sufficient mitigating circumstances to warrant a sentence of life imprisonment rather than the death penalty? Third, did the convicted person intentionally kill the victim of the offense?

A vote of yes/no/yes would send Rob Springsteen to death row. If jurors said no to the first question, they weren't required to answer the second two.

At the time, the Texas Penal Code didn't allow for a sentence of life without parole, so the prosecution and defense had agreed that, should the jury sentence Springsteen to life in prison, he would serve a mandatory thirty-five years, including time served, before being granted a parole hearing.

After explaining those options to the jury, Lynch called on the state to make its case for what it considered appropriate punishment.

To show that Yogurt Shop wasn't an anomaly, but part of an ongoing pattern of antisocial and violent behavior, the prosecution called a number of young men from West Virginia to testify to Springsteen's short fuse, his habitual drunkenness and the guns and knives they'd seen him carry and sometimes use to threaten people. One told of how Rob had kicked the bug shield of his pickup truck, scaring him so badly that he had to go after him with a nightstick. Another related a similar story of sudden and arbitrary violence. "I never did do nothing to him," he testified. "I'd never seen him, never heard of him or nothing."

Former McCallum High School principal Penny Miller spoke with some compassion and regret about Rob's time at McCallum and how she had failed to reach him. "We didn't succeed with all kids," she admitted. "We didn't with Rob."

A West Virginia policeman testified to an incident in 1995 when, during a DUI arrest, Springsteen became violent, resisted arrest and tried to kick several officers. Another described an arrest for disorderly conduct, when Rob told the cops, "Fuck it. Take me to jail." James Ramsbottom, from Charleston, described a night way back in 1990, when he was a doorman at a nightclub and Rob appeared, wearing a long dark coat, and asked Ramsbottom to hold a gun for him, a nine-millimeter that could be converted to a semiautomatic.

He also remembered Rob with a .380 and other guns, bragging about crimes he'd committed. During cross, this witness admitted to Sawyer that he was still on probation from a felony charge.

The last witness for the prosecution was Bob Ayers, who once again told tender stories about his daughter, how talented she was at riding and training horses, how much she loved cats, dogs, horses, rabbits and her FFA animals—how happy she made her family, how much they missed her. Robert Smith had photographs of a smiling, cowboy-hatted Amy projected onto the video screen, then announced that the prosecution rested.

Now it was time for the defense to mitigate those troubling testimonies. They might have presented witnesses to testify to Springsteen's basic strength of character and respect for life; his work ethic and his steadiness as a husband and stepfather—whatever they could come up with that might convince the jury that his life was worth sparing. They might have brought in a West Virginia psychologist to testify to the debilitating effects of his learning disabilities. His grandmother had gone home, saying she wouldn't testify because she knew she'd cry and didn't want to cry in front of those girls' parents; but his mother had taken her place, and might have been asked to talk about Rob as a child, much as Bob Ayers had about Amy. The defense might have projected the photo I saw much later of a blond, smiling baby in his mother's lap. Robert's wife might have told the jury about the "good and gentle" man she married. Bettis might have taken the stand to speak of Rob's honest desire to tell his story on the stand, whatever the risks and despite his lawyers' advice. The evidence the prosecution had presented to indicate future dangerous behavior was neither strong nor convincing; nonetheless, Sawyer had to find *some* way of convincing the jury *not* to kill his client.

It's easy to speculate what would've helped. What didn't was silence. But on punishment, the defense rested. Although this did not necessarily mean they'd given up on their client, a jury could easily assume they had. Even Lynch himself seemed taken aback, neglecting to ask the defendant if he agreed with this decision. In his journal, the judge would marvel at Sawyer's choice, especially because his client was seventeen when the offense occurred and, in the eight years since, had married, held a job and stayed out of serious trouble.

But Sawyer had been predicting the inevitability of a death sentence all day. When interviewed afterward, he'd tell reporters he couldn't imagine following up Bob Ayers's moving remembrances with a "Yes, but . . ." testimonial to their client's good character. At another time, he'd say Rob didn't want to involve his family in the mess he'd gotten himself into, and that he and Bettis respected that. He'd also call it strategy. Once the trial was over, Rob could request new counsel and a new trial, charging his attorneys with ineffective assistance of counsel, citing as proof the absence of mitigating testimony and the mistake of calling him to the stand.

However the decision was made, there was no turning back. One member of the defense team simply said, "Sawyer messed up and he knows it."

After a long lunch, Lynch read his charge to the jury, then went back over the special issues they were to consider and reminded them that the closing arguments were those of lawyers making a case, and if they felt unsure or conflicted on any point, they should trust the evidence they'd seen and heard.

Each side got half an hour. Efrain de la Fuente took the state's first fifteen minutes, stressing the need for accountability, Springsteen's no-good life in the years since the murders and the evil nature of the crime itself: "Hey, folks. They planned this thing out . . . knew what they were doing . . . didn't want to get caught, so . . . burn the bodies!" After reemphasizing the Ayerses' loss, he finished up by asking the jury to vote no to mitigating factors, because Robert Springsteen "ain't got no excuse for what he did."

Sawyer alone presented the defense argument. He characterized Rob's lack of remorse as a sign of his innocence. At a moment when biblical references were in order, he spoke of mercy and the New Testament. He encouraged the jurors, even if they believed him guilty, to have "the courage to spare his life." Once again, he chose brevity over persuasion. His argument took only six of his allotted thirty minutes.

Robert Smith countered with graphic details. "It took time to have those girls disrobe. It took time to tie them up and gag them. And at any point along the way Mr. Springsteen could go right out the door and not kill anybody. But that's not what he did. . . . You have to realize that there are people in this world, and one of them is sitting right there, who will come up close to you and press the muzzle of a gun to your head and kill you. So that's the person we are talking about here. He has that *core* in him. . . ."

To accompany his description of Springsteen shooting the wounded Amy Ayers in the head while she attempted to crawl away, he projected the photograph of Rob with his arm up, bent at the elbow as he described how she was positioned.

In the hall outside the courtroom, Sawyer told the *Statesman* he thought his client would be sentenced to death, even though he was innocent, but that they would win the case on appeal.

The jury asked for read-backs. Late in the afternoon, Lynch banged court into recess and everybody went home for the night, including the jury. The next afternoon, after eleven hours of deliberation, the bailiff informed the judge that the jury had come to a decision. Everybody filed back in, including the district attorney himself.

While at least one juror wept, the foreman handed the decision to Lynch, who read it aloud. The jury had unanimously voted yes to continuing threat, no to mitigating factors and yes to intentional murder. Following his mandate, Lynch imposed a sentence of death by lethal injection. Other jurors began to cry. The families of the girls linked arms. The APD officers in attendance tried to disguise their excitement. But Robert Smith and Ronnie Earle hung their heads, some thought to hide their response to a decision they'd worked to avoid by presenting the defendant with an offer they didn't think he'd refuse. Others disagree, having seen no sign of remorse in these two men's behavior.

After Lynch informed Springsteen that a death sentence automatically guaranteed an appeal, which he would quickly set in motion, he thanked the jurors, attorneys and spectators for their patience and cooperation, banged his gavel and—court adjourned—swooped out.

"This is not about killing Robert Springsteen," a sober Robert Smith maintained.

Barbara Ayres-Wilson said it wasn't that they wanted anybody to *die*. In years to come, however, she'd change her mind. "He got death," she told a reporter, "and we were happy about that, but it was still horrible we were hoping to take someone else's life."

Pam Ayers said they all needed some kind of ending.

The next day, flanked by the girls' families, Ronnie Earle held a press conference. "This is," he said, "a somber occasion. We are doing our job and we all together seek justice and truth."

Rob's mother: "I still think it was a railroad job. I'm appalled."

Bettis: "He's a proud man. He told the jury his story."

When pressed by a reporter for an interview, one departing juror said, "Leave me alone. I've been through hell." Jury foreman Phil Rodriguez said, "I think our whole community will appreciate this being over."

Lynch headed to Colorado for a fishing trip with his son.

Among closing arguments in a capital case, perhaps the best known is the one given by Clarence Darrow in 1924, when the state of Illinois wanted to hang Richard Loeb and Nathan Leopold for the Chicago "thrill killing" of young Bobby Franks. Local response to what was called "the crime of the century" closely resembled Austin's reaction to the Yogurt Shop Murders. The shocked city wanted an outcome; they wanted to understand; and they wanted blood.

On the first day of the trial, as the prosecution honed its opening statement and the press settled in for a long, juicy trial, Darrow—who represented both defendants—surprised the state, the judge and the world at large by issuing a last-minute guilty plea. The evidence against his clients was indisputable. If he couldn't protect the boys from a guilty verdict, he might at least be able to save their lives. Darrow's closing statement went on for a record twelve and a half hours. It has many quotable passages, some of which are applicable to Springsteen. Here is one that emphasizes the young age of Nathan Leopold and Richard Loeb, who were also teenagers at the time of the murder:

> *I know that these boys are not fit to be at large. I believe they will not be until they pass through the next stage of life, at forty-five or fifty. . . . I would not tell this court that I do not hope that some time, when life and age has changed their bodies, as it does, and has changed their emotions, as it does, that*

*they may once more return to life. I would be the last person
on earth to close the door of hope to any human being that
lives, and least of all to my clients.*

During his punishment argument, Sawyer had made a similar
plea: "If you genuinely believe he did this, as I know you do, then tell
me how important it is for him to at some point in his life discover
what he has done."

But Leopold and Loeb had entered a guilty plea. And they had
Darrow, who directed his argument not to a jury, but a judge, who
famously imposed a sentence of ninety-nine years plus life.

SCOTT

After Darla Davis read the grand jury indictment and Mike Scott's
plea of not guilty was recorded, Robert Smith followed his *Springsteen* opener pretty closely. He honed it stylistically, leaning even
more heavily on his habit of connecting terrible events with a repetitive, hypnotically understated conjunction: "Something happened.
And the ligature that was holding her hands together came loose,
and the gag that was on her mouth came loose. And she fought and
she tried to get away and they subdued her. And this defendant used
that sock gag as a ligature and choked her to death. And this defendant, Michael James Scott, shot her in the top of the head with a
.22-caliber revolver."

His statement went on much longer this time—well over an hour
and a half—leading Lynch to call for a break before he'd finished.

The defense attorneys divided their opening into three parts: Garcia first and last, Gilford in the middle.

Carlos began with a thesis: "This case is about one thing—the
crime scene and the physical evidence. The two objective things leading to one real simple truth. Michael James Scott is innocent of this
crime. Robert Springsteen is innocent. Forrest Welborn is innocent
and Maurice Pierce is innocent." And while he intended to stay on
point with that, he kept veering off into unmapped territory and then
had to backtrack. Once he got to the Paul Johnson task force, he
managed to return to his main strategy, emphasizing that everything
that *could* be manipulated, changed, pressured, persuaded—even

memories, discrepancies and perceptions—*had been,* and for one purpose only: to make them fit this crime. He finished by reminding the jury that the prosecution's mandate was to prove guilt beyond reasonable doubt.

Gilford's statement focused on the interrogation, covering false confessions, memory, coercive tactics and time itself. More colloquial than Garcia, he addressed the jurors as "friends" and told them that, hey, he'd been a prosecutor himself down in Bexar County. He'd prosecuted criminal cases; he'd heard confessions. But what the state had here, he assured them, "ain't a confession." Nearing the finish, he reminded the jury to "watch the theory of memory that they posit to Mike over and over again. Just as sure as God made little green apples, that is not how our memory works. We do not have a VCR in our heads and anybody that has studied it will tell you that . . . these are people who haven't studied memory one lick, but they convinced him of it."

By this time the two lawyers had gone on for two and a half hours, with Garcia's finisher still to come. Lynch gave him half an hour, not a minute more, and when issued a five-minute warning, he quickly summed up. "They will do whatever it takes . . . to make these boys fit. The truth is that when this thing is over, we are going to be able to prove what we said this afternoon. You are going to understand why there will be no conviction in this case. There will be no conviction because if you are honest and if you are an independent thinker, if you are objective you will see, you will recognize reasonable doubt. You will see it. You will know it. Because it's all over the place in this case."

They'd gone on too long and they knew it. "Three hours?" Garcia says today. "If we'd have been ready, we'd have finished in an hour."

The girls' families will never forget one image he created that day. Describing the photos the jury would examine, Carlos said, "It was so hot in this area that that heat charred the body, sometimes splitting it, much like if you put a hot dog on a skillet and you put the flame under the skillet and it blackens and it bursts open, that's what you are going to see." As one, the families recoiled at the insensitivity of this phrasing. "So," he says now, "after that the families hated me." He regrets having made the remark but knows that apologies will get him nowhere. "We all make mistakes," he tells himself.

Lynch thinks that while Carlos and Dexter were too long-winded and sometimes rambled far afield, they made sound points. And the prosecution knew it. The next morning, when Smith called his first witness, everybody in the courtroom—including the judge—expected Bob Ayers. Instead, he summoned Manuel Fuentes.

"This was not their original intent," Lynch wrote, "and it took the defense by surprise; everyone expected a more chronological approach, as in the first trial. . . ." When asked about this tactic, Efrain de la Fuente smiled. "We learned some things from the first trial," he said. "And we wanted to start strong." A skeptical journalist thought this fairly represented Paul Johnson's investigative approach, putting final results first and letting the backup details follow.

Fuentes read Scott's eight-page statement to the jury and, when asked to identify the person who made it, pointed out the defendant.

Because the defense wasn't at all prepared for this strategy, Garcia's cross took up most of the afternoon. Noting the many discrepancies between Scott's written statement and the videotaped interrogation, he asked about a cutting knife Mike said he'd taken from the shop and thrown off a bridge, even though no knife had been mentioned in earlier statements and none had been reported missing; did Fuentes know about that? He did not. And in the statement, Mike said he remembered what happened to the .380. This didn't appear in the videotape, nor did his erroneous description of the ICBY cash register drawer "being lifted and slammed back" or his memory of shoving a paper towel into a girl's mouth. He also originally said the girls were naked when they were shot, then later remembered one of them wearing a white shirt. Was Mike given an opportunity to check the statement for mistakes? Yes, he went through each page, initialed corrections and signed the statement in the presence of witnesses.

These were excellent points, but Garcia's cross-examination had rambled and stuttered.

"We didn't have a choice," he explains without sounding defensive. "We were figuring out what to do as we went along and had no choice but to cover every base, which meant we might get tedious and excessive."

Scott opened on August 14, 2002, and would not end until September 24, making it the longest-running criminal trial in Travis

County history. Lynch cast most of the blame for this on the defense's "excruciatingly tedious and often repetitive" cross-examinations.

After Fuentes, the prosecution returned to chronology: the girls, the crime, the investigation. Bob Ayers, Barbara Ayres-Wilson, James and Maria Thomas; Sam Buchanan, Troy Gay, Garza, Deveau, Pennington. The next day, Irma Rios, Reese Price, Melvin Stahl, Marshall Littleton, the fingerprint expert Rachel Riffe, the medical examiner Dr. Tommy Brown.

Garcia did particularly well dismantling Reese Price's testimony about the lock on the back door, especially after she identified the photograph of an obviously new device as the one that had been in the door on the night of the murders. Was she sure? Positive. Carlos pointed out that the lock was brand-new, whereas the only close-up photo taken that night showed one that was scarred and dull. In addition, the brass plate on the inside of the door had unusual scratches and gouges, perhaps having been damaged by a screwdriver or crowbar. Could the killers have perhaps become stuck in the back room? Did they have to pry open the back door? Did she know of anybody else using a crowbar? She couldn't say. Bottom line, he reminded her, the original lock had been lost and nobody even remembered what kind of lock it was, right? And so there was no way of knowing whether or not Rob Springsteen had wedged the door open or if it had remained locked until the killers forced it open, right? Right.

A productive, if costly, cross-examination. Although Price's perfect certainty had been slightly dislodged, Garcia had again gone on far too long. As one juror told a newspaper reporter, "I thought if I heard one more word about that back door lock I would *scream*." Ironically, one detail that went unmentioned was the receipt from Cothron's Safe and Lock for that new lock and bolt, which had been purchased for $28.52 on December 7 by Jesse Vasquez and charged to APD Homicide. Garcia didn't forget about it; the receipt had not been given to either defense team.

Melvin Stahl returned to give his change-of-heart testimony about the origin of the fire. On cross, Garcia pushed him hard. His conclusion of December 7, 1991, was that the fire appeared to have originated somewhere off the floor, maybe on the second shelf next to the south wall, near Jennifer Harbison's body, yes? Yes. And he'd stuck with that conclusion from 1991 until he retired in 1997, and in all that time none of the other arson investigators he'd met with had questioned it, correct? Yes. How many times had he met with them? Five times, maybe ten. Then 1999 rolled around and Paul Johnson wanted him to talk to a person named Marshall Littleton, right? Stahl couldn't remember who had called him; his report says it was somebody from the DA's office. And he met with Littleton and at first refused to change his opinion, correct? Yes. And again, that meeting occurred in October 1999, maybe on the fourteenth? He didn't recall the exact date, but that was close. And that was just after the police had gotten Mike to agree that he'd set these girls on fire, correct? Stahl believed it was. And by then there was also an eight-page statement Mike had signed, saying he'd piled the girls up and poured Zippo lighter fluid on them and lit it, right? Stahl hadn't read the confession. Then he met with Marshall Littleton again, true? Yes. And his conclusions changed? After viewing photographs and reading additional reports, yes. Even though he was there on December 7, 1991, and Littleton was not, even though Littleton never saw what he'd seen with his own eyes, even though Littleton knew only what Paul Johnson had told him? No response.

"Mr. Stahl, in your opinion as of December 7, 1991, was the likely source of origin of that fire somewhere along those shelves?"

"That is correct."

After more fire testimony from Marshall Littleton, followed by the ME's presentation of autopsy reports, photographs and Styrofoam heads with rods poked through to demonstrate the path of the projectiles, the state was ready to show the videotapes. Smith called Ron Lara. Once again the jury had been given transcripts, Garcia's objection overruled. Lynch issued instructions and the lights dimmed and the tape ran. White room, white table, Lara, Hardesty, ponytailed Mike. On and on. By Thursday, August 29, a weary Lynch asked Darla Davis how many more of "these things" there were. The final tape ran that day.

During the next few days, the prosecution called Robert Springsteen III, who again didn't remember calling Teleserve, and then Mary Ann Hueske, who recalled that he had. Then Kelly Hanna, Amanda Statham, her sister Sarah and their mother. On cross, Amanda said that when Mike told her he'd killed the girls, "the whole world sunk in on me." But when Garcia reminded her that she'd said nothing of Mike's confession until after his arrest, Statham simply said, "Correct." On September 4, Chandra Morgan returned, this time to testify that the .380 was tucked into the waistband of *Mike's* jeans, not Rob's. She'd also been brought up to speed on the make and model of Maurice's car. During cross, Gilford asked detailed questions about her previous version of the night's events, her heroin addiction and her ten-hour session with APD officers after the arrests. Once again, the loopy Morgan proved less than helpful to the state's case.

The prosecution revisited ballistics, unidentified hairs, mitochondrial DNA and Johnny Holder's "sale" of the .22 to Maurice Pierce. Lusella Jones described what it was like to view the lineup photos, and APD Sgt. Bruce Boardman presented a sketchy account of his 1991 interviews with Scott and Springsteen.

On Friday, September 6, after many contentious exchanges and at least one defense motion for mistrial, Lynch characterized the afternoon recess as a cease-fire. The prosecution would close on Wednesday. That gave Gilford and Garcia extra time to update their files in preparation for the state's final witnesses and to refine their own. At one point, Carlos told the judge he didn't know how he'd be able to finish this "friggin' case."

The next day, Lynch wrote in his journal that "we're now over three weeks into the trial. It has been extremely slow-going with the tension between the attorneys and sometimes, between attorneys and me." They'd already heard more than fifty witnesses and the state wouldn't rest until two days later. He didn't recall a case, he noted, with so many close and often novel questions to be decided, and *Scott* was even tougher than *Springsteen* because the defense lawyers were "anal-retentive" on questions relating to evidence and the law; plus, they had the benefit of having reviewed the record from *Springsteen*. "Also," he wrote, "they have constantly pushed the envelope on cross-examination, often well past proper outer limits."

In addition to standard and not-so-standard objections, he'd had to deal with "suggestive photo spreads, relevance of codefendants' acts loosely connected to but not part of the murders; prior consistent statements used to rehabilitate a witness; questions of hearsay and more complex 'back door' hearsay; admissibility of statements made as part of standard jail-booking procedures, admissibility of statements casually made to jail guards and others I've already lost track of."

When the time came to present Springsteen's West Virginia statement, the prosecution called Merrill. Because Rob hadn't signed anything, Lynch had ordered the state to paraphrase his videotaped confession in some ten to fifteen sentences to be read aloud in no more than five minutes. As in *Springsteen*, the defendant's name would be redacted.

But before Merrill could reach the stand, Garcia rose to hotly object to "every line" of the prepared summary. Overruled. Holding a single sheet of paper, Merrill entered the witness box. The first part of his testimony was standard setup: who was there, how the clock-camera worked, how long the interview lasted, at what point the Nagra tape ran out, what they did to assure Mr. Springsteen he was not in custody. Satisfied he'd covered due-process requirements, Smith asked Merrill if Mr. Springsteen had admitted participation in the Yogurt Shop Murders, to which Merrill replied, "Yes, sir." And when Smith asked what, exactly, the suspect had said, Merrill read this:

> He originally said that he did not know about the murders, did not even know they had occurred until he had been interviewed by the police. As the interview continued, he remembered he bought a newspaper and read it in a stolen Pathfinder on the way to San Antonio. During the interview, Robert Springsteen admitted involvement in the murders by telling us that he went into the yogurt shop prior to the robbery and opened the back door so he had a way to get in. Robert Springsteen said he went through the front door, then went to the bathroom. Robert Springsteen said when no one was looking he unlocked and opened the back door. Robert Springsteen said he propped it open by using a folded pack of cigarettes or a rock to keep the door from shutting all the way, saying it wasn't noticeable unless you were looking right at it. Robert Springsteen said at some point in time he went back that evening. He said he went through the back door. Robert Springsteen said there was a silver .380 automatic handgun used in the yogurt shop. Rob-

ert Springsteen said he raped a girl; stated he did not think he ejaculated. He said he shot a girl in the back of the head with the .380 as she was crawling, screaming, and crying. He demonstrated the position that Amy Ayers died, which was the position we found her in after the fire was extinguished. Robert Springsteen talked about hearing a total of five shots, maybe six, but remembered five. And after the robbery, Robert Springsteen said he left the yogurt shop, went to a bridge where he got out of the car and threw up. Then he ended the interview before we were complete.

After a few more quick questions, Robert Smith passed the witness to Garcia, who was intense and intelligent, but as always, Merrill took the heat with equanimity. When asked if in fact the interrogation segment of an interview wasn't a fact-finding expedition but an accusatory one, the unruffled cop said he would think that was correct, yes. When asked why police found it necessary to question a suspect in a controlled, face-to-face environment, Merrill replied, "Well, you can look at him, read his body, how he's answering, what he's saying. Because you're thinking ahead of him. You're thinking behind him. . . ."

Garcia: "You think he did it, don't you?"

Merrill: "Yes, sir."

On redirect, Smith pushed for the admission of a still photo taken from the Springsteen videotape, even though the two sides had agreed that no pictures from the interrogation would be shown. Garcia strenuously objected but was overruled and the clip of Rob demonstrating the position of Amy Ayers's body appeared on the screen.

On Wednesday, September 11, the state rested its case and Lynch called for the defense.

Garcia's strategy diverged considerably from Sawyer's.

"There was no way to win, taking that tack," Carlos says now. And that if "nobody was prepared to investigate a homicide like this, so what? So they didn't do a great job with the evidence, so DPS blew it, so what? John Jones did the best he could with what he had. We can talk about that forever, but what's to gain for our client?"

Instead, the *Scott* defense attacked what Garcia calls the Paul Johnson Show's "back-engineering," in which the detective came up with a scenario he liked and then did whatever it took to pile up a case around it to make it workable enough to sell. To shore up that theory and prove how many other people knew what Mike and Rob had done—and therefore might well have ended up at the top of Johnson's pyramid of guilt themselves—the two lawyers had submitted requests for some of the 1992 confessions: Saavedra and Cortez, Alex Briones and Shawn Smith, among others. And they dug up media stories, looking for quotes, leaks and rumors that might have fed Mike Scott's imagination with scraps of information he eventually became convinced were his own. They would call expert witnesses who could explain how memory really worked and how and why false confessions sometimes occurred.

They began by returning to the crime scene. Questioning firefighters, they made quick jumps from that night's play-by-play to what they were really after: information about visits Hardesty and other cops had made *after* the arrests and the answers the firefighters had given them about whom they might have told what they'd seen. Most said they'd described certain details—the ice scoop, the number of victims, the position of the bodies, who was burned the worst, what the place looked like—to wives or other firefighters. One said he'd told his wife "about the bodies of three of the victims being stacked in the rear of the business and about Amy Ayers's location." Another remembered saying that the "precise" piles of clothing meant that the disrobing must've taken a long time. But the court ruled that without firsthand knowledge, these witnesses could not speculate how far their news might have traveled *beyond* their immediate circle, so the lawyers had to hope jurors would make that leap on their own.

Then the defense brought back Reese Price and Amy Dreiss, the ICBY workers; Jorge Barney, from the Party House; an FBI ballistics expert; and two of Mike's friends. The next day, they called on John Jones to read Shawn Smith's confession and on Mike Huckabay to read Alex Briones's. Manuel Fuentes again acknowledged that he hadn't reviewed the videotapes, and Gilford himself took the stand to read a summary the defense had put together of the numerous crime-scene details reported by the *Statesman*. Afterward, outside the jury's presence, there was a storm of disagreements as both sides and the judge argued about the importance of tips and rumors. Every time the defense asserted its need to further pursue the possibility that Mike Scott had derived many of his so-called memories from information on the street and in the newspapers, the state shouted "irrelevant." Exchanges grew spiky. Once Garcia insulted Lynch, Gilford took over and touched on several instances: that two of the girls were "stacked in a certain way" and one was separate from the others; that one girl was choked and strangled; that money was left in the cash register; that the girls were tied up with their own underwear . . . and other bits of information that were every bit as accurate as Mike Scott's.

Late one afternoon after the jury had been dismissed, Gilford previewed for Lynch and the prosecution the testimony they expected to hear from their first expert witness, Richard Leo, the next morning. At the time, only criminologists and attorneys knew who Leo was, but in the next few years he would become widely known, having coauthored *The Wrong Guys: False Confessions and the Norfolk Four*, a book about four U.S. Navy sailors who, under intense police pressure and without any forensic evidence tying them to the crime, confessed one by one, in domino fashion, to a 1997 rape and murder they didn't commit. Three were tried and convicted; the fourth pleaded guilty; all four went to Virginia state prison until DNA results and a more cogent confession revealed the identity of the real killer-rapist. They were released but not exonerated, which means that to this day they live as legally designated sex offenders and murderers. *The New Yorker* and PBS's *Frontline* coverage would feature Richard Leo.

Explaining why they'd chosen him, Gilford reminded Lynch that when jury panelists were asked if they could imagine confessing to a crime they didn't commit, the answer was a nearly unanimous no. And if the defense was to prove its main premise—that Mike Scott did exactly that—the jury needed to hear a sound theory based on case studies and an anecdotal explanation of how this counterintuitive thing could happen. Gilford did a good job describing Leo's expertise, but the judge wasn't sold. False confession was one thing; what he didn't like was testimony aimed at drawing conclusions about the effect of coercive questioning on a potential suspect. And as Gilford struggled to make his case, Lynch's questions became edgier.

Like many judges, Mike Lynch harbored a faint distrust of expert witnesses, considering them hired guns, often academics flown in to lecture the rubes. And while he recognized the importance of specialized knowledge, he was inclined to get touchy when a witness produced anecdotes and called them science. *Soft* science was as far as he'd go. Thinking people, he maintained, had their own "specialized knowledge" and didn't need somebody like "the alleged false confession expert, Richard Leo from Berkeley," to help them draw conclusions. What's also pretty clear is that, unfortunately for the defense, Lynch couldn't get past Leo's close association with Richard Ofshe.

Gilford handled the judge well, having a quicker instinct for deference than Garcia. And the prosecution said they had no problem acknowledging that false confessions existed, but as they'd already made clear, they strongly objected to the need for an expert and would hold out against Leo's appearance for as long as it took.

Lynch requested case law and more information. The defense provided two hundred pages of Leo's testimony in another case, as well as a number of articles and examples of case law on false confessions, suggestibility and the effect of police interrogation tactics on decision making. Labeling Leo's field of expertise junk science, the prosecution presented Lynch with *their* articles and examples of case law.

The defense also wanted to call a memory specialist. Their first choice, Elizabeth Loftus, who'd written highly respected books on the subject, had to cancel at the last minute, and so they'd turned to Robert Shomer.

Lynch agreed to study the Leo information that night, and would hear arguments for and against admitting the two experts the next day. The exhausted lawyers finally left the courthouse at seven-thirty that night, but the judge headed back to his office.

Taking to his couch, he began reading; at ten, he drove to a nearby twenty-four-hour diner and, over a late meal, kept reading. At home, he reviewed the prosecution's transcripts and articles. Obviously, Leo was prepared to tell the jury not just *how* false confessions occurred but also *why* a person who'd given one didn't quickly recant, as most of us would expect. Sometimes, he maintained, the suspect remained in a "post-admission narrative" of guilt despite being convinced of his innocence—a theory that would give the defense room to explain why Mike Scott kept going back to be interviewed.

The Supreme Court had set the standard for the admission of expert witnesses in the 1993 decision on *Daubert v. Merrell Dow Pharmaceuticals, Inc.,* in which it established four criteria of reliability: testing, peer review, error rates and acceptability in the relevant scientific community. As gatekeeper of those standards, Lynch struggled. "Ordinarily," he wrote, "I might let it all come in just to be sure I give the defense every opportunity to develop a full and proper defense." He also wanted to make sure they got every legitimate dollar's worth out of the experts they'd hired. But this one rubbed him the wrong way. He didn't want to give the Berkeley professor a stage on which to parade opinions supporting what Lynch believed was his obvious agenda: to change police interrogation tactics.

The judge lost a lot of sleep trying to figure out "an honest reflection of the state of the law as best as [he] could determine it." But he still had questions. "Whatever [you] do in these tough situations," he wrote, "there is always residual doubt, guilt and second guessing."

The next morning, outside the jury's presence, he swore in the two experts. Richard Leo went first and, unlike Ofshe, he wore his expertise lightly. On the stand, he identified himself as a criminologist and social psychologist whose specialty was the study of "coercive persuasion or extreme influence in decision-making"; in other words, how an individual makes decisions in a high-pressure environment. He described modern interrogation techniques as psychological methods meant to shape and change a suspect's perceptions and to convince him that the most rational and sensible decision, given what the interrogator is telling him and what he has come to believe, is to say, "Okay, you're right, I did it. Now can I go home?"

He went on to explain the basic methods—again, Reid—used in the Scott interrogation. In order to create a context for their strategies, by first accusing the suspect of lying, and then attacking his denials and his belief in the reliability of his memory, Lara and the others had created a situation in which the suspect could lose only by denying his culpability. Not everybody could be broken in this manner, but it did happen. In time, some people came to think they might have committed the crime without remembering the act itself.

And then—isolated, alone, with no outside support to urge them to quit talking—they began to speculate, guess, imagine, toss out possibilities, incorporating street rumors as well as information from the press. They might even look to their interrogators for answers.

Garcia then took on memory expert Robert Shomer, who provided a long list of credentials, publications and research studies. He proposed to first discuss how memory worked and then to gauge the validity of theories held by polygraphers and the police. Shomer had seen the videotapes of Scott's interrogation; he'd also read the transcripts. The defense plan was to present video clips—the one in which Bruce Stevenson gave Scott his memory-as-VCR lesson, the trance induction of Sal Abreo, the visualization exercise—so that Shomer could refute the hypotheticals.

Robert Smith acknowledged the probable reliability of Shomer's expertise but didn't see the need to show video clips, since the jury had already seen the tapes. At one point, when Garcia disingenuously asked Smith which evidence they *were* prepared to admit, Lynch curtly pointed out that he was the one to decide, not the prosecution.

Lynch ruled that Shomer could talk about how memory worked and how persuasion and suggestion might encourage people to remember things that didn't happen. No video clips. As for Leo, he could talk about decision making under pressure and how people decided to confess to crimes they didn't commit, but he would not be allowed to discuss "persuaded false confessions" or "post-admission narratives." Considering *Daubert* and his own conscience, the judge had decided that while false confessions did occur, Leo's theory that police interrogation tactics caused regular folks to believe they were guilty of crimes they hadn't committed was pure guesswork.

Gilford protested. The entire case against their client was based on an interrogation the defense believed was coercive. To take away the information Leo could provide—with backup support from case studies, wrongful convictions, exonerations and other criminal trials—would gut their defense. When Lynch wouldn't budge, Gilford threw in the towel. Fine, then they wouldn't call Leo at all.

As lead counsel, Garcia didn't have to go along with this, but by then, both men were pretty used up and he didn't challenge Gilford's decision. Later, he admitted he should have pulled rank and convinced Dexter to take what they could get. But he didn't. And so Richard Leo headed back to California that afternoon, as the prosecution had hoped.

Lynch considers Richard Leo a smart man who's doing important work and thinks that, even hobbled by his decision, his testimony could have helped the defense. But he stands by his ruling. Based on all the literature he could absorb that night, he believes the witness was prepared to venture past the outer limits of good science into conjecture, speculation and "what he thought sometimes happened."

After the jury was seated, Shomer testified as expected, and afterward the defense called Paul Johnson again to ask him about phone interviews he'd had with Scott in 1998, and the conversations he'd had with Chandra Morgan before the four boys were arrested, in which she told many stories about the night of the murders but never once mentioned Springsteen, Scott or the other two and never said anything about going to the yogurt shop that afternoon. The last defense witness of the day was APD polygrapher Bruce Stevenson, whose revivification theory had been pretty much obliterated, not just by Shomer but also by ordinary common sense.

The defense had two more expert witnesses to present on Thursday. Smith wanted to schedule closing arguments the following day, but Garcia asked that they wait until Monday, giving them the weekend to work on theirs. Lynch—his patience frayed—preferred Friday, but there was a potential problem. On Saturday, the University of Texas Longhorns were playing a home game and, football being the great Texas pastime, he wasn't sure he could find motel space for the jurors that night. He'd have to check.

Known as a bloodstain pattern analyst (BPA) and crime-scene reconstructionist (CSR)—job titles familiar to fans of *The Closer* and the *CSI* series—the defense's next-to-last expert witness, Ross Martin Gardner, had worked in federal law enforcement for twenty-nine years before taking over a small metropolitan department in suburban Atlanta as chief of police. After that, instead of retiring, he got into forensics, studied at Scotland Yard, became active in the International Association of Bloodstain Pattern Analysts, took thousands of hours of technical training, wrote articles on crime-scene analysis and reconstruction and became, in time, a nationally recognized expert.

After establishing these credentials, Garcia asked Gardner to tell the jury what crime-scene reconstructionists did. The job, as he described it, was one of simple logic and deduction, using the scientific method. They gathered evidence, examined every available piece and explored the relationship between these items. For example, in Yogurt Shop, one piece of evidence was the phone receiver, found hanging from the melted body of the telephone. Why was it off the hook? Phone records revealed that no outgoing calls were made after the shop closed. A reasonable assumption would be an interrupted call, perhaps one of the girls attempting to call 911 when someone took control of the receiver or forced her to drop it.

"We take pieces of physical evidence, we put them in as much order as possible . . . and when we're done what we have is a skeleton . . . pieces that fit in a certain order."

In 1988, Gardner had taken a course from the defense's next expert, Tom Bevel, the country's leading blood-spatter analyst. Before long, they joined forces and developed a method of teaching what they'd learned to cops, private investigators, prosecutors, defense attorneys and whoever else wanted to know. In 1997, after coauthoring *Bloodstain Pattern Analysis with an Introduction to Crime Scene Reconstruction*, they expanded their teaching into a business. Operating out of Bevel's home state of Oklahoma, Bevel, Gardner & Associates was soon scheduling seminars all over the country; in the next fifteen years, they hired many more consultants and teachers, most of them retirees from law enforcement.

Ironically enough, in December of 2000, during Yogurt Shop pretrials, when the state was working hard to match crime-scene evidence with details of the codefendants' confessions, Tom Bevel had been hired by the Travis County DA's office to—in his words—examine "documentation relative to Amy Ayers's death, and to try to identify the most probable sequence of events relative to the physical evidence surrounding her body." It was Efrain de la Fuente who had made contact with Bevel and subsequently sent photographs, diagrams and the autopsy report. The package included no photographs of the storage room, the doors, the front room or the other girls. Bevel studied the material and in April 2001, when *Springsteen* was getting under way, submitted his findings. The only response he got was a letter from de la Fuente saying he might be called as a witness. He'd heard nothing more. Those findings have never been made public.

As requested, Carlos had sent Gardner a notebook filled with the original incident reports, autopsy and private-lab DNA reports, crime-scene and autopsy photographs and the conflicting arson conclusions. What Gardner specifically did *not* want were statements, whether from suspects, witnesses or the victims' families. It didn't matter what the victims had done that afternoon or what people who'd been to the shop remembered. He wanted only physical evidence and firsthand official reports. He'd even made a trip to Austin to view and take his own pictures of items stored in the APD evidence room in order to follow a "basic process . . . of crime scene analysis and crime scene reconstruction."

If this sounds at once sensible and somewhat oversimplified, it is both, though if the success of the Bevel-Gardner partnership points out anything it's that there are gaping holes in the forensic capabilities of police departments all across the country. That cops aren't scientists goes without saying, but it's also important to understand that they're *local*. Their job requires them to respond not just to their chief but also to the DA and the mayor, as well as—in a high-profile case like Yogurt Shop—to the families of the victims and a clamoring public. And then there are the inevitable skirmishes and power plays within any homicide department.

Ideally, an outsider can provide a more balanced response. Gardner might have gone on too long from time to time, but his was probably the most interesting and most nearly objective account of the Yogurt Shop crime scene that anybody had offered thus far. Having been prepped on Lynch's attitudes, he described the reconstructionist's methodology as scientific and objective.

"We're not guessing," he told the judge. "We're not going, *Well, I kind of have a gut feeling.*" On the contrary, they looked for "*defined events that occurred during . . . the incident,*" each of which they listed as a specific "event segment."

Because their arson expert had canceled his appearance, the defense also depended on Gardner to talk about fire origin and cause.

Although he wasn't an expert on software modeling, he'd studied fire science and was certain that the evidence showed that the girls' bodies suffered direct burns from falling ceiling tiles. The records and photographs showed no evidence of napkins or cups on or around the bodies, nor the use of an accelerant.

Garcia also wanted Gardner to present a flowchart comparing the videotaped and written statements of Michael Scott, noting the consistencies and inconsistencies between them, but de la Fuente objected. An expert witness could not testify to the credibility of a witness, particularly the defendant on trial. To refute this objection, Gilford cited Texas Rule of Evidence 704, which allowed expert testimony on an "ultimate issue," in this instance guilt or innocence. Objection overruled.

After warning the witness not to tell the jury how to perform its function, Lynch ruled that if Gardner stuck to *specific* statements by the defendant, compared them to *specific* findings he'd made and rendered an opinion *only* on whether or not that statement was consistent with *his* findings, he could be of assistance to the jury. He could not, however, make direct suggestions about the defendant's credibility. Gardner agreed to comply.

The defense next called Tom Bevel. Aiming to show that the APD and the prosecution weren't after the truth, but a confirmation of the case they'd built, Garcia asked immediately about the consultation Bevel had made in December 2000. When on cross de la Fuente accused him of claiming "scientific certainty" for his conclusions, Bevel didn't bite. All scientists, he said, including himself, were wary of making claims of certainty.

Later that afternoon, when de la Fuente re-called Gardner, his questioning was sharp, but his dependence on sarcasm often led him to make charges he had to back away from. Gardner remained calm, answered his questions and certainly earned the fee he'd been paid. Though the jurors didn't buy everything he said, he might well have planted seeds of doubt in their minds.

To emphasize once again that by early 1992 information about Yogurt Shop was floating freely throughout the city, especially among young people, the defense had hoped to bring in a man named Aaron Chadwick, who'd been interviewed then by both Hector Polanco and John Jones. But the pierced and tattooed Chadwick seemed to have vanished. All they had was an e-mail address, and he wasn't answering. Maybe they could conduct an interview via e-mail? Maybe the judge would give them more time? Bitterness and exhaustion produced a vicious exchange over these last-minute motions and requests.

The final day of testimony was a jumble of repeat appearances and requests from the defense for time and a reconsideration of Lynch's previous rulings—all denied. The state called several people in black to ask what they'd heard and from whom; some said they'd gotten everything they knew from one woman, who'd claimed to have inside sources. They then brought in some of Shawn "Buddha" Smith's gang to refute their leader's allegations. The defense called Mike Scott's Boy Scout leader to testify that he had indeed attended the craft meeting that Saturday, December 7, and no, he hadn't acted strange or nervous, just normal Mike. Garcia asked again for continuance, so they could take the weekend to write a proper closing argument. No deal. The jury was told to bring a suitcase, toothbrush, regular medications and change of clothing in with them the next day. Lynch had booked motel rooms, and after closing arguments the case would be theirs.

SCOTT: CLOSINGS, VERDICT, PUNISHMENT

As in *Springsteen,* Lynch gave each side two hours, the state to open and close, the defense in the middle. Mike wore a light gray suit and had his hair combed back. His pale clothes matched his natural coloring, giving him the appearance of a man who wished to vanish.

To begin the closings, Efrain de la Fuente reviewed the two confessions and urged jurors to find them honest and credible. Everything else, he said, was invention. He imagined Scott saying, "Gee, it's a false memory and they implanted this stuff in my mind and it never happened."

Dexter Gilford began his final argument by striking a note of humility. "I don't propose," he said, "to understand all of the ways in the workings of a human heart and human mind. I can't say and speak with as dogmatic conviction as my colleague Mr. de la Fuente does about when somebody is lying or when somebody is not, or when somebody had been frightened or when somebody has been deceived or tricked. I can't do it. I don't know how he is able to. . . . But it is something that I have noticed that has been characteristic throughout this case. Detectives Merrill, Lara, Hardesty, Meyer, all of them that have testified [who] had any contact with Mike. . . . They all propose the same sort of omniscience. . . . I don't know where they get it. I don't know how they can decide on a hunch that somebody is lying to them. I don't know if anybody can do that. I'm a God-fearing man. I believe in God. I don't know if you all do. If you do, the idea of omniscience to me is something that it is hard for me to understand any of us taking for ourselves. . . ."

His use of *omniscience* was purposeful and effective, giving the power of all-knowing to God, leaving humans to cope with relativity, possibility and doubt.

After refuting many of the state's positions, Gilford pointed out inconsistencies between Mike's statement and the crime-scene evidence—reminding the jurors more than once that the reason Mike had gotten so many things wrong on his written statement was that Lara and Hardesty and the rest hadn't been with him to guide his answers. Wrapping up, Gilford reminded jurors that while the girls' families and the city of Austin deserved to know what happened that night, "Mike Scott should not be our easy way out."

And he again spoke of the unwavering omniscience of the interrogating officers, who had said no when asked if there was any possibility they were mistaken about Mike Scott killing those girls. And that's where Gilford insisted the investigation itself had gone wrong, with the absence of even the possibility of a flawed theory.

It was an admirable speech, and Lynch calls it one of the best closing arguments he'd heard in his twenty years on the bench.

Carlos Garcia's closing was equally impassioned, if somewhat less cohesive. While a Jim Sawyer or a Dexter Gilford can depend on an ingrained sense of order that enables them to speak in paragraphs, Garcia's a man of heat, passion and virtue, who knows he needs to rein himself in to make better points, but in this case he simply didn't have enough time to organize and edit. His final focus was on that worrisome lock on the back door, a photograph of which—the only one taken that night—he projected on the screen. It was a fuzzy photograph, and while Carlos saw an irrefutable key lock, not a thumb latch, to others the mechanism wasn't so clear. It's true you couldn't see a lever or a latch, nor could you, with any certainty, make out a keyhole.

"That's the acquittal right there," Carlos told the jury, perhaps a little too adamantly. "If that doesn't convince you, I don't know what will." And one last time, he presented the jury with the theory that the killers had gone in through the front door or hidden in the space above the ceiling and, when the killing was over and it was time to leave, they'd had to force open the back doors, leaving telltale scratches on the inside panel.

In her turn, Darla Davis asked jurors to return their attention to Michael Scott's written statement and to read it carefully, word by word, and "you will know you are reading the words of a killer." Robert Smith wrapped up by going back over details that both Scott and Springsteen had relayed to police officers, describing the crime as the prosecution envisioned its having happened and emphasizing the horrifying details, especially concerning Amy Ayers. He reminded jurors that both confessors had told police officers that somebody threw up over the side of a bridge just after the crime. And that their accounts were far too consistent for these to be coincidences.

During his final moments, Smith would make a significant mistake when he invited the jury to resolve whatever doubts it might have about the reliability of Scott's confession by noting how closely it corresponded to Springsteen's, both in the details of the offense itself and in other "neutral" aspects. He also urged them to consider that "unlike with [Scott], the interrogating officers had not suggested answers to Springsteen." These statements will come to haunt Smith and the DA's office when they are judged "harmful" and used in the eventual reversal of Scott's conviction.

On Friday afternoon, September 20, with seven hundred pieces of evidence to consider, these men and women retired to the jury room to begin deliberations. A few hours later—when they requested the photograph of the lock on the back door and, soon afterward, Scott's written statement—the defense took heart. Transported from the courthouse by shuttle bus, the jury spent that night and the next in motel rooms, where on Saturday night some might have listened to a radio broadcast of the sold-out football game. Wildly favored, the UT Longhorns won their fifteenth straight home game, beating the University of Houston Cougars 41–11.

The next afternoon, after deliberating for more than twenty-two hours, the nine women and three men reentered the courtroom, several of them wiping away tears, others red-faced. Not good for the defense. The foreperson handed the verdict to the bailiff, who handed it to the judge, who read it aloud: guilty of capital murder.

The defense requested a poll. One by one, each juror had to stand and answer Lynch's question: "Is this your individual and personal verdict?" Once they'd all said yes, the judge declared the verdict formally received. Court in recess, to resume the next morning at nine for lawyers, ten for jurors. Mike Scott was taken back to his holding cell. Garcia was heartsick. Families of the murdered girls huddled together, throwing arms around one another, clasping shoulders warmly. On the other side of the courtroom, the Scott family broke down. When everybody else had left, they were still there.

Once she pulled herself together, an enraged Jeannine Scott went out to face the press. "The state of Texas," she said, "has succeeded in putting another innocent man in prison. I only hope the jury has enough sense to realize it's not worth his life." Her husband was innocent and she would fight every day to bring him home. Later, when she'd calmed down, she told a reporter she wasn't angry with the jurors. She thought they'd been duped, and that the real killer was a sick psychopath who was still out there.

Garcia, Gilford and Diaz met to discuss the next step. Whatever happened, there were many reasons that this verdict could be overturned. When it was, they'd be ready. In the meantime, saving Mike from execution would constitute a victory.

Arguing for the death penalty, the prosecution called friends from Mike's past, including one who remembered Mike bragging about being the "Mushroom King" of Austin, making big bucks—six figures—selling hallucinogenic fungi from his fanny pack. But under defense questioning, the witness admitted that he thought Scott was blowing smoke, especially about the money. The state also produced a county correctional officer who'd found contraband under Mike's mattress, a pencil with a scrap of razor blade inserted into the eraser end and a couple of paper clips that might be used to pick a lock; the guard had confiscated the items but hadn't bothered to report the incident. Others said sometimes Mike's temper could get the best of him, that they'd seen him steal money from the cash register in the bookstore where he'd worked. A woman described having a "hollering match" with him in her store.

The last prosecution witness was Bob Ayers, and because in a death-penalty case Texas law limits testimony that compares the victim's life to the defendant's, his descriptions of his daughter had to be curtailed. Lynch ruled that of the thirty photographs the state had hoped to exhibit, it should choose three.

The prosecution had taken less than an hour to argue that Scott presented a future danger.

The Scott team made a strong case to mitigate the death sentence, after which a local television reporter would refer to them as a legal "dream team." As witnesses, they called family, colleagues, former employees and friends to testify that Mike was a good son, a good father and husband, a good friend, a good Boy Scout, a hardworking employee. Jeannine Scott emphasized his patience and his respect for others, especially Jasmine, their daughter. Yes, he could be a little drifty from time to time, but he was her gentle giant, and she loved him for his sense of wonder, which counterbalanced her own natural cynicism. While in county jail, he had cut out and sent her articles from the newspaper every day: photographs, stories and recipes, perhaps using that pencil with the razor blade mentioned by the correctional officer. Several people testified about Mike's involvement in the medieval reenactment society. Mike's father talked about the care and precision required to create the traditional American Indian attire Mike made by hand. In the end, Lynch wrote, the defendant came off as goofy, eccentric and immature, perhaps by nature a follower, but not preternaturally violent or dangerous.

To prove another point—that executing juveniles (under eighteen) was a violation of the Eighth Amendment, which outlaws cruel and unusual punishment—the defense also called a neuropsychologist to describe the development of the brain and to suggest that Judge Lynch should order a directed verdict of life in prison (an argument with which the Supreme Court will agree in 2005, when Springsteen's death sentence is overturned).

Studying Mike's school records going back to prekindergarten, the neuropsychologist found that Mike had skipped so many days of the fourth grade, he'd had to repeat it. One of his teachers categorized him as emotionally unstable and "immature, immature,

immature"; a really bright boy who never lived up to his potential. After he was diagnosed as having off-the-chart ADHD, it became clear why he was unable to "prune" reality. To a boy like Mike, the neuropsychologist explained, every sound and experience carried the same weight.

So? Efrain de la Fuente would shrug. Immaturity justifies murder?

After the jury went home for the night, the defense presented its last expert witness, Jordan Steiker, a former Supreme Court clerk now teaching law at the University of Texas. A death-penalty antagonist, Steiker is extremely knowledgeable about both the Eighth and Fourteenth Amendments. By allowing him to speak at length about the issue of proportionality in other Supreme Court rulings, Lynch revealed his inherent interest in capital punishment. But he would not extend it far enough to sustain the request of the defense to order a directed verdict.

As for closing speeches the next day, de la Fuente once again took the hothead role, carping and making evidence personal, sharpening his tongue for spiky attacks. Gilford emphasized the difficulty of the jury's job. Garcia asked jurors to choose life over death and reminded them that if Martin Luther King Jr., Gandhi, Mother Teresa or Jesus Christ were alive, any one of them would have chosen life. And he told the story of Saul of Tarsus on the road to Damascus, who, after being forgiven by Jesus for hundreds of killings, went on to become an apostle.

Robert Smith finished up by calling the murders of the four girls sufficiently brutal to indicate future dangerousness, and by asking the jury to revisit the crime itself and the events of that night minute by minute, flavoring his rundown with quotes from Mike Scott, the last of which described the pistol shots to the back of the girls' heads: "Quick easy kill."

The jury was out for less than three hours.

When it returned, Lynch read the first question aloud: From the evidence presented by the prosecution, did the jurors consider it *probable beyond a reasonable doubt* that the defendant would commit criminal acts of violence that would constitute a continuing threat to society?

Scott's jury voted no.

So as the law mandates, Lynch didn't pose the second two questions and pronounced Scott's sentence, life imprisonment and a minimum of thirty-five actual years, which, considering time served, came to about thirty-two.

It took a minute for Carlos Garcia to take it in, but the response in the courtroom brought him around. "Oh," he said. "We won."

Mike Scott hugged his attorneys. After he was cuffed and hustled away, defense lawyers shook hands and hugged one another.

Ronnie Earle hung his head. Smith, Davis and de la Fuente gathered up their papers and left without commenting. Bob Ayers bolted without a word for the waiting press corps. When asked if she had anything to say to the jurors, Barbara Ayres-Wilson said, "Nothing nice."

Jeannine Scott and Mike's family rejoiced. "All we have to do now," she told reporters, "is bring him home."

So, what was it? Did Springsteen's lifted chin and his unfortunate eyebrows or his arrogant stride into the courtroom convince jurors of his future dangerousness? Did he simply look like a killer and when Sawyer didn't present evidence that he *wasn't,* the jury ended up trusting appearances? In one of the *48 Hours* interviews, Barbara Ayres-Wilson offered a simple explanation. Springsteen, she declared, should not have taken the stand. "He was not received well," she told Erin Moriarty in 2010. "He was the evil person in front of us." Sitting beside her, Maria Thomas energetically agreed. "Cocky," she said. "Arrogant."

"Slimy," Ayres-Wilson added.

Mike Lynch says the jury gave Scott life mainly because when the prosecution presented their argument that Mike Scott was irremediably violent, they didn't come up with much. He also thinks the videotape of his long, painful interrogation might actually have helped him.

Three months later, Lynch received a letter from Juanita Tijerina, who'd served on the *Scott* jury and, during the twenty-two-hour deliberations, had been the lone holdout for a not-guilty verdict. She was writing him, she said, because of the many things that bothered her about "the evidence, confessions and testimonies" presented at the trial, especially the potentially coercive actions of the detectives conducting the interrogation. It was Tijerina who—despite the impatience and anger of her fellow jurors—asked for the videotapes to be brought to the jury room for review. In the end, she told Lynch, having concluded that Scott's confession had been made "under high pressure tactics and not coercion," she changed her vote. By then the jurors were so wrung out, they all wept openly. But the main reason she wrote was to express her fear that sloppy APD investigative strategies might send an innocent person to prison or to death row or, by tainting the evidence, might even compromise the jury system and provide a technicality that could set a guilty person free. As a prescriptive measure, she recommended the creation of a special department to oversee police investigations, then thanked the judge for his impartiality and fairness.

Garcia thought Tijerina's letter was a sad testament to the jury's disinclination to "determine whether the substance of the 'confession' matched the evidence." Which, he insisted, it didn't. In truth, he admitted, blaming jurors was unfair, and in this particular instance they were hamstrung by his and Dexter's inability to "simplify the information/interrogation into manageable chunks." But the case was unwieldy at best: "information overload at a scale I had never nor have ever seen before and since."

Judge Lynch did not respond to this letter.

ALWAYS PIERCE

On September 25, 2002—with Scott in a holding cell awaiting transfer and Springsteen on death row—the DA's office went to work. Maurice Pierce was next, and, in December, Lynch announced his trial date as April 21, 2003. But the state had little to go on and Pierce still wasn't talking. A few weeks later, Springsteen returned to Austin for a two-day psychological workup, ordered by his appellate attorneys, Mary Kay Sicola and Robert Ford, who had already filed a brief citing the violation of their client's Sixth Amendment rights. By then, Garcia had arranged for Ariel Payan to file Michael Scott's appeal, and because of his life sentence, this would be directed to the Texas Third Court of Appeals.

In November, Christopher Ochoa and the family of Richard Danziger filed separate lawsuits in federal court, accusing former APD homicide investigators Hector Polanco, Bruce Boardman and Jamie Balaiga of illegal acts, including threatening violence, fabricating a confession and hiding and destroying exculpatory evidence. They also cited the negligence of Police Chief Jim Everett. City councilman and future mayor Will Wynn called Danziger's case the most troubling thing he'd had to deal with in his two and a half years on the job. "Ultimately," he said, "the justice system broke down."

Guillermo Gonzalez and the other members of Pierce's team began preparing for a trial, as did the girls' families, Judge Lynch and the DA's office. Finally, everybody on the prosecution side thought it was time to bring the ringleader to justice.

———

B ut this wasn't to be. Within four months of Scott's conviction, on January 9, 2003, Ronnie Earle held a surprise press conference. Looking grimly hangdog, he wasted no time getting to the point: "It is without pleasure that I announce today that the Yogurt Shop capital murder cases against Maurice Pierce have been dismissed."

Nobody knew it was coming. Neither Guillermo Gonzalez nor Pierce and his family. Nor the *Statesman*.

"The primary witnesses against Maurice Pierce," Earle continued, "are Robert Springsteen and Michael Scott. Juries have convicted both of them of capital murder for what they did," but they had a Fifth Amendment right not to testify and had made statements that couldn't be used without violating the "constitutional right of Maurice Pierce to confront the witnesses against him." Although the case remained open and the investigation active—murder having no statute of limitations—the evidence they'd hoped would prove guilt beyond a reasonable doubt had not developed, so the state was "unable to proceed at this time."

After calling Yogurt Shop the most difficult case in Austin's history, the DA made a special point of praising the APD's investigative work, calling the teamwork of police officers and prosecutors "close to miraculous." And while he still believed Pierce had participated in the murders, if they put him on trial and he was found not guilty, they would forever be barred from holding him to account for "what the evidence shows that he did."

As for the convicted murderers: "We had hoped they would come forward and tell the truth." Earle shrugged. "Hope springs eternal" and "life is long." This crime, he said, had left a "scar on Austin's soul" that had partly been healed by the convictions of Scott and Springsteen, but "we're not through and we won't rest until justice is done in full measure." He urged people who had information to come forward.

What the DA didn't say was that, in fact, he had nothing to offer. Convictions weren't final until the last appeal had been filed, so why would either man make a deal now? And as Mary Kay Sicola pointed out, if Springsteen had been willing to perjure himself and testify against the others, he wouldn't be on death row.

Although Pierce had been imprisoned for more than three years, Earle said nothing about his constitutional right to a speedy trial, which had kicked in the minute he was indicted. Local lawyers and legal scholars also wondered why it took so long to release him if Earle had known all along that Scott and Springsteen wouldn't testify. "There is," a UT law professor said, "an ethical obligation to drop charges, to seek dismissal when there is no longer a reasonable possibility that there will be a trial that will result in conviction."

Others also noted the irony inherent in Earle's mention of Pierce's constitutional—Sixth Amendment—rights when Springsteen and Scott had been denied theirs. And as for Earle's reference to "the evidence" that showed what Pierce did, what evidence? If proof existed, why couldn't they try him? Clearly, somebody had convinced the DA that solid proof leading to a conviction was forthcoming. Safe to say, that person had to have been Paul Johnson, whom Earle trusted utterly.

Even more obvious was the DA's exhaustion with his job. There's a moment when you can tell that an elected official's finished, his energy depleted, his zest for the game gone flat. Ronnie Earle had probably reached that point long before now.

Released from the Travis County Correctional Complex, Pierce made his first appearance as a free man in a clean white T-shirt hanging outside his jeans. Incarceration hadn't visibly changed him. He looked scrubbed and energetic. Bombarded by the press, he had only one thing to say: "Happy."

The next day, with his lawyer and his family in attendance, he read a prepared statement. His three-and-a-half-year imprisonment had been, he said, "a very difficult time," especially since "when I was detained and arrested I proclaimed my innocence of all the charges that [were] filed against me, and I am standing here today with that same proclamation. I am innocent of any and all charges pertaining to the Yogurt Shop case." He would now go home with his wife and daughter and try to pursue the many aspirations he had prior to his incarceration. He had no plans to sue the city or the district attorney. He, Kimberli and Marisa wanted to move on with their lives.

Without taking questions, he wrapped up with a winning statement: "I thank you very much and Godspeed to you all." And he shook a few hands and then was gone.

But easy times didn't follow his release as Maurice had hoped. Within eleven months, he had received three moving traffic violations—for not having insurance, for failing to control his speed and for driving on a highway shoulder—all issued in tough-on-crime counties close to Dallas. When Pierce paid none of the tickets, a warrant was issued for his arrest.

In May 2003, Mary Kay Sicola argued before the Texas Court of Criminal Appeals that the inclusion of Scott's confession in Springsteen's trial violated her client's Sixth Amendment rights, reminding the justices that the Supreme Court had ruled a number of times that the testimony of a nontestifying witness could not be used without the defendant's having an opportunity to confront, or cross-examine, him. Robert Smith presented the opposing argument, claiming that since Michael Scott confessed voluntarily, his testimony could be considered reliable and therefore admissible under the kind of "firmly rooted hearsay exception" the Supreme Court had judged acceptable in 1980.

Yogurt Shop also remained newsworthy in other respects. In October of that same year, the *Statesman* reported, Scott's friend Patrick Davidson was arrested on a four-count indictment handed down by a federal grand jury, claiming that Davidson had received, concealed and disposed of a firearm used in the murder of Amy Ayers, namely the missing .380 semiautomatic. Charged with being an accessory after the fact, failing to report a felony, making false statements to law officers and obstructing justice, he pleaded guilty five months later of conspiring to mislead officers by concocting stories about getting rid of a gun. He made stuff up, he testified, out of loyalty to his friend. He was then sentenced to a year in federal prison by District Judge Sam Sparks, who said Davidson's stories had authorities "shimmying up flagpoles when there's no flag."

SCALIA

In March 2004, while the Springsteen appeal awaited an opinion and Scott's appellate attorney prepared for his scheduled appearance before the Texas Third Court of Appeals, *Michael D. Crawford v. Washington* came before the Supreme Court; at issue, interpretation of the Confrontation Clause.

During Crawford's trial for the murder of a man he thought was about to rape his wife, prosecutors had used a statement his wife had made to police to help convict him. But because she couldn't be compelled to testify against her husband, her testimony had been read to the jury by a police officer, arguably robbing the defendant of his right to cross-examine his accuser. When the Washington State Court of Appeals agreed, Crawford's conviction was overturned. But when the prosecution appealed, the state supreme court reversed the decision, declaring his wife's testimony admissible under the 1980 *Ohio v. Roberts* ruling. This held that the Confrontation Clause did *not* bar the admission of out-of-court statements of witnesses unavailable for cross-examination, as long as they bore "adequate indicia of reliability," which could be "inferred" by what the court called "firmly rooted hearsay exception"—in other words, the same tactic Smith had used against Sicola the previous May.

Since *Roberts,* case law had allowed trial judges some leeway in deciding when a nontestimonial statement could be considered reliable, either because it fell within the hearsay exception or contained "particularized guarantees of trustworthiness." But in its March 2004 *Crawford* ruling, the Supreme Court overturned twenty-three years of case law in a unanimous decision reasserting the original limitations of the Confrontation Clause.

Judge Antonin Scalia wrote the majority opinion.

"Where testimonial statements are at issue," he wrote, "the *only* indicium of reliability sufficient to satisfy constitutional demands is the one the Constitution actually prescribes: confrontation. . . . Dispensing with confrontation because testimony is obviously reliable is akin to dispensing with jury trial because a defendant is obviously guilty. This is *not* what the Sixth Amendment prescribes."

Crawford overturned convictions all over the country. To gauge Scalia's passion about this issue, it's instructive to read the blistering dissent he would write in 2011's *Michigan v. Bryant,* a case in which police officers had been allowed to take the stand to recall the words of a crime victim who'd identified his assailant only minutes before dying. The vote was 6–2 against the petitioner, Elena Kagan abstaining, and Scalia began, "Today's tale—a story of five officers conducting successive examinations of a dying man with the primary purpose *not* of obtaining and preserving his testimony regarding his killer but of protecting him, them and others from a murderer somewhere on the loose—is so transparently false that professing to believe it demeans this institution. . . . Today's opinion distorts our Confrontation Clause jurisprudence and leaves it in a shambles. Instead of clarifying the law, the Court makes itself the obfuscator of last resort. . . ."

Mary Kay Sicola was confident that *Crawford* rendered Lynch's decision in *Springsteen* wrong. Scott's statement "is testimonial hearsay under *Crawford,*" she said, "and requires a finding of error. There is no way around it."

Equally optimistic, Jim Sawyer said the ruling would finally put an end to a practice that had been "standing the Constitution on its ear."

Carlos Garcia remained cautious. The state, he said, was likely to argue that the Yogurt Shop cases were different.

Bryan Case, head of the appellate division of the DA's office, said that because his office redacted the statements so they reflected only the declarant's guilt, they represented a different kind of "firmly rooted hearsay." *Crawford,* he blithely maintained, would not apply.

A wary Lynch fervently hoped not to be overturned.

In June, Ariel Payan argued before the Third Court of Appeals, citing *Crawford,* and Bryan Case appeared for the prosecution.

EVERYTHING HAPPENS IN THE SPRING

Things kept happening. On March 1, 2005, a year less a week after *Crawford,* the U.S. Supreme Court made another landmark decision when it ruled 5–4 that execution of offenders under eighteen years old at the time of the crime constituted cruel and unusual punishment, violating the Eighth and Fourteenth Amendments. The decision on *Roper v. Simmons*—written by Anthony Kennedy, joined by Souter, Ginsburg, Stevens and Breyer—stated, "When a juvenile offender commits a heinous crime, the State can exact forfeiture of some of the most basic liberties but the State cannot extinguish his life and his potential to attain a mature understanding of his own humanity. . . ."

Retribution, Kennedy declared, echoing the opinion of Jordan Steiker, was not proportional if the law's most severe penalty was imposed on one whose culpability or blameworthiness was diminished to a substantial degree by reason of youth and immaturity. The decision also noted the need to consider "evolving standards of decency that mark the progress of society" and, further, that since 1990 the United States stood alone in allowing the execution of juvenile offenders and that only one other country—Somalia—had not ratified Article 37 of the United Nations Convention on the Rights of the Child, which expressly prohibited the practice.

Roper canceled the death sentences of seventy-two inmates, including Robert Burns Springsteen IV. Once his sentence had been officially commuted by Governor Rick Perry, Springsteen was transferred from the death row section of the Allan B. Polunsky Unit in East Texas to a maximum-security unit closer to Austin.

Three weeks later, the Third Court of Appeals upheld Mike Scott's conviction, ruling that while his Sixth Amendment right to cross-examine witnesses had been violated, the error did not contribute to his conviction; therefore, admission of the redacted Springsteen testimony constituted "harmless" error.

Ariel Payan refiled the appeal, this time with the Texas Court of Criminal Appeals.

O n May 25, 2006, the TCCA reversed Robert Springsteen's conviction and remanded the case to Travis County District Court 167 for possible retrial. The ruling, written by Judge Paul Womack, stated, "Based on U.S. Supreme Court case law decided after defendant's trial, the admission [of Mike Scott's statement] violated the Confrontation Clause. A statement taken by police officers in the course of interrogation was exactly the kind of testimonial statement prohibited under a *Crawford* analysis. The error was not harmless because there was no physical or forensic evidence connecting defendant to the crime, there was no witness that tied him to the crime, and defendant had repudiated his videotaped confession." In conclusion, "introduction of Scott's statement was . . . vital to the State's case."

Presiding Judge Sharon Keller wrote the dissenting opinion, in which she concluded that trial testimony revealed *beyond a reasonable doubt* that the admission of Scott's written statement "did not contribute to the jury's conclusion that Robert Springsteen murdered Amy Ayers."

Mary Kay Sicola: "It's been an exceptionally long wait to get a ruling. For all the reasons, for the sake of the integrity of our justice system, the sake of our community, I'm so happy the court has finally issued a ruling."

John Jones: "Here we go again. This is going to be tough on the parents to have to live through all of this again."

Ronnie Earle: "We are reviewing the opinion and the issues it presents."

In a press release, the APD restated its belief in Springsteen's guilt and vowed to work closely with the DA's office to ensure that he "continues to be held accountable for these horrific murders."

According to Bryan Case, prosecutors now had three choices: ask the court for a new hearing, appeal the case to the U.S. Supreme Court or retry it in the same courtroom with the same judge.

In fact, there were two other options. Earle could offer Springsteen another deal and hope for better results this time. Or he could dismiss the charges and hope to try him again at a later date. But in order to get an indictment, they'd have to go before a new grand jury with a case that didn't depend on Scott's statement, and they didn't have one.

Earle requested a TCCA rehearing, but when the court refused to review its decision he was down to retry, dismiss or deal.

Sensing a decisive shift in the weather, Springsteen's attorneys were in no mood to accept any offer Ronnie Earle came up with, leaving him with only the dismiss or retry options.

SCIENCE

In the early spring of 2007, in a last-ditch effort to come up with biological evidence linking all four arrested men to the crime, the DA's office hired the Fairfax Identity Laboratories of Richmond, Virginia, to conduct DNA tests on six items recovered from the body of Amy Ayers, some taken at the scene, others at the morgue. This time around, the lab would test for "Short Tandem Repeat (STR) loci specific to the Male Y Chromosome, or Y-STR." This kind of male-specific DNA testing had not been available in 1991 or even in 2001–2 during the trials. Put simply, the Y-STR test separates out male, or Y-chromosome, DNA from female and is therefore especially useful in situations in which the majority of the DNA is female—as would be the case in a vaginal swab. If the Y-STR tests revealed the presence of DNA from at least one of the four suspects, the prosecution would have the forensic evidence they were lacking.

In June, the TCCA also threw out Michael Scott's conviction, reversing the decision of the Third Court and sending the case back to the 167th District Court.

Once again, Sharon Keller's dissent proclaimed the admission of the statement harmless.

Mike Lynch signed a bench warrant remanding Springsteen to the Travis County jail, where Scott arrived soon after. The judge then began scheduling pretrials. Barbara Ayres-Wilson said the reversals were due to a "loophole." Her husband said anybody who'd sat in the courtroom knew those guys were guilty.

Lynch said he wouldn't impose a gag order during the retrials, because he trusted the attorneys and, besides, they were dealing with a different set of circumstances. He didn't explain further. Efrain de la Fuente—who had become lead prosecutor after the Smith-Davis team moved on—argued against the judge's ruling, attributing the leak to the press in 2000. In response, the *Statesman* said it procured its information not from the defense team, but from official sources. In any case, Lynch didn't change his mind.

As for the "mastermind," Maurice Pierce had been arrested for those unpaid traffic tickets in Flower Mound, a prettified town not far from Lewisville, where he and his family lived. Police released him once he'd paid the fines, but within a year he'd been issued another citation: two hundred dollars for disorderly conduct after clobbering a motorist in a traffic dispute. Kimberli Pierce said the other guy threw the first punch.

DOWNHILL ROLL

In March 2008, both defense teams were told to report to Lynch's chambers. When Sawyer, Bettis, Garcia and Gilford arrived, de la Fuente and Darla Davis were already there, waiting to tell them about the swabs they'd submitted to Fairfax labs. The results had been surprising: This up-to-date Y-STR testing had revealed a previously undetected full male DNA profile in Amy Ayers's vaginal swab.

Defense took in the information, asked a few questions and waited for the other shoe to drop. After all, *previously undetected* was momentous and so was *full profile*. But the state's wrap-up was even more significant: This full profile matched none of the defendants'. And so the state was now in search of an unknown *fifth* assailant who hadn't been tested. As far as the prosecutors were concerned, nothing had changed. They were still planning for a *Scott* retrial in May.

The defense lawyers retired to a quiet place where they could fashion a new, more aggressive strategy.

On April 15, after acknowledging receipt of the new tests, Lynch honored a defense request for a hearing, in which Gilford would argue that they should have the right to hire their own lab to conduct Y-STR testing—not just on Amy but on all four girls. Despite objections from de la Fuente and Darla Davis's replacement, ADA Gail Van Winkle, the judge agreed to turn over what he termed a *laundry list* of physical evidence to the defense, including the DNA tests.

The next day, Maurice Pierce reentered the fray when a police officer in Plano pulled over a Ford Mustang GT for going thirty miles over the posted speed limit. Plano's in the Dallas suburbs, another province not known for softhearted law enforcement. When she asked the driver why he was so nervous about an ordinary speeding ticket, the jittery young man said that in the past he'd been accused of offenses he hadn't committed and so police made him nervous. When a second officer arrived, he reviewed the driver's record and, discovering an outstanding warrant issued by the Irving police, asked Pierce to step out of his car.

Instead, he threw the Mustang into reverse and peeled out, allegedly injuring one of the officers, and managed to get away. When officers arrived at his house, his wife said she hadn't seen him all day. A new warrant charged Maurice Pierce with aggravated assault on a police officer, a felony. By then, everybody knew exactly who he was.

The APD was pretty sure where he'd gone and soon confirmed its suspicions that indeed he was staying with the same sister he'd babysat for on the afternoon and evening of the Yogurt Shop Murders. Renee Reyna had moved farther west out MoPac, not far from where Barbara and Frank Suraci used to live on Tamarack Lane. Within a couple of weeks, the APD had put together a task force that included local officers and federal marshals. Reyna later claimed that when she walked into her living room at midnight with a child in her arms, armed men in uniforms ordered her and her family out of the house. One unconfirmed report said Maurice was hiding in a closet and that when police opened the door he came out swinging a baseball bat and had to be subdued with a Taser. Cops from the Travis County Sheriff's Office drove him, handcuffed, back to Collin County, where he'd been pulled over, to face charges and almost certainly to be given another chance to open up about Springsteen, Scott and Welborn.

Less than twenty-four hours after Mike Lynch ordered prosecutors to turn over DNA evidence to the defense, Jim Sawyer submitted a petition that would require the Travis County sheriff to bring the applicant (Springsteen) before the court and show cause why he shouldn't be released on a "reasonable bond." Back in 1999, when his client was charged with capital murder, no bond was set because a judge was given the option of denying bail to a suspect who seemed more likely than not to be found guilty and sentenced to death. According to Sawyer's petition, because new DNA tests excluded all four accused men, his client should be offered bail and released.

Lynch denied the request. But Yogurt Shop was back in the news. In the *Austin Chronicle*, Jordan Smith quoted "unnamed prosecutors" who said they already knew the identity of the newly discovered DNA contributor, and that he was more than likely "someone known to Amy Ayers," suggesting that the thirteen-year-old girl might have been sexually active at the time of the murders. The Ayerses made no comment.

Sawyer argued that science had eclipsed the state's theory and wondered, if Scott and Springsteen were guilty, where was the proof? If Springsteen's statement about putting his dick in Amy Ayers's pussy turned out to be a lie, given the absence of his DNA in her vaginal swab, what justified the prosecutors' white-hot pursuit of him?

In late May, Lynch scheduled a *Scott* pretrial, during which Garcia requested whatever new evidence the prosecution had gathered. When de la Fuente said they shouldn't have to give it up, the judge asked him why not—and clearly a chastened Mike Lynch had emerged. When the two sides continued to bicker about swabs, ligatures and other items of evidence, he said, "I am transfixed by this extraordinary difficulty you all have in working with each other on this case!" And he instructed them to "lock yourselves in a room and arm-wrestle."

Next day's headline in the *Statesman:* JUDGE TELLS YOGURT LAW-YERS TO ARM WRESTLE.

By the middle of the summer, prosecutors were still insisting that testing was incomplete. And when Lynch signed a gag order barring attorneys connected to the case from publicly discussing evidence, Sawyer protested: "The state went out and told the public they knew whose DNA this was. They don't. It's a misimpression and we're entitled to rebut it."

August 20 *Statesman* headline: YOGURT SHOP DEFENSE GROWS MORE AGGRESSIVE.

Jordan Smith, *Austin Chronicle*, August 29: "It's been more than four months since Travis County prosecutors said they expected to quickly find the donor of the unknown male DNA found in the body of Amy Ayers. No match has been found but apparently not because the state hasn't been looking." She quoted "courthouse sources" who said that as many as five dozen people had been tested, with no match, and yet prosecutors seemed "weirdly confident" despite the deep blow this delivered to their case.

Also in late August, ADA Van Winkle said the state's investigation was nearly completed, and in September Lynch announced that he was ready to retry Scott and Springsteen back-to-back, probably just after the first of the year. Sawyer requested money for the defense to resubmit a host of DNA evidence using Y-STR testing, stood his ground when Lynch protested the cost, and the money came through. Sawyer sent the evidence to Orchid Cellmark, an internationally known DNA-testing firm.

In late September, after Jordan Smith reported that after "eliminating sixty-three males," Travis County prosecutors still didn't have a clue whose DNA they'd found, contrary to earlier claims, letters to the *Chronicle* began to turn against the APD and Ronnie Earle's office.

At the end of October, Lynch set another date for the *Scott* retrial, December 10, but the date kept getting postponed.

By now, Sawyer said, "We all *knew* it wasn't going to happen."

The day after Christmas, Ronnie Earle abruptly announced his retirement at the end of the month, after thirty-two years in office, leaving First Assistant District Attorney Rosemary Lehmberg in charge until a special election could be held in March. He called the Yogurt Shop Murders a "hard slap at the laid-back image the city cultivates," and said that the savage nature of the crimes still gnawed at Austin's psyche. As for the suspects: "We thought we had the right guys." And so he swapped a DA's certainty—*We remain convinced*—for a regretful *We thought we had . . .*

Four days later, Orchid Cellmark informed the defense that, in addition to the full profile found in Amy Ayers's vaginal swab, Y-STR testing revealed the discovery of two, possibly three, unknown partial male profiles in swabs taken from Jennifer and Sarah Harbison. Orchid sent test results to Lynch and the DA's office.

Van Winkle argued that the results didn't disprove the state's case.

Sawyer saw it differently: "To a scientific certainty, we have excluded all four of these [men] and . . . we know that the DNA in these little girls' vaginas has nothing to do with consensual sex." And Garcia added that when DNA *excludes* a suspect, the prosecution must come up with a theory of the crime that explains the contradiction.

Lynch called for a meeting.

On that day, as Garcia, Sawyer and other defense lawyers stood waiting before an elevator in the Blackwell-Thurman Criminal Justice Center, the doors opened and out came members of the murdered girls' families.

"I'll never forget that moment," Garcia told me. "They'd just learned that their daughters had all been raped. It was horrible. Horrible."

Included in the *Statesman*'s list of the year's ten biggest stories was "Yogurt Shop Prosecutions Fall Apart."

ROSE

On January 1, 2009, Sawyer announced that because of the new DNA reports, he wanted his client out of jail. But Van Winkle wanted additional testing to be performed.

On January 7, Lynch set March 4 for a hearing to determine whether Springsteen and Scott should be released and said he would probably allow two "New York lawyers" with specialized knowledge of forensics to assist the Scott defense team.

After winning a four-candidate Democratic primary with no Republican opponents, Rosemary Lehmberg was sworn in as Travis County's first female DA. A native Texan, Rose is warm, straightforward and accessible and makes no bones about her long-term personal relationship with a woman. During her thirty-six years in the DA's office, she had focused to a great extent on child abuse and helped establish a county unit to investigate those crimes and to care for mistreated children.

Two weeks after taking office, when asked about Yogurt Shop, she acknowledged the possibility that there could be more than one unknown DNA donor; there was still work to be done. If further testing didn't dispel reasonable doubt, she'd "step up and suggest a bond." But she denied the validity of Sawyer's suggestion that science had passed her people by. Both her father and brother were doctors, and she cited the case of a local man who, after being convicted of rape, was cleared through DNA testing.

By the middle of May, the state seemed headed for a *Scott* retrial in July, and Garcia was eager to "vindicate our client with science."

After the defense requested more time for their experts to pre-pare affidavits, Lynch finally set Springsteen's bail-reduction hearing for June 19, the day Jim Sawyer donned glasses before reading the Orchid Cellmark report, which had been entered into the record:

1. DNA from an unknown male in Amy Ayers, a full Y-STR profile from a swab taken at the scene, as also reported by the DA's results from Fairfax. All four suspects arrested for the murders were excluded.

Sawyer looked up at the judge, removed his glasses and said the prosecutorial side hadn't tested vaginal swabs from the other girls, in his view because they were seeking only to prove Springsteen's state-ment that he had raped Amy Ayers. And so they focused strictly on her. He then returned to the Orchid reports.

2. The same DNA found in a scene-vaginal sample from Amy Ayers was also found in Jennifer Harbison's sample from the Medical Examiner's office, in addition to the DNA of [Jennifer's boyfriend] Sammy Buchanan. All four suspects excluded.
3. DNA from Sammy Buchanan and another male found in Sarah Harbison.
4. A third male's DNA found on clothing used to bind Eliza Thomas's wrists.
5. DNA from Sammy Buchanan found in both Jennifer and Sarah Harbison, indicating the likelihood that the same man raped both sisters, *transferring his own DNA as well as Buchanan's to Sarah after raping Jennifer* [italics added].

After Lynch asked the state for comment and Van Winkle said their tests were continuing, he said he'd probably decide early the next week whether to lower Springsteen's bail; but on Monday he said the test results needed a fuller analysis, and anyway his number-one priority was to begin jury selection for Mike Scott's retrial on July 6. When asked if her people were ready to go to trial, Rose Lehmberg confined her comments to the usual, rather hopeful assurances: that they had two of the individuals responsible for the murder in custody and would continue to investigate the identity of the unknown male donor or donors.

Lynch's preference was to conduct a robust review of the test results at trial, not in a hearing. But he needed to hear from the prosecution that they were ready. And so on June 23, he curtly reminded them that, absent emergency conditions, a motion for continuance (postponement) would *not* be entertained. "As previously stated on the record," he wrote, "any such motion by the state would, if granted, result in this Court granting both this defendant [Michael Scott] and Robert Springsteen release on personal recognizance bonds."

The next day, when the state reluctantly acknowledged that it wasn't prepared to go to trial as scheduled, Lynch briskly ordered that Springsteen and Scott be released immediately and set August 12 as the date when prosecutors would be asked to update their progress. He expected them to show up with "a more definite game plan," and if they didn't, the court would provide one.

Their release was front-page news, reported in banner headlines, along with photographs of Springsteen and Scott leaving the courthouse: Mike with Jeannine and his three lawyers, Rob with Sawyer and Bettis. Mike was wearing a light-colored suit and Rob a dark blue polo shirt and rimless glasses, his long hair tied back in a ponytail. TV stations issued special bulletins. Responding to the press, Rob thanked God, his lawyers and his family. Mike said nothing.

There were restrictions on their freedom—no alcohol, no guns, no associating with each other, no leaving Travis County—but they were out, wearing their own clothes and living their own lives.

Lehmberg gave a prepared statement. Because reliable scientific evidence presented an unknown male donor whom the state had not been able to identify, despite testing 130 people, she could not in good conscience allow the case to go to trial before the full truth was known, even though she remained fully confident, etc., etc. She called the Y-STR evidence powerful, and spoke of the search for the fifth man.

Police Chief Art Acevedo assured the public that his detectives would continue to work the case and that he, too, believed they had the right suspects in custody, and, echoing his boss, he referred to the possibility of a fifth man.

Jeannine Scott wanted a trial, not more delaying tactics. When asked if this was a big day for Mike and her, she said it would be a big day when twelve people declared her husband not guilty, so their family's nightmare would end and "the state can start pursuing the actual perpetrators and give those girls' families some peace and the truth."

Sawyer, Gilford and Garcia agreed.

According to the *Statesman:* "It is unclear whether the men once convicted in the 1991 killings . . . will ever face retrials . . . considering the questions raised about the prosecution's theories."

Maria Thomas, in Oregon: "I can't believe they let them go."

In early August, Lynch granted a postponement; the DA's office had until October 28 to decide if it was ready to proceed with a trial in January. But the court would entertain no further delays. In other words, if they didn't have a case, there wouldn't be a trial. In the meantime, *48 Hours* (now called *48 Hours Mystery*) was working up a third show on Yogurt Shop.

W hat Jim Sawyer left out of his Y-STR presentation was that, according to the lab report, further DNA testing might well produce additional results, especially from Eliza Thomas's swabs. And while Tony Diaz wanted to pursue this possibility and then initiate a suit demanding that the state also submit DNA samples from all *four* girls for Y-STR testing—including a secondary process called "re-amplification" to lock in the results—the other lawyers disagreed and the vote went against him. "We've done our job," Sawyer told the others. "Our clients have been freed." Garcia agreed. "We decided to let these little girls and their families rest," he says today.

ROSE'S CHOICE

Walking up to Blackwell-Thurman on October 28, 2009, when the DA's office would make its announcement, I noted the TV trucks, the video cameras poised and ready on the sidewalks, cameramen in work clothes, newsmen and -women facing the doors from which lawyers and family members would exit, hoping to catch a quick clip and an interview.

Beyond the metal detectors, elevators were crammed with people heading to the eighth floor. In the hall outside District Court 167, those who'd come to know one another during the trials chatted and looked around to see who else was there.

I took my seat—this time on the defendants' side of the room. Bob Ayers, the lone parent to attend, entered wearing full western regalia, boots and jeans, snap-button shirt, cowboy hat in his hands. Saying nothing, he sidled into a row on the prosecution's side. Minutes later, Art Acevedo came in and sat beside him.

Sawyer was in an elegant black suit, a crisp white handkerchief in his breast pocket, gold cuff links shining. Knowing what was ahead, he gave us spectators his perfect smile.

No longer an incarcerated defendant, Michael Scott entered the courtroom through the main doors, with Jeannine beside him, her hand resting on his arm. He was wearing his usual ill-fitting sport coat, this time with dark trousers. He'd grown heavy and his hairline had receded even more. Jeannine stood erect and confident, hair streaming down her back.

Springsteen came in accompanied by attorney Alexandra Gauthier. He looked sharp, in a dark blue suit and white shirt and a satiny tie. His mullet had been transformed into a new hipster cut, his goatee trimmed, his glasses fashionably rimless. Once again, no one from his family attended.

Garcia rolled in, wearing a sport coat, tie and gray pants, everything rumpled and a little tight.

When the court reporter and judge's aides filed in, the defendants and their attorneys took the table they'd been assigned to during their trials, Sawyer on the far left, then Springsteen, Tony Diaz and Mike Scott. Standing behind them, Garcia, Gilford, Gauthier and Bettis.

De la Fuente and Van Winkle came to the state's table. Rose Lehmberg and First Assistant District Attorney John Neal sat down directly in front of Ayers and Acevedo. Once the entire cast had entered, the bailiff called "All rise!" and the judge swept in, trailed by his black robe. Once everyone was seated, he issued a quick greeting and then spoke formally and a little curtly to the prosecutors, reminding them that today was their deadline to bring in a good-faith determination of whether or not they'd be ready to begin a jury trial in January. He had been and remained clear on this point, that there would be no continuance. Were they ready?

De la Fuente stood. The state, he said, was doing a wide testing of the vaginal swabs but so far had nothing new to offer. Since the judge had made it clear in August that he would grant no further postponements, "we have no other option than to file for a dismissal of the charges against these two men."

Lynch thanked the ADA and announced the court would therefore dismiss both indictments. This he accomplished straightaway by briskly signing each document, then banging his gavel and exiting the courtroom. He was planning to retire in January 2012, so unless he changed his mind about that, today's ruling would likely be his final association with Yogurt Shop.

Scott hugged Garcia, bending his head toward the attorney's shoulder. When the defendants shook hands, Scott smiled broadly, while Springsteen seemed reserved. Looking on, Gauthier smiled softly at them. Somebody snapped a picture of all three, which would appear on the front page of the next morning's *Statesman*.

Jeannine pulled at her husband's arm, and they walked out together.

In the hall outside, Sawyer praised the DA for the integrity of her decision. "This is no victory for anyone," he told reporters. We should, he added, reserve our sympathy for the families of those girls, and "I hope someday we will find the ones who killed their daughters."

Garcia commented that "this has been a long ten years for these guys." And in conventional cop-speak he addressed whoever had left his DNA at the scene. "Because of you, four innocent young men who had nothing to do with this . . . were punished. . . . We have your DNA. . . . One day we'll match a face to it."

Scott told reporters he was glad to be where he now was. When asked what he'd been doing the past few months, he ducked his head and said, "Staying out of trouble." He might have continued, but Jeannine nudged him and answered the question properly: "We've been a family again, the way we should have been for the past ten years." She then spoke of the girls' families. "I'm a mother. I can't imagine what they've been through."

Would Mike and Jeannine stay in the Austin area? At the time, they made no comment, but lawyers had already told them they'd never be safe in Texas. Somebody would always be hoping to make a score by taking Mike out. Cops would stop him for the least infraction, or none at all.

After the courtroom cleared, Rose Lehmberg held a press conference. Arrayed in a semicircle around her were Acevedo, de la Fuente, Van Winkle, Ron Lara and John Neal. An aide passed out printed copies of her statement, which began, "Today, I presented to Judge Mike Lynch motions to dismiss the cases against Robert Springsteen and Michael Scott."

Speaking carefully, she reminded reporters that in June they had filed a motion for continuance in order to conduct more tests and investigations. Judge Lynch had granted that motion, but on August 11, he had delivered a written order "stating that he would not grant another delay in the case if we again requested more time based on the same grounds." Therefore, "we have no choice but to announce that we are not ready to proceed to trial and ask for a dismissal of the cases pending further investigation. Make no mistake . . ."

Her voice broke. She took a deep breath, then looked up and completed her thought.

"This is a difficult decision for me and one I would rather not have to make. I believe it is the best legal and strategic course to take and is the one that leaves us in the best possible posture to ultimately retry both Springsteen and Scott."

After a few more statements and an avowal of commitment by representatives from her office, Art Acevedo and then Ron Lara, now head of the Cold Case Unit, uttered a few confident words, and finally it was over.

"I can't believe I lost my composure," she told me a few days later. "Lehmbergs don't lose their composure."

But she knew why. The day before the hearing, she'd invited the four girls' parents to her office to tell them what was about to happen. She'd set up a conference call with family members who couldn't be there and got them on speakerphone before giving everyone the news. The dismissal didn't mean that Springsteen, Scott and the other two men would never come to trial, or that the state thought they weren't guilty. Her team and the police department would continue to pursue justice for their murdered children. She felt confident that in the end justice would prevail and that the four men who they all agreed had murdered their children would be brought to justice and punished for their crimes.

In the middle of her press conference, she'd thought again of the families seated around her desk, pledging their loyalty, assuring her of their trust in the work she and her staff had done. That was when her voice broke.

"They're all so strong," she said. "Each in a different way."

Because Rob had no family in Austin, Jim Sawyer drove him to San Antonio, where he could stay with his brother before returning to West Virginia. He didn't really want to go back there, though. His wife had divorced him and he would rather stay in Texas, maybe San Antonio. But his lawyer said he should get out of Texas and stay out.

Four days later—on Sunday, November 1—the *Statesman* ran an editorial entitled YOGURT CASE IS FAR FROM CLOSED, casting most of the blame for the lack of resolution on the police and the state, specifically citing "investigators who overzealously sought confessions and prosecutors who, to date, have been unable to successfully make the case." Victims, it declared, included "everybody for whom the system has not worked . . . from the slain young girls to the defendants and suspects . . . and everybody who counts on a functional criminal justice system."

In the months following the dismissal, Sawyer, Lehmberg, Springsteen and members of the girls' families were interviewed by various reporters, including Erin Moriarty. Here are some of their responses:

Barbara Ayres-Wilson: "I do not want anyone in the community to feel like we have got the wrong guys because that was not the issue. . . . They have confessed. They did the murders."

Maria Thomas: "[When I heard the news] I felt like my head was gonna spin right out of my body. And it was because *their* rights were violated. Every time I hear those words, that *their* rights were violated, I feel like I'm gonna go insane. Pretty angry about that, you know. . . . To live it on a daily basis is very difficult."

Robert Springsteen: "I was berated and berated and berated by the police officers until they obtained what it was they wanted to hear. They basically broke me down."

Rose Lehmberg: "Y-STR is an accurate test for determining male DNA and mixtures of male and female . . . but as for the profiles inside Amy and the others, it could have come from contamination. Or transfer."

Jim Sawyer: "What does it take to make people say, 'I was wrong'?"

Robert Springsteen: "I wish we were going to trial right now. I want my name cleared."

Barbara Ayres-Wilson: "We can't go to trial without that DNA. It would devastate what we have left of the case."

Bob Ayers: "This thing is not near over. Believe me, it's just starting. And if it takes a little more time to find the information we need, so be it."

Barbara Ayres-Wilson: "You take a breath and you think, okay this is just one more thing to deal with."

Maria Thomas: "When I heard they were let out I just wanted to hit something."

———

In 2012, Springsteen would call Sawyer to ask about filing a claim for "actual innocence." In Texas and twenty-six other states, wrongfully convicted inmates had received compensation when solid evidence such as DNA tests proved them innocent of the crimes they'd been found guilty of. Texas law states that a "wrongfully convicted person is entitled to $80,000 per year of wrongful incarceration, as well as $25,000 per year spent on parole or as a registered sex offender." They also are eligible for child-support compensation, specific tuition payments and the opportunity to buy into the Texas State Employee Health Plan. But Springsteen's conviction had been voided, and because he was neither incarcerated nor exonerated, "wrongful" didn't precisely apply. On the other hand, as far as anybody knew, the state wasn't pursuing new charges. So his case fell between the cracks, and Texas law provided no remedy for this particular situation.

Jim Sawyer convinced respected civil attorney Broadus Spivey to see what he could do. In his original petition—there have been three so far—Spivey outlined Springsteen's eight-plus years in prison followed by the 2009 dismissal and described his current life as one in which the sword of Damocles hangs over him, with only a thread between him and another arrest. Lawyers dine often on that metaphorical sword, but in this instance it seems appropriate.

Mike Scott declined to participate in the suit.

As of this writing, Spivey's still actively pursuing Rob's case, but so far the thread still holds.

IV

UNANSWERED QUESTIONS

WHO KILLED THESE GIRLS?

How do we know what we know (or even remember) and when can we be, if not certain, at least reasonably persuaded that we've hit on the truthful version of what really happened? Maybe doubt is never reasonable and memories are closer to dreams than accurate recollections. Perhaps facts and solutions exist only in the science lab—and not always even then—and the best we can hope for is a perception that suits our individual temperament. In other words, what we're *prone* to believe, given genes, upbringing, class, culture and all the rest. And perhaps there's no such thing as closure, in which case nothing ever ends anyway.

Uncertainty, on the other hand, has its own kind of attraction, from the mysterious fifth (or sixth) man to countless other unknowns, from the Zodiac Killer to Jack the Ripper, from JonBenét Ramsey to Nicole Simpson, Tupac Shakur to Jimmy Hoffa. Some would add John F. Kennedy to the list. And will we ever, ever know?

"People talk about justice," Barbara Ayres-Wilson said recently. "I just want to know the *truth*. That's all I care about."

Answers fly away like fruit flies. We clutch the air and close up a fist, but they're already gone.

WHAT REALLY HAPPENED?

ACCORDING TO THE PROSECUTION

On the first day of *Springsteen,* Robert Smith began his opening statement with the assurance of a man into whose ear God was whispering the truth: "On Friday night, December 6, 1991, two high school senior girls were working . . ." And he went on from there, throughout the speech repeating the phrase "as the evidence will show you," even though there wasn't any. Seventeen months later, he made the same promise to the *Scott* jury, but this time he took a little longer and added a few new details. He wound up in fine fashion: "Something happened. And the ligature that was holding her hands together came loose and the gag that was on her mouth came loose and she fought and she tried to get away and they subdued her and this defendant used that sock, gag, as a ligature and choked her to death and this defendant, Michael James Scott, shot her in the top of the head with a .22 caliber revolver."

As if he'd been there. But then, Smith was just doing his job, and to trump reasonable doubt he had to convince the jury that the truth was simple and he knew what it was. *This is what happened and then this and then that.*

ACCORDING TO THE APD

In December 2011, the twentieth anniversary of the murders, the local NBC affiliate KXAN-TV ran a three-part series on Yogurt Shop, and one episode featured a visit to the APD Homicide Cold Case Unit, created by Rosemary Lehmberg in 2000 and supervised by Sgt. Ron Lara, with assistance from four homicide detectives. Housed in the same towers where Manuel Fuentes had taken Mike Scott's statement, the offices were lined with file cabinets and photographs of the victims of unsolved crimes, including the billboard shots of the Yogurt Shop girls.

Lara was still certain they'd arrested the right guys, and when the newscaster called for a show of hands from his team, the vote was unanimous. They had, Lara claimed, information they weren't sharing with the public. Paul Johnson made a brief appearance. Although retired, he still visited the unit once a week, specifically to discuss Yogurt Shop. His confidence, he said, had never wavered. Every time he and the others revisited the files, it seemed, they confirmed the truth of what they already knew.

ACCORDING TO THE CRIME RECONSTRUCTIONIST

Ross Martin Gardner might have been the only witness who proved objective, not on *who* committed the murders but *what happened*, based exclusively on evidence. There was physical evidence, he said, that store operations had ceased and the yogurt machines were being taken down when the incident began, though there was no video camera to show us when the intruders entered or the incident exactly began. The telephone was either knocked off the hook as the girls struggled or a call was disrupted. The latter was a good possibility, but there was no proof. First, the criminals had to bring the girls under control. Only once they were no longer able to act on their own could what followed be set in motion, using guns, threats and the surprise of the perpetrators' very presence.

Based on material from the APD evidence room, photographs and forensic analyses, Gardner's account lacks voice, eyewitness immediacy, characterization of the victims and literary references. While certainly unsettling—especially to the girls' families—this intentional coolness lends authority to his testimony and makes it worthy of our patient attention.

"We see evidence that the girls have been forced to undress. . . . There is no evidence of forcible undressing—tearing of clothes, jeans inside out. . . . The clothes are folded and neatly stacked. Several of the items have cuts in them, not to help disrobe a girl but as a kind of aggressive penetration, another measure of terror and control. And since all of the girls' clothes and shoes were found in the far west area close to the back doors and not elsewhere, we can see that they were brought under control in that part of the back room."

We also know, he said, that Sarah, Jennifer and Eliza were gagged with items of their own clothing, that the gags were knotted at the backs of their heads and "because three are gagged and only two are bound . . . it looks like the gagging started first."

Gardner's analysis follows the direction of blood flow as determined by gravity and the size, shape and placement of drops, spray, swipes and spatter. Evidence from the medical examiner's report shows that the rounds from the .22 that killed Sarah, Eliza and Jennifer came from back to front and low to high, indicating that these three girls were facedown on the floor when they were shot. The only other way that particular path of the projectile might have occurred was if the girls were on their hands and knees, and "we know that Sarah and Eliza could not have been in that position because their hands were tied." The placement of those two girls as they were shot is also denoted by two separate "blood-spatter events" on the northwest back door, directly across the room from the top of the girls' heads, after a "blood source [vein or artery] received some kind of force or energy [gunshot wound]," which then broke the source into droplets that projected out onto whatever surface was closest.

There were bloodstains on one of Jennifer's shoes, stains that looked like possible spatter on two articles of the girls' clothing and numerous stains and droplets on the door, but because the Department of Public Safety didn't sample the stains or test them for DNA, there was no way of knowing whose blood it was or even if they *were* of blood. Sarah's injuries on her labia and vulva indicate with some certainty that she was alive when she was vaginally assaulted. And because DNA from Eliza was found in the anal cavity of Sarah, "this leads us to think that Eliza was assaulted prior to the assault of Sarah."

And then?

"After Sarah was shot, she had to have been repositioned." Because blood follows gravity and there is evidence of blood on the back of her gag but none along her neck or in her ears or on the floor, it follows that she was quickly moved onto her back, while blood was still flowing. And subsequent to that, Eliza was also repositioned, to lie on her back across Sarah, which we know because in photographs of the two girls as they were discovered by the firefighters, both lie with hands tied behind their backs and their heads toward the back doors. Gardner said the placement of the ice scoop between Sarah's thighs didn't just happen. It was placed between her legs after she was repositioned.

He seemed a little hesitant to talk about Jennifer, except to say that she did not die as she was found, with her left leg in the air. He didn't know where she was when the fire started or if the three girls were lined up in a row, but her eventual position was unnatural, an indirect result of her proximity to the shelves as ceiling tiles, girders and shelving burned and fell on top of her.

Unlike other witnesses, who assumed Jennifer's wrists had been bound with a ligature that had burned away, Gardner didn't believe Jennifer's hands had been tied. If we look carefully, he said, apologizing for having to show the awful photograph, we can see that her hands are far apart, one curled against her spine, close to the thoracic area of her back, while the other one was lower down her back. And he placed his own hands against his spine to demonstrate. Also, he pointed out, if she'd been tied, there would be some remnant of the ligature, if only a tiny scrap.

He didn't say much about the order of the murders, except to note that since blood matching Jennifer's DNA was found under Amy's fingernails, Jennifer must have still been alive when the transfer occurred, perhaps as Amy grabbed for support or help. And although he couldn't state this as an outright certainty, he thought there was reason to believe Amy was the last one killed. Since her clothing was found in the same area as the other girls', and because she was exposed to the same or similar process as they were, Gardner felt confident, however, that the four girls were together when the incident began.

Like Jennifer's, Amy's wrists were not bound, but a ligature was tied with a loose half hitch at the back of her neck, so slack that it seemed to have been used more for control than silence, a speculation further borne out by the abrasions on the front of her neck. The best possibility—by no means a certainty—is that having been forewarned of her fate by the other girls' murders, Amy somehow managed to avoid a fatal injury when she was shot with the .22, perhaps by jerking her head away; and subsequent to that, she was more than likely taken, or forced, into the middle area of the storage room. There were swipes and stains of her blood on both the office wall and on a trash bucket beside it, indicating that she had already been shot and might have stumbled or fallen in that direction, possibly to her knees as she was being moved by someone pulling her by the sock around her neck. There were also light smears of her blood on the wall, perhaps from her hand.

The shot from the .380 was then administered to the side of her head and—although Amy was found lying on her right arm—at the moment of receiving the fatal shot she fell onto her *left* side and stayed there for at least a few moments. This was evident from the blood flow saturating that side of her ligature and her face and scalp. There was also blood on the floor beneath where she lay, but not on the right side of her face or under her body in the position in which she was discovered.

If Gardner was certain about anything, it was that Amy did not fall into that odd position while running and she didn't fall with her right arm fully extended beneath her. "The easiest way to explain what we are seeing in terms of Amy's final position is that as she lay left-side down . . . someone grabs her right arm. They then pulled it and extended it, dragging her out into this area and she was rolled up onto her right side."

When questioned about "pulled" and "rolled," Gardner modified his description: "She was repositioned." Since the first shot didn't kill her, they wanted to make sure she was dead after they fired the second one.

Carlos Garcia conducted the direct examination of Ross Gardner. It's hard to know what effect such an unemotional rundown might have had on the jury, but from this far out—so many years later—his seems the most likely account of what happened.

REGARDING THE RAPES, ACCORDING TO THE DEFENSE

In the June 2009 bail-reduction hearing, after reading the Orchid Cellmark DNA report, Jim Sawyer said, "From the Y-STR findings

I can tell you exactly in what order the girls were raped. First Amy, perhaps from behind, the sock-ligature used as a kind of steadying device, like a rope around a horse's neck. The first man left a full DNA profile inside her. The other guy did Jennifer, leaving a partial profile along with Sammy Buchanan's full profile inside of her. Then to Sarah, leaving both partials inside of her. Eliza probably last; her lower body was too horribly burned to capture any biological evidence."

Two *different* guys. But not Rob, Mike, Maurice or Forrest.

FROM CARLOS GARCIA AND AMBER FARRELLY, A NEW THEORY

In Jordan Smith's December 16, 2011, cover story in the *Austin Chronicle,* marking the twentieth anniversary of the murders, Garcia and Farrelly proposed a hypothesis based principally on crime-scene photographs and the eyewitness accounts of late-night customers Margaret Sheehan and Tim Stryker. This theory has received general support from the other Yogurt Shop defense attorneys and—to a lesser extent—from John Jones.

When Garcia began reworking his defense for Mike Scott's retrial, he organized the crime-scene photographs in a sequence that made sense to him. He then coordinated the pictures with statements by police, firefighters and eyewitnesses, noting the changes made in those statements before and after the arrests. He gave all this to Farrelly, who created an illustrated time line across an accordion-like foldout of white cardboard poster boards, using photographs from various magazines to represent the customers who'd come in during Eliza and Jennifer's shift. She then drew arrows connecting customers whose paths might have crossed, and at the bottom of the board inserted their testimony. The two lawyers visited the ICBY's back room again and afterward paid more attention to customers who hadn't noticed anything unusual but were nonetheless there. Within a few weeks, after paying particular attention to the Sheehan and Stryker accounts, they came up with some ideas.

The *Chronicle*'s cover featured a full-page photograph taken from inside the front doors just after the girls' bodies had been discovered. The original photo, used as a prosecution exhibit in both trials, shows three wooden tables lined up in the middle of the room, each with two chairs pulled up to it and two placed upside down on top. The paper napkin holder in the middle of each table is full, having been replenished for the next day's business, as Brice rules required. Each of the booths along the north wall has one chair upside down on its built-in table, and the napkin holders are full. The first four booths on the other side of the room look the same.

The fifth booth, however, the one closest to the cash register, has no chair on it, and by zooming in, you can see the napkin holder is empty. The clear implication—that this booth hadn't been cleaned, even though Jennifer had taken care of all the rest and had moved on to other jobs behind the counter—had not been mentioned by either side during the trials.

To illustrate the story's premise, the *Chronicle*'s art director, Jason Stout, superimposed a ghostly white drawing on the photograph: a pencil-like sketch of two figures in hooded jackets, caps, jeans and heavy-soled, lace-up work boots. They are grown men, not teenage boys, and they float there sitting across from each other, outlined but not fleshed out. The man closest to the cash register is large, bald, thick-necked and hulking. Wearing a kind of Michelin Man jacket he sits hunched over, elbows on the table, head down, so that while we see only a slice of his face, his bulk and obvious boredom make him seem dumb and scary.

His partner, a thinner man, lounges royally on the other bench, his right arm on the seat back, the left one placed casually on the table. From beneath his ball cap, his shaggy and straight hair drifts to his jacket collar, and he's wearing glasses of some kind, maybe with darkened lenses. He seems as relaxed as if he owned the shop and could do whatever he pleased. The legs of his jeans reach to the shoelaces of his thick-soled work shoes, and he's hiked up his right knee so he can rest that foot flat on the seat. The figures have the quick-sketch look of people who are both there and not, as if done with swipes of Wite-Out.

Inside the tabloid, Garcia and Farrelly delivered a theory derived from specific bits of evidence: the unopened Coke can by the cash register; the sweating Styrofoam cup; the booth with the empty napkin holder and no chair on top; and the credible testimony of Tim Stryker and Margaret Sheehan. In their version of what happened, once Sheehan and Stryker had taken their yogurt sundaes and gone home, Jennifer locked the front door, flipped over the OPEN sign and continued with her cleaning routine. The two men were still sitting there. The girls were chatting. They would unlock the front door when their last two customers were ready to leave.

The rest is speculation: A few minutes later, at about 11:00 p.m., one of the men went to the cash register and ordered a Coke. Eliza (cashier 13) took the can from the refrigerator, placed it on the counter and, after selecting a large Styrofoam cup, turned away from the customer and bent toward the small, low freezer to her right. When she'd filled the cup with ice, she turned back to find a gun pointed at her. She set the cup down beside the can of Coke.

The first time Carlos showed me blowups of this photograph, I couldn't believe what I was seeing. "They were already there," I said, more to myself than to him. "They didn't have to open the back door."

After Eliza rang up "No Sale," she gave the man whatever cash there was and then handed him the till. By this time, Jennifer would have stepped down from the stool beside the vanilla dispenser can. And maybe the other guy had already gone into the back room, where he pulled the second gun on the younger girls. Once all four of them were in the storage area, the men did everything they could to further humiliate and terrorize them. Since the .22 bullets traveled in an upward pattern from the base of their skulls through the brain and into the bone of their foreheads, Garcia and Farrelly speculated that the killer forced them to their knees, then bent their heads forward before pulling the trigger, and that everything happened quickly: Jennifer, then Sarah, then Eliza, 1-2-3. Perhaps because Amy was last and had time to react, she jerked her head to the side, as Ross Gardner had suggested, causing the bullet to go sideways, wounding but not killing her.

And so the rest happened and Amy was shot again, this time with the .380. After the cartridge went through and she fell down, they grabbed her right hand and flipped her over to make sure she was dead. And there she lay, half on her stomach, with her arm under her body in that odd, torqued posture. Although Eliza's wrists were still bound, her body lay at a slant, her right elbow pulled sharply away from her body. Sarah's arms mirrored Eliza's, her left elbow angled out, her right tucked behind her back. Did they pull Sarah into position by her elbow, splay her legs and place the ice scoop between her thighs, then drag Eliza by her right elbow and stack her on top of Sarah?

And then they set fire to the shelves where the flammable products were. And once it flared up, they had to escape through the back door. Were the scratches on the door plate from their efforts to pry it open? Carlos thinks so.

And finally the men vanished into the night, perhaps even passing Troy Gay as he drove east from MoPac looking for drunk drivers.

Amber Farrelly doesn't doubt this is how it all went down, and she scoffs at the notion of stoned high school boys putting these particular girls under their control. She says those girls would've laughed in their faces. Jim Sawyer's willing to go further, that they "would've kicked their asses." This was, he insists, "a man's crime."

Still, the proof Farrelly and Garcia presented is like unearthed bones placed in a skeleton shape without any connective tissue. When I asked John Jones what he thought, he said their scenario had *flow,* which was a good thing. But there was no way to know how the scene might have been affected by the water or the firemen—who testified they'd stumbled over the bodies—and minus a weapon, any theory remained speculation.

Of the pictures accompanying the *Chronicle* story, two yearbook photos are particularly interesting. One is the 1992 picture of Robert Springsteen looking soft and young, quite alert and sparky. The other is of Mike Scott, who's even wearing a tie for the occasion; he's smiling widely, his hair's in a high crew cut and he looks altogether okay, maybe even hopeful. It's easy to think of how they looked when they were arrested, but these are the hapless boys that Paul Johnson's task force built a case against, the ones they claimed overpowered four girls they then gagged, raped, murdered and burned.

The article also included a snappy quote from John Jones, who reminded readers that Hector Polanco had interviewed and cleared Maurice Pierce in 1991. "My story is, if Hector couldn't get Pierce to confess, then he didn't do it. Trust me." As for Welborn, "Forrest couldn't organize a two-car parade."

———

Other possibilities, still seriously discussed among players and various locals:

A crime of opportunity. Truckers or motorcyclists on MoPac, passing through.

The serial Ice Cream Killer on death row in Tennessee, who specialized in shops where frozen desserts were sold. No real proof. Also, serial killers generally work alone, and Yogurt Shop required at least two people.

Kenneth McDuff. Even though he told Chuck Meyer if he'd killed the yogurt girls he'd be proud to admit it, the conventional line on him is, *he had it in him to do it*. After all, he had mercilessly raped, tortured and killed at least thirteen young women, probably more.

If not him, then perhaps his disciples. Mightn't they have operated on his orders, the way Manson's people did?

A man who in 1992 took out regular classified ads aimed at girls who wanted to pose for glamour shots and was arrested for taking nude photographs of young girls between thirteen and fourteen in a house near the ICBY shop.

The Mexican nationals. Admitted criminals, drug dealers, rapists, they fit all the conventional assumptions. Just as Porfirio Saavedra had predicted.

The driver of the red Jeep Mike Scott claimed he saw. Driver of the white car. Driver of the van. A Satanist. And don't forget Shawn "Buddha" Smith.

The four guys.

The three men whose DNA was found inside the girls.

PAUL JOHNSON AND THE DISEASE OF CERTAINTY

Since 2009, Austin has had a Public Safety Commission, an appointed seven-member board that acts as an advisory body to the city council on budgetary and policy matters related to the APD, AFD and EMS. In 2011, a week after Yogurt Shop's twentieth anniversary, one commissioner, Dr. Kim Rossmo, asked his colleagues to consider establishing what he wanted to call the "External Review Board," made up of experienced criminal investigators with no prior connection to Austin who would cast fresh eyes on unsolved murders stored in the Cold Case Unit files, beginning, of course, with what happened at the ICBY.

A native Canadian and naturalized citizen, Rossmo worked in Vancouver law enforcement for more than twenty years and is internationally regarded as an expert on cold-case work, having served as a consultant on many high-profile investigations, including the Green River Killer in Washington State and the sniper attacks in D.C. A professor of criminology at Texas State University in San Marcos, he's also the author of several books, including one entitled *Criminal Investigative Failures.*

Having read the *Chronicle* article and seen the KXAN-TV broadcast, Rossmo described what he feared might be a possible lack of independent thinking concerning Yogurt Shop, reminding his fellow commissioners that "we have the same agency investigating a case and coming to the same conclusions they have in the past." He talked about tunnel vision: when investigators lock in on an early suspect and consider only evidence that supports their scenario; "group-think," a reluctance to challenge the dominant theory once it gets going; and the "disease of certainty." He also pointed out that in the UK, which has a 90 percent rate of homicide clearance, local departments are given *one year* to solve a crime, after which outside agencies are brought in, and compared this to the eight-year lag between the ICBY murders and the arrests and trials. One comment he found particularly disturbing was when District Attorney Lehmberg said, after Scott's and Springsteen's release, that she still believed the four men arrested were responsible for the crime, even though the DNA tests excluding them were far and away the most compelling evidence yet.

Rossmo also cited the *America's Most Wanted* Web site, which had posted only two theories about the 2009 Y-STR DNA profiles: one, that the sample was tainted; and two, that there was a fifth man. The program had not mentioned even once the possibility that none of these four men had been involved. All of which had prompted Rossmo's ongoing concern, especially since *America's Most Wanted* worked exclusively with local police departments. The commissioners agreed to study Rossmo's recommendation and vote on it later in the year.

Every meeting of the Public Safety Commission includes a slot for "Citizens Communications," when Austin residents who have a beef are given three minutes to speak. People who wish to take advantage of this opportunity must sign up at least ten minutes before the meeting is called to order, and only the first five who do so are given the floor. In May, retired APD detective Paul Johnson signed up early enough to be that month's second speaker. When his turn came, the chairman announced, "Our next speaker is Paul Johnson and his topic is Yogurt Shop."

Johnson wore a slightly wrinkled long-sleeved white shirt, pens in the pocket, reading glasses halfway down his nose and his thinning hair smoothed back. After introducing himself, he said he had come to challenge two statements made by Co–Vice Chair Rossmo in support of getting new investigators to work on this case. Not that he was resistant to the idea of bringing in new people; he himself had asked for outside evaluations when working as case agent. "I just don't want," he said, reading from a sheet of paper, "people in positions of authority"—he paused for emphasis without looking up—"*lying* about the case."

The next citizen waiting to speak sat directly behind Johnson, and when he said "lying," her jaw dropped; then she placed her hand over her mouth. As one, the commissioners lifted their heads.

Johnson's first complaint was Rossmo's description of the evidence that brought Scott and Springsteen to trial as "quite weak." In fact, Johnson contended, it was strong enough to convince twenty-four jurors of their guilt, and that proved it *wasn't* weak. "For the Co-Vice-Chairman to declare that the evidence was weak after it had been determined not to be weak by twenty-four people is"—he looked up—"just a *lie*."

His reasoning was reckless and his defensive bluster more than a little embarrassing, but he didn't care. While the commissioners were used to outrageous statements during Citizens Communications, labeling a fellow commissioner a liar invited blowback.

The second thing Johnson wanted to challenge was Rossmo's contention that said evidence was "basically two individuals pointing fingers at each other." If the commissioner knew anything about these trials, it would be that not once in Michael Scott's trial did Robert Springsteen mention Scott's name *at all,* and vice versa. And so, Johnson concluded, when Rossmo said they were pointing fingers at each other, he was *lying*.

Johnson ended by saying that although Co-Vice Chair Rossmo believed that judges, juries and the police should base their beliefs only on evidence, he was asking the police department and this commission to make a decision based not on evidence, but on *lies*. Folding his paper, he said thank you and prepared to step down.

Rossmo was absent that day, but Commissioner Mike Levy—the former publisher of *Texas Monthly*—spoke in his stead. Sir, he said, he knew Professor Rossmo as an honorable man. He might certainly misinterpret, misunderstand or make a mistake. He might be misinformed. But lying involves intent, and he would not lie.

Johnson would have none of it. Rossmo knew the law and knew that it was juries who determined whether evidence was weak or convincing. "And for him to say anything different . . . is just a *lie*."

Levy thanked him for coming out of retirement to keep working on the case, and Johnson once again prepared to leave. But the chairman had a final question: If Commissioner Rossmo so desired, would Johnson be willing to sit down and talk with him about his objections?

Johnson smiled. Since Rossmo had "made that suggestion," he'd stopped working on the case, so it wouldn't be proper for him to speak about it beyond the public statements he'd made today. Finally, he left. But like a spurned lover, he couldn't let well enough alone. A week later, he sent an e-mail to members of the Public Safety Commission. "Kim Rossmo," he wrote, "did lie to the commission and public and he knew the statements he made were not true, which shows his intent to deceive. He was making public statements (that were not true) about my investigation that implied that the investigation was flawed, which was attacking my professional integrity and competency. Making those kind of false statements from his position of presumed authority effects not only me, but the victims' families, the press and the entire public."

The e-mail said it all. He was irked by what he saw as a personal attack on *his* investigation, integrity and competency.

At the June meeting, Rossmo gave his presentation. While his backup material came from newspapers, magazines and television, not trial transcripts or personal interviews, he did quote ADA Robert Smith as saying, "There never was a fifth man."

After a short discussion, the commission voted. Wanting more time to study the resolution, the chairman abstained, but everybody else was in favor and it was passed to the city council.

Barbara Ayres-Wilson called Rossmo's idea a "slap in the face," and Bob Ayers phoned him to ask a few questions.

Some months later, the council rejected the proposal.

Rossmo remains hopeful. He thinks there's about a 15 percent chance the guys who got arrested are guilty.

THE STORAGE ROOM

Pictures often make things look bigger than they are. To understand the true dimensions of the back room of the ICBY shop, you have to go there, which I did in 2012, the year after a Vietnamese family renovated the shuttered shop and turned it into a nail salon called Classy Nails and Spa.

The front part looks completely different now. No more Mexican tile or wood-paneled walls, and the counter where frozen-yogurt toppings were once displayed has been removed. Just inside the front door, a recycling waterfall makes a splashing sound as water travels up one side of a tall sheet of bubbled Plexiglas and down the other; beyond it are ten mani-pedi chairs and several nail stations. The walls have been painted a soft mint green and are decorated with photos of idyllic beach scenes and, between them, flat-screen TVs tuned to either C-SPAN or a muted sports channel. There are orchids and soft background music.

Toward the rear, the women's bathroom—now unisex—is the same as it was in 1991, but the men's room has become a place where employees either take breaks or do laundry. Across from it, where the sink was attached to the wall leading to the walk-in cooler, are two small massage rooms, one for individuals, the other for couples. The storage room itself, however, is eerily the same: dark, dank, the concrete floor painted gray, and along the south wall, steel storage shelves.

When firefighters and police officers speak of Amy's being alone and speculate that perhaps the other three girls had already been killed and she was running away, they seem to indicate a flight from one room into another. In fact, there was no other room. Amy's body lay only four feet from Sarah's.

When I asked one of the Classy manicurists if she knew what the shop had been before they moved in, she replied quickly, "Cash 'n Advance." And before that?

"Yogurt shop," she said. Asked if she knew what had happened there, she removed a small ceramic pot from a nearby shelf and held it out for me to see. It was filled with incense sticks. They burn one on the memorial plaque every morning, she said, in memory of the girls. "We hope," she said, "if we remember them, when we die someone will remember us." When I left, I walked across the parking lot to the bronze plaque. A number of blackened incense sticks lay on it.

I once heard Barbara Ayres-Wilson say she wished somebody would burn the ICBY shop to the ground, but when I told her about the nail salon and the incense, she relented somewhat. "Well," she said, "I guess that's about as good as it could be."

JONES AT THE EMBASSY SUITES

In the spring of 2014, when his old friend Howard Williams asked if he'd give a talk at the Texas Citizens Police Academy convention in San Marcos, John Jones said, "Talk about *what*?" Williams had been the San Marcos police chief for eleven years, but he'd begun his career in Austin and he and Jones had worked together.

Williams said Yogurt Shop, what else? As for the specific topic, it could be anything Jones wanted to talk about. Hour and a half, July 29. Embassy Suites Conference Center. I-35 South. Eight in the morning. Probably between sixty and eighty people in attendance. It didn't take Jones long to figure out what he had to say that hadn't already been talked to death, so he said yes.

The TCPA is a statewide organization of citizens who want to learn about and support police work. To become members, they attend a course that lasts anywhere from ten to thirteen weeks and covers what an officer has to know in order to do his job. The instruction is free and lectures include DWI procedures, the use of force, patrol tactics, the protocol and procedures used in drug enforcement, criminal investigations and evidence collection. How to be a cop, in other words. After graduating, members are sometimes asked to participate in neighborhood-watch activities and ride out with cops. Vigilantism is not encouraged, but keeping vigilant is.

When the convention schedule was released, Jones's talk was announced as the feature presentation. His subject, "Police-Officer Stress in a High-Profile Investigation: A Case Study, the Yogurt Shop Murders of 1991." He'd decided to take the conventioneers "behind the curtain" and talk about the toll taken not just on police officers but on their whole families. He'd initially convinced his ex-wife, Yolanda, to participate, but she pulled out two days before the meeting. Though their four daughters tried to persuade her to go, she refused. That time, she said, was too painful. She didn't want to relive it.

Just as well. There must have been three hundred people sitting eight to a table in the ballroom, waiting for techies to set up Jones's PowerPoint presentation. Jones said he'd gone to smaller rooms first, looking for where he was supposed to speak. He'd hoped to wander through the audience while images flashed by on the screen, then found himself onstage with little room to move—and all those people out there. I sat in a chair pushed against the wall, too far away from the lectern to see much, but I did notice he was wearing a bow tie and a black suit jacket with wide, satiny lapels. I knew he was a spiffy dresser—but a tux and patent-leather shoes at eight in the morning?

The computer guys got the software ready to go, but Jones didn't use it much. He just talked, and mostly rambled. "My rambling," he said, "may give you an idea of what goes on inside." Yogurt Shop, he said, had had a profound, ineradicable effect on him. When his wife sued him for divorce on grounds of nonperformance as a husband, he agreed with her charges. Since the night he became case agent of the multiple murders at the ICBY shop, he had been obsessed, single-minded, snarly, socially incapacitated and a total loser as both husband and father. He'd converted to Catholicism in 1994, and his wife was a lifelong Catholic; even so, for the divorce he had to go to court and face the music. "Cops hate to admit they're wrong. And they hate to fail." He'd done both, and was here to tell us that the reason was Yogurt Shop. The pressures of living in a glass house that was more in a political spectrum than one of law enforcement, then coming home to a family in chaos, with two daughters in their teens and two who were three and four at the time of the murders, then in the early years of elementary school as the case dragged on. He'd never believed it when people said they stayed together because of the children, but that's what he and Yolanda had done. Then, three of the victims' parents had come to him to say he wasn't looking so good, that maybe he should go see somebody, and he thought, Wait, *they're* the victims' parents, not me. So he'd taken their advice and been officially diagnosed as having PTSD and ADHD. He listed some of the symptoms: insomnia, inability to trust or show love, inwardness, tension. After he was taken off the case, he went into hiding. Stayed away from folks. Didn't make friends. All of the symptoms he'd shown at the time of his diagnosis still affected his life and made him who he was. And so, he said, "I ramble."

Most of the members of his audience weren't from Austin, and many who were didn't know the details of Yogurt Shop, so people began squirming in their seats. But Jones recaptured their attention when he told the story of his first newsworthy case, which came in 1989, when a 180-year-old live oak—said to have been the site of an important treaty signing between Texas hero Stephen F. Austin and local Indian leaders—was poisoned and began to die, the culprit having used enough of the powerful herbicide Velpar to kill a hundred trees. Jones's assignment was considered a joke by his supervisor, a kind of initiation when he moved from Assault and Family Violence to Robbery. They called the crime an "arborcide." But the poisoning of the Treaty Oak went viral, and as the APD spokesperson, he found himself interviewed day and night. They solved the case pretty quickly after a woman called and said she thought her ex-boyfriend had done it. When they went to the guy's apartment, he immediately confessed.

"He was a member of the *Aryan Nation*," John said. "So me and him, we got along *real* good." This—his only reference to his race—got a big laugh, and from then on, the audience was with him.

Calling himself a "supervisory nightmare," he compared a stint in Homicide with an assembly-line job, but there, "you measure time by the number of bodies that roll by." He had seen 150, he said, and the last four were the girls at the yogurt shop.

He told about that night and the television reporter who rode out with him and how the footage the videographer shot of him driving to the ICBY shop was later used on *48 Hours*. And he described the "hideous green-and-white shirt" he had on when he got the calls saying a fire, a homicide, three girls . . . no, four . . . as he drove north up the interstate, and about Troy Gay getting to the yogurt shop within five minutes of a flashover, which would have destroyed whatever evidence they could manage to collect. He explained why he'd automatically been made case agent and quickly chose Mike "Huck" Huckabay as his partner and told of their mutual agreement that if you didn't solve a crime in three days, you were going backward in a hurry. And also that because this was an unusual case requiring unusual methods, they would not file for an arrest warrant until they had a suspect or suspects they felt sure were guilty beyond a reasonable doubt, even though they didn't need to be that certain. All they needed to arrest a suspect in a criminal investigation was probable cause, and in civil cases, a preponderance of evidence. Probable cause wasn't that hard to come by, and the DA's office expected cops to supply only that level of certainty. But he and Huck decided between themselves not to go that route. And that's how they operated during their years on the case.

Then he told about the Mexican nationals and the six written confessions, the 240 witnesses, the 203 affidavits and the 159 apartments they'd searched, the moving violation citations they'd gone through, the people in black, the witches and Satanists. But what got him in trouble with his boss was getting too close to the families of the victims, especially after he okayed that letter they wrote to the Mexican attorney general.

As for the harsh criticism he, Huck and the others received for their conduct at the crime scene and collecting the evidence, he defended himself and all the agencies that worked with him that night by saying, "Look. Back then we called the DPS evidence-collecting unit the 'fingerprint team.' That's what they had in 1991. But in fact, everybody did their job." Might not have been perfect. But they did their job.

When an official held up a ten-minute warning sign, Jones mentioned his attire. He'd decided to wear his tux this morning, he said, admitting that he did have a flair for the dramatic. "But I hate jackets," he said, removing his coat, folding it carefully and setting it aside. "This is me," he said, holding his arms out. "Bow tie, suspenders, white T-shirt, no sleeves." Beneath the jacket his arms were bare. "I brought out the guns," he said later, laughing.

He ended on a final note about the effect of PTSD on a human being, whether a police officer or a soldier. "Damage," he said. "Damage, damage, damage."

And when someone asked if he thought those four guys were guilty, he said, "I don't know. I just don't know."

It wasn't a great talk, but it pretty much summed up the effect of Yogurt Shop on every single person involved in the case in any way. Nobody escaped unscathed: not cops, firefighters, FBI and BATF agents, lawyers, the judge, the families and friends of the girls, other ICBY employees, customers. . . .

Carlos Garcia agrees. "Of *course* he has PTSD," he says. "Everybody who was at the crime scene has it, him probably the worst."

As I made my way out of the hotel, a conferee sidelined me and asked why I was leaving. Wasn't I going to the body farm?

I'd read about the impending TCPA trip to Texas State University's Forensic Anthropology Research Facility, where donor bodies are allowed to decompose in various conditions of climate and topography.

I said I had to get home.

Oh, she said, she wouldn't miss it for anything.

2015

Austin's population is up to around a million today, give or take, about twice the size it was in 1991. We have high-rises downtown, gridlock during rush hour and a light-rail system. Statistics say sixty-five people move here every day, a figure that keeps going up along with the real estate values. A beautiful white-stone boardwalk is connected to the Lady Bird Johnson hike-and-bike trail, allowing us to walk the full ten miles around the lake bearing that great lady's name. In a city of festivals, we can choose from South by Southwest's Film and Interactive festivals, followed by its Music Festival, the Fusebox Festival, the Austin City Limits Festival, the Texas Book Festival, the Republic of Texas Motorcycle Rally, the Reggae Festival, the Art Outside Festival, the Fun Fun Fun and Frontera fests, and the newest—the Formula 1 Grand Prix—which is attended mostly by Europeans and South Americans. There are triathalons, marathons, dog parades. Eeyore's Birthday Party doesn't attract the crowds it used to, but it's still on the calendar. In my neighborhood, an outdoor venue called Festival Beach hosts weekend celebrations—without an actual beach—whose themes include Celtic and Pachanga music, raw food and, when summertime temperatures reach into the three digits, a Hot Sauce Festival.

Some of us wonder how long the city can support the weight of all those visitors and new citizens, and we're swallowing up towns in every direction. I didn't grow up here, go to UT or live here during the glory days of the Armadillo World Headquarters and Janis Joplin, but a friend who did, and now lives in Baltimore, said, "I'd move back to Austin, but I don't like what's happening here." And I had to wonder, compared to what—Baltimore? And when I asked another friend who lived here then if he felt nostalgic, he said, "Why wouldn't I? It was fabulous!"

Some things remain the same. Except for the debilitating heat in July and August, outdoor life couldn't be better, swimming especially. Houstonians still sniff at what they consider our local self-obsession and the absence of world-class cultural institutions, but here we are, still emerging. We aren't big enough to have a professional sports team, so many of those who yearn for that either travel to San Antonio or root for the Longhorns. Casual dress is an art form, and we're competing with Portland, Oregon, to be the most tattooed and pierced, dog-friendly and proudly weird city in the country.

Maria Thomas died abruptly, if not unexpectedly, last spring, but the family managed to keep the manner of her passing under wraps, and I didn't find out about it for months. Barbara Ayres-Wilson was with Maria in her last days and helped her daughter Sonora make funeral arrangements. The *Statesman*'s obituary was brief, and few people involved in Yogurt Shop seemed to have read it, but two members of the DA's staff did attend the funeral, and one of them approached Barbara afterward to say he hoped they'd done right by the girls and their families.

Barbara and her husband, Manley, run an on-call legal protection business out of their home in Kyle, one of those small towns being quickly swallowed up by Greater Austin. She also spends a lot of time with two step-grandbabies, twin girls who, because one is chubby and one tiny, remind her of Sarah and Jennifer.

Bob and Pam Ayers live and work west of Austin. They mostly keep to themselves, although if anything broke in the case, Bob would surely be the first parent to show up.

Sidney Lanier High School has installed sturdy pens, troughs and other amenities for the use of FFA members. The ag farm visited by Jennifer, Sarah and Eliza on the morning of December 6, 1991, is now an open, weedy field.

Divorced in 2015, Michael and Jeannine Scott live far apart: Mike in Florida, where he works for a structural steel company; Jeannine in Iowa with Jasmine. Their parting, according to Jeannine, was not friendly. All Mike will say about that stuff back there is he had nothing to do with it, and if anybody wants to know anything else or ask him to participate in the innocence thing, they should talk to his lawyer, Tony Diaz.

Broadus Spivey and his three colleagues—Jim Hackney, Amber Farrelly and retired judge Charlie Baird—await word from the Third Court of Appeals regarding their April oral argument, asking that Robert Springsteen be given the day in court they maintain he deserves. Because the law doesn't specifically cover Rob's situation, they are arguing for a novel approach, in which their client would present his case—including the DNA evidence that disproves his confession about raping Amy Ayers—before a civil judge, who would then rule on the validity of his appeal. Two staff members from Rose Lehmberg's office argued fiercely against Spivey's position, accusing his team of making an "end run around the law." In response, Spivey said prosecutors are stonewalling because "they don't want to admit they screwed up." He also believes Springsteen's appeal could open an avenue for others struggling to establish their innocence. "All these people need," he told a television reporter, "is some forum in which to test whether they are innocent or not, otherwise they're in limbo." If granted, Springsteen would become eligible for more than $700,000, in addition to the other benefits; if not, Spivey plans to present his argument before the Texas Supreme Court.

Remarried, Springsteen still lives in West Virginia. On the Sunday before his case came before the Third Court, the *Statesman* ran the story on the front page. Headlined SUSPECT IN YOGURT SHOP KILLINGS: CLEAR MY NAME, the report rehashed the entire saga and featured a number of photographs, including the ones taken of the four suspects after their 1999 arrests and another of a man on a ladder putting up the original WHO KILLED THESE GIRLS? billboard. Most online comments to the story lambasted Springsteen for daring to make his appeal since he was obviously guilty. A few weeks later, Broadus Spivey received a handwritten letter from a woman in Walla Walla, Washington, naming the Yogurt Shop killers and warning him to watch his back because the two men were contract killers who also liked to commit "recreational murder." Soon after that, John Jones received a call from a relative of Amy Ayers saying she wanted to fight Springsteen's suit.

And so the controversy and the intransigent position-taking rock on. And on.

On his current Facebook page, Forrest Welborn lists Austin as his home and Patriot Fence Company as his employer. He has bulked up significantly in the six years since his *48 Hours* interview with Erin Moriarty and has shaved his head and grown a thick goatee. His profile photo shows him looking straight into the camera lens, frowning, his eyes in an angry squint. When one of his friends asks why he looks so mad when he's alive and should be happy, Forrest replies, "That's me smiling." In June, Forrest agreed to talk with me about his current life and the effects of Yogurt Shop, but didn't show up for the meeting. His lawyer, Robert Icenhauer-Ramirez, wasn't surprised. He said it was really hard to get Forrest to talk about this case, and besides, he thought they'd proved out his client's innocence during the cert hearings, so no wonder.

Though retired, Jeanne Meurer and Mike Lynch maintain a connection with the Travis County court system as visiting judges. In 2014, Lynch wrote the blueprint for an overhaul of the county indigent criminal defense system, resulting in the creation of the Capital Area Private Defender Service, a carefully structured organization whose job is to select and appoint counsel for criminal defendants who can't afford to pay for an attorney. This is something he's thought about for a long time, feeling that, in his experience, defendants often became convinced that judges selected lawyers who'd get the work done quickly by agreeing to a plea deal, thereby moving the docket along. He's proud of having made this happen. "It isn't easy to convince judges to give up anything," he says now, but eventually most of them went along. They still get to appoint counsel in capital cases. Lynch also works in the public school system, helping teenage kids learn about the law. So he's busy.

After her arrest on a shocking DWI charge—the videotape of which quickly reached the Internet—as part of her plea agreement, Rosemary Lehmberg agreed to step down in November, when she will be replaced.

John Jones applied for a job as Cap Metro's head of security, but the job went to an applicant from Arizona. *"Hmmm,"* Jones murmured in mock contemplation. "Isn't Arizona the state that refused to honor Martin Luther King Day?"

Carlos Garcia—who's returned to private practice—says every time he looks at his ICBY hard files, he thinks about burning them, just to get them out of his life. "But," he says and shrugs, "I've digitized them all so I'd still have them." He's back on the short list of capital case–certified attorneys and is working on two, in one of which the DA is asking for death.

Tony Diaz speaks often to Michael Scott and regrets not pursuing a civil case against the state. He fights back tears when recalling how Mike looked during his incarceration in county jail—handcuffed and hopeful—and says Jeannine Scott is his "hero" for refusing, ever, to back down from her belief in her husband's innocence.

Sawyer's still on the short list as well, but he's less inclined to take on a capital case these days, partly because they take so much time and also because they're just so personally intense and difficult. He's become friendly enough with Efrain de la Fuente to ask about Yogurt Shop. "Oh," he says de la Fuente replied. "That's all over."

In addition, Amber Farrelly swears that, walking into the courthouse one afternoon, she passed two guys struggling with a flat roller-cart stacked with banker's boxes marked "YSM," with the *Scott* and *Springsteen* case numbers. "The famous thirty-three boxes," she says. She wasn't in the courthouse long, but when she came out, the guys were still wrestling with the boxes and loading them into a van. She called Alexandra Gauthier—now a magistrate judge in Williamson County—who said the boxes were probably heading for storage.

Two defense lawyers, friends of Ronnie Earle, say the retired DA has told them in confidence that he doesn't think the four guys they arrested for Yogurt Shop were the real killers. That being the case, we have to wonder, why doesn't he say so publicly? Broadus Spivey has assured the courts that his plan does not preclude Springsteen's future arrest, but we also have to wonder if the state is really planning ever to charge him and Michael Scott again. Or will the thirty-three boxes gather dust in some dark basement from now on?

As of mid-2016, we have no answers to those questions, and we still don't know who killed those girls.

Over lunch one day, I asked John Jones if he thought we ever would.

Like most cops, he's a confirmed skeptic. So his answer surprised me.

"Oh, yeah," he said with a little shrug, "we'll know. Someday."

Epilogue

There are several ways to look at it. It was Maurice Pierce, after all, who set the ball rolling when he showed up at Northcross Mall with a loaded .22 pistol in his waistband and sixteen rounds of ammunition in his jeans pocket, then told Hector Polanco that his friend Forrest Welborn had borrowed the gun and might have used it to kill the yogurt girls. And when the cop asked Maurice what he'd been up to on the night of the murders, he said hanging out with his friends Forrest, Rob Springsteen and Mike Scott. So there they were, the four guys.

If Maurice hadn't pulled that prank, who knows? Paul Johnson might have found somebody else in the tips file to pursue and this whole story might have gone off in a completely different direction. But Maurice was Maurice, and that's pretty much all there is to say about what he did and why he did it.

On Friday, December 23, 2010, he was living part-time in Austin with his sister, Renee Reyna, and part-time in Lewisville with his wife, Kimberli, and daughter, Marisa, who'd graduated from high school the previous June and was almost nine months pregnant with his first grandchild. In the spring, he'd face a felony charge for assaulting the Plano police officer. One reason he was commuting was that people in Collin County now knew who he was, which made jobs even harder to come by than before; also, he and Kimberli were having problems. So when one of her relatives offered him work in his Austin landscaping business, Maurice moved in with Renee.

They'd closed early that day because of the Christmas holiday, and then he'd gone out to have some drinks with friends. He was heading back to his sister's—the same house where the task force Tasered him in 2007—to spend the night before driving home the next morning to spend Christmas with his daughter.

Marisa said she and her father spoke on their cell phones every night, and that night was no different from any other. Maurice was talking away when, at about 10:54, he exited Highway 183 and turned into Renee's neighborhood on Parmer Lane. Most of the medium-size ranch-style houses had several big cars or pickup trucks parked in their driveways. When Maurice got to the stop sign at Shreveport and Carrera, the streets were empty and so, slightly zonked, talking to Marisa, he slid right through.

Who could have predicted that two cops would be staked out in the next block, watching for speeders? Who would have believed this coincidence, if that's what it was? In fact, we might wonder why cops were patrolling a dark, quiet neighborhood in northwest Austin that late, only two nights before Christmas. When the story broke the next day, newspaper and television reporters would refer to the neighborhood as Metric. A couple of young people I know told me that drug dealers had moved to Metric because it was safe and out of the way. Maybe that was why a seasoned five-year veteran, Frank Wilson, had chosen that particular neighborhood as a training ground for his partner, Bradley Smith.

According to the incident report, when a black SUV ran that stop sign, the cops turned on their flashers. Later, Renee's husband will say he actually saw the whirling lights from their living room window. Because Maurice was due back at any minute and was always getting in trouble, he wondered if it was happening again. When investigators listened to Marisa Pierce's cell-phone conversation with her father, they reportedly heard Maurice say he was almost home and then noted a change in his voice. "They're after me again," he told his daughter.

"And then," Marisa said later, "he told me he loved me and that he would never see me again." Maurice kept going for a couple of blocks before pulling over. Wilson and Smith pulled up behind him.

The press will refer to this as a "routine traffic stop," but as John

Jones often says, no police work is routine unless you're sitting at a desk doing paperwork. Once you're on the street, anything can happen.

Maurice got out of his car. Police don't like it when drivers do that, and he certainly had enough experience with cops to know that. But he thought he was in big trouble again and had already told Marisa she'd never see him again, so he did what he felt like. He *exited his vehicle,* as the police would say. Wilson approached on foot, with one hand on his holster, as protocol required.

There have been a number of shootings in Austin when a police officer has shot an unarmed man, claiming the victim had moved in a threatening manner or was holding something that looked like a gun. Usually, after an internal investigation, the cop is cleared. The chief finds a justification for the shooting; the family of the dead man raises a ruckus; life moves on. But to be on the safe side, Art Acevedo had ordered dashboard cameras installed in all police cruisers so that even minor traffic stops could be recorded.

The dash camera in Wilson's car was running.

At this point, Marisa says she began wildly texting her father, who didn't respond. She texted Reyna, who, in turn, texted Maurice and got no answer. "I think they're after him," her husband said. Pierce didn't answer these texts for a simple reason, because instead of standing by his car waiting, he did what he always did when he was in trouble: He ran.

Frank Wilson pursued on foot, Smith following close behind in the cruiser.

When asked, Ron Lara will admit that the Cold Case Unit had certainly kept up with Maurice; they knew where he lived, what jobs he'd held, what kind of car he drove and, of course, all about his troubles in Collin County. Maybe they were still hoping to make a Yogurt Shop deal with him before he went on trial for the assault, but Lara and other officers insisted they weren't actively tracking him. As for Frank Wilson, he hadn't lived in Austin at the time of the murders, the arrests or the trials, so the name Maurice Pierce meant nothing to him. He was simply pursuing someone who'd aroused his suspicion by running from a straightforward traffic stop.

Everybody I've talked to or who was quoted in the press thinks

Wilson was telling the truth. It all happened so fast, and the night was dark. Even people who don't believe in coincidences think maybe this might be the exception.

In no time, Wilson caught up with the runner and they tussled. Wilson wore a utility knife on his duty belt for backup, and Pierce grabbed for it.

Aside from the policemen's testimony and the dash-cam video, you can't really tell what happened. There were no witnesses, and while the dash camera captured the struggle, details are fuzzy. What is clear is that at some point Maurice snatched Wilson's knife from his belt and slashed the right side of his neck, nicking his carotid artery. Pierce then ran off, but before falling to the ground, the officer grabbed his revolver and fired one round.

Maurice Pierce made it through a few front yards before collapsing in a driveway only a block or so from his sister's home.

Renee Reyna says she heard the pop.

Smith called for assistance and applied pressure to Wilson's neck to stanch the blood flow. An ambulance arrived within minutes. Transporters from the ME's office soon zipped Maurice in a body bag and drove him to the morgue. On the Christmas Eve news, a man who lived nearby told a reporter that he'd heard a gunshot and had gone to his front door and looked out in time to see a man fall into a driveway and not get up. When the station's video camera panned the neighborhood, you could see Christmas lights in the windows of every house.

Five hours after the shooting, a detective came to Carrera Lane to tell Reyna that a police officer had shot a man they were almost certain was her brother.

After a night in intensive care, Frank Wilson was released; he went home to spend the holidays with his family.

Victims' Services sent e-mails to the families of the four girls that evening to inform them of the shooting before they read about it in the paper or heard it on TV. One girl's father texted his ex-wife to say, "Ding Dong the witch is dead!"

On Christmas Day, the *Statesman*'s lead story was headlined YOGURT SHOP SUSPECT DIES IN SHOOTING. There were photos of Pierce, Wilson and Smith, and a map of the area where the traffic stop and shooting had occurred.

Five months later, on May 22, 2011, the *Statesman* ran another front-page story—headlined WHO WAS MAURICE PIERCE?—which was accompanied by the photo taken the day he was released from jail in 2003, when, in his loose white T-shirt and blue jeans, he sprinted away from reporters. That was the day before he wished the press and the city of Austin "Godspeed." The paper then told Maurice's story, mostly from his family's perspective. Ever since the Yogurt Shop arrest, they said, his life was about the murders and nothing else. He couldn't get work or sign a lease without somebody saying, *Aren't you the one . . .* He was afraid of the police and saw them coming after him everywhere, even when the family took trips out of the state. Marisa said she tried to convince her father to live within the limits of the law and that if he was ever pulled over, he should simply "take the ticket" and move on. But that's something he would never do.

On September 22, 2011, after a Travis County grand jury declined to indict Frank Wilson, investigative details were revealed that, as the *Statesman* put it, shed new light on Pierce's mind-set the night he died. Apparently, after having dinner with a nephew, he'd gone to the apartment of a woman who provided police with a written statement saying that she and Maurice had been in an intimate and tumultuous relationship off and on for six months, but she'd pretty much ended it because of his fierce fits of jealousy, which once had led him to strike her in the face. On December 23, he'd arrived, uninvited, at her house around six-thirty and had begun drinking and "getting very jealous." When he got out of line, she'd poured a can of beer over his head. He'd left at about ten. Among the papers sent to the grand jury by the DA's office was a toxicology report showing that when Pierce was shot he had a blood-alcohol level of 0.14, well above the 0.08 legal driving limit.

It's possible to take an ironic narrative slant on the life of Maurice Pierce as the story of a risk-taking boy who would not live to see his first grandchild or ever get out from under the sway of his demons, who could never manage to follow his daughter's advice and just take the ticket. People convinced he was the Yogurt Shop ringleader might well have imagined that a vengeful God had finally delivered justice.

Others might wonder if, had he lived, he could've cleaned up his act and moved on.

My guess is, Maurice knew all along what lay ahead for him. Behind the high-wire shine in his eyes was pure sadness, obvious in every photograph as he sits there looking beyond the camera lens into what seemed to be his inevitable future, eyebrows pressed down at the outer edges like a soulful clown's. Maybe it's only because I know what was going to happen that I see something in that gaze that says, This will never end well, not for me.

Appendices

Appendix 1. Michael Scott Written Statement

[After giving his phone number, address and Social Security information and confirming that he has been read his rights, he continues.]

My name is Michael James Scott. I was born on 2-6 of '74. I'm currently at the Austin Police Department homicide office at the Twin Towers giving this statement to Detective Manuel Fuentes and Texas Ranger Sal Abreo. I am giving this statement about my involvement in the death of the four girls at the yogurt shop on December 6th, 1991. I have previously given accounts of what happened in 1991 and afterwards to Detective Fuentes, Texas Ranger Sal Abreo, Detective Merrill, Detective Ron Lara and other detectives. Today I told Detective Fuentes and Texas Ranger Sal Abreo that now that I have confessed to my father and my best friend Patrick Davidson in my part in the girl's death, I have been able to remember and I want this statement to be correct and truthful. These things I will clear up in this statement such as what I threw off the bridge after the murders. I had previously said that I threw a set of keys off the bridge. It was actually a cutting knife that I got from inside the yogurt shop.

When I told you that I didn't really remember what happened to the second gun, that small semiautomatic pistol, I do remember that I gave it to my friend Patrick Davidson in December of 1992 so that he could get rid of it. I did not want to pull him into this and that is why I had been so hesitant to tell you what happened to the gun. If something happens to him, he has nothing to fall back on. I will explain this more in detail later.

On December 6, 1991, I was with my friends Maurice, Rob Springsteen and Forrest. I wasn't sure about Maurice and Forrest's last name. I had been living with Robert Springsteen at his father's condominium on Dry Creek Drive. I think the apartment was right across from the swimming pool. We were at the Northcross Mall sitting at a round table at the food court. Maurice brought up that he needed to get some money. I don't remember the specifics about what was discussed, but I do know that this is what brought—what brought what all this to be.

Maurice and Rob talked about robbing a place. They said this would be the easiest way to get some money. I got up and walked around the mall. I remember being in the arcade, and then I remember coming back to the table and sitting down. Maurice got up and walked around with somebody. I don't know who it was. I had seen him before, but didn't know who he was. Ranger Abreo asked me what time was this happening. I don't remember exactly what time it was, but it was still daylight. We were all at the table when Maurice said we needed to go and look around. I believed him to mean he wanted to find a place to rob. When we left, Maurice was driving his dad's gray Ford LTD. Rob was sitting in the right front seat. I sat back behind the driver. Forrest was in the back seat with me. We drove around and looked at the businesses around the North-cross area. We drove up to the strip mall where the I Can't Believe It's Yogurt shop was at. We looked at the businesses that were at the mall. Maurice was the one that said something like "let's go inside and take a look at the yogurt shop." Maurice went in and bought a yogurt swirl, chocolate and vanilla. I followed Rob inside.

I sat down, and Rob came over and said something to me and we got up and made it look like we were going to the restroom. Maurice was up at the counter talking to at least one of the girls. I remember that he was talking to the dark-haired girl. Maurice was supposed to distract them. Rob and I walked out the back and walked around to the front of the building. When we got around to the front, Maurice was already in the car eating his yogurt. We drove back to the mall and we sat at the same table. It was the same table we always sat at. Detective Fuentes asked me if we were armed at the time we cased the store. No, the guns were left inside the car at the time. We sat at the table and—BS'ing with Forrest. We were just talking, not about what was fixing to happen. I remember eating some curly fries, and it was strange that I remember a large Mexican boy that we all knew in passing who had come—sit down with us. The Mexican boy picked up the container of catsup and started drinking it. I walked around the mall with Rob. We ran into Maurice again when we were walking around. Maurice told us that it was time to go. We got back into his car. Maurice was driving. I was in the back seat, and Rob and Forrest were in the car with us. We drove around the neighborhood more. I think we were looking for a route to take and there was talk about how often the cops drove around and if there was a general route they drove around in.

I know it was dark when we left Northcross Mall. Most of the businesses were closed when we got over to the yogurt shop. We drove across the parking lot and drove through the alley behind the stores. We wanted to see if there was [sic] any vehicles parked in the back, or if there were any people back there. I believe we even wanted to see if the back double doors were still slightly open. We drove back through the parking lot and then back to the rear of the store. I remember the building was on the driver's side, the left side of the car. We stopped just past the double doors, not more than 50 feet past the doors. Maurice told Forrest that the only thing that he had to do was honk the horn if anyone was coming. Maurice pulled out his gun. I believe that he had it in between the seat. I know Rob had a gun because he looked at it before we went inside to make sure it was loaded.

Before we went in, Maurice told me to make sure that I brought the can of Zippo lighter fluid. It was the bigger metal can. Texas Ranger Sal Abreo asked me why I thought we brought the can of lighter fluid. I believe Maurice wanted to use it to cover our tracks. We went into the back door. Maurice went in first, then Rob, and then I followed them. One of the girls said something like, Hey, you, what are you doing? You don't belong in here. This girl was wearing a T-shirt I believe that had the name "I Can't Believe It's Yogurt" on it. I believe that she was working in the back room when we entered the back. Rob told me to stop and stay right there and not let anyone out the back. We were all surprised because we expected to find only two girls inside the store and there were two other girls up at the front in the dining room area sitting down. I could see the commotion going on up front. I remember Maurice told me to check the front door to make sure it was locked. He also told me to check to see if there was anyone out front that could see us. I checked the door and it was locked. There was one key in the lock. The door was locked. I looked outside to make sure no one was looking in.

As this went along I got more and more scared. I heard the cash register open. I heard the drawer being lifted and slammed back. I saw Maurice at the cash register and I saw him put something in his pocket. I thought to myself that he had just put money in his pocket. All the girls were in the back with Rob. I looked out to check the front again. I heard Maurice say something like "Where in the fuck is the rest of the money?" I heard the girls crying and one of the girls said, "That's all there is. It's already been dropped and you can't get to it." I heard Rob say, "Come help me with this." I went back there and he wanted help tying them up. When I went back there I saw that all four girls were naked. I believe this is the way that it was because I don't remember pulling their clothes off. I went to the pile of clothes and picked up some clothes to use to tie them up. I remember a T-shirt and a bra that we used to tie them up. The girls were crying and whimpering. They were begging for us not to kill them. They said they didn't want to die. I got a paper towel and put it inside one of the girls' mouth. I remember that my finger pushed through the towel when I was trying to stuff it in her mouth. This may not have worked so I may have had to use something else to stuff in her mouth. It was white like terry cloth. The girls were on their knees. I don't believe they were standing up because I was looking down at them. Rob told me to check the front. I went up front and remember what sounded like one of the girls trying to scream. Maurice was screaming, saying, "Where the fuck is the rest of the money?" I heard a bang, a crack. It sounded like a gun going off. I checked the lock one last time and I turned around to see what happened. One of the girls was already dead. I think Maurice shot that one. After the shot, Maurice said again, "Where in the fuck is the rest of the money?" And there was a second shot. I went to the back and saw Rob, and he had one of the dark-haired girls on her hands and knees and he's raping her, raping her hard. I told Rob that this wasn't

right. That's not what he came here for. Rob stood up, and I don't
know if he finished. I did not see his dick. I know that Maurice was
not back there with Rob. Maurice had gone into an office and he had
one of the girls with him. He was squatting down and I think she was
trying to open a safe or something.

Rob told me to do one of the girls. I believe it was the one that
he had just did. He told me not to be a pussy and told me if I didn't,
then I was next. We laid the girl on the floor and I got on top of her.
I tried to do her from the front. I looked at her. I didn't want to look
at her face. She had a piece of white terry cloth towel on her mouth.
I looked away because I didn't want to see her. I couldn't get it up
because I knew what—that what I was doing was wrong. I sort of
faked it to make Rob think I did her. I got up and remember either
Maurice or Rob telling me to finish her. I remember grabbing the
revolver from Maurice. He told me to finish her. The girl was still on
the floor and I pointed the gun at her and tried to shoot it first but
couldn't. Maurice told me to do it or I would be next.

I pointed the gun again at the girl and fired once into her head.
I remember Rob pushed me toward Maurice. Maurice was in the
other room with the other girl. I don't remember seeing a safe, but I
don't remember what she was doing down on the floor. I remember
looking in the doorway and the gun is still in my hand. Maurice
asked Rob if I did it, and Rob said, "Yeah, he finished her." Maurice
told me, you are in this neck-deep already. I saw the side profile of
this girl. She had like a white shirt on. I think she had dark hair. Rob
was standing right there and he had the small semiautomatic gun.
Rob told me not to be a puss. I think I shot her in the head. I've been
not wanting to remember this. I know I have told you had something
different, but I did her too because Maurice and Rob were pressur-
ing me. I dropped the revolver. Maurice was mad at me. He asked
me where the lighter fluid was and I had thought I had left it in the
car. He told me to go out to the car and get it. I looked at Forrest
and then I looked at the floorboard and picked up the lighter fluid.
Forrest did not say a word. I went back inside. Rob told me to burn
the place. I saw the girls laying there and I pulled one of the girls on
top of the other.

Rob was watching me as I gathered up napkins, cups and paper
towels and piled them on top of the three girls. I sprayed Zippo

fluid on top of girls. I emptied the can of lighter fluid. I had a Zippo lighter with me and I lit the fire. I heard a whoosh sound of the accelerant when it caught fire. I don't remember what I did with the can. I could have threw it on the pile of stuff in the back of the store. I remembered that my only thought was to get out. I went outside and remembered that Forrest was not in the car anymore. I had taken a knife from inside the shop. I believe I got it off the counter. It was a nice knife. I told you all before that I had taken a set of keys, but it was a knife. I remember now that it was a knife. Rob and I were already back in the car when Maurice got there. I asked Maurice where Forrest was. He said that he must have took off.

Texas Ranger Sal Abreo asked me how long were we in the shop. I think we were in there about 20 to 25 minutes. I'm not sure. We were in the car, and on the way out we saw Forrest. He was in the parking lot somewhere, and we picked him up. I remember driving, but I don't remember what direction we went. We stopped at some bridge. It was about 10 to 15 minutes away from the shop. I got out and threw up over the railing of the bridge. I took the knife and threw it over the rail also. I made sure it was gone. I remember trees and I don't remember seeing any water. I got back into the car. I don't know what happened next. I remember being back at the apartment. Detective Fuentes asked me to describe the two guns. The gun that Maurice had was a black .22 caliber revolver, small. I think it had wood grips. The gun that Rob had was a small semiautomatic pistol. It had a clip. I think it was a .38. Some of the writing on the gun was scratched off. Rob and I split up from Maurice and Forrest. Rob and I spent some time at the apartment.

I remember on the weekend that I got into a yellow or gold jeep to see Mary. Mary is a girl I met at music camp who lives in Helotes, which is near San Antonio. Maurice was driving and I think Forrest was with us. Rob and I rode with them to San Antonio. We stayed there maybe an hour. I got a hold of a newspaper, and I remember reading about the fire and the yogurt shop murders. I read it out loud to everybody. We drove back to Austin. I remember getting back home and wanting to do nothing more than sleep. Several days after we got back from San Antonio, Rob came into the room we sleep in and told me that Maurice got popped with the gun that they had used at the yogurt shop. The semiautomatic pistol was lying on the bed. I knew that I had to get rid of it. I picked it up and left the apartment. I remember walking past a dumpster and thinking I should just throw it in the dumpster. I walked into the creek in the apartment complex. I put it in a hole in the side of a wall in the creek. I wedged another rock in it. I stacked some rocks near it as a marker to remind me where it [*sic*] put it. I went back and told Rob that I got rid of it and no one would ever find it. Less than a month later, Rob took off. I had moved out from Dry Creek and was staying at my parents' house. When I went back to Rob's apartment to get some of my things, Rob's dad told me that Rob went back to wherever he came from. I used to remember where that was but don't remember now.

A couple of months later I met this guy named Patrick Davidson that I met at Double Daves. We moved in with things—guys—we moved in with these guys named Danny and Daniel in December of 1992. I was smoking a lot of pot. I had been drinking a lot too, and started having flashbacks. I went back out to the creek and found the gun. I took the gun and put it in a brown paper sack that I found in the creek. I took the gun back to the—south Austin to our apartment. I told Pat a little. I don't remember how much I told him, but I do remember that I told him I wouldn't have done it if I hadn't—if I had not been forced to do it. I told Pat that I needed to get rid of what was in the sack. I didn't tell him. I asked him if he wanted to know, and he said no. He told me that he put it out in the trash. Yesterday when I told him what was going on and told him that I was in trouble, he said that he pretty much knew that there was a gun in that sack when I gave it to him in 1992.

Detective Fuentes asked me who I have told about the murders. My dad came over to my house this past Sunday. I told him what was going on but did not give him a lot of details. He is a smart man and he figured out what I was talking about when I told him that it happened back around seven years ago. I think he had always suspected that I was somehow involved back in 1991 because of who I was hanging out with. We hugged several times and he kind of started to cry. I cannot tell my mother because this would destroy her. I told my wife, but I did not give her details. She is real upset with me right now. We talked about whether I should get a lawyer right now, and I told her that that was the last thing I needed right now. Yesterday right after I dropped my daughter off at day-care, I went next door to use the pay phone, and I called the attorney, Betty Blackwell. I told her that it involved the yogurt shop murders and that I was talking to the police. She recommended that I stop talking to you all. She told me whoever they pin this on, they are looking for the death penalty. She told me she did not handle cases like this. She told me that I didn't sound too good and I should seek help by checking into Shoal Creek or something like that. I told my best friend Patrick Davidson and he was pissed off at me. When we got rid of the gun—when he got rid of the gun for me in 1992, he didn't know what I had done with it. He said that he pretty much knew it was a gun when he threw it away. The other day when I was being interviewed by Detective Lara and Detective Merrill, they showed me digital photographs on their computer of the people I had been talking about when I used the names Maurice, Robert Springsteen and Forrest. I recognized Maurice and Rob, but I had a hard time with Forrest's photograph. I had known Maurice for about two or three months before the murders. I met Maurice through Rob. I had seen Maurice almost every two or three days during that time period. I had known Robert Springsteen about maybe six months and he had been staying with—and had been staying with him for about a couple of months. Forrest is a guy that I knew from McCallum High School. I would see him at school and Northcross Mall. I remember when we were in Maurice's car leaving the shop, Maurice had threatened everybody in the car. I don't remember exactly what he said. Later Rob told me when we were at his apartment if I ever said anything it would all come back to me. He said he would deny everything. I can read write and understand the English language, and the above statement I have read, and it is true and correct to the best of my knowledge and belief.

Appendix 2. Redacted Michael Scott Statement

[Beginning on page 3, after the Manuel Fuentes introduction and Michael Scott's acknowledgment of his Miranda rights.]

On December 6, 1991, I don't remember exactly what time it was. It was still daylight. Drove up to the strip mall where the I Can't Believe It's Yogurt shop was at. Go inside and took a look at the yogurt shop. Got up and make it look like going to the restroom. Walked out the back and walked around to the front of the building. Drove back to the mall. Left Northcross Mall. Drove through the alley behind the stores to see if the back double doors were slightly open. The building was on the driver's side, the left side of the car.

I brought the can of Zippo lighter fluid. It was the bigger metal can. Went into the back door. One of the girls said something like "Hey, you. What are you doing? You don't belong in here." This girl was wearing a T-shirt. I believe that it had the name I Can't Believe It's Yogurt on it. Believe that she was working in the back room.

Expected to find only two girls inside store, and there were two other girls up front in the dining room sitting down. I could see the commotion going on up front. I checked the door, and it was locked. There was one key in the lock. The door was locked. I looked outside to make sure no one was looking in.

As this went along, I got more and more scared. I looked out to check the front again. I heard the girls crying and one of the girls say that that's all there is. It's been dropped and you can't get to it. I went back there. I saw that all four girls were naked. I went to the pile of clothes and picked up some clothes to use to tie them up.

I remember a T-shirt and a bra used to tie them up. The girls were crying and whimpering. They were begging not to kill them. They said that they didn't want to die. I got a paper towel and put it inside one of the girl's mouth. I remember that my finger pushed through the towel when I was trying to stuff it in her mouth. This may not have worked, so I might have had to use something else to stuff in her mouth. It was like terry cloth.

The girls were on their knees. I don't believe they were standing up, because I was looking down at them. I went to the back and saw one of the dark-haired girls on her hands and knees. I got on top of her. I tried to do her from the front. I looked at her face. I didn't want to look at her face. She had a piece of white terry cloth towel on her mouth. I looked away because I didn't want to see her. I couldn't get it up because I knew what I was doing was wrong. I sort of faked it. The girl was sitting on the floor. I pointed the gun at her and tried to shoot at first but couldn't. I pointed the gun again at the girl and fired once into her head.

I don't remember seeing a safe, but I don't remember what she was doing down on the floor. I remember looking in the doorway, and the gun is still in my hand. I saw the side profile of the girl. She had like a white shirt on. I think I shot her in the head. I have been not wanting to remember this. I know I told you something different, but I did her too. I dropped the revolver.

I saw the girls laying there and I pulled one of the girls on top of the other. I gathered up napkins, cups, paper towels, and piled them on top of the three girls. I sprayed Zippo—Zippo fluid on top of the girls. I emptied the can of lighter fluid. I had a Zippo lighter with me and lit the fire. I heard a whoosh sound of the accelerant when I, when it caught fire. I don't remember what I did with the can. I could have threw it in the pile of stuff in the back of the store.

I remember that my only thought was to get out. I went outside. I had taken a knife from inside the shop. I believe I got it off the counter. It was a nice knife. I told you all before that I had taken a set of keys but it was a knife. I remember now that it was a knife.

I remember driving but I don't remember what direction. I got out and threw up over the railing of the bridge. I took the knife and I threw it over the rail also. I made sure it was gone. I remember trees, and I don't remember seeing any water. I got back into the car. I don't know what happened next. I remember being back at the apartment.

Detective Fuentes asked me to describe the two guns. A black .22-caliber revolver, small; I think it had wood grips. A small, semi-automatic pistol; it had a clip. I think it was a .38. Some of the writing on the gun was scratched off.

On the weekend I rode to San Antonio. I got hold of a newspaper and I remember reading about the fire and the yogurt shop murders. I read it out loud. I remember getting back home and wanting to do nothing more than sleep.

The semiautomatic was lying on the bed. I knew that I had to get rid of it. I picked it up and left it at the apartment. I remember walking past a dumpster and thinking I should just throw it in the dumpster. I walked into the creek in the apartment complex. I put it in a hole in the side of a wall in the creek. I wedged another rock in it. I stacked some rocks near it as a marker to remind me where [I] put it.

In December of 1992 I was smoking a lot of pot. I had been drinking a lot to[o] and started having flashbacks. I went back out to the creek and found the gun. I took the gun and put it in a brown paper [s]ack that I found in the creek. I took the gun back to south Austin to our apartment. I told Pat that I needed to get rid of what was in the sack. I didn't tell him. He told me that he put it out in the trash.

I can read, write and understand the English language in the above statement I have read, and it is true and correct to the best of my knowledge and belief.

Acknowledgments

I could not have pulled this together without the help of a whole slew of people, many of whom would have preferred never to even *think* about this terrible crime again, much less talk about it.

First off, John Jones, who—over Kerbey Lane and Magnolia Café omelets and Frisco fried catfish—willingly shared his memories, his stories and biographical information and, perhaps even more significantly, his APD files and his copies of the three episodes of *48 Hours,* all accompanied by his snappy wit and lingering anger at how things have turned out.

Equally generous was Barbara Ayres-Wilson, a sister in grief who holds nothing back, no matter the situation. Our many meetings—at Barbara's home and the Motley Menagerie Tea Room, Gift & Resale Shop in Kyle, Nonna Gina's Italian in Buda, Hyde Park Bar & Grill South and Cenote in Austin, among other spots—were always charged with emotion, information and laughter. Thanks to her also for the introduction to Maria Thomas.

Also—first at Romeo's, then their home, then Baker Street and, most recently, the sports bar and restaurant Cover 3—Jim Sawyer whose memory, generosity and narrative gifts are a wonder, and his whip-smart partner, Deirdre Darrouzet, who supplied important documents, contacts, hot corrections and passionate opinions.

Carlos Garcia—at his office, his home, Threadgill's, Angie's and Buffet Palace—for the CDs, DVDs, photographs, transcripts, Reid information, false-confession sources and memories he'd snuff out if he could; also for the introduction to the great Anthony Graves.

Mike Lynch (his chambers and Buenos Aires Café) for information, warmth, honesty and his wonderfully written journal.

John Hardesty, old friend—at Güero's, Texas French Bread and El Naranjo—for connections, phone numbers and open-ended conversations about the APD interrogations, the arrests and the certification hearings.

The late Dr. Gerald Hurst for tea, cookies and a long and fascinating conversation in his home.

Robert Springsteen for talking freely with me on his back porch in Cross Lanes, West Virginia.

Michael Scott and Jeannine Scott, who in an unnamed midwestern city willingly spent many hours over two days' time with me, rehashing painful memories and relating happier present times.

Also: District Attorney Rosemary Lehmberg. ADA Efrain de la Fuente. Lawyers Guillermo Gonzales, Alexandra Gauthier, Amber Farrelly, Broadus Spivey, Jim Hackney, Tony Diaz, Robert Icenhauer-Ramirez, Hugh Lowe, Malcolm Greenstein and Dave Richards. Retired APD policeman J. W. Thompson. From the Travis County Courthouse, Melissa Moreno and Karen Kiker; from Victims' Services, Ellen Halbert. Also cold-case specialist and Texas State University professor Dr. Kim Rossmo. Brandon Ariel for the McCallum information. Maggie Halliday, Peggy Sanders, Kate Wallace McClung and her mother, Rebecca Wallace (with a nod to Sue Ellen Harrigan for the introduction). The helpful staff in the records room of the Texas Court of Criminal Appeals. Bridget Weiss, Dorothy Brown, Gary Cartwright, Bill Wittliff, Dagoberto Gilb, Mercedes Pena, Lou Dubose, Richard Lu.

Friends John Davidson, Nancy Smith, David Burnham and Dave Richards for reading early drafts. Claire Brulator for transcriptions. Kenny Braun for the photo.

From Knopf: GF of course. Also, his fabulous assistant, Ruthie Reisner, and true-crime enthusiast and publicist Jordan Rodman. Plus assistant publicist Tammy Tarng, marketer Danielle Plafsky and production editor Ellen Feldman. Oliver Munday for the great cover. And the whole blooming Knopf organization for its work, its loyalty and its enthusiasm. Also for sticking out tough times for all these years.

My agent, Betsy Lerner.

And of course, Colin Lowry and Andrea Ariel, my family, for unqualified support, encouragement and home-cooked meals.

Bibliography

In addition to the resources noted within the text of this book, a number of additional books have been particularly helpful in my effort to understand some of the legal and psychological issues of this case, especially those involving memory, interrogations and false confessions. Here are some that I found particularly instructive:

Burns, Sarah. *The Central Park Five: A Chronicle of a City Wilding.* New York: Alfred A. Knopf, 2011.

Garrett, Brandon L. *Convicting the Innocent: Where Criminal Prosecutions Go Wrong.* Cambridge, Mass.: Harvard University Press, 2011.

Leo, Richard A. *Police Interrogation and American Justice.* Cambridge, Mass.: Harvard University Press, 2008.

Loftus, Elizabeth, and Katherine Ketcham. *Witness for the Defense: The Accused, the Eyewitness, and the Expert Who Puts Memory on Trial.* New York: St. Martin's Press, 1991.

Scheck, Barry, Peter Neufeld and Jim Dwyer. *Actual Innocence: When Justice Goes Wrong and How to Make It Right.* New York: New American Library, 2003.

Simon, David. *Homicide: A Year on the Killing Streets.* Boston: Houghton Mifflin, 1991.

Vollen, Lola, and Dave Eggers, comps. and eds. *Surviving Justice: America's Wrongfully Convicted and Exonerated.* San Francisco: McSweeney's Books, 2008.

Warden, Rob, and Steven A. Drizin, eds. *True Stories of False Confessions.* Evanston, Ill.: Northwestern University Press, 2009.

Wells, Tom, and Richard A. Leo. *The Wrong Guys: Murder, False Confessions, and the Norfolk Four.* New York: The New Press, 2008.

A NOTE ABOUT THE AUTHOR

Beverly Lowry is the author of six novels and three previous works of nonfiction. Her writing has appeared in *The New Yorker, The New York Times, The Boston Globe, Vanity Fair, Rolling Stone, Mississippi Review, Granta,* and many other publications. She has received awards from the National Endowment for the Arts, the Guggenheim Foundation, the Texas Institute of Letters, and the Mississippi Institute of Arts and Letters. She lives in Austin, Texas.

A NOTE ON THE TYPE

The text of this book was set in Sabon, a typeface designed by Jan Tschichold (1902–1974), the well-known German typographer. Based loosely on the original designs by Claude Garamond (ca. 1480–1561), Sabon is unique in that it was explicitly designed for hot-metal composition on both the Monotype and Linotype machines as well as for filmsetting. Designed in 1966 in Frankfurt, Sabon was named for the famous Lyons punch cutter Jacques Sabon.

Typeset by Scribe,
Philadelphia, Pennsylvania

Printed and bound by Berryville Graphics,
Berryville, Virginia

Designed by Betty Lew